CATALOGUE

OF THE

STATE LIBRARY

OF WISCONSIN.

1872.

Prepared under the direction of the State Librarian.

MADISON, WIS.:
ATWOOD & CULVER, STATE PRINTERS, JOURNAL BLOCK.
1872.

PREFACE.

THIS catalogue is issued in pursuance of the provisions of section 3, chapter 105, general laws of 1871.

"The State Library had its origin in the generous appropriation of $5,000 out of the general treasury, by Congress, contained in the seventeenth section of the organic act, creating the Territory of Wisconsin. At the first session of the territorial legislature, held at Belmont in 1836, a joint resolution was adopted, appointing the Hon. John M. Clayton, of Delaware (through whose instrumentality the clause in the organic act making the appropriation was inserted), Hon. Lewis F. Linn, of Missouri, Hon. G. W. Jones, then delegate in Congress from this territory (which at that time included what now constitutes the state of Iowa, as well as Wisconsin,) and Hon. Peter Hill Engle, the speaker of the first territorial House of Representatives, a committee to select and purchase a library for the use of the territory, and authorizing them to draw the sum appropriated for that purpose from the federal treasury. Mr. Engle was the active member of the committee, and made the selections and purchases, with the approval of the other members. James Clarke, publisher of the Belmont *Gazette*, and first territorial printer, was the first librarian."

"The first appropriation, by the State, to replenish the library, was made in 1851. The sum of $2,500 was then appropriated to be expended under the direction of Gov. Dewey, in the purchase of law books. No report of this expenditure seems to have been made to the legislature. Subsequently, in 1854, the sum of $3,000 was appropriated for law and miscellaneous works; and in 1857 the additional appropriation of $1,000 was made for the same purpose, together with a standing appropriation of $250 for such additions to the law and miscellaneous departments of the library as might from time to time be deemed desirable."*

* The paragraphs above quoted, are taken from the preface to the catalogue of 1858.

The annual appropriation was, in 1864, increased to $500. In 1866, an additional fund of $600 per annum was put at the disposal of the Governor, for the purpose of supplying deficiencies in the law department of the library. This appropriation was in the first instance limited to two years; but the act has been re-enacted from time to time, and is still in force. By the provisions of the acts of 1866 and 1868, also, purchases for this library are now confined to "law books, books of reference, and works on political science and statistics;" except that the librarian is permitted to continue and complete any sets of valuable works already contained in the library.

For some years past the design has been steadily pursued of collecting in the state capitol (so far as the appropriations made for the purpose will permit,) a State Law Library, proximately complete, and adequate to the ever-growing wants of the bench and bar of Wisconsin; and at the same time procuring such works bearing upon political science as may render the Library useful to the legislative and executive departments of the state government. The present catalogue will show what progress has been made in the execution of this design; and will at the same time show to any one who studies it carefully, what large deficiencies remain to be supplied before this collection can claim the character of a first-rate State Law Library.

Counsel and others who contemplate a visit to the capitol for the purpose of consulting this library, frequently wish to know beforehand just what authorities can here be found. Copies of this catalogue will be furnished to such persons, on application therefor; and to render it more useful to them, the titles of the books have been given with considerable fullness. At the end of Part First will be found an Index of Subjects, which will show the inquirer at a glance what treatises the library contains upon any given topic of the law. In connection with Part Second are given Chronological Lists of the Reporters in the various courts of England, Ireland and Scotland, and also a Table of the Regnal Years of the English Sovereigns. Under the name of each State will also be found a chronological list of its Reports. These adjuncts of the catalogue may be found convenient in determining readily the exact period of a reported decision, or in tracing from its origin the stream of judicial authority upon any legal question which may be the subject of investigation.

JULY, 1872. O. M. C.

CONTENTS.

LAWS AND REGULATIONS.

I. EXTRACTS FROM THE STATUTES.

Revised Statutes, 1858, *Chapter X.*

SECTION 9. The Governor shall appoint a Librarian, who shall have charge of the State Library; he shall hold his office for the term of one year, to commence on the first day of April thereof, and until his successor shall be appointed and qualified. Before entering upon the duties of his office, he shall give a bond, with good and sufficient surety in the penal sum of ten thousand dollars, in such form as the Governor shall approve, conditioned for the performance of all the duties required of him by law and for the observance of all the rules prescribed by the Trustees of the State Library. He shall give his personal attendance upon the library during the hours it shall be directed to be kept open, and shall perform such duties as shall be imposed on him by law, or shall be prescribed by the rules and regulations of the trustees aforesaid. He may appoint an assistant by the approval and consent of the Governor, but such appointment shall not excuse him from personal attendance at the Library, unless from necessity, and then but for such time as said Governor may limit.

SECTION 10. The salary of the Librarian shall be one thousand dollars per annum, nor shall any extra amount be paid for any Assistant Librarian.

R. S. 1858, *Chapter* 26.

OF THE STATE LIBRARY, AND OF THE DISTRIBUTION OF THE PUBLIC DOCUMENTS TO THE SEVERAL COLLEGES AND ACADEMIES OF THIS STATE.

SECTION 1. The Governor, Secretary of State, and Superintendent of Public Instruction, shall be ex-officio Trustees of the State Library.

SECTION 2. The said Trustees shall have full power to make and carry into effect such rules and regulations for the superintendence and care of the books, maps, charts, paper and furniture contained in the State Library, and for the arrangement and safe keeping of the same, as they may deem proper.

SECTION 3. [It shall be the duty of said Trustees to provide in their rules and regulations that any member of the Legislature, during the session thereof, or any member or attorney of the Supreme Court, during the session of the same, shall be permitted, under proper restrictions, penalties and forfeitures, to take to his rooms any book belonging to the said library, excepting such as the Trustees shall deem it improper to permit to be removed]; but no member of the Legislature shall be allowed to take more than five books at one time, nor to retain the same for a longer time than five days.

SECTION 4. The State Library shall be kept open every day during the sessions of the Supreme Court and of the Legislature, and during such other days as the Trustees or Governor shall direct, except Sundays, and during such hours as shall be directed by the Trustees. The State Librarian shall perform such duties as are or shall be prescribed by law, by the rules and regulations of the Trustees, and by the Governor, and the penalty of his official bond shall be ten thousand dollars.

SECTION 5. The Trustees of the Library shall, as soon as may be, and before any additional purchases are made, make an examination of the State Library, and cause their Librarian to make out a complete list or catalogue of all books contained in the same; and they shall also report the same, together with such additions as may hereafter be made by virtue of any law, to the next legislature.

SECTION 6. The Librarian shall make report five days before the adjournment of any session of the legislature, of the number of the books that have been taken out of the Library by the members, giving the names of all members that have any books at the date of such report, with the name and number of such books.

SECTION 7. All fines, penalties and forfeitures imposed by the rules and regulations of the Trustees of the Library, for any violation of such rules and regulations, may be recovered in any proper action or proceeding, in the name of the State, before any court of competent jurisdiction; and all such fines, penalties, forfeitures and recoveries shall be applied to the use of the Library, under the direction of the Trustees.

[SECTION 8. There is hereby annually appropriated to the Governor of the State the sum of two hundred and fifty dollars, to be paid to him by the State Treasurer, out of any money in the treasury not otherwise appropriated, to be expended under the direction and approval of the Governor, by the State Librarian, in the purchase of such law reports and other books for the State Library as may be deemed necessary or advisable.]

SECTION 9. The Librarian is hereby authorized to deliver to each college, incorporated academy, and literary institution of this State, having a library of three hundred volumes, one copy of the revised statutes, one copy of the session laws of each session of the legislature, one copy of the journals of the Senate and Assembly, of each session, one copy each of the journals of [the] two constitutional conventions, one copy each of all documents printed by order of the legislature of this State, and one copy each of the revised statutes, laws, and journals of the council and house of representatives of the territory of Wisconsin, and the reports of the decisions of the Supreme Court of this State: *provided*, twenty-five copies of each document and book be retained in the Library.

SECTION 10. Whenever any books or documents mentioned in section nine of this chapter, shall be deposited in the office of the Governor, Secretary of State, State Superintendent, or Superintendent of Public Property, in quantities exceeding twenty-five copies, the institutions mentioned in said section shall be entitled to receive, from such excess, one copy of each of said volumes or documents, of whatever nature, the same as if deposited in the State Library.

SECTION 11. The said statutes, laws, journals, and documents may be delivered to any person authorized by the president or principal of said institutions.

SECTION 12. Said literary institutions shall also be entitled to receive from the Agricultural Society, and from the Historical Society, one copy of each volume of the transactions of said societies which are now or may hereafter be published: *provided always*, that twenty-five copies of each of said publications be retained by such societies in their respective libraries.

SECTION 13. All duplicates of historical and miscellaneous works, now or hereafter in the State Library, shall be transferred to the State Historical Society.

Chapter 135, *General Laws of* 1858.

SECTION 3. No work belonging to the State Library shall be borrowed or taken away from the same, except by the Executive, Judges of the Supreme or other Courts, Members or Officers of the Legislature, or State Officers, and in no case shall they be taken away from the capitol.

SECTION 4. The State Librarian is hereby authorized to sell or dispose of copies of the revised statutes or session laws, under the direction of the Trustees of said Library.

Note.—This is now done by the Secretary of State.

Chapter 321, *General Laws of* 1864.

SECTION 1. Section eight of chapter 26 of the revised statutes of this state, is hereby amended, so as to read as follows: "Section 8. There is hereby annually appropriated to the governor of the state the sum of *five hundred* dollars, to be paid to him by the state treasurer, out of any money in the state treasury not otherwise appropriated, to be expended under the direction and approval of the governor, by the state librarian, in the purchase of such law reports and other books for the state library, as may be deemed necessary or advisable."

Chapter 119, *General Laws of* 1866.

SECTION 1. The governor is hereby authorized to procure for the state library such volumes of English or American reports, statutes, parliamentary debates, or digests, published before the year 1860, as may be certified to him by the chief justice of the supreme court to be necessary or desirable for the purposes of said library.

SECTION 2. On the presentation to him of bills for such books, with the approval of the governor indorsed thereon, and a certificate of the state librarian that the books have been received in good condition at the state library, the secretary of state is authorized to audit such bills, and to issue warrants for the amounts thereof upon the state treasurer, in favor of the persons of whom such books are purchased, or the person authorized to receive payment therefor: *provided*, that the whole amount to be paid from the state treasury under the provisions of this act, shall not exceed six hundred dollars in any one year; *and provided, further*, that the authority conferred by this act upon the governor and secretary of state, shall cease and determine at the end of two years from the passage thereof.

SECTION 3. No books shall hereafter be purchased for the state library, except law books, [books] of reference, and works of political science and statistics.

SECTION 4. There is hereby appropriated from any moneys in the state treasury not otherwise appropriated, an amount sufficient to pay the expenditures authorized by this act.

Chapter 102, *General Laws of* 1867.

SECTION 1. The Secretary of State shall be authorized to purchase a sufficient number of such volumes of the Wisconsin Reports as are not owned by the State, to enable him to furnish complete sets of Reports to such of the United States as have or shall hereafter furnish full sets of Reports for the Library of the State of Wisconsin.

Chapter 68, *General Laws of* 1868,

Is in terms identical with chapter 119, General Laws of 1866, excepting the third section, which reads as follows:

SECTION 3. No books shall hereafter be purchased for the State Library, except Law Books, Books of Reference and Works on Political Science and Statistics: *provided*, that this shall not be construed to prevent the completion of any defective sets of valuable works now in the library.

By Chapter 136, *General Laws of* 1870,

The provisions of chapter 68, General Laws of 1868, are continued in force for two years longer.

Chapter 134, *General Laws of* 1872.

SECTION 1. Chapter sixty-eight, general laws of 1868, entitled "an act to provide for certain deficiencies in the law department of the State Library," as the same was revived by chapter one hundred and thirty-six, general laws of 1870, is hereby revived and continued in force for the period of five years.

SECTION 2. It shall be the duty of the Secretary of State to deposit in the State Library, for the use thereof, twenty-five copies of every volume of the laws, journals and documents of this state, and of every other volume published by the state printer, except the "transactions of the State Agricultural Society," and the "transactions and catalogue of the State Historical Society."

SECTION 3. It shall also be the duty of the Secretary of State to deposit in the State Library for the use thereof, twenty-five copies of Taylor's Compilation of the statutes of this state, and a like number of every volume which may hereafter be purchased for the use of the State by virtue of any act of the Legislature, in quantities exceeding one hundred copies, unless the act providing for the purchase thereof shall direct their distribution in a manner inconsistent with the provisions of this section.

II. RULES AND REGULATIONS.

Prescribed by the Trustees of the State Library.

RULE I.

The Library shall be open from 9 o'clock A. M. until 12½ o'clock P. M.; from 2 o'clock P. M. until 6 o'clock P. M.; from 7 o'clock P. M. till 9 o'clock P. M., during sessions of the Legislature or of the Supreme Court at the Capitol. On all other days (Sundays excepted), it shall be open from 9 o'clock A. M. till 12 o'clock M.; and from 2 o'clock P. M. till 5 o'clock P. M.

RULE II.

SECTION 1. The State Librarian shall be accountable for any book that is missing, and for every injury which a book, map, or chart may receive during his term of office, excepting such as may be occasioned by ordinary use, and he shall be relieved from such accountability only by showing that some other person is responsible for such book or injury, without any fault of the Librarian.

SECTION 2. He shall keep a catalogue containing all the books belonging to the State Library, a manuscript of which he shall deposit with the Secretary of State.

SECTION 3. He shall keep a book of record, in which the titles or names of all books, maps, or charts received by donation, exchange or purchase, shall be entered.

SECTION 4. He shall keep a memorandum book, in which he shall enter the title of every book taken from the Library, the date when taken, and the name of the person taking the same. For every violation of this rule, he shall forfeit one dollar, to be deducted from his salary.

SECTION 5. He shall see that the Library room is kept clean and in good order, and shall carefully preserve the books, maps, charts and furniture belonging thereto, and permit none to be taken therefrom, unless expressly authorized by law or the Trustees of the Library.

SECTION 6. He shall preserve order, and permit no talking incompatible with quiet reading or copying.

SECTION 7. He shall prevent smoking, and exclude, if necessary, any disorderly person.

SECTION 8. He shall report annually to the Governor, twenty days previous to the sessions of the Legislature, the title of every book, map or chart missing from the Library since the date of the last annual report, together with the names of persons who have borrowed and detained the same, that such report may be submitted to the Legislature.

RULE III.

SECTION 1. All persons are permitted to visit the Library and examine and read the books therein, but no person is allowed to take the same therefrom except those hereinafter specified.

SECTION 2. Any State officer, Judges of the Supreme or other courts, members or officers of the Legislature, may take any book from the Library, except those hereinafter specified, provided that in no case shall such books be taken from the Capitol.

SECTION 3. No book can be taken until its delivery has been entered by the Librarian.

SECTION 4. No person can have more than five books from the Library at the same time.

SECTION 5. No book can be detained more than five days, but the borrower may, after returning it, again take it out, unless some other person has, in the mean time, made application for it.

SECTION 6. A fine of twenty-five cents may be imposed for every day's detention beyond the time above specified.

SECTION 7. Every person taking a book shall be answerable for all damages it may sustain, and if it be destroyed or lost he shall pay the value thereof, or if it is one of a set, the value of the set to which it belongs.

SECTION 8. All fines, penalties and forfeitures shall be determined and collected by the Librarian.

SECTION 9. An appeal from the above fines, penalties and forfeitures may be made to the Trustees of the Library.

RULE IV.

SECTION 1. No map, chart, or book of maps and charts, Wilson's or Bonaparte's Ornithology, Wilkes' Exploring Expedition, together with such other works as may, from time to time, be specified by the Governor or Trustees, can be taken from the Library room.

SECTION 2. No lexicon, dictionary, cyclopedia, or any file of newspapers can be taken from the Library room except during the session of the Legislature, or of the Supreme Court; any member thereof may take the same to any room in the Capitol, to be returned the same day.

RULE V.

Visitors are requested not to seat themselves near the book shelves. They are also particularly requested to return all books taken from the shelves, to their *proper places*

RULE VI.

These regulations shall be conspicuously hung in frames in the Library and other rooms of the Capitol.

PART FIRST.

ELEMENTARY LAW BOOKS:

MANUALS, COMMENTARIES, TREATISES, GENERAL DIGESTS, ABRIDGMENTS, AND DICTIONARIES OF THE LAW.

ELEMENTARY LAW BOOKS.

ABBOTT (Charles, Lord Tenterden.) A Treatise of the Law relative to Merchant Ships and Seamen. 2d Ed. By William Shee. 6th Am. Ed. With the Notes of Mr. Justice Story, and additional Annotations by J. C. Perkins. Boston. 1850.

ABBOTT (Brothers.) A Collection of Forms of Pleadings in Actions under the Code of Procedure of the State of New York, with Copious Notes and Authorities. To which are added Forms in Submissions of Controversies without Action, in Proceedings against Joint Debtors, &c.; and of Judgments by Confession. New York. 1858.

The Same. 2 vols. New York. 1864.

A Treatise upon the United States Courts and their Practice. 2 vols. New York and Chicago. 1869–1871.

ABBOTT (Benjamin Vaughan) and ABBOTT (Austin.) A Collection of Forms of Conveyancing, Contracts, and Legal Proceedings. With Notes, Explanations and Authorities. 2d Ed. New York. 1867.

A General Digest of the Law of Corporations; presenting the American Adjudications upon Public and Private Corporations of every kind. Royal 8vo. New York. 1869.

ADAMS (John.) A Treatise on the Principles and Practice of the Action of Ejectment, and resulting Action for Mesne Profits. With Notes and References by Messrs. John L. Tillinghast, Thomas W. Clerke, and William Hogan. Additional Notes by Thomas W. Waterman. 4th Ed. New York and Albany. 1854.

ADAMS (John, Jun.) The Doctrine of Equity; being a Commentary on the Law as administered by the Court of Chancery. 2d Am. Ed. Notes and References by James R. Ludlow and John M. Collins. Philadelphia. 1852.

The Same. Philadelphia. 1850. Law Library, Vol. 66.

ADDISON (C. G.) A Treatise on the Law of Contracts and Rights and Liabilities Ex Contractu. Philadelphia. 1847.

ALBANY LAW JOURNAL. Vol. 1, January to July, 1870.

ALLEN (Otis.) The Duties and Liabilities of Sheriffs, in their various relations to the Public and to Individuals, as Governed by the Principles of Common Law, and Regulated by the Statutes of New York. Albany. 1845.

ALNATT (Charles Blake.) A Practical Treatise on the Law of Partition. Philadelphia. 1834. Law Library, Vol. 3.

AMERICAN JURIST. 28 vols. Boston. 1829–43.

AMERICAN LAW MAGAZINE. 6 vols. Philadelphia. 1843–46.

AMERICAN LAW REGISTER. 14 vols. 1853–66, and New Series, vols. 6, 7, 8, 9, 10, 1866–71. (The New Series begins at vol. 10 of the whole set.) Philadelphia.

AEERICAN LAW REVIEW. 5 vols. Boston. 1867–71.

AMOS (A.) and FERARD (J.) A Treatise on the Law of Fixtures and other Property, partaking both of a Real and Personal Nature. With Notes and References by William Hogan. New York and Albany. 1855.

ANDREWS (C. C.) A Practical Treatise on the Revenue Laws of the United States. Boston. 1858.

ANGELL (Joseph K.) An Inquiry into the Rule of Law which Creates a Right to an Incorporeal Hereditament by an Adverse Enjoyment of twenty years. Boston. 1827.

A Treatise on the Limitation of Actions at Law and Suits in Equity and Admiralty. 4th Ed.: Revised and Enlarged by J. W. May. Boston. 1861.

The Same. 5th Ed. By J. W. May. Boston. 1869.

The Same. 1st Ed. Boston. 1829.

A Treatise on the Law of Carriers of Goods and Passengers, by Land and by Water. 4th Ed.: Revised and Enlarged by John Lathrop. Boston. 1868.

The Same. 2d Ed. 1851.

A Treatise on the Right of Property in Tide Waters, and in the Soil and Shores thereof. Boston. 1826.

A Treatise on the Law of Fire and Life Insurance. 2d Ed., Enlarged. Boston. 1855.

A Treatise on the Law of Watercourses. 6th Ed.: Revised and Enlarged by J. C. Perkins. Boston. 1869.

The Same. 5th Ed. 1854.

ANGELL (J. K.) and AMES (Samuel). A Treatise on the Law of Private Corporations Aggregate. 7th Ed.: Revised, Corrected and Enlarged, by John Lathrop. Boston. 1816.

The Same. 5th Ed. 1855.

ANGELL (J. K.) and DURFEE (Thomas). A Treatise on the Law of Highways. 2d Ed. with Notes and References by G. F. Choate. Boston. 1868.

The Same. 1857.

ANTHONY (Elliott.) A Treatise on the Law of Consolidation of Railroad Companies. Chicago. 1865.

APPLETON (John.) The Rules of Evidence stated and discussed. Philadelphia. 1860. Law Library, Vol. 99.

ARCHBOLD (J. F.) The Law of Landlord and Tenant; with all the requisite forms. Philadlephia. 1846.

The Same. Law Library, Vol. 51.

The Practice of the King's Bench, and, incidentally, of the Common Pleas and Exchequer, in Personal Actions and Ejectment. 3d Ed. By Thomas Chitty. 2 vols. London and Dublin. 1833.

A Complete Practical Treatise on Criminal Procedure, Pleading and Evidence, in Indictable Cases. Notes by Thomas W. Waterman. 7th Ed. 2 vols. New York and Albany. 1860.

The Law of Nisi Prius. 2 vols. 2d Ed. Philadelphia. 1845. Law Library, Vol. 48.

ARNOLD (Joseph.) A Treatise on the Law of Marine Insurance and Average, 2d Ed., with annotations by J. C. Perkins. 2 vols. Boston. 1850.

ATHERLY (Edmund Gibson.) A Practical Treatise on the Law of Marriage and other Family Settlements. Philadelphia. 1840. Law Library, Vol. 25.

ATKINSON on Titles. Philadelphia. 1857. Law Library, Vol. 14.

ATTORNEY GENERAL. Opinions of. Vols. 1–12.

AUSTIN (John.) Lectures on Jurisprudence, or the Philosophy of Positive Law. 3d. Ed. Revised and Edited by Robert Campbell. 2 vols. London. 1869.

AVERY (EDWARD) and HOBBS (Geo. W.) The Bankrupt Law of the United States, approved March 2, 1867. Boston. 1868.

BABINGTON (Richard.) A Treatise on the Law of Set-off and Mutual Credit. From the London Edition. Philadelphia. 1834. Law Library, Vol. 14.

BACON (Nathan.) A New Abridgment of the Law. 7th Ed. 8 vols. Vols. 2, 3 and 4 (except the addenda) by Sir

Henry Gwilliam. Vols. 1, 5, 6, 7 and 8 and the addenda, by C. E. Dodd. London. 1832.

The Same. Vols. 9, 11. By Bird Wilson and John Bouvier. Philadelphia. 1854.

BAGLEY (William.) The Practice at the Chambers of the Judges of the Courts of Common Law, in Civil Actions. From the London Edition. Philadelphia. 1837. Law Library, Vol. 13.

BAILLIE (Neil B. E.) A Digest of Moohummudan Law on the subjects to which it is usually applied by the British Courts of Justice in India. Compiled and Translated from the Original Arabic. 2 vols. Vol. 1, Hanifeea. Vol. 2, Imameea. London. 1865–1869.

BALLANTYNE (Wm.) A Treatise on the Statute of Limitations, with Notes, etc., by John L. Tillinghast. Albany. 1829.

BARBOUR (Oliver L.) A Treatise on the Practice of the Court of Chancery. 2 vols. Albany and New York. 1843.

A Treatise on the Criminal Law of the State of New York; and upon the Jurisdiction, Duty and Authority of Justices of the Peace, and, incidentally, of the Power and Duty of Sheriffs, Constables, etc., in Criminal Cases. 2d Ed. Albany and New York. 1852.

A Treatise on the Law of Set Off. Albany and New York. 1841.

A Summary of the Law of Parties to Actions at Law and Suits in Equity. Albany. 1864.

BATEMAN (Wm. O.) The General Commercial Law as recognized in the Jurisprudence of the United States. Philadelphia. 1860.

BATTEN (Edmund). A Practical Treatise on the Law relating to the Specific Performance of Contracts. Philadelphia. 1850. Law Library, Vol. 65.

BEAMES (John). A Summary of the Doctrine of Courts of Equity, with respect to Costs, deduced from the Leading Cases. From the last London Ed. Philadelphia. 1838. Law Library, Vol. 20.

BEAUMONT (Joseph). The Law and Practice of Bills of Sale, and Bills of Sale of Ships, under the recent statutes. Philadelphia. 1860. Law Library, Vol. 101.

BECCARIA. On Crimes and Punishments. 2d Am. Ed. Philadelphia. 1819.

BECK (F. R. and J. B.) Elements of Medical Jurisprudence. 10th Ed. 2 vols. Albany. 1850.

BELL (Sydney Smith). The Law of Property as arising from the relation of Husband and Wife. Philadelphia. 1850. Law Library, Vol. 65.

BELL (G. J.) On the Contract of Sale of Goods and Merchandize. Philadelphia. 1845. Law Library, Vol. 48.

BEMIS (George). American Neutrality: its honorable past, its expedient future. Boston. 1866.

BENEDICT (E. C.) The American Admiralty; its Jurisdiction and Practice. New York and Albany. 1850.

BENET (S. V.) A Treatise on Military Law and the Practice of Courts-Martial. 3d Ed. with additions. New York. 1863.

BENJAMIN (J. P.) A Treatise on the Law of the Sale of Personal Property. London and Washington, D. C. 1868.

BENNETT (E. H.) and HEARD (F. F.) A Selection of Leading Cases in Criminal Law. 2 vols. Boston. 1856.

BENNETT (W. H.) A Short Dissertation on the Nature of the various Proceedings in the Master's Office in the Court of Chancery. Philadelphia. 1842. Law Library, Vol. 35.

BENTHAM (Jeremy). Rationale of Judicial Evidence, specially applied to English Practice. 5 vols. London. 1827.

BEST (W. M.) A Treatise on Presumptions of Law and Fact, with the Theory and Rules of Presumptive or Circumstantial Proof in Criminal Cases. Philadelphia. 1845. Law Library, Vol. 45.

A Treatise on the Principles of Evidence and Practice as to Proofs in Courts of Common Law. Philadelphia. 1849. Law Library, Vol. 64.

BICKNELL (G. A.) The Practice of the Supreme and Circuit Courts of the State of Indiana in Civil Cases. Cincinnati. 1864.

BILLINGS (Sydney). A Practical Treatise on the Law of Awards and Arbitrations. Philadelphia. 1846. Law Library, Vol. 49.

BINGHAM (A.) and COLVIN (A. J.) A Treatise on Rents, Real and Personal Covenants, and Conditions. Albany. 1857.

BINGHAM (Peregrine). The Law of Infancy and Coverture. 2d Am. from last London Edition. Notes and References by E. H. Bennett. Burlington. 1849.

The Law and Practice of Judgments and Executions. From the London Edition. Philadelphia. 1836. Law Library, Vol. 11.

BISHOP (J. P.) Commentaries on the Law of Marriage and Divorce, of Separations without Divorce, and of the evidence of Marriage in all issues. 4th Ed. 2 vols. Boston. 1864.

Commentaries on the Criminal Law. 4th Ed. Revised and Enlarged. 2 vols. Boston. 1868.

Commentaries on the Law of Criminal Procedure, or Pleading, Evidence and Practice in Criminal Cases. 2 vols. Boston. 1866.

The First Book of the Law. Boston. 1868.

BISSETT (A.) A Practical Treatise on the the Law of Partnership, including the Law relating to Joint Stock Companies. Harrisburg, Pa. 1847.

A Practical Treatise on the Law of Estates for Life. Philadelphia. 1843. Law Library, Vol. 40.

BLACKBURN (Colin.) A Treatise on the Effect of the Contract of Sale on the Legal Rights of Property and Possession in Goods, Wares, and Merchandize. Philadelphia. 1847. Law Library, Vol. 55.

BLACKWELL (R. S.) A Practical Treatise on the Power to sell Land for the non-payment of taxes. 2d Ed. Revised and Enlarged. Boston. 1864.

BLACKSTONE (William.) The Great Charter and Charter of the Forest, with other authentic instruments. To which is prefixed an introductory discourse containing the history of the Charters. Oxford. 1759.

Commentaries on the Laws of England; in four books. Chitty's Ed. Vol. 2.

The Same. From the 21st London Ed. With copious notes explaining the changes in the law down to 1844. Vol. 1, by J. F. Hargrave; Vol. 2, by G. Sweet; Vol. 3, by R. Couch; Vol. 4, by W. N. Welsby. With American Notes by John L. Wendell. 4 vols. New York. 1859.

The Same. With Notes selected from the Editions of Archbold, Christian, Coleridge, Chitty, Stewart, Kerr and others, Baron Field's Analysis, and additional notes and a life of the author, by George Sharswood. 2 vols. Philadelphia. 1868.

The Same. With such notes of enduring value as have been published in the several English Editions; a copious Analysis of the Contents; and additional notes, and some Considerations regarding the Study of the Law, by Thomas M. Cooley. 2 vols. Chicago. 1871.

BLAKE (D. T.) Practice of the Court of Chancery of the State of New York. 2d Ed. Albany. 1824.

BLAYNEY (Frederick.) A Practical Treatise on Life Annuities. London. 1817.

BLYDENBURGH (J. W.) A Treatise on the Law of Usury. New York. 1844.

BONNEY (C. C.) A Summary of the Law of Marine, Fire and Life Insurance. Chicago. 1865.

Rules of Law for the Carriage and Delivery of Persons and Property by Railway. Chicago. 1864.

BOUTWELL (George S.) A Manual of the Direct and Excise Tax System of the United States. Boston. 1863.

BOUVIER (J.) A Law Dictionary adapted to the Constitution and Laws of the United States of America, and of the several States of the American Union. 12th Ed. Revised and Enlarged. 2 vols. Philadelphia. 1863.

The Same. 3d Ed. 2 vols. Philadelphia. 1848.

Institutes of American Law. New Edition by Daniel N. Gleason. 2 vols. Philadelphia. 1870.

BOWYER (George.) Commentaries on Universal Public Law. Philadelphia. 1854. Law Library, Vol. 82.

BRACTON and his relation to the Roman Law. By Carl Güterbock. Philadelphia. 1866.

BRIGHT (J. E.) A Treatise on the Law of Husband and Wife as respects Property. Notes and References by Ralph Lockwood. 2 vols. New York and Albany. 1850.

BRIGHTLY (F. C.) The Bankrupt Law of the United States. Philadelphia. 1869.

BROOKE (Sir Robert.) Le Graunde Abridgement, folio, 1573.

BROOM (Herbert.) Commentaries on the Common Law, designed as an introduction to its study. Philadelphia. 1856.

The Same. Philadelphia. 1856. Law Library, Vol. 89.

Practical Rules for determining Parties to Actions. From the 2d London Ed. Philadelphia. 1847. Law Library, Vol. 54.

A Selection of Legal Maxims Classified and Illustrated. 3d Ed. Philadelphia. 1852.

The Same. Philadelphia. 1845. Law Library, Vol. 48.

BROWNE (Causten.) A Treatise on the Construction of the Statute of Frauds as in force in England and the United States. 2d Ed. Revised and Enlarged. Boston. 1863.

The Same. Boston. 1857.

BROWNE (Arthur.) A Compendious View of the Civil Law and the Law of the Admiralty. 2 vols. New York. 1840.

BROWNE (Rowland Jay.) A Practical Treatise on Actions at Law. Philadelphia. 1844. Law Library, Vol. 43.

BUCK (Edward.) Massachusetts Ecclesiastical Law. 12mo. Boston. 1866.

BUCKNILL (J. C.) Unsoundness of Mind in relation to Criminal Acts. Philadelphia. 1856.

The Same. Philadelphia. 1856. Law Library, Vol. 90.

BULLER (Sir Francis.) An introduction to the law relative to trials at Nisi Prius. Annotations by Richard W. Bridgman. 7th Ed. London, 1817.

BUMP (Orlando F.) The Bankrupt Law of the United States, with all the amendments, and the Rules and Forms as Amended. New York, 1868.

BUNYAN (Charles John.) A Treatise upon the Law of Life Assurance. Philadelphia, 1854. Law Library, Vol. 77.

BURGE (William.) Commentaries on the Law of Suretyship and the rights and obligations of Parties thereto, and herein of obligations *in Solido.* First American, from the London Edition. Boston, 1847.

BURLAMAQUI (J. J.) The Principles of Natural and Politic Law. 2 vols. Philadelphia, 1832.

BURRILL (A. M.) A Law Dictionary and Glossary. 2d Ed. 2 vols. New York, 1867.

A New Law Dictionary and Glossary. 2 vols. New York. 1850.

A Treatise on the Practice of the Supreme Court of the State of New York. 2d Ed. 2 vols. New York, 1846.

Appendix to the above. 2d Ed. New York, 1846.

A Treatise on the Nature, Principles and Rules of Circumstantial Evidence. New York, 1856.

A Treatise on the Law and Practice of Voluntary assignments for the benefit of Creditors. 2d Ed. New York. 1858.

BURTON (W. H.) An Elementary Compendium of the Law of Real Property. 2d Ed. London, 1834.

The Same. Law Library, Vol. 21.

BUTTERFIELD (J. W.) A Digest of the Decisions in the office of the Second Comptroller of the Treasury. 3d Ed. Washington, D. C. 1869.

BYLES (John Barnard.) A treatise of the Law of Bills of Exchange, Promissory Notes, Bank Notes, Bankers' Cash Notes and Checks. 3d Am. Ed., from 6th London Ed., with Notes by Hon. George Sharswood. Philadelphia, 1853.

The Same. 2d Am., from the 5th London Ed. Philadelphia, 1848. Law Library, Vol. 59.

CALDWELL (James Stamford.) A Treatise of the Law of Arbitration. 2d Am., from last English Ed., with Notes and References by Chauncey Smith. Burlington, 1853.

CALVERT (Frederic.) A Treatise upon the Law respecting Parties to Suits in Equity. From the London Ed. Philadelphia, 1837. Law Library, Vol. 15.

CARY (Henry A.) Practical Treatise on the Law of Partnership, with Precedents of Copartnership Deeds. From the London Ed. Philadelphia, 1834. Law Library, Vol. 3.

CHAMBERS (Charles Harcourt.) A Treatise on the Law of Landlord and Tenant. London, 1823.

CHICAGO LEGAL NEWS. 3 vols. From October, 1868 to September, 1871. Chicago, 1868–1871.

CHIPMAN (Daniel.) An Essay on the Law of Contracts for the Payment of Specific Articles. Middlebury, 1822.

CHITTY (J.) The Practice of the Law in all its Departments. 2d Am., from 2d London Ed. 3 vols. Philadelphia. 1836.

The Same. Vol. 4. Philadelphia. 1839.

CHITTY (Joseph.) A Practical Treatise on Bills of Exchange, Checks on Bankers, Promissory Notes, Bankers' Cash Notes, and Bank Notes. 8th Am., from 8th London Ed. Containing the American Notes of former editions; to which are now added Notes by Pierre Ogilvie Beebee. Springfield. 1836.

CHITTY (Joseph, Jr.) A Practical Treatise on the Law of Contracts not under Seal; and upon the usual Defenses to Actions thereto. 8th Am., from 4th London Ed. By John A. Russel. Notes by J. C. Perkins. Springfield. 1851.

CHITTY (Joseph.) A Practical Treatise on the Criminal Law. 5th Am., from the 2d and last London Ed. 3 vols. Notes and corrections by Richard Peters and Thomas Huntington. Additional Notes by J. C. Perkins. New York and Albany. 1847.

A Treatise on Pleading and Parties to Actions. 11th Am., from 6th London Ed. With the new matter incorporated of the Text of the Treatise in the 7th London Ed., by H. Greening. Notes and Additions, by John A. Dunlap and E. D. Ingraham, and additional Notes and References by J. C. Perkins. 3 vols. Springfield. 1857.

CHITTY (Joseph.) A Practical Treatise on the Law of Nations. Boston. 1812.

CITY HALL RECORDER. The New York City Hall Recorder for the years 1816–1820. 6 vols. in 3. New York, 1817–1821.

CLANCY (James.) A Treatise of the Rights, Duties and Liabilities of Husband and Wife, at Law and in Equity. 2d Am., from last London Ed. New York. 1837.

CODE NAPOLEON; or, the French Civil Code. Literally translated from the original and official edition, published at Paris in 1804. New York. 1841.

COKE (Edward.) Systematic Arrangement of Lord Coke's First Institute of the Laws of England, on the plan of Sir Matthew Hale's Analysis; with the annotations of Mr. Hargrave, Lord Chief Justice Hale, and Lord Chancellor Nottingham. New Notes and References. 3 vols. By J. H. Thomas. 2d Am., from last London Ed.; to which are added the Notes of Charles Butler, Esq. Philadelphia. 1836.

The Second Part of the Institutes of the Laws of England, containing the Exposition of many Ancient and other Statutes. 2 vols. London. 1797.

The Third Part of the Institutes of the Laws of England, concerning High Treason and other Pleas of the Crown, and Criminal Causes. London. 1797.

The Fourth Part of the Institutes of the Laws of England. Concerning the Jurisdiction of Courts. London. 1797.

The First Part of the Institutes of the Laws of England; or a Commentary upon Littleton. Revised and Corrected, with additions of Notes, References, and Proper Tables, by Francis Hargrave and Charles Butler, including also the Notes of Lord Chief Justice Hale and Lord Chancellor Nottingham; and an Analysis of Littleton, written by an unknown Hand in 1658–9. By Charles Butler Esq. First American, from the 19th London Edition, corrected. 2 vols. Philadelphia. 1853.

COLBY (John H.) A Practical Treatise upon the Criminal Law and Practice of the State of New York. 2 vols. Albany. 1868.

Cole (W. R.) The Law and Practice relating to Criminal Informations, and Informations in the Nature of Quo Warranto. Philadelphia. 1841. Law Library, Vols. 54 and 55.

Collier (R. P.) A Treatise on the Law relating to Mines. Philadelphia. 1853. Law Library, Vol. 75.

Collyer (John.) A Practical Treatise on the Law of Partnership ; with an Appendix of Forms. 3d Am. from the 2d English Ed., with large additions to the text and notes, by J. C. Perkins. Boston. 1848.

Comyn (Robert Buckley.) A Treatise on the Law of Usury. From the London Ed. Philadelphia. 1834. Law Library, Vol. 3.

A Treatise on the Law of Landlord and Tenant. 2d Ed. From the London Ed. Philadelphia. 1834. Law Library, Vol. 4.

Comyns (Sir John, Knight). A Digest of the Laws of England. The 1st Am., from the 5th London Ed., with the addition of the American Decisions. By Thomas Day, Esq. 8 vols. New York. 1824.

Comyn (Samuel). The Law of Contracts and Promises upon vaous subjects and with particular persons, as settled in the Action of Assumpsit. The 4th Am., from the last London Edition. New York and Albany. 1835.

Conkling (Alfred). The Jurisdiction, Law and Practice of the Courts of the United States in Admiralty and Maritime Causes, including those of Quasi Admiralty Jurisdiction arising under the Act of February 26, 1845. 2 vols. Albany and Boston. 1848.

A Treatise on the Organization, Jurisdiction and Practice of the Courts of the United States. 4th Ed. Revised, Corrected and Enlarged. Albany. 1864.

The Powers of the Executive Department of the Government of the United States. Albany. 1866.

Coode (George). On Legislative Expression ; or, the Language of the Written Law. Philadelphia. 1848. Law Library, Vol. 58.

Cook (R. D.) Manual of the Highway Laws of New York. Albany. 1870.

Cooke (George Wingrove). A Treatise on the Law of Defamation. Philadelphia. 1846. Law Library, Vol. 51.

Cooley (Thomas M.) Commentaries on the Laws of England ; in four books. By Sir William Blackstone, Knight. 2 vols. Chicago. 1871.

A Treatise on the Constitutional Limitations which rest upon the Legislative Power of the States of the American Union. Boston. 1868.

COOPER (Thomas.) The Institutes of Justinian. 2d Edition. New York. 1841.

COOTE (Richard Holmes.) A Treatise on the Law of Mortgage. Philadelphia. 1837. Law Library, Vol. 16. Law Library, Vol. 61.

The Same. 3d English Ed. 2d Am. Ed. Philadelphia. 1850.

CORD (Wm. H.) A Treatise on the Legal and Equitable Rights of Married Women; as well in respect to their Property and Persons as to their Children. Philadelphia. 1861.

CORNISH (William Floyer.) A Treatise on Purchase Deeds; consisting of brief and familiar Essays on the various assurances by which Freehold Property is transferred. London, Edinburgh and Dublin. 1828.

The Same. A New Ed. by George Horsey. Philadelphia. 1856. Law Library, Vol. 88.

An Essay on Uses. From the London Ed. Philadelphia. 1834. Law Library, Vol. 1.

CORPUS JURIS CIVILIS. 2 vols. 4to. Gottingen. 1776.

CORYTON (John.) A Treatise on the Law of Letters Patent, for the sole Use of Inventions in the United Kingdom of Great Britain and Ireland. Philadelphia. 1855. Law Library, Vol. 85.

COVENTRY (Thomas.) Concise Forms in Conveyancing. 2d Ed. London. 1827.

On Conveyancers' Evidence. Philadelphia. 1839. Law Library, Vol. 24.

COWEN (Esek.) A Treatise on the Civil Jurisdiction of Justices of the Peace in the State of New York. 3d Ed. 2 vols. Albany and New York. 1844.

The Same. 4th Ed. New York and Albany. 1863.

CRABB (George.) A History of English Law; or an attempt to trace the Rise, Progress and Successive Changes of the Common Law, from the earliest period to the present time. 1st Am. Ed. Burlington. 1831.

The Law of Real Property in its present state. 2 vols. Philadelphia. 1846. Law Library, Vols 52, 53.

CRARY (Charles.) The Law and Practice in Special Proceedings and in Special Cases, within the Courts, etc., of the State of New York. 2d Ed. 2 Vols. Albany. 1866.

The Same. New York. 1858.

CROCKER (John G.) The Duties of Sheriffs, Coroners and Constables. With Practical Forms. Albany and New York. 1855.

CROSS (John) A Treatise on the Law of Lien, and Stoppage in Transitu. Philadelphia. 1841. Law Library, Vol. 32.

CURTIS (George Ticknor.) Commentaries on the Jurisdiction, Practice, and Peculiar Jurisprudence of the Courts of the United States. Vol. 1. Philadelphia. 1854.

A Treatise on the Law of Copyright in Books, Dramatic and Musical Compositions, Letters and other manuscripts, Engravings and Sculpture, as enacted and administered in England and America; with some Notices of the History of Literary Property. Boston and London. 1847.

A Treatise on the Law of Patents for Useful Inventions as enacted and administered in the United States of America. 3d Ed. Boston. 1867.

The Same Work. 1st Ed. Boston. 1849.

CUSHING (Luther S.) An Introduction to the Study of Roman Law. Boston. 1854. 12mo.

Elements of the Law and Practice of Legislative Assemblies in the United States of America. Boston. 1865.

CURWEN (Maskell E.) A Manual upon the searching of Records, and the Preparation of Abstracts of Title to Real Property. Cincinnati. 1865. 12mo.

DANE (Nathan). A General Abridgment and Digest of American Law, with occasional Notes and Comments. 8 vols. Boston. 1823.

The Same. Vol. 9. Boston. 1829.

DANIÊLL (Edmund Robert). Pleading and Practice of the High Court of Chancery. 3d English Ed. by Thomas Emerson Headlam. 3d Am. Ed. by J. C. Perkins. 3 vols. Boston. 1865.

The Same Work. 1st Am. Ed. 3 vols. Boston. 1846.

DANIEL (John Warwick). The Law and Practice of Attachment, under the Code of Virginia; and of Bail and Injunction in analogous cases wherein Attachment is not available —with a variety of all necessary forms. Also: The Law of Attachment under the new Code of West Virginia, with explanatory references to the context. Lynchburg, Richmond and Philadelphia. 1869.

DART (J. Henry). A Compendium of the Law and Practice of Vendors and Purchasers of Real Estate. With Notes and References. Also, a Prefatory View of the existing law of Real Property in England and the United States. By Thomas W. Waterman. New York and Albany. 1851.

DAVIDGE (J. B. F.) and KIMBALL (J. G.) A Compendium of Internal Revenue Laws, with Decisions, Rulings, Instructions, Regulations and Forms. Washington, D. C. 1871.

DAVIS (Daniel). A Practical Treatise upon the Authority and Duty of Justices of the Peace in Criminal Prosecutions. 3d Ed. by F. F. Heard. Boston. 1853.

DAYTON (Isaac.) The office of Surrogate, Surrogates, and Surrogates' Courts, and Executors, Administrators, and Guardians, in the State of New York. New York and Albany. 1855.

DEAN (Amos.) A Manual of Law, for the use of Business Men. Albany and New York. 1838. 12mo.

Principles of Medical Jurisprudence. Albany and New York. 1850.

DEARSLY (Henry R.) Criminal Process. Philadelphia, 1854. Law Library, Vol. 79.

DELOLME (J. L.) The Constitution of England; or, an account of the English Government; in which it is compared both with the Republican form of Government, and the other Monarchies in Europe. London. 1822.

DEVEREAUX (John C.) The most material parts of Blackstone's Commentaries, reduced to Questions and Answers. New York. 1864.

The most material parts of Kent's Commentaries, reduced to Questions and Answers. New York. 1864.

DOMAT (Jean.) The Civil Law in its Natural Order. Translated from the French by William Strahan. Edited from the 2d London Ed., by Luther S. Cushing. 2 vols. Boston. 1850.

DRAKE (Charles D.) A Treatise on the Law of Suits by Attachment in the United States. 3d Ed. Boston. 1866.

The Same Work. 2d Ed. Boston. 1858.

DREWRY (Charles Stewart.) A Treatise on the Law and Practice of Injunctions. Philadelphia. 1842. Law Library, Vol. 34.

Supplement to the Law and Practice of Injunctions, containing the cases decided since 1841. Philadelphia. 1854. Law Library, Vol. 77.

DUER (John.) The Law and Practice of Marine Insurance. 2 Vols. New York. 1845.

DUER (William Alexander.) A Course of Lectures on the Constitutional Jurisprudence of the United States. 2d Ed. Boston. 1856. 12mo.

DUNLAP (Andrew.) A Treatise on the Practice of Courts of Admiralty in Civil Causes of Maritime Jurisdiction. Philadelphia. 1836.

DUNPHY & CUMMINS. Remarkable Trials of all Countries. New York. 1867.

DU PONCEAU (Peter S.) A Dissertation on the Nature and Extent of the Jurisdiction of the Courts of the United States. To which are added, a Brief Sketch of the National Judiciary Powers exercised in the United States prior to the adoption of the present Federal Constitution, by Thomas Sergeant; and the Author's Discourse on Legal Education. Philadelphia, 1824.

DWARRIS (Fortunatus.) A General Treatise on Statutes and their Rules of Construction. Philadelphia, 1835. Law Library, Vol. 7.

A General Treatise on Statutes, their Rules of Construction, and the Proper Boundaries of Legislation and of Judicial Interpretation. With American Notes and Additions, and with Notes and Maxims of Constitutional and of Statute Construction. Also a Treatise on Constitutional Limitations upon the National and State Legislative Power, with a chapter on Parliamentary Law and Parliamentary Privileges. By Platt Potter, LL. D. Albany, 1871.

EAST (Edward Hyde.) A Treatise on the Pleas of the Crown. 2 vols. Philadelpha, 1806.

EDEN (Robert Henley.) A Treatise on the Law of Injunctions. 1st. Am. Ed. Albany and New York, 1822.

The Same. By Waterman. 1852.

A Practical Treatise on the Bankrupt Law, as amended by the New Act of the 6 Geo. IV. c. 16. From the last London Ed. Philadelphia, 1841. Law Library, Vol. 32.

EDWARDS (Isaac.) A Treatise on Bills ot Exchange and Promissory Notes. Albany and New York. 1857.

A Treatise on the Law of Bailments. Albany and New York. 1855.

EDWARDS (Charles.) A practical Treatise on Parties to Bills and other Pleadings in Chancery; with Precedents. New York and Albany. 1832.

The Law and Practice of Referees, under the New York Code and Statutes generally. Albany. 1860.

On Receivers in Equity and under the New York Code of Procedure; with Precedents. 2d Ed. New York. 1857.

A Practical Treatise on the Stamp Act of July 1, 1862, and Amendatory Statutes to March 3, 1863. 2d Ed. New York. 1863.

ELLIOTT (Jonathan.) The American Diplomatic Code. Treaties and Conventions between the United States and Foreign Powers, from 1778 to 1834, with an Abstract of Important Judicial Decisions on points connected with our Foreign Relations; also a Concise Diplomatic Manual, etc., etc. 2 vols. Washington. 1834.

The Debates, Resolutions and other Proceedings, in Convention, on the Adoption of the Federal Constitution. Vol. 1, Massachusetts and New York. Vol. 2, Virginia. Vol. 3, North Carolina and Pennsylvania. Vol. 4, Journal and Debates of the Federal Convention, held at Philadelphia from May 14 to September 17, 1787. 4 vols. Washington. 1827–1830.

ELLIS (Charles.) The Law of Fire and Life Insurance and Annuities, with Practical Observations. 2d Am., from the last English Edition. With Notes, Additions and References, by Wm. G. Shaw. Burlington. 1854.

The Same. Philadelphia. 1834. Law Library, Vol. 2.

ELWELL (John J.) A Medico-Legal Treatise on Malpractice and Medical Evidence; comprising the Elements of Medical Jurisprudence. New Edition. New York. 1866.

EMERIGON (Balthazard Marie.) A Treatise on Insurance. Translated from the French; with an Introduction and Notes by Samuel Meredith. London and Boston. 1850.

ESPINASSE (Isaac.) A Digest of the Law of Actions and Trials at Nisi Prius. 3d Ed. 2 vols. London. 1798.

FARRAR (Timothy.) Manual of the Constitution of the United States of America. 2d Ed. Boston. 1869.

FARREN (George.) The common Forms and Rules for Drawing an Original Bill in Chancery. With Notes and References by Richard Stone; also, the Rules of Practice for the Courts of Equity of the United States, as in force at the present time; with annotations on the same, and an appendix, by John J. McKinnon. Chicago, 1866.

FEARNE (Charles.) An Essay on the Learning of Contingent Remainders and Executory Devises. 3d Am., from 8th London Edition, by Charles Butler. Philadelphia. 1826.

FELL (W. W.) A Treatise on the Law of Mercantile Guaranties, and of Principal and Surety in General.

FINLASON (W.) A Selection of Leading Cases on Pleading and Parties to Actions. From the London Edition. Harrisburg, Pa. 1847.

FISHER (William Richard.) The Law of Mortgages, as applied to the Redemption, Foreclosure and Sale in Equity of Incumbered Property. Philadelphia. 1857. Law Library, Vol. 92.

FITZ-HERBERT (Anthony.) The New Natura Brevium; together with the Authorities in Law and Cases in the Books of Reports cited in the Margin. 8th Ed. with the Writs translated into English. To which is added A Commentary by the late Lord Chief Justice Hale. London. 1755. 4to.

FLANDERS (Henry.) A Treatise on the Law of Shipping. Philadelphia. 1853.

FLETA. Seu Commentarius Juris Anglicani sic muncupatiq; etc., etc. Accedit Tractulus vetus de Agendi Excipiendiq: Formulis Gallicanus, FET ASSAVOIR dictus. Subjungitur JOAN. SELDINI ad *Fletam* Dissertatio Historica. Editio Secunda. Londini. 1685.

FLETCHER (Charles.) An Essay on the Estates of Trustees. From the London Ed. Philadelphia. 1835. Law Library, Vol. 8.

FONBLANQUE (John). A Treatise of Equity. 2 Vols. Dublin. 1793.

FORSYTH (William). History of Trial by Jury. London. 1852.

A Treatise on the Law relating to the Custody of Infants, in cases of difference between Parents and Guardians. Philadelphia. 1850.

The Same. Philadelphia. 1850. Law Library, Vol. 66.

FORTESCUE (Sir John.) De Laudibus Legum Angliæ. Translated into English; illustrated with the Notes of Mr. Selden, etc.; to which are prefixed Mr. Selden to the Reader, and a large Historical Preface, etc., etc. London. 1737. Folio.

Foss (Edward.) A Biographical Dictionary of the Judges of England from the Conquest to the Present Time. 1066–1870. Boston. 1870.

Foster (Sir Michael.) A Report of some Proceedings on the Commission for the Trial of the Rebels in the year 1746, in the County of Surry; and other Crown Cases; to which are added Discourses uponn a few Branches of the Crown Law. Third Ed. with an Appendix containing New Cases. With Additional Notes and References by Michael Dodson, Esq. London. 1792. (In Reports.)

Foster (Thomas Campbell.) A Treatise on the Writ of *Scire Facias*. Philadelphia. 1851. Law Library, Vol. 71.

Fry (Edward.) A Treatise on the Specific Performance of Contracts, including those of Public Companies. Philadelphia. 1858.

The Same. Philadelphia. 1858. Law Library, Vol. 98.

Gale (C. J.) and Whately, (F. D.) A Treatise on the Law of Easements. With American Notes by E. Hammond. New York. 1840.

Gardner (David.) Institutes of International Law, Public and Private, as settled by the Supreme Court of the United States, and by our Republic. New York, 1860.

Gibbons (David.) A Manual of the Law of Fixtures. From the London Ed. Philadelphia. 1836. Law Library, Vol. 11.

Gilbert (Lord Chief Baron.) A Treatise on Rents. 12mo. London. 1758.

Cases in Law and Equity, Argued, Determined and Adjudged in the King's Bench and Chancery in the Twelfth and Thirteenth Years of Queen Anne, During the time of Lord Chief Justice Parker, with Two Treatises, the one on the Action of Debt, the other on the Constitution of England. 2d Ed. Dublin. 1792.

The Law of Devises, Last Wills, and Revocations. Dublin. 1792.

The Law of Evidence. 7th Ed. By James Sedgwick. Philadelphia. 1805.

The Law and Practice of Distresses and Replevin. 2d Ed. Dublin. 1792.

The Law of Tenures. 3d Ed. London. 1757.

GOLDSMITH (G.) The Doctrine and Practice of Equity; or a Concise Outline of Proceedings in the High Court of Chancery. Philadelphia. 1843. Law Library, Vol. 38.

GOULD (James). A Treatise on the Principles of Pleading. 2d Ed. New York. 1836.

A Treatise on the Principles of Pleading, in Civil Actions. 4th Ed. Albany. 1861.

GOW (Neil). A Practical Treatise on the Law of Partnership. 3d Ed. with Notes and References by Edward D. Ingraham. Philadelphia. 1845.

GRADY (Standish Grove). The Law of Fixtures, with reference to Real Property and Chattels of a Personal Nature. Philadelphia. 1846. Law Library, Vol. 49.

GRAHAM (David, Jr.) A Treatise on the Organization and Jurisdiction of the Courts of Law and Equity, in the State of New York. New York. 1839.

GRAHAM (David). A Treatise on the Practice of the Supreme Court of the State of New York. 3d Ed. 2 vols. Vol. 1. New York and Albany. 1847.

An Essay on New Trials. New York and Albany. 1834.

GRAHAM (David) and WATERMAN (Thos. W.) A Treatise on the Law of New Trials, in Cases Civil and Criminal. 2d Ed. 3 vols. New York and Albany. 1855.

GRANT (James). A Practical Treatise on the Law of Corporations in general, as well aggregate as sole. Philadelphia. 1854. Law Library, Vol. 78.

A Treatise on the Law relating to Bankers and Banking. Philadelphia. 1851. Law Library, Vol. 91.

GRAPEL (William). Sources of the Roman Civil Law. Philadelphia. 1857. Law Library, Vol. 92.

GREENLEAF (Simon). An Examination of the Testimony of the Four Evangelists, by the Rules of Evidence Administered in Courts of Justice. With an account of the Trial of Jesus. 2d Ed. London and Edinburgh. 1847.

GREENLEAF (Simon.) A Treatise on the Law of Evidence. 12th Ed., by Isaac F. Redfield. 3 vols. Boston. 1866.

The Same. 3d. Ed. 3 vols. Boston. 1850.

A Digest of the Law of Real Property. By William Cruise. Revised and enlarged, by Henry Hopley White. Further revised and abridged, by Simon Greenleaf. 7 vols. in 3. Boston and London. 1849.

A Collection of Overruled, Denied, and Doubted Decisions and Dicta, both American and English. 4th Ed., by John Townshend. New York. 1867.

A Collection of Cases Overruled, Denied, Doubted, or Limited in their application, taken from American and English Reports. 3d Ed. New York. 1840.

GRESLEY (Richard Newcombe.) A Treatise on the Law of Evidence in Courts of Equity. 2d Ed., by Christopher Alderson Calvert. 2d Am. Ed. Philadelphia. 1848.

GROTIUS (Hugo.) His three books, treating of the rights of War and Peace. Translated into English, by William Evats, B. D. 4to. London. 1682.

GWYNNE (A. E.) A Practical Treatise on the Law of Sheriff and Coroner. Cincinnati. 1849.

HALE (Sir Matthew, Knt.) The History of the Pleas of the Crown. 1st Am. Ed., by W. A. Stokes and E. Ingersoll. 2 vols. Philadelphia. 1847.

HALLECK (H. W.) International Law; or, Rules regulating the Intercourse of States in Peace and War. New York and London. 1861.

HALSTED (Jacob R.) Digest of the Law of Evidence. 2d Ed. 2 vols. New York. 1859.

HAMMOND (Anthony.) On Forgery. The Criminal Code; including a Digest, Consolidation, and Collection of the Statutes, collated with the Original Record. Forgery. London. 1823.

HAMMOND (William A.) The Quarterly Journal of Psychological Medicine and Medical Jurisprudence. Vols. 1 and 2. New York. 1867–1868.

HARE (Thomas.) A Treatise on Discovery of Evidence by Bill and Answer, in Equity. 2d Am., from last London Ed. With Notes and References, by Robert S. Rowley. New York. 1849.

HARE (J. I. Clark) and WALLACE (H. B.) American Leading Cases. 2d Ed. 2 vols. Philadelphia. 1851.

A Selection of Leading Cases on various branches of the Law: with Notes by John William Smith. Additional Notes by J. I. Clark Hare and J. W. Wallace. 2 vols. in 3. Philadelphia. 1866.

HAWKINS (William). A Treatise of the Pleas of the Crown. 8th Ed. 2 vols. By John Curwood. London and Dublin. 1824.

HAYES (William). Principles for expounding Dispositions of Real Estate to Ancestor and Heirs in Tail, Parent and Issue, and solving the question, "Whether the first taker is Tenant for Life or in Tail?" With an Elementary Essay, and Dissertations on several of Mr. Fearne's Doctrines. From the London Ed. Philadelphia. 1835. Law Library, Vol. 5.

HENING (William W.) The American Pleader and Lawyer's Guide. To which is added the Merchant's, Clerk's, and Sheriff's Magazine, containing all the necessary forms appertaining to their respective pursuits. 2 vols. New York. 1811.

HENNELL (Charles). Forms of Declarations, &c., prepared in conformity with the New General Rules of all the Courts. From the London Ed. Philadelphia. 1834. Law Library, Vol. 1.

HIGHMORE (A.) A Treatise on the Law of Idiocy and Lunacy. Exeter, N. H. 1822.

HILDYARD (Francis). A Treatise on the Principles of the Law of Marine Insurances. From the London Ed. Harrisburg, Pa. 1847.

HILL (James). A Practical Treatise on the Law relating to Trustees, their Powers, Duties, Privileges, and Liabilities. 3d Am. Ed. With Notes and References by Francis J. Froubat and Henry Wharton. Philadelphia. 1857.

HILLIARD (Francis). The Law of New Trials and other Rehearings. Philadelphia. 1866.

The Law of Remedies for Torts, or Private Wrongs. Boston. 1867.

The Law of Torts or Private Wrongs. 2 vols. Boston. 1859.

The Law of Mortgages of Real and Personal Property. 2 vols. Boston and London. 1853.

The American Law of Real Property. 2d Ed. 2 vols. Philadelphia. 1846.

The Law of Injunctions. Philadelphia. 1865.

A Treatise on the Law of Bankruptcy and Insolvency. Philadelphia. 1863.

HILLIARD (Francis.) A Treatise on the Law of Sales of Personal Property. New York. 1841.

The Law of Contracts. 2 vols. Philadelphia. 1872.

The Law of Vendors and Purchasers of Real Property. 2d Ed. Boston. 1868.

The Same. 2 vols. in one. Boston. 1858.

HINDMARCH (W. M.) A Treatise on the Law relative to Patent Privileges for the Sole Use of Inventions: and the Practice of obtaining Letters Patent for Inventions. Harrisburg, Pa. 1847.

Observations on the Defects of the Patent Laws of this country; with suggestions for the Reform of them. Philadelphia. 1851. Law Library, Vol. 71.

HOFFMAN (David.) A Course of Legal Study. 2d Ed. 2 vols. Baltimore. 1836.

A Treatise upon the Practice of the Court of Chancery. 2d Ed. 2 vols. New York. 1843.

A Treatise upon the Practice of the Court of Chancery. In 3 vols. Vol. 3. New York. 1840.

The Provisional Remedies of the Code of Procedure. New York. 1862.

HOLCOMBE (James P.) An Introduction to Equity Jurisprudence. Cincinnati. 1846.

The Law of Debtor and Creditor, in the United States and Canada. New York and Philadelphia. 1848.

HOLMES & DISBROW. Practice in the Supreme Court of the State of New York in Common Law Actions upon Contracts. New York. 1859.

HORNE (Thomas Hartwell.) Diplomacy. Philadelphia. 1853. Law Library, Vol. 76.

HOUCK (Louis.) A Treatise on the Law of Navigable Rivers. Boston. 1868.

A Treatise on the Mechanics' Lien Law of tne United States. Chicago. 1867.

HOVENDEN (John Eykyn.) A General Treatise on the Principles and Practice by which Courts of Equity are Guided as to the Prevention or Remedial Correction of Fraud. 1st Am. Ed., by Thomas Huntington. 2 vols. New York. 1832.

HUBBACK (John.) A Treatise on the Evidence of Succession to Real and Personal Property. Philadelphia. 1845. Law Library, Vols. 45 and 46.

HOWARD (Nathan.) The Code of Procedure of Pleadings and Practice of the State of New York, in 1858-9. New York and Albany. 1859.

The Code of Procedure of the State of New York, unabridged. Including all the sections in full as originally passed and amended, to and including 1867. With full and copious Notes. Vol. 1. New York. 1867.

HUGHES (Edward.) The Equity Draughtsman. From the Second London Edition. New York. 1832.

HUGHES (David.) A Treatise on the Law relating to Insurance. New York and Philiadelphia. 1833.

HULL (Amos G.) A Treatise on the Powers and Duties other than Judicial of Town and County Officers in the State of New York. Albany. 1855.

HUMPHREYS (Charles.) A collection of Practical Forms in Suits at Law; also Precedents of Contracts, Conveyances, Wills, etc. 2 Vols. Albany and New York. 1845.

HUNTER (Sylvester Joseph.) An Elementary View of the Proceedings in a Suit in Equity. Philadelphia, 1860. Law Library, Vol. 102.

HURD (John Codman.) The Law of Freedom and Bondage in the United States. 2 Vols. Boston and New York. 1858.

HURD (Rollin C.) A Treatise in the Right of Personal Liberty, and on the Writ of *Habeas Corpus* and the Practice connected with it; with a view of the Law of Estradition of Fugitives. Albany. 1858.

HURLSTONE. (Edwin Tyrrel.) A Practical Treatise on the Law of Bonds, with an appendix of Forms, Declarations, and Pleas. From the London Edition. Philadelphia, 1835.

INGERSOLL (E.) The History and Law of the Writ of *Habeas Corpus*, with an Essay on the Law of Grand Juries. Philadelphia. 1849.

INGRAHAM (Edward D.) A View of the Insolvent Laws of Pennsylvania. 2d Ed. Philadelphia. 1827.

JAMES (Edwin.) The Bankrupt Law of the United States, 1867; New York. 1867.

JAMESON (John Alexander.) The Constitutional Convention; its History, Powers and Modes of Proceeding. New York and Chicago. 1867.

JARMAN (Thomas.) A Treatise on Wills. 2d American Edition, by J. C. Perkins. 2 Vols. Boston, 1849.

JENKINS (John S.) The New Clerk's Assistant, or Book of Practical Forms. New York and Buffalo. 1864.

JEREMY (George.) A Treatise on the Equity Jurisdiction of the High Court of Chancery. 1st Am. from last London Ed. Philadelphia.

JONES (Robert.) A History of the French Bar, Ancient and Modern. Philadelphia. 1856. Law Library, Vol. 88.

JONES (Sir William Knt.) An Essay on the Law of Bailments. From the last London Edition.

JOY (Henry H.) On the Admissibility of Confessions and Challenge of Jurors in Criminal Cases in England and Ireland. Philadelphia. 1843. Law Library, Vol. 38.

On the Evidence of Accomplices. Philadelphia. 1844.

JUSTINIAN'S Institutes. By Harris.

KAUFMANN (Philip Ignatius.) Compendium of Modern Civil Law. By Ferdinand Mackeldey. From the 12th German Ed. 2 vols. Vol. 1. New York. 1845.

KENT (James.) Commentaries on American Law. 11th Ed. By Geo. F. Comstock. 4 Vols. Boston. 1867.

The Same. 10th Ed. Boston. 1860.

The Same. 8th Ed. New York. 1854.

KELLY (James Birch.) A Summary of the History and Law of Usury. Philadelphia. 1853. Law Library, Vol. 73.

KELHAM (Robert.) A Dictionary of the Norman or old French Language. Philadelphia. 1843.

KERR (Robert Malcolm) An Action at Law. Philadelphia. 1854. Law Library, Vol. 79.

KERR (William Williamson.) A Treatise on the Law and Practice of Injunctions in Equity. Edited, with notes and references to American cases, by Wm. A. Herrick. Boston. 1871.

KYD (Stewart.) A Treatise on the Law of Awards. 1st Am. from 2d London Ed. Philadelphia. 1808.

LALOR (T. W.) The Law of Real Property of the State of New York. New York. 1866.

LAMBARD (William.) Archaionomia, sive de Priscis Anglorum Legibus Libri. Sermone Anglico * * conscripti, etc., etc. Cum Glossario, etc. Folio. Cambridge. 1644.

LAMBERT (Eli.) A Treatise on Dower. New York and Albany. 1834.

LANGDELL (C. C.) A Selection of Cases on the Law of Contracts. With references and citations. Prepared for use as a text-book in Harvard Law School. Boston. 1871.

LAWES (Edward.) A Practical Treatise on Pleading in Assumpsit. With decisions of American Courts, by Joseph Story. Boston. 1811.

LAW (Stephen D.) Digest of American Cases relating to Patents for Inventions and Copyrights from 1789 to 1862. Statute Laws of the United States of America relating to copyrights and Patents for inventions from 1791 to 1862. New York. 1866.

The Jurisdiction and Powers of the United States Courts, and the Rules of Practice of the Supreme Court of the United States and the Circuit and District Courts in Equity and Admiralty. Albany. 1852.

LAW LIBRARY (The). Edited by Thomas Sergeant and John C. Lowber. Philadelphia. 1834–1860. (The several Works contained in this Series are also separately catalogued.)

Adams' Doctrine of Equity, 66.
Allnat on Partition, 3.
Appleton on Evidence, 99 (6 S. Vol. 28).
Archbold's Landlord and Tenant, 51.
" Nisi Prius, 47, 48.
Atherley on Marriage Settlements, 25.
Atkinson on Titles, 14.

Babington on Set-Off, 4.
Bagley's Practice at Chambers, 13.
Batten on Contracts, 65.
Beames on Costs in Equity, 20.
Beaumont on Bills of Sale, 101 (6 S. Vol. 30).
Bell on the Contract of Sale, 48.
Bell on the Law of Real Property, 65.
Bennet's Practice in Master's Office, 35.
Best on Presumptions of Law and Fact, 45.
Best's Principles of Evidence, 64.
Billings on the Law of Awards, 49.
Bingham on Judgment and Execution, 11.
Bisset on Estates of Life, 40.
Blackburn on the Contract of Sale. 55.
Bowyer's Universal Public Law, 82 (6 S. Vol. 11).
Broom on Parties to Actions, 54.
Broom's Legal Maxims, 48.

Broom's Commentaries on the Common Law, 89 (6 S. Vol. 18).
Browne on Actions at Law, 43.
Bucknill on Criminal Lunacy, 90 (6 S. Vol. 19).
Bunyon on Life Assurance, 77.
Burton's Compendium of Law of Real Property, 21.
Byles on Bills of Exchange, 59.

Calvert on Parties to Suits in Equity, 15.
Cary on Partners, 3.
Cole on Criminal Informations, 54, 55.
Collier's Law of Mines, 75.
Comyn on Usury, 3.
Comyn on Landlord and Tenant, 4.
Coode on Legislative Expression, 58.
Cooke on Defamation, 51.
Coote on Mortgages, 16, 67 (2 Editions.)
Cornish on Uses, 1.
Cornish on Purchase Deeds, 88 (6 S. Vol. 17).
Coryton on Patents, 85 (6 S. Vol. 14).
Coventry on Conveyancer's Evidence, 24.
Crabb on Real Property, 52, 53.
Cross on the Law of Lien, 32.

Dearsley on Criminal Process, 79.
Drewry on Injunctions, 34, 77.
Dwarris on Statutes, 7.

Eden on the Bankrupt Law, 32, 33.
Ellis on Insurance, 2.

Fisher on Mortgages, 92 (6 S. Vol. 21).
Fletcher on the Estates of Trustees, 8.
Forsyth on the Custody of Infants, 66.
Foster's Writ of Scire Facias, 71.
Fry on Specific Performance, 98 (6 S. Vol. 27).

Gibbons' Law of Fixtures, 11.
Goldsmith's Equity, 38.
Grady's Law of Fixtures, 49.
Grant on Corporations, 78.
Grant on Banks and Banking, 91 (6 S. Vol. 20).
Grapel on the Roman Civil Law, 91 (6 S. Vol. 21)

Hayes on Estates Tail, 5.
Haynes' Outlines of Equity, 96 (6 S. Vol. 25).
Hennell's Forms, 1.
Hindmarch on the Patent Laws, 71.
Horne on Diplomacy, 76.
Hubback's Evidence of Succession, 45, 46.
Hurlstone on bonds, 7.
Hunter's Suit in Equity, 102 (6 S. Vol. 31).

Jones' History of the French Bar, 88 (6 S. Vol. 17).
Joy on the Admissibility of Confessions, 38.
Joy on the Evidence of Accomplices, 43.

Kelly on Usury, 73.
Kerr on Actions at Law, 79.

Lee on Abstacts of Title, 56.
Leigh & Dalzell on Conversion, 3.
Levi on Mercantile Law, 82 (8 S. Vol. 11).
Lewin on Trusts and Trustees, 22, 95 (6 S. Vol. 24).
Lewis on Perpetuity, 50, 64.
Lindley's Study of Jurisprudence, 84 (6 S. Vol. 13).
Lindley on Partnership, 100, 101 (6 S. 29, 30).
Locke on Foreign Attachment, 77.
Long's Discourses, 58.
Lovelass on Wills, 23.
Lund on Patents, 71.

McNamara on Nullities, 85 (6 S. Vol. 14).
McNaughton's Select Cases, 72.
McPherson on Infants, 39.
Mac Queen on Husband Wife, 57, 64.
Mansel on Demurrer, 24.
Matthews on Executors, 7.
Mayne on the Law of Damages, 90 (6 S. Vol. 19).
Miller's Law of Equitable Mortgages, 45.
Moore on Abstracts of Title, 75.

Norman's Law of Patents, 75.
Notes of Recent Leading Cases, 50, 60.

Oliphant on Horses and Horse-Racing, 56.

Paley on Agency, 26.
Park on Dower, 9.
Parsons on Wills, 84 (6 S. Vol. 13).
Perpigna on Patents, 2.
Petersdorf on Bail, 8.
Phear on Rights of Water, 98 (6 S. Vol. 27).
Phillimore on International Law, 81, 86, 93 (6 S. 10, 15, 22).
Phillimore on Domicil, 55.
Pitman on Principal and Surety, 38.
Platt on Covenants, 1.
Pollock on the Production of Documents, 75.
Polson's Law of Nations, 76.
Pothier on Partnership, 81 (6 S. Vol. 10).
Poynter on Marriage and Divorce, 11.
Powell on Devises, 19, 20.
Powell on Evidence, 94 (6 S. Vol. 23).
Preston on Estates, 40.
Pulling on Mercantile Accounts, 55.

Willcock on Municipal Corporations, 12.
Willcock's Office of Constable, 27.
Williams on Personal Property, 60.
Willis on Pleadings in Equity, 33.
Willis on Trustees, 8.
Wills on Circumstantial Evidence, 39.
Wilson on Springing Uses, 9.
Winslow on the Plea of Insanity, 40.
Wooddeson's Lectures, 36, 37.
Woolrych on Ways, 2.
Woolrych's Law of Waters, 76.
Wordsworth on Joint Stock Companies, 37, 38.
Worthington on the Power of Juries, 27.
Worthington on Wills, 58.

LEE (John Yate.) A Treatise on the Evidence of Abstracts of Title to Real Property. Philadelphia. 1847. Law Library, Vol. 56.

LEGAL OBSERVER. The Legal Observer or Journal of Jurisprudence. Published Weekly. November, 1830, to May, 1854. Bound in 54 vols. and 6 monthly parts in paper. London. 1830–1854.

LEIGH (J. H.) and DALZELL (R.) A Treatise on the Equitable Doctrine of Conversion of Property. Philadelphia. 1834. Law Library, Vol. 3.

LESTER (W. W.) Decision of the Interior Department in Public Land Cases, and Land Laws passed by the Congress of the United States; together with the Regulations of the General Land Office. Philadelphia 1860.

Land Laws Regulations and Decisions. Vol. 2. Philadelphia. 1870.

LEVI (Leone.) Manual of the Mercantile Law of Great Britain and Ireland. Philadelphia. 1854. Law Library, Vol. 82.

LEWIN (Thomas.) A Practical Treatise on the Law of Trusts and Trustees. Philadelphia. 1839. Law Library, Vol. 22.

The Same. 2d Am. from the 3d London Edition. Philadelphia. 1858. Law Library, Vol. 95.

LEWIS (William David.) A Practical Treatise on the Law of Perpetuity. Philadelphia. 1846. Law Library, Vols. 50 and 64.

LILLY (John.) A Collection of Modern Entries, or Select Pleadings in the Courts of King's Bench, Common Pleas and Exchequer. 6th Ed. 2 vols. Dublin. 1792.

LINDLEY (Nathaniel.) An Introduction to the Study of Jurisprudence. Philadelphia. 1855. Law Library, Vol. 84.

A Treatise on the Law of Partnership, including its application to Joint Stock and other Companies. 2 vols. Philadelphia. 1860. Law Library, Vols. 100 and 101.

LITTLETON (H. A.) and BLATCHLEY (J. S.) Digest of Fire Insurance Decisions in the Courts of Great Britain and North America. 2d Ed. By Stephen G. Clark. New York. 1868.

LIVERMORE (Samuel.) A Treatise on the Law of Principal and Agent; and of Sales by Auction. 2 vols. Baltimore. 1818.

LIVINGSTON (John.) The Law Register. New York. 1868.

LOCKE (John.) The Law and Practice of Foreign Attachment in the Lord Mayor's Court, under the New Rules of of Practice. Philadelphia. 1854. Law Library, Vol. 77.

LOCRE (M. le Baron.) La Legislation Civile, Commerciale et Criminelle de la France, ou Commentaire et Complement des Codes Francais. 12 Vols. Paris. 1827.

LOMAX (John Taylor.) Digest of the Laws respecting Real Property generally adopted and in use in the United States. 2d Ed. 3 Vols. Richmond, Va. 1855.

A Treatise on the Law of Executors and Administrators, generally in use in the United States; and adapted more particularly to the Practice of Virginia. 2 Vols. Philadelphia. 1841.

LONG (George.) A Treatise on the Law relative to Sales of Personal Property. 2d Ed., by Benjamin Rand. Boston. 1839.

Two Discourses delivered in the Middle Temple Hall. Philadelphia. 1848. Law Library, Vol. 58.

LOVELASS (Peter.) The Law's Disposal of a Person's Estate who dies without a Will or Testament. From the 12th London Ed. Philadelphia. 1839. Law Library, Vol. 23.

LUBE (D. G.) An Analysis of the Principles of Equity Pleading. 2d Am. from the last London Edition. By J. D. Wheeler. New York and Albany. 1846.

LUND (Henry.) A Treatise on the Substantive Law relating to to Letters Patent for Inventions. Philadelphia. 1851. Law Library, Vol. 71.

MACNAGHTEN (Stewart.) Select Cases Argued and Adjudged in the High Court of Chancery, before the late Lords Commissioners of the Great Seal, and the late Lord Chancellor King, from the year 1724 to 1733. 2d Ed. Philadelphia. 1851. Law Library, Vol. 72.

MACNAMARA (H.) A Practical Treatise on Nullities, and Irregularities in Law, their Character, Distinctions and Consequences. Philadelphia. 1855. Law Library, Vol. 85.

MACOMB (Alexander.) The Practice of Courts Martial. New York and Albany. 1847.

MACPHERSON (William.) A Treatise on the Law relating to Infants. Philadelphia. Law Library, Vol. 39.

MACQUEEN (John Fraser.) The Rights and Liabilities of Husband and Wife at Law and in Equity. Philadelphia. 1848. Law Library, Vol. 57.

The Same. Philadelphia. 1849. Law Library, Vol. 64.

MAINE (Henry Sumner.) Ancient Law; its connection with the early history of society, and its relation to modern ideas. 1st Am. from the 2d London Edition. New York. 1864.

MANSEL (George Barclay.) A Treatise on the Law and Practice of Demurrer to Pleadings and Evidence. Philadelphia. 1839. Law Library, Vol. 24.

MARSHALL (John). The Writings of John Marshall, late Chief Justice of the United States., upon the Federal Constitution. Boston. 1839.

MARSHALL (Samuel). A Treatise on the Law of Insurance. 2 vols. Philadelphia. 1810.

MARVIN (J. G.) Legal Bibliography, or a Thesaurus of American, English, Irish, and Scotch Law Books. Philadelphia. 1847.

MATTHEWS (John H.) A Treatise on the Doctrine of Presumption and Presumptive Evidence, as affecting the Title to Real and Personal Property. New York and Albany. 1830.

MATTHEWS (Richard). A Practical Guide to Executors and Administrators. From the London Edition. Philadelphia. 1835. Law Library, Vol. 7.

MAYNE (John D.) A Treatise on the Law of Damages. Philadelphia. 1856. Law Library, Vol. 90.

McCALL (H. S.) The New York Civil and Criminal Justice; a complete treatise on the Civil, Criminal, and Special Powers and Duties of Justices of the Peace in the State of New York. 3d Ed. Albany. 1866.

McMullen (Joseph F.) The New Wisconsin Form Book; a Compendium of Legal and Practical Forms, with Principles of Law adapted to the Statutes of Wisconsin. 3d Ed. Milwaukee. 1869.

Metcalf (Theron). Principles of the Law of Contracts, as applied by Courts of Law. New York and Philadelphia. 1868.

Miller (Samuel). The Law of Equitable Mortgages. Philadelphia. 1845. Law Library, Vol. 45.

Mitford (John). A Treatise on the Pleadings in Suits in the Court of Chancery, by English Bill. 4th Ed., by George Jeremy. 3d Am. Ed., by Charles Edwards. New York. 1833.

Monell (Claudius.) A Treatise on the Practice of the Supreme Court of the State of New York; adapted to the Code of Procedure, as amended by the Act of April 11, 1849, and the Act of April 16, 1852, and the Rules of the Supreme Court. 2d Ed. 2 vols. Albany and New York. 1855.

Montesquieu (Baron de.) The Spirit of Laws. 1st Am. from the 5th London Ed. 2 vols. Worcester. 1802.

Moore (Henry.) Instructions for preparing Abstracts of Titles. From the 2d London Ed. Philadelphia. 1853. Law Library, Vol. 7.

Morris (O. Pemberton.) A Practical Treatise on the Law of Replevin in the United States. Philadelphia. 1849.

The Same. 2d Ed. Philadelphia. 1869.

Morse (John F., Jr.) A Treatise on the Law relating to Banks and Banking; with an Appendix containing the National Banking Act of June 3, 1864, and Amendments thereto. Boston. 1870.

Moses (Halsey H.) The Law of *Mandamus* and the Practice connected with it. Albany. 1867.

National Bankrupt Registry; with Supplement, containing the Bankruptcy Decisions reported in the sixth volume of the "International Revenue Record," and the Leading Cases, etc., in Bankruptcy of the District Judges of the U. S. 4to. Vols. 1 and 2. June, 1867, to July, 1869. Bound in one volume. New York. 1869.

The Same. Vols. 3 and 4. New York. 1869–1871.

Nash (Simeon.) Pleading and Practice under the Civil Code. 2d Ed. Cincinnati. 1864.

New York Legal Observer. 12 vols. New York. 1843–1854.

Newland (John.) A Treatise on Contracts, within the Jurisdiction of Courts of Equity. Philadelphia. 1821.

Norman (John Parton.) A Treatise on the Law and Practice relating to Letters Patent for Inventions. Philadelphia. 1853. Law Library, Vol. 75.

Nott (Charles C.) A Treatise on the Mechanics' Lien Laws of the State of New York. Albany. 1856.

Noy (William.) The Principal Grounds and Maxims, with an Analysis of the Laws of England. 2d Am. from the 9th London Ed. By William Waller Hening. Richmond. 1824.

Oliphant (George Henry Hewit). The Law concerning Horses, Racing, Wagers, Gaming. Philadelphia. 1847. Law Library, Vol. 56.

Ordronaux (John). The Jurisprudence of Medicine in its relations to the Law of Contracts, Torts and Evidence, with a Supplement on the Liabilities of Vendors of Drugs. Philadelphia. 1869.

Page (Henry Folsom). A View of the Law relative to the subject of Divorce, in Ohio, Indiana and Michigan. Columbus. 1850.

Paine (Elijah) and Duer (William). The Practice in Civil Actions and Proceedings at Law in the State of New York, in the Supreme Court, and other Courts of the State; and also in the Courts of the United States. 2 vols. New York. 1830.

Paley (William). A Treatise on the Law of Principal and Agent, chiefly with reference to Mercantile Transactions. 3d Ed. By J. H. Lloyd. 3d Am. Ed. by John A. Dunlap. New York and Albany. 1847.

A Treatise on the Law of Principal and Agent. 2d Am. from the 3d London Ed. Philadelphia. 1840. Law Library, Vol. 26.

Park (Sir James Allan, Knt.) A System of the Law of Marine Insurance; with three chapters on Bottomry; on Insurances on Lives; and on Insurance against Fire. 8th Ed. by Francis Hildyard. 2 vols. London. 1842.

PARK (John James). A Treatise on the Law of Dower; particularly with a view to the Modern Practice of Conveyancing. From the London Ed. Philadelphia. 1836. Law Library, Vol. 9.

PARSONS (Theophilus). A Treatise on Maritime Law. 2 vols. Boston. 1859.

A Treatise on the Law of Marine Insurance and General Average. 2 vols. Boston. 1868.

A Treatise on the Law of Partnership. Boston. 1867.

A Treatise on the Law of Shipping and the Law and Practice of Admiralty. 2 vols. Boston. 1869.

The Law of Contracts. 5th Ed. 3 vols. Boston. 1864.

The Same. 4th Ed. 2 vols. Boston. 1860.

The Same. 1st Ed. Vol. 1. Boston. 1853.

A Treatise on the Law of Promissory Notes and Bills of Exchange. 2 vols. Philadelphia. 1863.

The Elements of Mercantile Law. Boston. 1856.

PARSONS (Theophilus.) The Laws of Business for Business Men, in all the States of the Union. Boston. 1851.

PARSONS (A. V.) Select Cases in Equity Argued and Determined in the Court of Common Pleas of the First Judicial District of Pennsylvania, from 1841 to 1850. Vol. 1. Philadelphia. 1859.

PARSONS (Arthur.) A Treatise on the Law of Wills. Philadelphia. 1855. Law Library, Vol. 84.

PASCHAL (George W.) The Constitution of the United States Defined and Carefully Annotated. 12mo. Washington, D. C. 1868.

PERPIGNA (A.) The French Law and Practice of Patents for Inventions, Improvements and Importations. From the Paris Ed. Philadelphia. 1834. Law Library, Vol. 2.

PETERSDORFF (Charles.) A Practical and Elementary Abridgment of the Cases Argued and Determined in the Courts of King's Bench, Common Pleas, Exchequer and at Nisi Prius; and of the Rules of Court, from the Restoration in 1660, to Michaelmas Term, 4 Geo. IV. With important Manuscript Cases; Alphabetically, Chronologically and systematically arranged and translated. 15 vols. London. 1825.

PETERSDORFF (Charles). A Practical Treatise on the Law of Bail, in Civil and Criminal Proceedings. From the London Edition. Philadelphia. 1835. Law Library, Vol. 8.

PHEAR (J. B.) A Treatise on the Rights of Water. Philadelphia. 1859. Law Library, Vol. 98.

PHILLIMORE (Robert). The Law of Domicil. Philadelphia. 1847. Law Library, Vol. 55.

Commentaries upon International Law. Vol. 1. Philadelphia. 1854. Law Library, Vol. 81.

The Same. Vol. 2. Philadelphia. 1855. Law Library, Vol. 86.

The Same. Vol. 3. Philadelphia. 1857. Law Library, Vol. 93.

The Same. 3 vols. in 2. Philadelphia. 1854.

PHILLIPPS (S. March) and ARNOLD (Thomas James). A Treatise on the Law of Evidence. 10th Eng. Ed. 4th Am. Ed. with Cowen and Hill's Notes. 3 vols. New York and Albany. 1859.

PHILLIPPS (S. March). A Treatise on the Law of Evidence. 6th American from 9th London Ed. 5 vols. With Notes by Esek Cowen and Nicholas Hill, Jr., also by J. Marsden VanCott. New York and Albany. 1849.

PHILLIPS (Willard). A Treatise on the Law of Insurance. 5th Ed. 2 vols. New York. 1867.

PIERCE (Edward L.) A Treatise on American Railroad Law. New York. 1857.

PITMAN (Edward Dix). A Treatise on the Law of Principal and Surety. Philadelphia. 1843. Law Library, Vol. 38.

PLATT (Thomas). A Treatise on the Law of Leases. 2 vols. London and Dublin. 1847.

A Treatise on the Law of Covenants. From the London Ed. Philadelphia, 1834. Law Library, Vol. 1.

POLLOCK (Charles Edward). A Treatise on the Power of the Courts of Common Law to Compel production of Documents for Inspection. Philadelphia. 1853. Law Library, Vol. 75.

POLSON (Archer). Principles of the Law of Nations. Philadelphia. 1853. Law Library, Vol. 74.

POMEROY (John Norton.) An Introduction to the Constitutional Law of the United States, New York. 1868.

An Introduction to Municipal Law. New York and London. 1864.

POTHIER (R. J.) A Treatise on the Law of Obligations or Contracts. Translated from the French, with an Introduction, Appendix, and Notes, illustrative of the English Law on the Subject. By William David Evans. 2 vols. Philadelphia. 1826.

Treatise on the Contract of Sale. Translated from the French by L. S. Cushing. Boston. 1839.

A Treatise on the Contract of Partnership. Translated from the French by Owen Davies Tudor. Philadelphia. 1854. Law Library, Vol. 81.

POWELL (J. J.) A Treatise on the Law of Mortgages. Reprinted from the 6th English Ed. by Thomas Coventry. Notes and References to American Cases by Benjamin Rand. 3 vols. Boston. 1828.

An Essay on Devises. Also a Treatise on the Construction of Devises. By Thomas Jarman. 2 vols. From the last London Ed. Philadelphia. 1838. Law Library, Vols. 19 and 20.

POWELL (Edmund). The Practice of the Law of Evidence. With a Chapter on the Measure of Damages. Philadelphia. 1858. Law Library, Vol. 94.

POYNTER (Thomas). A Concise View of the Doctrine and Practice of the Ecclesiastical Courts in Doctors' Commons, on various points relative to the subject of Marriage and Divorce. 2d Ed. London. 1824.

A Concise View of the Doctrine and Practice of the Ecclesiastical Courts in Doctors' Commons, on various points relative to the subject of Marriage and Divorce. 2d Ed. From the London Ed. Philadelphia. 1836. Law Library, Vol. 11.

PRESTON (Richard). An Essay in a Course of Lectures on Abstracts of Title. 2 vols. New York and Philadelphia. 1828.

An Elementary Treatise on Estates; with Preliminary Observations on the Quality of Estates. 2 vols. New York. 1828.

An Essay on the Quantity and Quality of Estates, with more immediate reference to the Law of Merger. From the 3d London Ed. Philadelphia. 1843. Law Library, Vol. 40.

PRESTON (William Scott). A Practical Treatise on the Law of Legacies. New York. 1827.

PULLING (Alexander). A Practical Compendium of the Law and Usage of Mercantile Accounts. Philadelphia. 1847. Law Library, Vol. 55.

RAFF (George W.) A Manual of Pensions, Bounty and Pay. 2d Ed. Cincinnati. 1865.

RAM (James). A Practical Treatise of Assets, Debts and Incumbrances. From the London Ed. Philadelphia. 1835. Law Library, Vol. 6.

A Treatise on the Exposition of Wills of Landed Property. From the London Ed. Philadelphia. 1835. Law Library, Vol. 6.

The Science of Legal Judgment. From the London Ed. Philadelphia. 1835. Law Library, Vol. 7.

RAWLE (William). A View of the Constitution of the United States of America. 2d Ed. Philadelphia. 1829.

RAWLE (William Henry). A Practical Treatise on the Law of Covenants for Title. 2d Ed. Philadelphia. 1854.

RAY (J.) A Treatise on the Medical Jurisprudence of Insanity. 3d Ed. Boston. 1853.

The Same. 5th Ed., with additions. Boston. 1871.

RAYMOND (John). The Bill of Exceptions. Philadelphia. 1848. Law Library, Vol. 60.

READ (G. W.) Modern Probate of Wills, containing an analysis of the modern Law of Probate in England and America. Boston. 1846.

REDFIELD (Isaac F.) Leading American Railway Cases. Boston. 1870.

The Law of Wills, embracing also the Jurisprudence of Insanity; the Effect of Extrinsic Evidence; the Creation and Construction of Trusts, as far as applicable to Wills; with Forms and Instructions for preparing Wills. Boston. 1864.

The Law of Wills. Part II. Embracing Devises, Legacies, and Charitable Trusts, and the Duties of Executors, Administrators, and other Testamentary Trustees. Boston. 1866.

The Law of Carriers of Goods and Passengers; also the Construction, Responsibility, and Duty of Telegraph Companies, the Responsibility and Duty of Innkeepers, and the Law of Bailments of every class, embracing Remedies. Cambridge, Mass., and New York. 1869.

The Law of Railways. 2d. Ed. Boston. 1858.

The Same. 1st Ed. Boston. 1858.

The Same. 2 vols. Boston. 1867.

REDFIELD (I. F.) and BIGELOW (M. M.) Leading and Select American Cases in the Law of Bills of Exchange, Promissory Notes and Checks; with notes and references. Boston. 1871.

REEVE (Tapping.) A Treatise on the Law of Descents, in the several United States of America. New York. 1825.

The Law of Baron and Femme, of Parent and Child, Guardian and Ward, Master and Servant, and of the Powers of the Courts of Chancery. 2d Ed. By Lucius E. Chittenden. Burlington. 1846.

The Same. 3d Ed., with notes and references to English and American Cases. By Amasa J. Parker and Charles E. Baldwin. Albany. 1867.

REEVES' History of the English Law, from the time of the Romans to the end of the reign of Elizabeth. A New Edition, in three volumes. By W. F. Finlason. London. 1869.

RICE (Clinton.) Manual of the United States Bankruptcy Act, 1867. Washington, D. C. 1867.

RIDDLE (Daniel S.) The Law and Practice in Proceedings Supplementary to Execution, under the New York Code. New York. 1866.

ROBERTS (William.) A Treatise on the Law of Wills and Codicils; including the Construction of Devises, and the Office and Duties of Executors and Administrators. 3d Ed. 2 vols. London and Dublin. 1826.

ROBERTS (William.) A Treatise on the Statute of Frauds. 3d Am. from last London Edition. Philadelphia. 1833.

A Treatise on the Construction of the Statutes relating to Voluntary and Fraudulent Conveyances, and on the nature and force of different considerations to support deeds and other legal instruments, in the Courts of Law and Equity. 2d Am. from last London Ed. Hartford. 1825.

ROBERTS (David.) A Treatise on Admiralty and Prize. New York. 1869.

ROBERTS (Thomas A.) The Principles of the High Court of Chancery, and the Powers and Duties of its Judges. From the 2d London Ed. Philadelphia. 1857. Law Library, Vol. 94.

ROBERTSON (David.) A Treatise on the Rules of the Law of Personal Succession. Edinburgh. 1836. Philadelphia. 1836. Law Library, Vol. 10.

ROBINSON (Conway.) The Practice in Courts of Justice in England and the United States. Volumes 5 and 6. Richmond, Baltimore and Philadelphia. 1868.

ROCKWELL (John A.) A Compilation of Spanish and Mexican Law in relation to Mines and Titles to Real Estate, in force in California, Texas and New Mexico. New York. 1851.

ROLLE (Henry.) Un Abridgment des plusieurs Cases et Resolutions del Common Ley, etc. Folio. London. 1868.

ROPER (R. S. Donnison.) A Treatise on the Law of Legacies. Re-arranged by Henry Hopley White. 1st Am. from 3d London Edition. 2 vols. Philadelphia. 1829.

A Treatise on the Law of Property arising from the relation between Husband and Wife. 2 vols. Philadelphia. 1841. Law Library. Vols. 29 and 30.

ROSCOE'S Digest of the Law of Evidence in Criminal Cases. By David Power. 6th Am. from 6th London Edition, with Notes and References by George Sharswood. Philadelphia. 1866.

The Same. Philadelphia. 1836.

ROSCOE (Henry.) A Digest of the Law of Evidence on the trial of Actions at Nisi Prius. 1st Am. from 2d London Edition, with Notes and References by James Bayard. Philadelphia. 1832.

A Treatise on the Law of Actions relating to Real Property. 2 vols. Philadelphia. 1840. Law Library, Vols. 26 and 27.

ROSS (George.) A Treatise on the Law of Purchasers and Venders of Personal Property; considered chiefly with a view to Mercantile Transactions. 2d Ed. By S. B. Harrison. From the London Edition. Philadelphia. 1836. Law Library, Vol. 10.

Leading Cases in the Commercial Law of England and Scotland. Vol. 1. Bills and Notes. Philadelphia. 1854. Law Library, Vol. 80.

The Same. Vol. 2. Contract of Sale. Philadelphia. 1855. Law Library, Vol. 83.

The Same. Vol. 3. Suretyship, Agency, Partnership and Insurance. Philadelphia. 1858. Law Library, Vol. 97.

RUSSELL (Sir William Ordnall.) A Treatise on Crimes and Misdemanors. By Charles Sprengel Greaves. 8th Am. Ed., with Notes and References by Daniel Davis and Theron Metcalf, and with aditional Notes and References by George Sharswood. In two volumes. Philadelphia. 1857.

RUSSELL (Francis.) A treatise on the Power and Duty of an Arbitrator, and the Law of Submissions and Awards. Philadelphia. 1849. Law Library, Vol. 61.

RUSSELL (John A.) A Treatise on the Laws relating to Factors and Brokers. Philadelphia. 1845. Law Library, Vol. 46.

RUSSELL (John, Earl.) An Essay on the History of the English Government and Constitution, from the Reign of Henry VII. to the present time. 12mo. London. 1866.

RUTHERFORD (T.) Institutes of Natural Law. 2d Am. Ed. Baltimore. 1832.

ST. GERMAIN. Doctor and Student: or, Dialogues between a Doctor of Divinity and a Student in the Laws of England; containing the Grounds of those Laws; together with Questions and Cases concerning the Equity thereof. The eighteenth edition. Corrected and improved by William Muchall, Gent. Dublin. 1792.

SANDERS (Francis William.) An Essay on Uses and Trusts, and on the Nature and Operation of Conveyances at Common Law, and of those which derive their effect from the Statute of Uses. 1st Am. from the 4th London Ed. 2 volumes in 1. Philadelphia. 1830.

SAUNDERS (John Simcoe.) The Law of Pleading and Evidence in Civil Actions. 2d Ed., by Robert Lush. 5th Am. Ed. 2 vols. Philadelphia. 1851.

SAUNDERS (Thorndike.) Bankruptcy Practice under the Law of the United States of 1867; together with the Amendatory Act of 1868, the General Orders, Forms, Rules of the Southern District of New York, the Rules of the Circuit Court for the Southern District of New York, in the Second Circuit; and a Digest of all the Decisions thereunder, to September, 1868. Annotated. New York. 1868.

SAVIGNY'S Treatise on Possession; or the *Jus Possessionis* of the Civil Law. 6th Ed. Translated from the French by Sir Erskine Perry. London. 1848.

SCHOULER (James.) A Treatise on the Law of the Domestic Relations. Boston. 1870.

SCHULTES (Henry.) An Essay on Aquatic Rights; intended as an illustration of the Law relative to Fishing, and to the propriety of ground or soil produced by alluvion and dereliction in the Sea and Rivers. Philadelphia. 1839. Law Library, Vol. 22.

SCRIBNER (Charles H.) A Treatise on the Law of Dower. 2 vols. Philadelphia. 1864.

SCOTT (William L.) and JARNAGIN (Milton P.) A Treatise upon the Law of Telegraphs. Boston. 1868.

SERGEANT (Thomas.) Constitutional Law. Being a view of the Practice and Jurisdiction of the Courts of the United States, and of Constitutional points decided. 2d Ed. Philadelphia. 1830.

SERGEANT (Henry J.) A Treatise on the Lien of Mechanics and Material Men, in Pennsylvania, with the Acts of Assembly relating thereto. 2d Ed. By E. Spencer Miller. Philadelphia. 1856.

SEDGWICK (Theodore.) A Treatise on the Measure of Damages. 4th Ed. By Henry Dwight Sedgwick. New York and London. 1868.

A Treatise on the Measure of Damages. 3d Ed. New York and London. 1858.

A Treatise on the Rules which Govern the Interpretation and Application of Statutory and Constitutional Law. New York. 1857.

SEWELL (Richard Clarke.) A Treatise on the Law of Sheriff. Philadelphia. 1845. Law Library, Vol. 44.

SHARSWOOD (George.) An Essay on Professional Ethics. 3d Ed. Philadelphia. 1869.

Law Lectures. Philadelphia.

Commentaries on the Laws of England. In four books. By Sir William Blackstone, Knt. With Notes and a Life of the Author, by George Sharswood. 2 vols. Philadelphia. 1868.

SHEARMAN (Thomas G.) and REDFIELD (Amasa A.) A Treatise on the Law of Negligence. New York. 1869.

SHELFORD (Leonard). The Law of Railways, including the Consolidation and other General Acts for regulating Railways in England and Ireland. 1st Am. from 3d London Ed., with Notes and References by Milo L. Bennett. 2 vols. Burlington. 1855.

A Practical Treatise of the Law of Marriage and Divorce. Philadelphia. 1841. Law Library, Vol. 31.

A Practical Treatise of the Law of Mortmain and Charitable Uses and Trusts. Philadelphia. 1842. Law Library, Vols. 34 and 35.

SHEPPARD's Touchstone of Common Assurances. From the last London Edition. 2 vols. Philadelphia. 1840. Law Library, Vols. 28 and 29.

SHERMAN (Henry). An Analytical Digest of the Law of Marine Insurance. New York. 1841.

SMITH (John William). The Law of Contracts. 5th Am. from 4th London Edition. By John George Malcolm. With Notes and References by William Henry Rawle, and additional Notes by George Sharswood. Philadelphia. 1869.

The Same. Philadelphia. 1847. Law Library, Vol. 54.

A Compendium of Mercantile Law. Philadelphia. 1837. Law Library, Vol. 15.

SMITH (John William). A Selection of Leading Cases on various branches of the Law. In two volumes. Vol. 2 in two parts. Philadelphia. 1838, 1839 and 1840. Law Library, Vols. 11, 21, 28.

The Same. With Notes by John William Smith, Esq. Am. Editors, J. I. Clarke Hare and H. B. Wallace. 5th Am. from the last English Edition. With Notes and References by J. I. Clarke Hare and J. W. Wallace. 2 vols. Philadelphia. 1855.

The Same. American Editors, J. I. Clarke Hare and H. B. Wallace. 6th Am. Edition, from the last English Edition. 2 vols. in 3. Philadelphia. 1866.

An Elementary View of the Proceedings in an Action at Law. From the 3d London Edition. Philadelphia. 1847. Law Library, Vol. 58.

SMITH (Charles Manley.) A Treatise on the Law of Master and Servant, including therein Masters and Workmen in every description of Trade and Occupation. Philadelphia. 1852. Law Library, Vol. 73.

SMITH (Chauncey) and BATES (Samuel W.) Cases relating to the Law of Railways, decided in the Supreme Court of the United States, and in the courts of the Several States. 2 Vols. Boston. 1854.

SMITH (Josiah W.) An Original View of Executory Interests in Real and Personal Property. Philadelphia. 1845.

A Manual of Equity Jurisprudence. 1st American from 9th London Ed. Washington. 1871.

A Compendium of the Law of Real and Personal Property, connected with Conveyancing. Philadelphia. 1856. Law Library, Vol. 87.

SMITH (John Sidney.) A Treatise on the Practice of the Court of Chancery. 2d Am., from the 2d London Ed.; with Notes and References by David Graham, Jr. 2 vols. Philadelphia. 1842.

SMITH (E. Fitch.) Commentaries on Statute and Constitutional Law and Statutory and Constitutional Construction. Albany and New York. 1848.

SNELL (Edmund Henry Turner.) The Principles of Equity. Philadelphia. 1868.

SPENCE (Geo.) The Equitable Jurisdiction of the Court of Chancery. 2 vols. Philadelphia. 1846.

STARKIE (Thomas.) A Practical Treatise on the Law of Evidence, and Digest of Proofs in Civil and Criminal Proceedings. 6th Am., from a new English Ed. 2 vols. Philadelphia. 1837.

A Practical Treatise on the Law of Evidence. 9th Am., from the 4th London Ed. By George Morley Dowdeswell, and John George Malcolm. Philadelphia. 1869.

The Same. 4th Ed., by George Morley Dowdeswell, and John George Malcolm. London and Dublin. 1853.

A Treatise on the Law of Slander and Libel, and incidentally of Malicious Prosecutions. From the 2d English Ed., of 1830. By John L. Wendell. 2 vols. in one. West Brookfield, Mass. 1852.

The Same. 1st Am. Ed., by Edward D. Ingraham. New York. 1826.

STEARNS (Asahel). A Summary of the Law and Practice of Real Actions. 2d Ed. Hallowell. 1831.

STEPHEN (Henry John). A Treatise on the Principles of Pleading in Civil Actions. 6th Am. Ed., by F. J. Troubat. Philadelphia. 1851.

New Commentaries on the Laws of England. 1st Am. Ed. 4 vols. New York. 1841.

Summary of the Criminal Law. Philadelphia. 1840. Law Library, Vol. 25.

STEVENS AND BENECKE. Treatises on Averages, and Adjustment of Losses in Marine Insurance. With Notes by Willard Phillips. Boston. 1833.

The Same. Boston. 1833.

STOCK (John Shapland). A Practical Treatise on the Law of *Non Compotes Mentis*, or Persons of Unsound Mind. Philadelphia. 1839. Law Library, Vol. 23.

STORY (Joseph). Commentaries on the Law of Partnership, as a Branch of Commercial and Maritime Jurisprudence, with occasional illustrations from Civil and Foreign Law. 5th Ed. Boston. 1859.

Commentaries on the Law of Bailments. 6th Ed. Boston. 1856.

The Same. 8th Ed. Revised, corrected and enlarged, by Edmund H. Bennett. Boston. 1870.

The Same. 1st Ed. Boston. 1832.

Commentaries on the Law of Promissory Notes, and Guaranties of Notes, and Checks on Banks and Bankers. 5th Ed. Boston. 1859.

Commentaries on Equity Pleadings, and incidents thereof, according to the Practice of the Courts of Equity of England and America. 6th Ed. Boston. 1857.

The Same. 7th Ed., by Isaac F. Redfield. Boston. 1865.

Commentaries on the Law of Bills of Exchange, Foreign and Inland, as administered in England and America. 2d Ed. Boston and London. 1847.

A Treatise on the Law of Sales of Personal Property. 2d Ed. Boston. 1853.

Commentaries on the Conflict of Laws, Foreign and Domestic, in regard to Contracts, Rights, and Remedies, and especially in regard to Marriages, Divorces, Wills, Successions and Judgments. 6th Ed., by Isaac F. Redfield. Boston. 1865.

The Same. 5th Ed. Boston. 1857.

The Same. 1st Ed. Boston. 1834.

STORY (Joseph). A Selection of Pleadings in Civil Actions, with occasional Notations. 2d Ed. by Benjamin L. Oliver, Jr. Boston. 1829.

Commentaries on the Constitution of the United States. 2 vols. 3d Ed. Boston. 1858.

The Same. 1st Ed. 3 vols. Boston and Cambridge. 1833.

Commentaries on the Law of Agency as a Branch of Commercial and Maritime Jurisprudence. 5th Ed. Boston. 1857.

The Same. 7th Ed. by Isaac F. Redfield and William A. Herrick. 1869.

Commentaries on Equity Jurisprudence, as administered in England and America. 9th Ed. by Isaac F. Redfield. 2 vols. Boston. 1866.

The Same. 6th Ed. 2 vols. Boston. 1853.

STORY (William W.) A Treatise on the Law of Contracts. 4th Ed. 2 vols. Boston. 1856.

STREET (Alfred B.) The Council of Revision of the State of New York; its History; History of the Courts with which its Members were connected; Biographical Sketches of its Members; and its Vetoes. Albany. 1859.

SUGDEN (The Right Hon. Sir Edward). A Practical Treatise of Powers. 2d Am. from 7th London Ed. 2 vols. in one. Philadelphia. 1847.

The Same. From the 6th London Ed. 2 vols. Philadelphia. 1837. Law Library, Vols. 13 and 14.

A Series of Letters to a Man of Property on Sales, Purchases, Mortgages, Leases, Settlements, and Devises of Estates. From the London Ed. Philadelphia. 1834. Law Library, Vol. 1.

A Practical Treatise of the Law of Vendors and Purchasers of Estates. From the 9th London Ed. 2 vols. in one. Brookfield, Mass. 1836.

A Treatise of the Law of Property, as administered by the House of Lords. Philadelphia. 1849. Law Library, Vol. 62.

SULLIVAN (Francis Stoughton). Lectures on the Constitution and Laws of England: with a Commentary on Magna Charta, and Illustrations of Many of the English Statutes. 2d Ed. Dublin. 1790.

SWAN. Pleadings and Precedents under the Code of Ohio.

TAMLYN (John.) A Treatise on the Law of Evidence, principally with reference to the Practice of the Court of Chancery and in the Master's Offices. Philadelphia. 1846. Law Library, Vol. 49.

TAPPING (Thomas.) The Law and Practice of the High Prerogative writ of *Mandamus*, as it obtains both in England and Ireland. Philadelphia. 1853. Law Library, Vol. 74.

TAYLOR (John.) Elements of the Civil Law. 4th Ed. London, Edinburgh and Dublin. 1828.

TAYLOR (John N.) A Treatise on the American Law of Landlord and Tenant. 5th Ed. Boston. 1869.

The Same. 2d Ed. Boston. 1852.

TAYLOR (Alfred S.) Medical Jurisprudence. 3d Am. from 4th London Edition. By Edward Hartshorne. Philadelphia. 1853.

THACHER (Peter Oxenbridge.) Reports of Criminal Cases tried in the Municipal Court of the City of Boston. Boston. 1845.

THIBAUT. (See LINDLEY.)

THOMPSON (Isaac Grant.) The Law and Practice of Provisional Remedies. Albany and New York. 1867.

The Supervisor's Manual: containing the Laws relating to the Powers and Duties of Supervisors. With an Appendix of Forms. 2d Ed. Albany. 1869.

The Assessor's, Collector's and Town Clerk's Manual. With an Appendix of Forms. Albany. 1870.

A Practical Treatise on the Law of Highways, including Ways, Bridges, Turnpikes and Plank Roads, at Common Law and under the Statutes. Albany. 1868.

THORNTON (James B.) A Digest of the Conveyancing, Testamentary and Registry Laws of all the States of the Union. Philadelphia. 1847.

THORPE (B.) Ancient Laws and Institutes of England; comprising Laws enacted under the Anglo-Saxon Kings, Laws of Edward the Confessor, of William the Conqueror, etc.; also, Monumenta Ecclesiastica Anglicana, from the seventh to the tenth century, etc. 2 vols. 1840.

THROOP (Montgomery H.) A Treatise on the Validity of Verbal Agreements, as affected by the Legislative enactments in England and the United States, commonly called the Statute of Frauds. 2 vols. Albany. Vol. 1. 1870.

TIDD (William.) The Practice of the Courts of King's Bench and Common Pleas, in Personal Actions and Ejectment. 2 vols. 9th Ed. London. 1828.

Supplement to The Practice of the Courts of King's Bench and Common Pleas, etc. London. 1830.

2d Supplement to the Same. London. 1832.

TIFFANY (Joel) and SMITH (Henry.) The New York Practice. 3 vols. Albany. 1864.

TIFFANY (Joel.) A Treatise on Government and Constitutional Law. Albany. 1867.

TIFFANY (Joel) and BULLARD (E. F.) The Law of Trusts and Trustees, as administered in England and America. Albany. 1862.

TILLINGHAST (John L.) and SHEARMAN (Thos. G.) Practice, Pleadings and Forms in Civil Actions in Courts of Record in the State of New York, adapted to the Code of Procedure of the State of New York. 2 vols. New York. 1861.

TOMLINS (T. E.) The Law Dictionary, defining and interpreting the Terms or Words of Art, and explaining the Rise, Progress and Present State of the English Law. 2 vols. London. 1810.

TOWNSHEND (John.) A Treatise on the Wrongs called Slander and Libel, and on Remedy by Civil Action for those Wrongs. New York and London. 1861.

The Law and Practice on Proceedings by Landlords to recover possession of demised premises, on the non-payment of Rent or Expiration of the Term. 2d Ed. New York. 1866.

TRAIN (Charles R.), and HEARD (F. F.) Precedents of Indictments and Special Pleas. Boston. 1855.

TROUBAT (Francis J.) The Law of Commandatary and Limited Partnership in the United States. Philadelphia. 1853.

TROWER (Charles Francis.) The Law of Debtor and Creditor. Philadelphia. 1861. Law Library, Vol. 102.

TURNBULL (Stephen H.) Practise of the District Courts of the City of New York; the Acts relative to the Marine Court, and an Appendix. New York. 1864.

TURNER (Samuel.) The Present Practice and Costs in the High Court of Chancery. 6th Ed., by Robert Venables. 2 vols. London. 1825.

TYLER (Ransom H.) A Treatise on the Remedy by Ejectment, and the Law of Adverse Enjoyment, in the United States. Albany. 1870.

Commentaries on the Law of Infancy, including Guardianship and Custody of Infants, and the Law of Coverture, embracing Dower, Marriage and Divorce, and the Statutory Policy of the several States in respect to Husband and Wife. Albany. 1868.

American Ecclesiastical Law; the Law of Religious Societies, Church Government and Creeds, disturbing Religious Meetings, and the Law of Burial Grounds in the United States. Albany. 1866.

UPTON (Francis H.) A Treatise on the Law of Trade Marks, with a Digest and Review of English and American Authorities. Albany. 1860.

The Law of Nations affecting Commerce during War; with a Review of the Jurisdiction, Practice and Proceedings of Prize Courts. New York. 1863.

VAN SANTVOORD (George.) A Treatise onPleading under the New York Code. 2d Ed.

Precedents of Pleadings in Civil actions under the New York Code of Procedure. Albany. 1858.

A Treatise on the Practice in the Supreme Court of the State of New York in Equity actions, adapted to the Code of Procedure. 2 vols. Albany. 1860, 1862.

VATTEL (Monsieur De.) The Law of Nations. 4th Am. Ed. From the New Edition, by Joseph Chitty. Philadelphia. 1835.

The Same. With additional Notes and References by Edward D. Ingraham. Philadelphia. 1856.

VERPLANCK (Julian C.) An Essay on the Doctrine of Contracts. New York. 1825.

VINER (Charles.) A General Abridgement of Law and Equity. 24 vols. folio. Aldershot. 1751.

VOORHIES. New York Code, with Notes, etc. 4th Ed. New York. 1855.

The Same. 8th Ed. New York. 1864.

The Same. 10th Ed. New York. 1871.

WAIT (William). The Code of Procedure of the State of New York, as amended to 1871, with Notes on Practice, Pleadings and Evidence; Rules of the Courts, fully annotated, etc. Albany. 1871.

The Law and Practice in Civil Actions and Proceedings in Justices' Courts in the State of New York. 2 vols. 2d Ed. Albany. 1867.

WALFORD (Frederick). A Summary of the Law of Railways. 2d Ed. Boston and London. 1850.

WALKER (James W.) The Theory of the Common Law. Boston. 1852.

WALKER (Timothy). Introduction to American Law. 4th Ed. Boston. 1860.

WALLACE (John William). The Reporters, Chronologically Arranged, with occasional remarks upon their respective Merits. 3d Ed. Philadelphia. 1855.

WARD (William.) A Treatise on Legacies; or Bequests of Personal Property. Philadelphia. 1837. Law Library, Vol. 16.

WARD (Robert). An Enquiry into the Foundation and History of the Law of Nations in Europe, from the time of the Greeks and Romans, to the Age of Grotius. 2 vols. London. 1795.

WARREN (Samuel). A Popular and Practical Introduction to Law Studies. Edited by Isaac Grant Thompson. Albany. 1870.

The Same. Philadelphia. 1837. Law Library, Vol. 12.

The Moral, Social and Professional Duties of Attorneys and Solicitors. Albany. 1870.

WASHBURN (Emory). A Treatise on the American Law of Easements and Servitudes. Philadelphia. 1863.

A Treatise on the American Law of Real Property. 2 vols. Boston. 1860.

The Same. 3 vols. 3d Ed. Boston. 1868.

WATERMAN (Thomas W.) A Compendium of the Law and Practice of Injunctions, and of Interlocutory Orders in the Nature of Injunctions. By Robert Henley Eden. 3d Ed. 2 vols. New York and Albany. 1852.

A Treatise on the Law of Set-Off, Recoupment and Counter-Claim. New York. 1869.

WATERMAN (Joshua). The Wisconsin and Iowa Justice, being a Treatise on the Civil and Criminal Jurisdiction of Justices of the Peace, written expressly for the states of Wisconsin and Iowa. Revised by Thomas W. Waterman. New York and Albany. 1853.

WATKINS (Charles). Principles of Conveyancing: designed for the use of students. 7th Ed. London. 1829.

WATSON (William Henry). A Practical Treatise on the Law relating to the Office and duty of Sheriff. From the London Edition. Philadelphia. 1835. Law Library, Vol. 5.

A Treatise on the Law of Arbitration and Awards. From the last London Ed. Philadelphia. 1836. Law Library, Vol. 9.

The Same. From the 3d London Ed. Philadelphia. 1848. Law Library, Vol. 57.

WEDGEWOOD (William B.) and HOMANS (Smith). A Law Manual for Notaries Public and Bankers. New York. 1859.

WENDELL (John L.) Blackstone's Commentaries on the Laws of England. 4 vols. New York. 1859. See BLACKSTONE.

WENTWORTH (Thomas). The Office and Duty of Executors. From the 14th London Ed., by Henry Jeremy. Notes and References by E. D. Ingraham. Philadelphia. 1832.

WENTWORTH (John). A Complete System of Pleading; Comprehending the most approved Precedents and Forms of Practice. 9 vols. Dublin. 1799.

WESTLAKE (John). A Treatise on Private International Law, or the Conflict of Laws. Philadelphia. 1859. Law Library, Vol. 9.

WHARTON (Francis) and STILLE (Moreton). A Treatise on Medical Jurisprudence. Revised and Corrected by Alfred Stille. 2d Ed. Philadelphia. 1860.

WHARTON (Francis). State Trials of the United States during the Administrations of Washington and Adams. Philadelphia. 1849.

A Treatise on the Law of Homicide in the United States. Philadelphia. 1855.

A Treatise on the Criminal Law of the United States. 4th Ed. Philadelphia. 1857.

The Same. 6th Ed. 3 vols. Philadelphia. 1868.

Precedents of Indictments and Pleas, adapted to the Use both of the Courts of the United States and those of the several States. Philadelphia. 1848.

WHARTON (J. J. S.) The Law Lexicon, or Dictionary of Jurisprudence. From the London Edition. Harrisburg. 1848.

WHARTON (J. J. S.) The Principles of Conveyancing. Philadelphia. 1851. Law Library, Vol. 72.

WHEATON (Henry.) History of the Law of Nations in Europe and America, from the earliest times to the Treaty of Washington, 1842. New York, Albany and Dublin, 1845.

Elements of International Law. 3d Ed. Philadelphia. 1846.

The Same. 8th Ed. By Richard Henry Dana, Jr. Boston. 1866.

The Same. Annotated by William Beach Lawrence. 2d Ed. Boston and London. 1863.

An Abridgment of the Law of Nisi Prius. By William Selwyn. 4th Am. from the 7th London Ed., with Notes and References by Thomas J. Wheaton. 2 vols. New Haven and Philadelphia. 1831.

WHEELER (Jacob D.) Reports of Criminal Law Cases decided at the City Hall of the City of New York and Albany. 1823.

A Practical Treatise on the Law of Slavery. New York and New Orleans. 1837.

WHITE (Frederick Thomas) and TUDOR (Owen Davies.) A Selection of Leading Cases in Equity. 2 vols. Vol. 1. Philadelphia. 1849. Law Library, Vol. 63.

The Same. Vol. 2. Philadelphia. 1851. Law Library, Vols. 69 and 70.

The Same. With Annotations by J. J. Clark Hare and H. B. Wallace, and additional Notes by J. J. Clark Hare. 3d Am. from the 2d London Ed. 3 vols. Philadelphia. 1859.

WHITMAN (Charles Sidney.) Patent Laws, and the Practice of obtaining Letters Patent for Inventions in the United States and Foreign Countries, including Copy-Right and Trade-Mark Laws. Washington. 1871.

WHITTAKER (Henry.) Practice and Pleading in actions in the Courts of Record in the State of New York, under the Code of Procedure, and other Statutes, when applicable. 3d Ed. 2 vols. New York. 1863.

WHITWORTH (John.) Equity Precedents. Philadelphia. 1848. Law Library, Vol. 60.

WIGRAM (James.) Points in the Law of Discovery. 1st Am. Ed., from 2d London Edition. Boston. 1842.

The Same. From the London Edition. Philadelphia. 1836. Law Library, Vol. 11.

WILDMAN (Richard.) Institutes of International Law. 2 vols. Philadelphia, 1850. Law Library, Vols. 66, 68.

WILKINSON (James John.) The Practice in the Action of Replevin. From the London Ed. Philadelphia. 1834. Law Library, Vol. 4.

WILLARD (John.) A Treatise on Equity Jurisprudence. Albany and New York. 1855.

A Treatise on the Law of Real Estate, and of the Mode of Alienation thereof. Albany. 1861.

A Treatise on the Law of Executors, Administrators and Guardians, and of Remedies by and against them, in the Surrogates' Courts of the State of New York; together with an account of the Jurisdiction and Practice of those Courts in the Admeasurement of Dower. Albany. 1859.

WILLCOCK (J. W.) The Office of Constable. Philadelphia. 1840. Law Library, Vol. 27.

The Law of Municipal Corporations; with a brief sketch of

their History, and a Treatise on *Mandamus* and *Quo Warranto*. Philadelphia. Law Library, Vol. 12.

WILLIAMS (Joshua.) Principles of the Law of Real Property. 3d Am., from 7th Eng. Edition; with Notes and References by William Henry Rawle and James T. Mitchell. Philadelphia. 1866.

Principles of the Law of Real Property, intended as a first book for the use of Students of Conveyancing. London. 1845.

WILLIAMS (Joshua.) Principles of the Law of Personal Property. 2d Am., from the 2d English Ed. With Notes and References by Benjamin Gerhard and Samuel Wetherill. Philadelphia. 1855.

The Same. Philadelphia. 1848. Law Library, Vol. 60.

WILLIAMS (Edward Vaughan.) A Treatise on the Law of Executors and Administrators. 4th Am., from the last London Ed. With Notes and References by Asa J. Fish. 2 vols. Philadelphia. 1855.

The Same. With Notes and References by Francis J. Troubat. 2 vols. Philadelphia. 1832.

WILLIS (John Walpole.) A practical Treatise on the Duties and Responsibilities of Trustees. From the London Ed. Philadelphia. 1835. Law Library, Vol. 8.

Pleadings in Equity. Philadelphia. 1842. Law Library, Vol. 33. (See Vol. 41.)

WILMOT (Sir John E. Eardley, Bart.) A Digest of the Law of Burglary. London. 1851.

WILLS (William.) An Essay on the Principles of Circumstantial Evidence. From the 3d London Ed. Philadelphia. 1853.

An Essay on the Rationale of Circumstantial Evidence. Philadelphia. 1843. Law Library, Vol. 39.

WILSON (John.) A Treatise on Springing Uses, and the Limitations by Deed, corresponding with Executory Devises; according to the arrangement in Mr. Fearne's Essay. From the London Ed. Philadelphia. 1836.

WILSON (O. M.) A Digest of Parliamentary Law; also, the Rules of the Senate and House of Representatives of Congress; with the Constitution of the United States, and Amendments thereto, and their History. 2d Ed. Philadelphia. 1869.

WINSLOW (Forbes.) The Plea of Insanity in Criminal Cases. Philadelphia. 1843. Law Library, Vol 49.

WOOD (Thomas.) Institute of the Laws of England; or, the Laws of England in their Natural order, according to common use. Folio. [Title page gone.]

WOODDESSON (Richard.) Lectures on the Law of England. 2d Ed. With Notes and Additions, by W. R. Williams. 3 vols. London. 1834.

The Same. 3 vols. Philadelphia. 1842. Law Library, Vols. 36 and 37.

WOODFALL'S Practical Treatise on the Law of Landlord and Tenant. 2d Ed. By S. B. Harrison. London and Dublin. 1834.

WOOLRYCH (Humphrey W.) A Treatise on the Law of Ways, including Highways, Turnpike Roads and Tolls, Private Rights of Way, Bridges and Ferries. From the London Ed. Philadelphia. 1834. Law Library, Vol. 2.

A Treatise of the Law of Waters. 1st Am. from 2d London Ed. Philadelphia. 1853. Law Library, Vol. 76.

WOOLSEY (Theodore D.) Introduction to the Study of International Law. 2d Ed. New York. 1864.

WORTHINGTON (George.) An Inquiry into the Power of Juries to decide incidentally on Questions of Law. Philadelphia. 1840. Law Library, Vol. 27.

A General Precedent for Wills. From the 4th London Ed. Philadelphia. 1848. Law Library, Vol. 58.

WORDSWORTH (Charles.) The Law of Joint Stock Companies. From the 3d London Ed. Philadelphia. 1843. Law Library, Vols. 37 and 38.

YATES (John V. N.) A Collection of Pleadings and Practical Precedents, with Notes thereon, and Approved Forms of Bills of Costs. Albany and New York. 1837.

INDEX.

CIVIL LAW.
Browne, Burlamaqui, Code Civile, Code Napoleon, Cooper's Justinian, Corpus Juris Civilis, Cushing, Domat, Gueterbock's Bracton, Grapel, Justinian's Institutes, Lindley, Livingstone, Locre, Long, Mackeldy, by Kaufman, Maine, Rutherford, Savigny, Taylor.

CLERK'S ASSISTANT. See FORMS.
Abbott, Jenkins, McCall.

CODE. See CIVIL LAW, PLEADING, PRACTICE.
Abbott, Howard, Voorhies, Waite.

COMMENTARIES.
Blackstone, Bowyer, Broom, Coke, Kent, Phillimore, Smith (E. F.,) Stephen, St. Germain, Smith, Story, Sullivan, Wood, Wooddesson.

COMMERCIAL LAW. See AGENCY, BILLS AND NOTES, CONTRACTS, SALES, PARTNERSHIP, ETC., ETC.
Bateman, Fell, Holcombe, Levi, Montefiore, Parsons, Roccus by Ingersoll, Ross, Smith, Wedgwood and Homans.

COMMON LAW.
1. HISTORY. Crabb, Reeves.
2. COMMENTARIES. See Commentaries.

CONDITIONS.
Bingham and Colvin.

CONFESSIONS. See CRIMINAL LAW.
Joy.

CONFLICT OF LAWS.
Bowyer, Story, Westlake.

CONSTABLES.
Barbour, Crocker, Willcock.

CONSTITUTIONAL CONVENTION.
Jameson.

CONSTITUTIONAL LIMITATIONS.
Cooley, Potter's Dwarris.

CONSTITUTIONAL LAW, ENGLISH.
Blackstone, Broome, De Lolme, Gilbert, Russell, Stephen, Sullivan, Wynne (Eunomus.)

CONSTITUTIONAL LAW, AMERICAN.
Binney, Calhoun, Clay, Curtis, Cooley, Conklin, Duer, Elliott, Farrar, Federalist, Hurd, Jameson, Kent, Marshall, Rawle, Paschal, Pomeroy, Sergeant, Sedgwick, Smith, Story, Tiffany, Webster, Whiting.

CONSTRUCTION OF STATUTES.
Coode, Dwarris, Sedgwick, Smith.

CONTINGENT BEMAINDERS.
Fearne.

CONTRACTS. See BILLS OF SALE, BILLS AND NOTES, COVENANTS, DEEDS, LEASES, MERCANTILE LAW, MORTGAGES, SALES, SPECIFIC PERFORMANCE.
Addison, Bateman, Batten, Bell, Blackburn, Byles, Chipman, Chitty, Comyns, Fell, Fry, Hilliard, Hurlstone, Langdell, Metcalf, Newland, Parsons, Pitman, Pothier, Ross, Smith, Story, Verplanck.

CONVERSION, EQUITABLE.
Leigh and Dalzell.

CONVENTION, CONSTITUTIONAL.
Jameson.

DIGESTS. See CATALOGUE OF DIGESTS.
Abbott, Bacon, Comyns, Cruise, Dane, Espinasse, Law, Lomax, Halsted, Petersdorff.

DIPLOMACY.
Horne.

DIPLOMATIC LAW.
Elliott.

DIRECTORY.
Livingston.

DISCOVERY. See CHANCERY.
Hare, Wigram.

DISTRESS.
Gilbert.

DIVORCE.
Bishop, Page, Poynter, Shelford.

DOCUMENTS, PRODUCTION OF.
Pollock.

DOMESTIC RELATIONS. See HUSBAND AND WIFE, INFANCY.
Bingham, Reeve, Schouler, Tyler.

DOMICILE. See CONFICT OF LAWS.
Phillimore.

DOWER. See REAL PROPERTY, HUSBAND AND WIFE.
Lambert, Park, Scribner, Tyler, Willard.

EASEMENT. See ADVERSE ENJOYMENT, HIGHWAYS, REAL PROPERTY
Gale & Whateley, Washburne.

ECCLESIASTICAL LAW.
Buck, Tyler.

EJECTMENT.
Adams, Archbold, Tyler.

ELECTIONS.
Brightly.

ENGLISH LAW.
Blackstone, Bracton, Britton, Broom, Coke, Crabb, Fleta, Fortescue, Lambard, Reeve, Russell, St. Germain, Stephen, Thorpe, Wendell, Wood, Wooddesson, Wynne.

ENTRIES. See FORMS AND ENTRIES.
Lilly.

EQUITY. See CHANCERY.

ESTATES. See REAL PROPERTY, TRUSTS AND TRUSTEES.
Preston, Sugden.

ESTATES FOR LIFE. See ESTATES, REAL PROPERTY.
Bissett.

ESTATES TAIL. See ESTATES, REAL PROPERTY.
Hayes.

EVIDENCE. See CONFESSIONS.
Appleton, Archibold, Bentham, Best, Bishop, Burrill, Coventry, Elwell, Gilbert, Greenleaf, Gresley, Halsted, Hare, Hubback, Joy, Lee, Matthews, Phillipps and Arnold, Pollock, Powell, Roscoe, Saunders, Starkie, Tamlyn, Wigram, Wills.

GUARANTIES.
Fell.

GUARDIAN AND WARD. See DOMESTIC RELATIONS.
Dayton, Willard.

HABEAS CORPUS. See TRIALS.
Binney, D'Hauteville Case, Hurd, Ingersoll.

HIGHWAYS. See WAYS.
Angell and Durfee, Cook, Thompson, Woolrych.

HINDOO LAW. See MOOHUMMUDAN LAW.

HISTORY OF LAW. See MAGNA CHARTA, FRENCH BAR, TRIAL BY JURY.
Blackstone, Crabb, Fleta, Forsyth, Gutenbock, Hale, Maine, Montesquieu, Reeves, Spence, Street.

HOMICIDE. See CRIMINAL LAW.
Wharton.

HORSES AND HORSE RACING.
Oliphant.

HUSBAND AND WIFE. See COVERTURE, DOMESTIC RELATIONS, FAMILY SETTLMENTS, MARRIAGE AND DIVORCE, MARRIAGE SETLEMENTS.
Atherly, Bell, Bishop, Bright, Clancy, Cord, McQueen, Reeve, Roper, Schouler, Tyler.

IDIOTS. See INSANITY.
Highmore.

IMPEACHMENT TRIALS. See TRIALS.

INCUMBRANCES. See MORTGAGE.
Fisher, Ram.

INDICTMENTS. See CRIMINAL LAW.
Train and Heard, Wharton.

INFANCY. See DOMESTIC RELATIONS.
Bingham, Forsyth, McPherson, Schouler, Tyler.

INFORMATION. See CRIMINAL INFORMATIONS, QUO WARRANTO.

INJUNCTIONS.
Drewry, Eden, Hilliard, Kerr.

INN-KEEPERS. See BAILMENT.
Redfield.

INSANITY. See MEDICAL JURISPRUDENCE.
Bucknill, Highmore, Ray, Redfield, Stock, Winslow.

INSOLVENCY. See ASSIGNMENTS, BANKRUPTCY AND INSOLVENCY.

INSTITUTES.
Bouvier, Coke, Cooper, Gardner, Hargrave, Justinian, Rutherford, Wood.

INSURANCE.
Angell, Arnould, Bigelow, Bonney, Bunyon, Duer, Ellis, Emerigon, Hildyard, Hughes, Littleton & Blatchley, Marshall, Park, Parsons, Phillips, Ross, Sherman, Stevens & Benecke.

INTERNATIONAL LAW.
Chitty, Burlamaqui, Bowyer, Elliott, Gardner, Grotius, Halleck, Horne, Kent, Marten, Phillimore, Polson, Puffendorf, Upton, Vattel, Ward, Westlake, Wheaton, Wildman, Woolsey.

LEGAL DIRECTORY.
Livingston.

LEGAL EDUCATION.
Anthon, DuPonceau, Hoffman, Warren.

LEGAL ETHICS.
Sharswood, Warren.

LEGAL MAXIMS.
Broom, Noy and Francis.

LEGISLATIVE ASSEMBLIES, RULES OF.
Cushing, Wilson.

LEGISLATIVE POWER. See CONSTITUTIONAL LAW.
Cooley.

LETTERS PATENT. See PATENTS.

LEXICONS. See DICTIONARIES.

LIBEL AND SLANDER.
Cooke, Starkie, Townshend.

LIEN.
1. *Of Vendor of Goods.* Cross.
2. *Of Mechanics.* Houck, Nott, Sergeant.

LIFE ASSURANCE. See INSURANCE.

LIMITATION OF ACTIONS.
Angell, Ballentine.

LUNACY. See INSANITY.

MAGNA CHARTA.
Blackstone, Sullivan.

MALICIOUS PROSECUTION.
Starkie.

MANDAMUS.
Moses, Tapping.

MANUAL OF LAW.
Bishop, Dean, Devereux, Walker.

MARITIME LAW. See ADMIRALTY.

MARINE INSURANCE AND AVERAGE. See ADMIRALTY, INSURANCE.

MARRIAGE AND DIVORCE.
Bishop, Page, Poynter, Shelford, Tyler.

MARRIAGE SETTLEMENTS. See DOMESTIC RELATIONS, HUSBAND AND WIFE, MARRIAGE AND DIVORCE.
Atherly.

MARRIED WOMEN. See HUSBAND AND WIFE.
Bishop, Clancy, Cord.

MARTIAL LAW. See COURTS MARTIAL, HABEAS CORPUS, MILITARY LAW.

MASTER AND SERVANT.
Smith (C. M.)

MAXIMS.
Broom, Noy and Francis.

MEASURE OF DAMAGES. See DAMAGES.
Powell, Sedgwick.

MECHANICS' LIEN.
Houck, Nott, Sergeant.

OFFICERS. See CONSTABLE, CORONER, SHERIFFS, TOWN AND COUNTY OFFICERS.

OVERRULED CASES.
Greenleaf, Lockwood.

PARENT AND CHILD. See DOMESTIC RELATIONS, INFANCY.

PARLIAMENTARY LAW.
Cushing, Wilson.

PARTIES.
Barbour, Broom, Browne, Calvert, Chitty, Edwards, Finlason.

PARTITION. See REAL PROPERTY.
Allnatt.

PARTNERSHIP. See MERCANTILE LAW.
Bissett, Cary, Collyer, Gow, Lindley, Parsons, Ross, Pothier, Story, Troubat.

PATENTS.
Coryton, Curtis, Hindmarch, Law, Lund, Norman, Perpigna, Robb, Whitman.

PENSIONS.
Raff.

PERIODICALS. See LAW PERIODICALS.

PERPETUITIES. See REAL PROPERTY.
Lewis.

PERSONAL PROPERTY. See CONTRACTS.
Hilliard, Long, Robertson, Ross, Smith, Story, Sugden, Williams.

PLEADING. See ACTIONS, NISI PRIUS, PRACTICE.
Abbott, Archbold, Bishop, Chitty, Daniell, Finlason, Gould, Hare, Hennell, Hening, Hughes, Humphreys, Hunter, Lawes, Lilly, Lube, Mansel, Mitford, Nash, Saunders, Stephen, Story, Swan, Train and Heard, Van Santvoord, Wentworth, Wharton, Whitworth, Whittaker, Willis, Winslow, Yates.

PLEAS OF THE CROWN.
East, Hale, Hawkins.

POSSESSION.
Savigny.

POWERS.
Blackwell, Sugden.

PRACTICE. See ACTIONS, BANKRUPTCY, BILL OF EXCEPTIONS, CODE, FORMS AND ENTRIES, NISI PRIUS, PLEADING.
1. *American.* Abbott, Bagley, Barbour, Bicknell, Bingham, Bishop, Blake, Burrill, Conkling, Crary, Curtis, Dunlap, Graham, Hoffman, Holmes and Disbrow, Law, Monell, Nash, Paine and Duer, Riddle, Robinson, Tiffany and Smith, Tillinghast and Shearman, Thompson, Townshend, Turnbull, Van Santvoord, Whittaker, Yates.
2. *English.* Archbold, Bennett, Chitty, Daniell, Dearsley, Espinasse, Farren, Gilbert, Goldsmith, Maddock, Raymond, Smith, Tidd, Turner and Venables, Wheaton's Selwyn.

PRECEDENTS. See FORMS, PLEADINGS, PRACTICE.

PRECEDENTS OF INDICTMENTS.
Train and Heard, Wharton.

RENTS.
Bingham and Colvin, Gilbert.

REPLEVIN.
Gilbert, Morris, Wilkinson.

REPORTERS.
Marvin, Wallace.

REVENUE LAWS OF UNITED STATES.
Andrews, Boutwell, Davidge and Kimball, Edwards.

RIVERS. See WATERS.
Houck.

ROMAN LAW, See CIVIL LAW.

SALES. See REAL PROPERTY.
Beaumont, Rell, Benjamin, Blackburn, Hilliard, Long, Livermore, Pothier, Ross, Story, Sugden.

SCIRE FACIAS.
Foster.

SEA LAWS. See ADMIRALTY.

SEAMEN. See SHIPPING.
Abbott.

SELECT CASES. See LEADING AND SELECT CASES.

SERVITUDES. See EASEMENTS, REAL PROPERTY.

SET-OFF.
Babington, Barbour, Waterman.

SHERIFFS.
Allen, Barbour, Crocker, Gwynne, Sewell, Watson.

SHIPPING. See ADMIRALTY, INSURANCE, MARITIME LAW.
Abbott, Flanders, Parsons.

SLAVERY.
Hurd, Wheeler.

SPANISH AND MEXICAN LAW.
Rockwell.

SPECIFIC PERFORMANCE. See CONTRACTS, EQUITY.
Batten, Fry.

STAMP ACT.
Edwards.

STATE TRIALS. See TRIALS.

STATUTE OF LIMITATIONS. See LIMITATION OF ACTIONS.

STATUTORY CONSTRUCTION.
Dwarris, Sedgwick, Smith.

STOPPAGE IN TRANSITU. See LIEN.
Cross.

STUDY OF LAW. See LEGAL STUDIES.

SUBROGATION. See AGENCY.

SUCCESSION. See DESCENTS.
Hubback, Robertson.

SUPPLEMENTARY PROCEEDINGS.
Riddle.

PART SECOND.

REPORTS OF JUDICIAL DECISIONS.

A TABLE OF REGNAL YEARS,

FOR CONVENIENCE OF REFERENCE TO THE STATUTES AND LAW REPORTS.

SOVEREIGNS.	Commencement of Reign.	L'ngth of Reign.
William I.	October 14, 1066.	21
William II.	September 26, 1087.	13
Henry I.	August 5, 1100.	36
Stephen	December 26, 1135.	19
Henry II.	December 19, 1154.	35
Richard I.	September 23, 1189.	10
John.	May 27, 1199.	18
Henry III.	October 28, 1216.	57
Edward I.	November 20, 1272.	35
Edward II.	July 8, 1307.	20
Edward III.	January 25, 1326.	51
Richard II.	June 22, 1377	23
Henry IV.	September 30, 1399.	14
Henry V.	March 21, 1413.	10
Henry VI.	September 1, 1422.	39
Edward IV.	March 4, 1461.	23
Edward V.	April 9, 1483.	..
Richard III.	June 26, 1483	3
Henry VII.	August 22, 1485.	24
Henry VIII.	April 22, 1509.	38
Edward VI.	January 28, 1547.	7
Mary	July 6, 1553.	6
Elizabeth	November 17, 1558	45
James I.	March 24, 1603.	23
Charles I.	March 27, 1625.	24
The Commonwealth.	January 30, 1649.	11
Charles II.*	May 29, 1660.	37
James II.	February 6, 1685.	4
William and Mary.	February 13, 1689.	14
Anne	March 8, 1702.	13
George I.	August 1, 1714.	13
George II.	June 11, 1727	34
George III.	October 25, 1760.	60
George IV.	January 29, 1820.	11
William IV.	June 26, 1830	7
Victoria.	June 20, 1837	—

* Although Charles II. did not ascend the throne until 29th May, 1660, his regnal years were computed from the death of Charles I., January 30, 1649, so that the year of his restoration is styled the twelfth of his reign.

REPORTS OF JUDICIAL DECISIONS.

ABBOTT (Brothers). Reports of Practice Cases determined in the courts of the State of New York: with a Digest of all Points of Practice embraced in the standard New York Reports issued during the period covered by this volume; with References to the Amendatory Acts of 1855. 19 vols. New York. 1855–1865.

ABBOTT (Benjamin Vaughan) and ABBOTT (Austin). Reports of Practice Cases determined in the courts of the State of New York: with a Digest of all Points of Practice embraced in the standard New York Reports issued during the period covered by this volume. New Series. 10 vols. New York. 1866–1871.

ABBOTT (Brothers). Reports of Cases in Admiralty, argued and determined in the District Court of the United States for the Southern District of New York. Vol. 1. Boston. 1857.

ABBOTT (Benjamin Vaughan). Reports of Decisions rendered in the Circuit and District Courts of the United States. Vol. 1. New York. 1870.

ACTON (Thomas Harman). Reports of Cases argued and determined before the Lords Commissioners of Appeals in Prize Causes; also on Appeal to the King in Council. With an Appendix containing Orders in Council, Notifications, Instructions, etc. 2 vols. (English Admiralty Reports, Vol. 5).

ADAMS (Nathaniel). Reports of Cases argued and determined in the Superior Court of Judicature for the State of New Hampshire, from September, 1816, to February, 1819. Exeter, 1819. (New Hampshire Reports, Vol. 1.)

ADAMS (John Milton). Reports of Cases in Law and Equity determined by the Supreme Judicial Court of Maine. 2 vols. Hallowell. 1858. (Maine Reports, Vols. 41, 42).

ADDAMS (J.) Reports of Cases argued and determined in the Ecclesiastical Courts, at Doctors' Commons; and in the High Court of Delegates. 3 vols. (English Ecclesiastical Reports, Vol. 2).

ADDISON (Alexander). Trial of, President of the Courts of Common Pleas in the Circuit Court consisting of the counties of Westmoreland, Fayette, Washington and Alleghany, on an Impeachment by the House of Representatives, before the Senate of the Commonwealth of Pennsylvania. Lancaster. 1803.

ADDISON (Alexander). Reports of Cases in the County Courts of the Fifth Circuit and in the High Court of Errors and Appeals of the State of Pennsylvania. Washington. 1800.

ADMIRALTY. See ENGLISH ADMIRALTY REPORTS.

ADOLPHUS (John Leycester) and ELLIS (Thomas Flower). Reports of Cases argued and determined in the Court of King's Bench. Containing the cases from Easter Term, 1834, to Michaelmas Vacation, 1841. (Eng. Com. Law Reps., Vols. 28–31, 33–37, 39, 40.)

Queen's Bench Reports. New Series. Containing the cases determined from Hilary Term, IV. Vict., to Trinity Term, XV. Vict. (Eng. Com. Law Reps., Vols. 41–43, 45, 48, 51, 53, 55, 58, 59, 63, 64, 66, 68, 69, 71, 79, 83.)

AIKENS (Asa). Reports of cases argued and determined in the Supreme Court of the State of Vermont. 2 vols. Windsor. 1827, 1828.

ALABAMA.

Minor's Reports. 1820–26. 1 vol.
Stewart's Reports. 1827–31. 3 vols.
Stewart and Porter's Reports. 1831–1834. 5 vols.
Porter's Reports. 1834–1839. 9 vols.
Alabama Reports (N. S.) 1840–1870. Vols. 1–3, 5, 9, 10, 13–45.

Vols. 1, 2, 3, 5, 9, 10, 22, 23, by the Judges of the Court.
Ormond. (Vols. 13–15.)
Cocke. (Vols. 16–18.)
Shepherd. (Vols. 19–21.)
Shepherd. (Vols. 24–41.)
Danner. (Vol. 42.)
Jones. (Vols. 43–45.)

ALEYN (John). Select Cases in B. R., 22, 23, and 24, Car. I. Regis. Reported by John Aleyn, late of Grey's Inn Esq. Folio. London. 1681.

ALLEN (Charles). Reports of Cases argued and determined in the Supreme Judicial Court of Massachusetts. 14 vols. Boston. 1861–1869.

AMBLER (Charles). Reports of Cases argued and determined in the High Court of Chancery, with some few in others. 2d Ed. By John Elijah Blunt. 2 vols. London. 1828.

AMES (Samuel.) Reports of Cases argued and determined in the Supreme Court of Rhode Island. 4 vols. Boston and Providence. 1858–1865. (Rhode Island Reports, Vols. 4–7.)

AMES (Samuel), KNOWLES (John P.) and BRADLEY (Charles S.) Reports of Cases argued and determined in the Supreme Court of Rhode Island. Providence. 1871. (Rhode Island Reports, Vol. 8.)

AMES (Michael E.) Michigan Reports, Vol. 1. See OFFICER.

ANDERSON (Edmund.) Les Reports du Treserudite Edmund Anderson, Chivalier, Nadgairs, Seigniour Chief Justice del Common Bank. Folio. London. 1664.

ANDREWS (George.) Reports of Cases argued and adjudged in the Court of King's Bench, in the Eleventh and Twelfth Years of the Reign of his present Majesty King George the Second. Folio. In the Savoy. 1754.

ANGELL (J. K.) Reports of Cases argued and determined in the Supreme Court of Rhode Island. Vol. 1. 1847.

ANSTRUTHER (Alexander.) Reports of Cases argued and determined in the Court of Exchequer, from Easter Term, 32 George III. to Trinity Term 33 George III., both inclusive. 3 vols. London. 1796.

ANTHON (John.) The Law of Nisi Prius, being Reports of Cases determined at Nisi Prius in the Supreme Court of New York, with Notes and Commentaries on each case. With Introductory Essay. New York. 1820.

APPEAL CASES. (See House of Lords Cases.)

APPEAL CASES. Privy Council. (See "Law Reports.")

APPLETON (John.) Reports of Cases determined in the Supreme Judicial Court of Maine. 2 vols. Hallowell. 1842–43. (Maine Reports, Vols. 19–20.)

ARCHER (James T.) Reports of Cases argued and adjudged in the Supreme Court of Florida, January Term. 1848. 1 vol. Tallahassee. 1848. (Florida Reports, Vol. 2.)

ARKANSAS.
- Pike's Reports. (1–5 Ark.) 1837–1842.
- English's Reports. (6–13 Ark.) 1843–1853.
- Barber's Reports. (14–24 Ark.) 1853–1867.
- Cox's Reports. (25 and 26 Ark.) 1867–1871.

ASHMEAD (John W.) Reports of cases adjudged in the Courts of Common Pleas, Quarter Sessions. Oyer and Terminer, and Orphan's Court, of the First Judicial District of Pennsylvania, with Notes and References. Vol. 2. Philadelphia, 1841.

ATKYNS (John Tracy.) Reports of Cases argued and determined in the High Court of Chancery, in the time of Lord Chancellor Hardwicke. 3d Ed. 3 vols. 1st Am. from the 3d London Ed. New York. 1826.

ATWATER (Isaac.) Michigan Reports, Vol. 1. See OFFICER.

BAGLEY (David T.) and HARMON (——.) Reports of Cases determined in the Supreme court of California. 4 vols. Sacramento. 1861–62. (California Reports, Vols. 16–19.)

BAIL COURT.
- Chitty. 2 vols. 1819–1820.)
- Dowling. 9 vols. 1830–1840.
- Dowling (N. S.) 2 vols. 1841–1842.
- Dowling and Lowndes. 7 vols. 1846–1849.
- Saunders and Cole. 2 vols. 1842–1848.
- Lowndes, Maxwell and Pollock. 2 vols. 1850–1851.
- Maxwell. 1 vol. (Bail Court Cases.) 1852.

BAILEY (H.) Reports of Cases argued and determined in the Court of Appeals of South Carolina, on Appeal from the Courts of Law. 2 vols. 1828–1832. Charleston, S. C. 1858.

Reports of Cases in Equity, argued and determined in the Court of Appeals of South Carolina. Vol. 1. Containing the Cases from January 1830 to April, 1831, inclusive. Charleston. 1841.

BALDWIN (Henry.) Reports of Cases determined in the Circuit Court of the United States in and for the Third Circuit, Comprising the Eastern District of Pennsylvania and the State of New Jersey. Vol. 1. Philadelphia. 1837.

BALL (Thomas) and BEATTY (Thomas.) Reports of Cases argued and determined in the High Court of Chancery in Ireland, during the time of Lord Chancellor Manners, from the Sittings after Michaelmas Term, 48 Geo. III, 1807 to the Sittings after Trinity Term, 57 Geo. III, 1811. 2 vols. 1st American from the last London Ed. Philadelphia. 1839.

BANKRUPTCY AND INSOLVENCY (Eng.)
- Rose, 2 vols. 1810–1816.
- Buck, 1 vol. 1816–1820.
- Glyn and Jameson, 2 vols. 1821–1828.
- Montagu and McArthur, 1 vol. 1828–1830.
- Montagu, 1 vol. 1830–1832.
- Montague and Bligh, 1 vol, 1832–1833.
- Montagu and Ayrton, 3 vols. 1833–1838.

Montagu and Chitty, 1 vol. 1838–1840.
Deacon and Chitty, 4 vols. 1832–1835.
Deacon, 4 vols. 1836–1839.
Montagu, Deacon and DeGex, 3 vols. 1840–1844.
DeGex, 1 vol. 1845–1848.

Bankruptcy Reports (See "Law Times Reports.")

Banks (Elliot V.) Reports of Cases argued and determined in the Supreme Court of Kansas. 4 vols. Leavenworth, Kansas. 1865–71. (Kansas Reports, Vols. 2–5.)

Barber (L. E.) Reports of Cases at Law and in Equity, argued and determined in the Supreme Court of Arkansas, from the July Term, 1853, to June Term, 1867. 11 vols. Little Rock, Ark. 1854–1867. (Arkansas Reports, Vols. 14–24.)

Barbour (Oliver L.) Reports of Cases argued and determined in the Court of Chancery of the State of New York. 3 vols. New York and Albany. 1847–1849.

Barbour (Oliver L.) Reports of Cases in Law and Equity in the Supreme Court of the State of New York. 54 vols. New York and Albany. 1848–1870.

Barnardiston (Thomas). Reports of Cases determined in the High Court of Chancery from April 25, 1740, to May 9, 1741. Folio. In the Savoy. 1742.

Barnardiston (Thomas). Reports of Cases determined in the Court of King's Bench, together with some other Cases; from Trin. 12 Geo. I. to Trin. 7 Geo. II. 2 vols. Folio. In the Savoy. 1744.

Barnes (Henry). Notes of Cases in Points of Practice, taken in the Court of Common Pleas at Westminister, from Michaelmas Term, 1732, to Hilary Term, 1756, inclusive. To which is added a Continuation of Cases to the End of the Reign of George the Second. 3d Ed. London. 1790.

Barnewall (Richard Vaughan) and Alderson (Edward Hall.) Reports of Cases argued and determined in the Court of King's Bench, from Michaelmas Term, 58th Geo. III. (1817) to Trinity Term, 2d Geo. IV. (1821.) 4 vols. Boston. 1820–1822.

The Same. From Michaelmas Term, 1817, to Trinity Term, 1822. 5 vols. London. 1818.

The Same. Containing the Cases from Michaelmas Term, 60 Geo. III., 1819, to Michaelmas Term, 12 Geo. IV., 1821, inclusive. Vols. 3–5. (Eng. Com. Law Reps., Vols. 5–7.)

BARNEWALL (Richard Vaughan) and ADOLPHUS (John Leycester.) Reports of Cases argued and determined in the Court of King's Bench, from Trinity Term, 11th Geo. IV., 1830, to Hilary Term, 4th William IV., 1834. 5 vols. London. 1831–1835.

The Same. Philadelphia. 1832–1836. (Eng. Com. Law. Reps., Vols. 20, 22–24, 27.)

BARNEWALL (Richard Vaughan) and CRESWELL (Creswell.) Reports of Cases argued and determined in the Court of King's Bench, from Michaelmas Term, 3d Geo. IV., 1822, to Easter Term, 11th Geo. IV., 1830. 10 vols. London. 1823–32.

The Same. Containing the cases from Michaelmas Term, 3d Geo. IV., 1822, to Trinity Term, 11th Geo. IV., 1830. (Eng. Com. Law Reps., Vols. 8–11, 13–15, 17, 21.)

BARR (Robert M.) Pennsylvania State Reports, containing Cases Adjudged in the Supreme Court, from May Term, 1845, to May Term, 1849. 10 vols. Philadelphia. 1846–1849. Pennsylvania Reports, Vols 1–10.

BARRON (Arthur) and ARNOLD (Thomas James). Reports of Cases of Controverted Elections, before Committees of the House of Commons, Fourteenth Parliament of the United Kingdom, and of Cases upon Appeal from the Decisions of Revising Barristers in the Court of Common Pleas, from Michaelmas Term, 1843, to Easter Term, 1846, both inclusive. Vol. 1. 1843–1846. London. 1846.

BARRON (Arthur) and AUSTIN (Alfred). Reports of Controverted Elections in the Fourteenth Parliament of the United Kingdom. 1842. London. 1844.

BASHFORD v. BARSTOW. The Trial in the Supreme Court of the information in the nature of a *Quo Warranto* filed by the Attorney General, on the relation of Coles Bashford, v. Wm. A. Barstow, contesting the right to the Office of Governor of Wisconsin. Madison, Wis. 1856.

BAY (S. M.) Reports of Cases argued and decided in the Supreme Court of the State of Missouri from 1837 to 1845. 7 vols. Fayette, Mo., and St. Louis, Mo. 1840–1845. (Missouri Reports, Vols. 1–3, 5–8.)

BAY (Elihu Hall). Reports of Cases argued and determined in the Superior Courts of Law in the State of South Carolina, since the Revolution. 2 vols. New York. 1809–1811.

BEASLEY (Mercer). Reports of Cases argued and determined in the Court of Chancery and on Appeal in the Court of

Errors and Appeals of the State of New Jersey. 2 vols. Trenton. 1863.

Beatty (Francis). Reports of Cases argued and determined in the High Court of Chancery in Ireland, during the time of Sir Anthony Hart. Dublin. 1829.

Beavan (Charles). Reports of Cases in Chancery argued and determined in the Rolls Court during the time of Lord Langdale, Master of the Rolls, from 1 Victoria (1838) to 29 Victoria (1866). With Index. 36 vols. London. 1840–69.

Beavan (Charles.) The same. Vols. 1, 2, 7 and 3. (English Chancery Reports, Vols. 17, 29 and 43.) New York. 1845–1857.

Bee (Thomas.) Reports of Cases adjudged in the District Court of South Carolina. Philadelphia. 1810.

Bellewe (Richard.) Les ans du Roy Richard le Second. Conlect ensembl' hors les abridgments de Statham, Fitzherbert et Brooke. Per Richard Bellewe de Lincoln's Inn. London. 1869.

Benloe (Gulielme) et Dalison (Gulielme.) Les Reports de Gulielme Benloe Sergeant de Ley des divers Pleadings et Cases en le Court del Comon bank, en le several Roignes de les tres Hault and Excellent Princes le Roy Henry VII. Henry VIII. Edw. VI et le Roignes Mary and Elizabeth. Folio. London. 1689.

Bendloes (Gulielme.) Les Reports de Gulielme Bendloes, Sergeant de la Ley: Des Divers Resolutions et Judgments donne par les Reverendes Judges de la Ley: De certeine Matieres en la Ley en le Temp del Raigne de Roys et Roignes Hen. VIII. Edw. VI. Phil. et Mary et Elizab. avec que Autres Select leases en la Ley adjudges et resolves en le temps del Regne de Tresillustres Roys Jacques et Charles le premier Jammais par cy devant imprimee. Folio. London. 1661.

Benedict (Robert D.) Reports of Cases Argued and Determined in the District Court of the United States within the Second District. 3 vols. New York. 1869–1871.

Bennett (Samuel A.) Reports of Cases Argued and Determined in the Supreme Court of the State of Missouri. 6 vols. St. Louis. 1853–1856. Missouri Reports Vols. 16–21.

Bennett (Nathaniel). Reports of Cases argued and determined in the Supreme Court of the State of California. 1 vol. San Francisco and New York. 1851. (California Reports, Vol. 1.)

BEST (William Mawdesley) and SMITH (George James Philip). Reports of Cases argued and determined in the Court of Queen's Bench, and the Court of Exchequer Chamber on Appeal from the Court of Queen's Bench, from Easter Term 24th Victoria (1861) to Michaelmas Term 32d Victoria (1868). With some Cases of subsequent Terms. 9 vols. London. 1862–70.

The Same. Vol. 10. London. 1870.

The Same. Containing the cases from Easter Term, 24th Vict. 1861, to Hilary Term, 27th Vict. 1864. 4 vols. Philadelphia. 1863–66. (Eng. Com. Law Reps. Vols. 101, 110, 113, 116.)

BIBB (Geo. M.) Reports of Cases at Common Law and in Chancery argued and decided in the Court of Appeals of the Commonwealth of Kentucky, from the Fall Term, 1808, to the Spring Term, 1817. 2d Ed. 4 vols. Frankfort, Ky. 1840.

BINGHAM (William) and BINGHAM (Peregrine). Reports of Cases argued and determined in the Court of Common Pleas and other Courts, from 1822–1834. Philadelphia. 1835, 1836. (Eng. Com. Law Reps., Vols. 8, 9, 11, 13, 15, 19, 20, 21, 23, 25.)

BINGHAM (Peregrine.) New Cases in the Court of Common Pleas and other Courts. Containing the Cases from Trinity Term, 1834 to Michaelmas Term, 1840, inclusive. Philadelphia. 1836–41. (Eng. Com. Law Reps. Vols. 27, 29, 32, 33, 35,-37.)

BINNEY (Horace.) Reports of Cases adjudged in the Supreme Court of Pennsylvania. 6 vols. Philadelphia. 1809–1823.

BLACK (J. S.) Reports of Cases argued and determined in the Supreme Court of the United States from December Term, 1861, to December Term, 1862. Washington, D. C. 1862–3.

BLACK (James B.) Reports of Cases argued and determined in the Supreme Court of Judicature of the State of Indiana. 4 vols. Indianapolis. 1869–1871. (Indiana Reports, Vols. 30, 33.)

BLACKFORD (Isaac.) Reports of Cases argued and determined in the Supreme Court of Judicature of the State of Indiana. Containing the Cases from May Term, 1817, to November Term, 1847. 8 vols. Indianapolis. 1830–1850.

BLACKSTONE (Henry.) Reports of Cases argued and determined in the Courts of Common Pleas and Exchequer Chamber, from Easter Term, 28th George III. (1788,) to Hilary Term 36th, George III. (1796,) both inclusive. 2 vols. 2d Am. from the last London Ed. Philadelphia. 1849.

BLACKSTONE (Sir William, Knt.) Reports of Cases determined in the several Courts of Westminister Hall, from 1746 to 1779. 2d Ed. By Charles Keneage Elsley. 2 vols, London and Dublin. 1828.

BLAND (Theodorick.) Reports of Cases decided in the High Court of Chancery of Maryland. 3 vols. Baltimore. 1836–1841.

BLATCHFORD (Samuel.) Reports of Cases argued and determined in the Circuit Court of the United States for the Second Circuit. 7 vols. Auburn and New York. 1852–1871.

Reports of Cases in Prize, argued and determined in the Circuit and District Courts of the United States, for the Southern District of New York. 1861–1865. New York. 1866.

BLATCHFORD (Samuel) and HOWLAND (Francis) Reports of Cases argued and determined in the District Court of the United States for the Southern District of New York. Vol. 1. New York. 1855.

BLECKLY (Logan E.) Reports of Cases in Law and Equity argued and determined in the Supreme Court of Georgia. 2 vols. Atlanta, Ga. 1867–1868. (Georgia Reports, Vols. 34–35.

BLIGH (Richard.) Reports of Cases heard in the House of Lords, on Appeals and Writs of Error; and decided during Sessions of 1819, '20, '21. 3 vols. London. 1823.

The Same. Vol. 4, Part 1. Cases decided during the Session of 1821.

New Reports of Cases heard in the House of Lords, or Appeals and Writs of Error; and decided during the Sessions from 1827 to 1837. 11 vols. London. 1829.

BOORAEM (H. Toler.) Reports of Cases argued and determined in the Supreme Court of the State of California. San Francisco and Sacramento. 1858. (California Reports, Vols. 6–8.)

BOSANQUET (John Bernard) and PULLER (Christopher.) Reports of Cases argued and determined in the Court of Common Pleas, and other Courts, from Easter Term, 36 Geo. III., (1796), to Trinity Term, 47 Geo. III., (1807.) A

New Edition. By Thomas Day. 5 vols. Hartford. 1810.

BOSWORTH (Joseph S.) Reports of Cases argued and determined in the Superior Court of the City of New York. 10 vols. Albany. 1859–1865.

BRADFORD (Alexander W.) Reports of Cases Argued and determined in the Surrogate's Court of the County of New York. 4 vols. New York. 1851–1857.

BRANCH (Joseph.) Reports of Cases argued and determined in the Supreme Court of Florida: January Terms. 1846–7. Tallahassee. 1847. (Florida Reports, Vol. 1.)

BRAYTON (William.) Reports of Cases adjudged in the Supreme Court of the State of Vermont. Middlebury. 1821.

BREESE (Sidney.) Reports of Cases of Common Law and in Chancery, argued and determined in the Supreme Court of the State of Illinois, from its first organization in 1819, to the end of December Term, 1831. Second Edition, with additional notes, by Edwin Beecher. Hartford, Ct. 1861. (Illinois Reports, Vol. 1.)

BREVARD (Joseph.) Reports of Judicial Decisions, in the State of South Carolina, from 1793 to 1816. 3 vols in 2. Charleston, S. C. 1857.

BREWER (Nicholas). Maryland Reports, containing Cases argued and determined in the Court of Appeals of Maryland, from June Term, 1862, to October Term, 1866. 8 vols. Annapolis. 1864–1869. (Maryland Reports, Vols. 19–26.)

BREWSTER (F. Carroll). Reports of Equity, Election, and other important Cases, argued and determined principally in the Courts of the County of Philadelphia. 3 vols. Philadelphia. 1869–1871.

BRIDGMAN (Sir John). Reports of that Grave and Learned Judge, Sir John Bridgman, Knight; Serjeant at Law, some time Chief Justice of Chester. Folio. London. 1659.

BRIDGMAN (Sir Orlando). Reports of Judgments delivered by Sir Orlando Bridgman, when Chief Justice of the Common Pleas, from Michaelmas, 1660, to Trinity, 1667. By S. Bannister. London. 1823.

BRIGHTLY (Frederick C.) Reports of Cases decided by the Judges of the Supreme Court of Pennsylvania, in the Court of Nisi Prius at Philadelphia, and also in the Supreme Court. Philadelphia. 1851.

Brisbin (John B.) Michigan Reports, Vol. 1. See Officer.

British Crown Cases. (Am. Reprint.) 6 vols. Philadelphia. 1839–53.

Vol. 1. Russell & Ryan. 1799–1823.
Vol. 2. 1st Moody. 1824–1837.
Vol. 3. Jebb (Irish). 1822–1840.
Vol. 4. 2d Moody. 1837–1844.
Vol. 5. 1st Dennison. 1844–1850.
Vol. 6. Dennison & Pearce. 1850–1852.

Brockenbrough (John W.) Reports of Cases decided by the Honourable John Marshall, late Chief Justice of the United States, in the Circuit Court of the United States for the District of Virginia and North Carolina, from 1802 to 1833, inclusive. 2 vols. Philadelphia and Pittsburgh. 1837.

Broderip (William John) and Bingham (Peregrine). Reports of Cases argued and determined in the Court of Common Pleas, and other Courts, from Easter Term, 59 Geo. III. (1819) to Easter Term, 3 Geo. IV. (1822), both inclusive. 3 vols. London and Dublin. 1820–2.

The Same. Containing the cases from Easter Term, 59 Geo. III. (1819) to Easter Term, 3 Geo. IV. (1822). Philadelphia. 1822–1836. (Eng. Com. Law Reps., Vols. 5–7.)

Brook (Sir Robert). Some New Cases of the years and time of King *Hen.* 8, *Edw.* 6, and Qu. *Mary.* Written out of the Great Abridgement, composed by Sir Robert Brook, Knt., &c., there dispersed in the Titles, but here collected under years. Translated into English by John March. 16mo. London. 1651.

Brown (William). Reports of Cases argued and determined in the High Court of Chancery, during the time of Lord Chancellor Thurlow, and of the several Lords Commissioners of the Great Seal, and Lord Chancellor Loughborough, from 1778 to 1794. 1st Am., from the 5th London Edition. By J. C. Perkins. 4 vols. Boston. 1844.

Brown (Josiah). Reports of Cases upon Appeals and Writs of Error determined in the High Court of Parliament. 2d Ed. By T. E. Tomlins. 8 vols. London and Dublin. 1803.

Browne (Peter A.) Reports of Cases adjudged in the Court of Common Pleas of the First Judicial District of Pennsylvania. 2 vols. Philadelphia. 1811–1813.

Browne (Albert G., Jr.) Reports of cases argued and determined in the Supreme Judicial Court of Massachusetts.

8 vols. Boston. 1868–1872. (Massachusetts Reports, Vols. 97–104.)

BROWNLOW (Richard) and GOLDSBOROUGH (John). Reports of Divers Choice Cases in Law. First and Second Parts. 3d Ed. London. 1675.

BUCK (J. W.) Cases in Bankruptcy. Vol. 1. Containing Reports of Cases decided by Lord Chancellor Eldon, and by Vice Chancellors Sir Thomas Plumer, and Sir John Leach. From Michaelmas Term, 1816, to Michaelmas Term, 1820. London, Dublin and Edinburgh. 1820.

BURNETT (T. P.) Reports of the Supreme Court of the Territory of Wisconsin; for 1842 and 1843. Madison, 1844.

BURR (Aaron.) The Trial of Aaron Burr for High Treason, in the Circuit Court of the United States for the District of Virginia, Summer Term, 1807. By J. J. Coombs. Washington, D. C.

BUNBURY (William.) Reports of cases in the Court of Exchequer, from the beginning of the Reign of King George the First until the Fourteenth Year of the Reign of King George the Second. 2d Ed. Dublin, 1793.

BURROW (Sir James, Knt.) Reports of Cases argued and adjudged in the Court of Kings Bench, during the time of Lord Mansfield's presiding in that Court, from Michaelmas Term 30 Geo. II. (1756) to Easter Term 12 Geo. III. (1772.) 5 vols. 1st. Am. from 4th London Ed. Philadelphia. 1808.

The Same. 5 vols. in 3. New York. 1833.

Decisions of the Court of King's Bench, upon Settlement Cases, from the death of Lord Raymond, in March, 1732, to June, 1776, inclusive. During which time Lord Hardwicke, Sir William Lee, Sir Dudley Ryder, and Lord Mansfield, presided in that Court. The Second Edition. London. 1786.

BUSBEE (Perrin.) Reports of Cases at Law argued and determined in the Supreme Court of North Carolina, from December Term, 1853, to August Term, 1853, both inclusive. Raleigh. 1853.

Reports of Cases in Equity, argued and determined in the Supreme Court of North Carolina, from December Term, 1852, to August Term, 1853, both inclusive. Raleigh. 1854.

BULSTRODE (Edward.) The Reports of Edward Bulstrode of the Inner Temple Esquire, His Highness Chief Justice of North Wales. Of divers Resolutions and Judgments in the Court of King's Bench in the Time of King James. London. 1657.

Bush (W. P. D.) Reports of Selected Civil and Criminal Cases decided in the Court of Appeals of Kentucky. 7 vols. Frankfort, Ky., and Louisville, Ky. 1868–1871.

Caines (George.) New York Term Reports of Cases argued and determined in the Supreme Court of that State. Second Edition. 3 vols. New York. 1813–1814.

Cases argued and determined in the Court for the trial of Impeachments and Correction of Errors in the State of New York. 2 vols. New York. 1805–1807.

California.

California Reports. 1850–1871. 40 vols.
Bennet. (Vol. 1.)
Hepburn. (Vols. 2–4.)
Morris. (Vol. 5.)
Booraem. (Vols. 6–8.)
Lee. (Vols. 9–12.)
Harmon. (Vols. 13–15.)
Bagley and Harmon. (Vols. 16–19.)
Hillyer. (Vols. 20–22.)
Tuttle. (Vols. 23–32.)
Hale. (Vols. 33–37.)
Robinson. (Vol. 38.)
Thompson. (Vols. 39–40.)

Call (Daniel.) Reports of Cases argued and adjudged in the Court of Appeals of Virginia. Second Edition. 6 vols. Richmond. 1824–1833.

Calthrop (Sir H.) Reports of Special Cases touching several Customs and Liberties of the City of London. Whereunto is annexed divers Ancient Customs and Usages of the said City of London. London. 1670.

Cameron (Duncan) and Norwood (William.) Reports of Cases ruled and determined by the Court of Conference of North Carolina. Second Edition, with notes by William H. Battle, Esq. Bound with Taylor's N. C. Reports. Raleigh. 1844.

Campbell (James Mason.) Reports of Cases at Law and Equity and in the Admiralty, determined in the Circuit Court of the United States for the District of Maryland, by Roger Brooke Taney, Chief Justice of the Supreme Court of the United States. April Term, 1836, to April Term, 1861. Philadelphia. 1871.

CAMPBELL (John). Reports of Cases determined at Nisi Prius, in the Courts of King's Bench and Common Pleas, and on the Home Circuit, from the Sittings after Michaelmas Term, 48 Geo. III. (1807), to the sittings after Hilary term, 49 Geo. III. (1818), both inclusive. 4 vols. New York. 1810.

CAROLINA LAW REPOSITORY. Containing Opinions of American Jurists, and Reports of Cases adjudged in the Supreme Court of North Carolina. Vols. 1 and 2. Second Edition, with Notes by William H. Battle, Esq. Raleigh. 1844. Bound with Taylor's Term Reports.

CARRINGTON (F. A.) and KIRWAN (A. V.) Reports of Cases argued and ruled at Nisi Prius, in the Courts of Queen's Bench, Common Pleas, and Exchequer; together with Cases tried on the Circuits and in the Central Criminal Court; from Hilary Term, 6 Vict., to Easter Term, 16 Vict. 3 vols. London and Dublin. 1845.

The Same. Containing the cases from Hilary Term, 6 Vict., to Hilary Term, 13 Vict. 2 vols. Philadelphia, 1846–1850. (Eng. Com. Law Reports,Vols. 47, 61.)

CARRINGTON (F. A.) and MARSHMAN (J. R.) Reports of Cases argued and ruled at Nisi Prius, in the Courts of Queen's Bench, Common Pleas and Exchequer, together with the Cases tried on the Circuits, and in the Central Criminal Court, from Easter Term, 4 Vict., to Hilary Term, 6 Vict. Philadelphia. 1843. (Eng. Com. Law Reps., Vol. 41).

CARRINGTON (F. A.) and PAYNE (J.) Reports of Cases argued and ruled at Nisi Prius in the Courts of King's Bench and Common Pleas, and on the Circuit; from the Sittings in Michaelmas Term, 1823, to Easter Term, 1841. Vols. 1–9. Philadelphia. 1828–1841. (Eng. Com. Law Reps., Vols. 11, 12, 14, 19, 24, 25, 32, 34, 38.)

CARTER (Horace E.) Reports of Cases argued and determined in the Supreme Court of Judicature of the State of Indiana, being an official continuation of Blackford's Reports. Containing the Cases from May Term, 1847, to May Term, 1851, both inclusive. Indianapolis. 1852–1853. (Indiana Reports, Vols. 1–2).

CARTER (S.) Reports of several Special Cases argued and resolved in the Court of Common Pleas in the 16th, 17th, 18th and 19th years of King Charles II., in the time when Sir Orlando Bridgman sate Chief Justice there. To which are added some cases adjudged in the time of Chief Justice Vaughan, never before printed. Folio. London. 1688.

CARTHEW (Thomas). Reports of Cases adjudged in the Court of King's Bench from the third year of King James the Second to the twelfth year of King William the Third. Folio. In the Savoy. 1728.

CARY (Sir George). Reports in Chancery. 16mo. [No Title Page.]

CASEY (Joseph.) Pennsylvania State Reports. Comprising Cases adjudged in the Supreme Court of Pennsylvania, from May Term, 1855, to May Term, 1860. 12 vols. Philadelphia. 1857-1861. (Pennsylvania State Reports, Vols. 25-36.)

CASES IN CHANCERY. Cases argued and decreed in the High Court of Chancery, (1660-1677.) Two parts in one volume. With the Duke of Norfolk's Case, or the Doctrine of Perpetuities, etc., etc. New York and Philadelphia. 1828.

CASES IN EQUITY ABRIDGED. A General Abridgement of Cases in Equity argued and adjudged in the High Court of Chancery, etc. By a Gentleman of the *Middle Temple.* The Fourth Edition, Corrected. 2 vols. Folio. In the Savoy and London. 1756-1769.

CASES TEMP. HARDWICKE. Cases argued and determined in the Court of King's Bench at Westminster, in the 7th, 8th, 9th and 10th years of the reign of his late Majesty, King Geo. the Second. During the time the late Lord Chief Justice Hardwicke Presided in that Court. To which are added some Determinations of the Lord Chief Justice Lee, and also two Equity Ones by Lord Chancellor Hardwicke. Folio. 2 vols. London. 1770.

CASES TEMP. TALBOT. Cases in Equity during the time of the late Lord Chancellor Talbot. Folio. In the Savoy. 1741.

CHANCERY APPEAL CASES. (See "Law Reports.")

CHANCERY (Eng.) See English Chancery Reports.

CHANDLER (David H.) Reports of Cases argued and determined in the Supreme Court of the State of Wisconsin. 4 vols. Milwaukee. 1850-1854.

CHANDLER (William E.) Reports of Cases argued and determined in the Superior Court of Judicature of New Hampshire. 8 vols. Concord. 1859-1864. (New Hampshire Reports, Vols. 20, 28-34.)

CHARLTON (Robert M.) Reports of Decisions made in the Superior Courts of the Eastern District of Georgia. Savannah. 1838.

CHASE (Samuel.) Trial of Samuel Chase, an Associate Justice of the Supreme Court of the United States, impeached by the House of Representatives for High Crimes and Misdemeanors before the Senate of the United States. 2 vols. Washington. 1805.

CHEVES (L.) Cases of Law argued and determined in the Court of Appeals of South Carolina. Vol. 1. Columbia, S. C. 1840.

CHIEF JUSTICE MARSHALL'S DECISIONS. (See BROCKENBROUGH.)

CHIPMAN (Daniel.) Reports of Cases argued and determined in the Supreme Court of the State of Vermont. Vol. 1. Middlebury. 1824.

CHITTY (Joseph). Reports of Cases principally on Practice and Pleading, determined in the Court of King's Bench. Containing the Cases in Hilary, Easter, Trinity and Michaelmas Terms, A. D. 1819. 2 vols. Philadelphia. 1831. (Eng. Com. Law Reps., Vol. 18.)

CHOYCE CASES IN CHANCERY. Reprinted from the Edition of 1672. London. 1870.

CITY HALL RECORDER, The New York, for the years 1816–1821. Containing Reports of the most interesting Trials and Decisions which have arisen in the various Courts of Judicature, for the trial of Jury Cases in the Hall, during those years, particularly in the Court of Sessions. With Notes, Critical and Explanatory. By Daniel Rogers. 6 vols. bound in 3. New York. 1817–1821.

CLARK (Charles) and FINNELLY (W.) The House of Lords, Cases on Appeals and Writs of Error, Claims of Peerage and Divorces during the sessions of 1847–1866. 11 vols. Boston. 1870–71.

CLARKE (Charles L.) Reports of Chancery Cases, decided in the Eighth Circuit of the State of New York, by the Hon. Frederick Whittlesey, Vice Chancellor. Vol. 1. Rochester. 1841.

CLARKE (Hovey K.) Michigan Reports. Reports of Cases determined in the Supreme Court of Michigan, from July 7, 1869 to April Term, 1870. 2 vols. Detroit. 1870. (Michigan Reports, Vols. 19, 20.)

CLARKE (W. Penn). Reports of Cases in Law and Equity, determined in the Supreme Court of the State of Iowa. 8 vols. New York, Albany and Davenport. 1856–1859. (Iowa Reports, Vols. 1–8.)

CLIFFORD (William Henry). Reports of Cases determined in the Circuit Court of the United States for the First

Circuit, from April Term, 1858, to October Term, 1867, by Hon. Nathan Clifford, LL.D., Associate Justice of the Supreme Court, assigned to said Circuit. 2 vols. Boston. 1869–1870.

COBB (Thos. R. R.) Reports of Cases in Law and Equity, argued and determined in the Supreme Court of the State of Georgia, from Savannah Term, 1849, to Athens Term, 1856, inclusive. 15 vols. Athens. 1849–1857. (Georgia Reports, Vols. 6–20.)

COCKBURN (A. E.) and ROWE (W. Carpenter). Cases of Controverted Elections determined in the Eleventh Parliament of the United Kingdom, being the first session after passing the Reform Acts. Vol. 1. London. 1833.

COCKE (N. W.) Reports of Cases argued and determined in the Supreme Court of Alabama, from January Term, 1849, to January Term, 1851. 3 vols. Montgomery. 1849–1857. (Alabama Reports, Vols. 16–18.)

CODE REPORTER, The. A Monthly Law Journal, Containing Reports of the Decisions on the Code, Articles on Legal Topics, and Miscellaneous Information concerning Legislation, Law and Lawyers. 3 vols. in 2. New York. 1853.

CODE REPORTS. New Series. Reports of Decisions on the Code of Procedure. Vol. 1. New York. 1852.

COKE (Sir Edward, Knt.) The Reports of, A New Edition. By John Henry Thomas and John Farquhar Frazer. 6 vols. London. 1826.

COLDWELL (Thomas H.) Reports of Cases argued and determined in the Supreme Court of Tennessee, during the years 1860–1869. 6 vols. Nashville, Tenn. 1867–70.

COLEMAN & CAINES CASES. Reports of Cases of Practice determined in the Supreme Court of Judicature of the State of New York, from April Term, 1794, to November Term, 1805, both inclusive. To which is prefixed all the Rules and Orders of the Court to the present time. New York. 1808.

COLLES (Richard.) Reports of Cases, upon Appeals and Writs of Error, in the High Court of Parliament; from the year 1697 to the year 1713. Dublin. 1789.

COLLYER (John.) Reports of Cases decided in the High Court of Chancery, by the Right Honorable Sir J. L. Knight Bruce, Vice Chancellor. With Notes by John A. Dunlap and E. Fitch Smith. 2 vols. New York and Albany. 1851–1853. (English Chancery Reports, Vols. 28 and 33.)

COMBERBACH (Roger). The Report of Several Cases argued and adjudged in the Court of King's Bench at Westminster; from the first year of King James the Second, to the tenth year of King William the Third. Folio. In the Savoy. 1724.

COMMON BENCH REPORTS.. Vols. 1–9. Cases argued and determined in the Court of Common Pleas, from Hilary Term, 1845, to Michaelmas Term, 1850. By James Manning, T. C. Granger, and John Scott. Philadelphia. 1846–53. (Eng. Com. Law Reps., vols. 50, 52, 54, 56, 57, 60, 62, 65, 67.)

COMMON BENCH REPORTS. Vols. 10–18. By John Scott. Containing the Cases from Michaelmas Term and Vacation, 1850, to Trinity Vacation, 1856. Philadelphia. 1853–57. (Eng. Com. Law Reps., vols. 70, 73, 74. 76, 78, 80, 81, 84, 86.)

COMMON BENCH REPORTS. New Series. By John Scott. Containing the Cases from Michaelmas Term, 1856, to Trinity Vacation, 1865. 20 vols. Philadelphia. 1857–66. (Eng. Com. Law Reps., vols. 87, 89, 91, 93, 95, 97, 100, 103, 104, 106, 108, 109, 111, 112, 114, 115, 117.)

COMMON LAW REPORTS. See English Common Law Reports.

COMSTOCK (George F.) Reports of Cases argued and determined in the Court of Appeals of the State of New York. 4 vols. Albany and New York. 1849–1850. (New York Reports, Vols. 1–4.)

COMYNS (Sir John.) Reports of Cases argued and adjudged in the Courts of King's Bench, Common Pleas, and Exchequer. To which are added some Special Cases in the Court of Chancery; and before the Delegates. 2d Ed. By Samuel Rose. 2 vols. London. 1792.

CONDENSED REPORTS of Cases in the Superior Court of the Territory of Orleans, and in the Supreme Court of Louisiana; containing the Decisions of these Courts from the Autumn Term, 1809, to the March Term, 1830, and which were embraced in the twenty volumes of Fr. Xavier Martin's Reports. With Notes. Edited by J. Burton Harrison. 4 vols. New Orleans. 1839–1840.

CONFERENCE REPORTS. North Carolina. Bound with Taylor's Reports.

CONOVER (O. M.) Reports of Cases argued and determined in the Supreme Court of the State of Wisconsin. Containing the Cases Decided from June Term, 1864, to June Term, 1870. Madison, Wis., and Chicago. 1865–1872. Wisconsin Reports, Vols. 16–26.

CONNECTICUT.
Root's Reports. 1789–1798.
Day's Reports. 1802–1813.
Connecticut Reports. 1814–1870.
Day. (Vols. 1–21.)
Watson. (Vols. 22–24.)
Hooker. (Vols. 25–38.)

CONSPIRACY TRIAL for the Murder of the President and the attempt to overthrow the Government by the Assassination of its Principal Officers. Edited with an introduction, by Ben. Berley Poore. 3 vols. Boston. 1865.

CONSTITUTIONAL. (S. C.) See MILLS.

COOKE (William Wilcox.) Reports of Cases decided in the Supreme Court of Tennessee and in the Federal Court for the District of West Tennessee. Vol. 1. Nashville, Tenn. 1814.

COOLEY (Thomas M.) Michigan Reports. Reports of Cases heard and decided in the Supreme Court of Michigan, from January 1, 1858, to October 18, 1864. 8 vols. Detroit and Ann Arbor. 1858–1864. (Michigan Reports, Vols. 5–12.)

COOPER (William Frierson.) Reports of Cases argued and determined in the Highest Courts of Law and Equity of the State of Tennessee. A new Edition from Overton to Meigs, inclusive, in ten volumes. Vol. 1, containing 1st and 2d Overton's Tennessee Reports; and Vol. 4, containing Peck's Reports and Martin and Yerger's Reports. St. Louis. 1870–1871.

COOPER (George). Cases argued and determined in the High Court of Chancery, during the time of Lord Chancellor Eldon; in Hilary, Easter and Trinity Terms, 55th Geo. III. (1815); with a few cases of an earlier period. London. 1815.

CORBETT (Uverdale) and DANIELL (Edmund Robert). Reports of Cases of Controverted Elections in the Sixth Parliament of the United Kingdom. London. 1821. "Election Cases, 1819."

COURT OF CLAIMS.
Vol. 1. See DEVEREUX.
Vols. 2–5. See NOTT & HUNTINGTON.

COWEN (Esek). Reports of Cases argued and determined in the Supreme Court, and in the Court for the Trial of Impeachments and the Correction of Errors, of the State of New York. 9 vols. Albany and New York. 1830–1835.

COWPER (Henry). Reports of Cases adjudged in the Court of King's Bench, from Hilary Term, the 14th of Geo. III. (1774) to Trinity Term, the 18th of Geo. III. (1778), both inclusive. 2d American from the last London Ed. 2 vols. By J. Prescott Hall. New York. 1833.

COX (Samuel Compton). Cases determined in the Courts of Equity, from 1783 to 1796 inclusive, with a few of an earlier date, by Lord Hardwicke and Lord Northington. 2 vols. London. 1816.

COXE (Richard S.) Reports of Cases argued and determined in the Supreme Court of New Jersey. From April Term, 1790, to November Term, 1795, both inclusive. Vol. 1. Burlington, N. J. 1816.

COX (Norval W.) Reports of Cases at Law and in Chancery argued and determined in the Supreme Court of Arkansas. Containing the cases decided from December Term, 1867, to June Term, 1871. Little Rock. 1870–1872. (Arkansas Reports, Vols. 25 and 26.)

CRABBE (William H.) Reports of Cases argued and adjudged in the District Court of the United States, for the Eastern District of Pennsylvania. From May Sessions, 1836, to May Sessions, 1846, inclusive. Philadelphia. 1853.

CRAIG (R. D.) and PHILLIPS (F. J.) Reports of Cases argued and determined in the High Court of Chancery during the time of Lord Chancellor Cottenham. Vol. 1. 1840–1, 3 and 4 Victoria. London. 1842.

The Same. New York. 1847. (English Chancery Reports, Vol. 18.)

CRANCH (William). Reports of Cases argued and adjudged in the Supreme Court of the United States, from August Term, 1801, to February Term, 1815. 9 vols. in 8. Vols. 1 and 2 in one. 3d Ed. Philadelphia. 1815. Vols. 3 and 4, 2d Ed. New York. 1812. Vols. 5 and 6. New York. 1812. Vols. 6–9. Washington. 1816 and 1817.

CRANCH (William). Reports of Cases Civil and Criminal, in the United States Circuit Court for the District of Columbia, from 1801 to 1841. 6 vols. Boston and New York. 1852–1853.

CRITCHFIELD (L. J.) Reports of Cases argued and determined in the Supreme Court of Ohio. New Series. 16 vols. New York, Albany, and Cleveland. 1858–1872. (Ohio State Reports, Vols. 5–20.)

CROKE (Sir George, Knt.) Reports of. 5th Ed. 3 vols. Dublin. 1791.

Vol. 1. Elizabeth.
Vol. 2. James.
Vol. 3. Charles.

CROMPTON (Charles) and JERVIS (John). Reports of Cases argued and determined in the Courts of Exchequer and Exchequer Chamber, from Easter Term, 11 Geo. IV., to Trinity Term, 2 Will. IV., both inclusive. 2 vols. Philadelphia. 1854.

CROMPTON (Charles) and MEESON (R.) Reports of Cases argued and determined in the Courts of Exchequer and Excheqer Chamber, from Michaelmas Term, 3 Will. IV., to Trinity Term, 4 Will. IV., both inclusive. 2 vols. Philadelphia. 1854.

CROMPTON (Charles), MEESON (R.) and ROSCOE (H.) Reports of Cases argued and determined in the Courts of Exchequer and Exchequer Chamber, from Trinity Term, 4 Will. IV., to Michaelmas Term, 6 Will. IV., both inclusive. 2 vols. Philadelphia. 1854.

CROWN CASES RESERVED. See BRITISH CROWN CASES.

CURRY (Thomas). Reports of Cases argued and determined in the Supreme Court of the State of Louisiana. With marginal references, by Thomas Gibbs Morgan. 7 vols. New Orleans. 1854. (Louisiana Reports, vols- 17–19; or of the Reprint, vols. 4–10.)

CUNNINGHAM (T.) Reports of Cases argued and determined in the Court of King's Bench, in the Seventh, Eighth, Ninth and Tenth Years of King George the Second. During which time the Right Honorable the Earl of Hardwicke was Lord Chief Justice of that Court. 3d Ed. By Thomas Townsend Bucknill. London. 1871.

CURTIES (W. C.) Reports of Cases argued and determined in the Ecclesiastical Courts at Doctors' Commons. Vol. 1. Containing the Cases from Michaelmas Term, 1834, to Michaelmas Term, 1838. Philadelphia. 1841–1845. (English Ecclesiastical Reports, Vols. 6 and 7.)

CURTIS (B. R.) Reports of cases argued and determined in the circuit Court of the United States for the First Circuit, 1851–1856. 2 vols. Boston. 1853–1857.

CUSHING (Luther S.) Reports of Cases argued and determined in the Supreme Court of Massachusetts. 12 Vols. Boston. 1850–1860.

CUSHMAN (John F.) Reports of Cases argued and determined in the High Court of Errors and Appeals for the State Mississippi. 7 vols. Boston. 1852–1855. (Mississippi Reports, vols. 23–29.)

DALLAS (A. J.) Reports of Cases ruled and adjudged in the Courts of Pennsylvania, before and since the Revolution. 4 vols. Philadelphia. 1830–1835.

DALY (Charles P.) Reports of Cases argued and determined in the Court of Common Pleas for the City and County of New York. 2 vols. New York. 1866–1870.

DANA (James G.) Reports of Select Cases decided in the Court of Appeals of Kentucky. 9 vols. in 5. Containing all the Cases reported from 1833 to 1840. Second Edition. Cincinnati. 1851.

DANNER (John L. C.) Reports of Cases argued and determined in the Supreme Court of Alabama, during January and June Terms, 1868. Montgomery, Alabama. 1870. (Alabama Reports, vol. 42.)

DANIEL (EDMUND ROBERT.) Reports of Cases argued and determined on the Equity side of the Court of Exchequer, before the Right Honorable Sir Richard Richard, Knight, Lord Chief Baron, during the years 1817, 1818, 1819, and 1820. London. 1824.

DAVIES (Edward H.) Reports of Cases determined in the District Court of the United States for the District of Maine, with some Opinions of the District Judge in Cases determined in the Circuit Court. 1839–1849. 1 vol. Portland. 1849.

DANSON (F. M.) and LLOYD (S. N.) Reports of Cases relating to Commerce, Manufactures, etc. etc., determined in the Courts of Common Law, at Nisi Prius and in Banc, in 1827–1829. Vol. 1, London. 1830.

DAVIS (Sir John.) Les Reports des Cases et Matters en Ley, Resolves et Adjudges en les Courts del Roy en Ireland. London. 1674.

DAVISON (Henry) and MERIVALE (Herman.) Reports of cases argued and determined in the Court of Queen's Bench, and upon Writs of Error from that Court to the Exchequer Chamber, in Trinity and Michaelmas Terms, 1843, and Hilary and Easter Terms, 1844. Vol. 1. London and Dublin. 1844.

DAY (Thomas.) Reports of Cases argued and determined in the Supreme Court of Errors of the State of Connecticut. 21 vols. Second Edition. New York, Albany and Hartford. 1848–1853. (Connecticut Reports, Vols. 1–21.

Reports of Cases argued and determined in the Supreme Court of Errors of the State of Connecticut, in the years 1802, 1803 and 1804. Second Edition. 5 vols. Hartford and Philadelphia. 1823–1830.

DEACON (Edward E.) Reports of Cases in Bankruptcy argued and determined in the Court of Review, and on Appeal before the Lord Chancellor. 4 vols. London. 1857.

The Same. (Eng. Com. Law Reports, Vol. 38.)

DEACON (Edward E.) and CHITTY (Edward.) Reports of Cases argued and determined in the Court of Review, and on Appeal before the Lord Chancellor. 4 vols. London. 1833.

DEANE (John F.) Reports of Cases argued and determined in the Supreme Court of the State of Vermont. 3 vols. Bellows Falls and Brattleboro. 1853–1855. (Vermont Reports, Vols. 24–26.)

DEGEX (John P.) Reports of Cases in Bankruptcy decided by the Court of Review, the Vice Chancellor, Sir James Lewis Knight Bruce, and the Lord Chancellors, Lord Lyndhurst and Lord Cottenham. London. 1852.

DE GEX (J. P.) and JONES (H. Cadman.) Reports of Cases heard and determined by the Lord Chancellor and the Court of Appeals in Chancery, from 1857 to 1859. 4 vols. London. 1858–61.

DEGEX (J. P.), JONES (H. Cadman) and SMITH (R. Horton.) Reports of Cases heard and determined by the Lord Chancellor, and the Court of Appeals in Chancery, from 1863 to 1865. 3 vols. London. 1865–6.

DEGEX (J. P.), FISHER (F.) and JONES (H. Cadman.) Reports of Cases heard and determined by the Lord Chancellor and the Court of Appeal in Chancery, 1857–62. 4 vols. London. 1861–1870.

DE GEX (J. P.), McNAUGHTEN (S.) and GORDON (A.) Reports of Cases heard aud determined by the Lord Chancellor, and the Court of Appeals in Chancery, from 1851 to 1857. 8 vols. London. 1853–64.

DE GEX (John P.) and SMALE (John.) Reports of Cases decided in the High Court of Chancery, from Michaelmas Term, 1846, to the end of Trinity Vacation, 16 Vict., 1852. 5 vols. London and Dublin. 1849–53.

DELAWARE.

Harrington's Reports, 1832–1855. 5 vols.

Houston's Reports. 1856–1858. 1 vol.

DENIO (Hiram.) Report of Cases argued and determined in the Supreme Court and in the Court for the Correction of Errors of the State of New York. 5 vols. Albany and New York. 1846–1849.

DENISON (Stephen Charles.) Crown Cases Reserved for Consideration and decided by the Judges of England, from the year 1844 to the year 1850. With Notes by George Sharswood. Vol. 1. Philadelphia. 1853. (British Crown Cases, Vol. 5.)

The Same. From the year 1850 to the year 1851. Continued from Trinity Term, 1851, to Trinity Term, 1852, by Robert Rouiere Pearce. Vol. 2. Philadelphia. 1853. (British Crown Cases, Vol. 6.)

DESAUSSURE (Henry William.) Reports of Cases argued and determined in the Court of Chancery of the State of South Carolina, from the Revolution to December, 1813, inclusive. New Edition. 4 vols. in 2. Philadelphia. 1854.

DEVEREAUX (John C.) Court of Claims. Reports and Digest of Opinions Delivered since the Organization of the Court. With an Appendix. New York. 1856.

DEVEREUX (Thomas P.) Equity Cases argued and determined in the Supreme Court of North Carolina, from June Term, 1828, to June Term, 1834. Second Edition. 2 vols. Raleigh and Fayetteville. 1849–1855.

Cases argued and determined in the Supreme Court of North Carolina, from December Term, 1826, to June Term, 1834. 4 vols. Second Edition. Raleigh. 1836–1851.

DEVEREUX (Thomas P.) and BATTLE (Wm. H.) Reports of Cases at Law argued and determined in the Supreme Court of North Carolina, from December Term, 1834, to June Term, 1839, both inclusive. Second Edition. 4 vols. in 3. Fayetteville. 1857.

Reports of Cases in Equity, argued and determined in the Supreme Court of North Carolina, from December Term, 1834, to December Term, 1839, both inclusive. 2 vols. Second Edition. Fayetteville. 1858–1860.

D'HAUTEVILLE'S CASE. Report of the D'Hauteville Case: the Commonwealth of Pennsylvania, at the Suggestion of Paul Daniel Gonsalve Grand D'Hauteville, *versus* David Sears, William C. Sears and Ellen Sears Grand D'Hauteville. *Habeas Corpus* for the Custody of an infant child. Philadelphia. 1840.

DICKENS (John.) Reports of Cases argued and determined in the High Court of Chancery. 2 vols. London and Dublin. 1803.

DISNEY (William.) Reports of Cases adjudged in the Superior Court of Cincinnati at Special and General Terms, from

October, 1853, to January, 1860. 2 vols. Cincinnati. 1867–1871.

DODSON (John.) Reports of Cases argued and determined in the High Court of Admiralty, commencing with the Judgments of the Right Hon. Sir William Smith, Trinity Term, 1811. 2 vols. Boston. 1853. (English Admiralty Reports, Vol. 6.)

DOUGLAS (Samuel T.) Reports of Cases argued and determined in the Supreme Court of the State of Michigan. 2 vols. Detroit. 1846–1849.

DOUGLAS (Sylvester, Right Hon.) Reports of Cases argued and determined in the Courts of King's Bench, in the 19th, 20th, 21st, 22d, 23d, 24th and 25th years of the reign of George III. 4th Ed. By William Frere. 4 vols. London. 1813.

The Same. Vols. 3 and 4. Containing the cases from Michaelmas Term, 1781, to Trinity Term, 1785, inclusive. Philadelphia. 1835. (Eng. Com. Law Reports, Vol. 26.)

DOUGLAS (The Right Hon. Sylvester, Lord Glenbervie.) The History of the Cases of Controverted Elections, which were tried and determined during the First and Second Sessions of the 14th Parliament of Great Britain, 15 and 16 George III. 4 vols. Second Edition. London. 1802. "Election Cases, 1776–1777."

DOW (P.) Reports of Cases upon Appeals and Writs of Error in the House of Lords, during the 1st, 2d, 3d, 4th, 5th and 6th Sessions of the Fifth Parliament of the United Kingdom, from 53 Geo. III., (1813), to 58 Geo. III., (1818.) 6 vols. London. 1814–9.

DOW (P.) and CLARK (C.) Reports of Cases upon Appeals and Writs of Error in the House of Lords, and decided during the Sessions of 1827, 1828, 1829, 1830, 1831–32. 2 vols. London. 1830–2.

DOWLING (Alfred S.) Reports of Cases argued and determined in the King's Bench Practice Court; with the Points of Practice Decided in the Courts of Common Pleas and Exchequer, from Michaelmas Term, 1830, to Michaelmas Term, 1841. 9 vols. London. 1833–42.

DOWLING (Alfred) and DOWLING (Vincent). Reports of Cases argued and determined in the Queen's Bench Practice Court; with the Points of Pleading and Practice decided in the Courts of Common Pleas and Exchequer; from Trinity Term, 1841, to Easter Term, 1843. 2 vols. New Series. London and Dublin. 1843–4.

DOWLING (Alfred) and LOWNDES (John James). Reports of Cases argued and determined in the Queen's Bench Practice Court; with the Points of Pleading and Practice decided in the Courts of Common Pleas and Exchequer; from Easter Term, 1843, to Michaelmas Term, 1849. 7 vols. London and Dublin. 1845–51.

DOWLING (James) and RYLAND (Archer). Reports of Cases argued and determined in the Court of King's Bench, from Hilary Term, 2d Geo. IV., 1822, to Trinity Term, 1827. 9 vols. Philadelphia. 1830–33. (Eng. Com. Law Reps., Vols. 16, 22.)

Reports of Cases argued and determined at Nisi Prius, in the Court of King's Bench, and on the Home Circuit. (Being part of Vol. 1 of Dowling & Ryland's Reports.) Philadelphia. 1830. (Eng. Com. Law Reps., Vol. 16.)

DREWRY (Charles Stewart). Reports of Cases decided in the High Court of Chancery, 1852–59, by Sir Richard Torin Kindersley, Vice-Chancellor. 4 vols. London. 1853–60.

DUER (John). Reports of Cases argued and determined in the Superior Court of the City of New York. 6 vols. Albany. 1854–1858.

DUDLEY (G. M.) Reports of Decisions made by the Judges of the Superior Courts of Law and Chancery of the State of Georgia. New York. 1837.

DUDLEY (C. W) Reports of Cases at Law argued and determined in the Court of Appeals of South Carolina, 1837–38. Charleston, S. C. 1858.

Reports of Cases argued and determined in the Court of Appeals of South Carolina, on Appeal from the Courts of Equity, containing the Decisions from December, 1837, to May, 1838, inclusive. Charleston, S. C. 1858.

RNFORD (Charles) and EAST (Edward Hyde.) Term Reports in the Court of Kings Bench, from Michaelmas Term, 26 Geo. III., 1785, to Trinity, 38 Geo. III, 1798, inclusive. 8 vols. in 4. 3 Am. from 5th London Ed. New York. 1834.

DURFEE (Thomas.) Reports of Cases argued and determined in the Supreme Court of Rhode Island. 1 vol. Providence. 1854. (Rhode Island Reports, Vol. 2.)

DUTCHER (Andrew.) Reports of Cases argued and determined in the Supreme Court and the Court of Errors and Appeals of New Jersey. 5 vols. Trenton. 1856–1863. (New Jersey Law Reports, Vols. 25–29.)

DUVAL (Alvin.) Reports of Selected Civil and Criminal Cases, decided in the Court of Appeals of Kentucky. Vol. 1. Containing the Cases decided at the Winter Term, 1863, and Summer and Winter Terms, 1864. Frankfort, Ky. 1865.

DYER (Sir James.) Reports of Cases in the Reigns of Henry VIII, Edw. VI, Q. Mary, and Q. Eliz. by John Vaillant. 3 Parts. Dublin. 1794.

EAST (Edward Hyde.) Reports of Cases argued and determined in the Court of King's Bench, from the 41st year of George III. (1800) to the 53d year of George III. (1812.) Philadelphia and London. 1810–16.

ECCLESIASTICAL. (See ENGLISH ECCLESIASTICAL REPORTS.)

EDEN (Hon. Robert Henley.) Reports of Cases in the High Court of Chancery, from 1757 to 1766. 2d Ed. 2 vols. London. 1827.

EDMONDS (John W.) Reports of Select Cases decided in the Courts of New York, not heretofore reported or reported only partially. Vol. 1. New York. 1868.

EDWARDS (Charles.) Reports of Chancery Cases decided in the First Circuit of New York, by the Hon. Wm. T. Mc-Coun. 4 vols. New York and Albany. 1833–1851.

EDWARDS (Thomas.) Reports of Cases argued and determined in the High Court of Admiralty, commencing with the Judgments of Sir William Scott, Easter Term, 1808. 1 vol. Boston. 1853.

ELLIS (Thomas Flower) and BLACKBURN (Colin). Reports of Cases argued and determined in the Court of Queen's Bench, and the Court of Exchequer Chamber on Error from the Court of Queen's Bench. Containing the Cases from Michaelmas Term, 1852, to Hilary Term and Vacation, 1858. (Eng. Com. Law Reps., Vols. 72, 75, 77, 82, 85, 88, 90, 92.)

ELLIS (Thomas Flower), BLACKBURN (Colin) and ELLIS (Francis). Reports of Cases argued and determined in the Court of Queen's Bench, and the Court of Exchequer Chamber on Error from the Court of Queen's Bench. Containing the Cases determined in Easter, and Trinity Term and Vacation. 1858. Philadelphia. 1861. (Eng. Com. Law Reps., Vol. 96.)

ELLIS (Thomas Flower) and ELLIS (Francis). Reports of Cases argued and determined in the Court of Queen's Bench, and the Court of Exchequer Chamber on Error, from the Court of Queen's Bench. Containing the Cases from Michaelmas Term and Vacation, 1858, to Hilary Term and Vacation, 1861. 3 vols. Philadelphia. 1864–68. (Eng. Com. Law Reps., Vols. 102, 105, 107.)

ENGLISH (E. H). Reports of Cases at Law and in Equity, argued and determined in the Supreme Court of Arkansas. 1845–1853. Little Rock, Ark. 1846–1853. (Arkansas Reports, Vols. 6–13.)

ENGLISH ADMIRALTY REPORTS. American Edition. Edited by George Minot. 9 vols. Boston. 1853.

Vol. 1. Robinson (Chr.) Vols. 1 and 2.
Vol. 2. Robinson (Chr.) Vols. 3 and 4.
Vol. 3. Robinson (Chr.) Vols. 5 and 6.
Vol. 4. Edwards (Thomas), Hay (Sir George) and Marriott (Sir James), and Cases selected from Vol. 7 of Moore's Privy Council Reports.
Vol. 5. Acton (Thomas Harman). Vols. 1 and 2, and Cases selected from Vol. 4 of Notes of Cases.
Vol. 6. Dodson (John). Vols 1 and 2.
Vol. 7. Haggard (John). Vols. 1 and 2.
Vol. 8. Haggard (John). Vol. 3. Robinson (William). Vol. 1.
Vol. 9. Robinson (William). Vol. 2 and Parts 1 and 2 of Vol. 3; and Table of Cases.

ENGLISH CHANCERY REPORTS. Condensed Reports of Cases decided in the High Court of Chancery in England. Edited by Richard Peters. 43 vols. Philadelphia, New York and Albany. 1831–57.

Vol. 1. Simons and Stuart. 2 vols.
Vol. 2. Simons, Vols. 1 and 2.
Vol. 3. Russell, Vols. 2, 3 and 4, with Index containing Vol. 1.
Vol. 4. Jacob, Vol. 1. Russell & Mylne, Vol. 1.
Vol. 5. Simons, Vol. 3. Tamlyn, Vol. 1.
Vol. 6. Simons, Vols. 4 and 5. Russel and Mylne, Vol. 2. Mylne & Keene, Vol. 1.
Vol. 7. Mylne & Keene, Vols. 1 and 2. Simons, Vol. 5.
Vol. 8. Mylne & Keene, Vols. 2 and 3. Coopers Select Cases, Vol. 1.
Vol. 9. Mylne & Keene, Vol. 3. Simons, Vols. 6 and 7.
Vol. 10. Simons, Vol. 7. Mylne & Keene, Vol. 3. Lloyd & Goold, Vol. 1.
Vol. 11. Turner & Russell, Vol. 1. Simons, Vol. 8.
Vol. 12. Molloy, Vols. 1, 2.
Vol. 13. Russell & Mylne, Vol. 2. Mylne & Craig, Vol. 1.
Vol. 14. Mylne & Craig, Vols. 2 and 3.
Vol. 15. Keen, Vols. 1 and 2.

Vol. 16. Simons, Vols. 9 and 10.
Vol. 17. Beavan, Vols. 1 and 2.
Vol. 18. Mylne & Craig, Vol. 4. Craig and Phillips, Vol. 1.
Vol. 19. Phillips, Vol. 1.
Vol. 20. Younge & Collyer, Vol. 1.
Vol. 21. Younge & Collyer, Vol. 2.
Vol. 22. Phillips, Vol. 2.
Vol. 23. Hare, Vol. 1.
Vol. 24. Hare, Vol. 2.
Vol. 25. Hare, Vol. 3.
Vol. 26. Hare, Vol. 5.
Vol. 27. Hare, Vol. 7.
Vol. 28. Collyer, Vol. 1.
Vol. 29. Beavan, Vol. 7.
Vol. 30. Hare, Vol. 4.
Vol. 31. Hare, Vol. 6.
Vol. 32. Hare, Vol. 8.
Vol. 33. Collyer, Vol. 2.
Vol. 34. Simons, Vol. 11.
Vol. 35. Simons, Vol. 12.
Vol. 36. Simons, Vol. 13.
Vol. 37. Simons, Vol. 14.
Vol. 38. Simons, Vol. 15.
Vol. 39. Simons, Vol. 16.
Vol. 40. Simons, Vol. 1. N. S.
Vol. 41. Hare, Vol. 1.
Vol. 42. Simons, Vol. 17. Simons, Vol. 2. N. S.
Vol. 43. Beavan, Vol. 3.

ENGLISH COMMON LAW REPORTS. Reports of Cases argued and determined in the English Courts of Common Law. Edited by Thomas Sergeant and John C. Lowber. 117 vols. Philadelphia. 1834–66.

Alphabetical List of Reporters in Johnsons' Edition of the English Common Law Reports.

Volume of original Reports.	Title of Reports.	Abbreviations	Name of Court.	Date of Reports.	Volume of English Common Law Reports.
1	Adolphus and Ellis.....	A. & E. or	King's Bench.	1834	28
2	..........do............	Ad. & E.	......do......	1834–5	29
3	..........do............	....do....	......do......	1835–6	30
4, 5	..........do............	....do....	......do......	1835–6	31
6	..........do............	....do....	......do......	1837	33
7	..........do............	....do....	......do......	1837–8	34
8	..........do............	....do....	Queen's Bench.	1838	35
9	..........do............	....do....	......do......	1839	36
10	..........do............	....do....	......do......	1839	37
11	..........do............	....do....	......do......	1839–40	39
12	..........do............	....do....	......do......	1840–41	40

English Common Law Reports—continued.

Vol. of original Reports.	Title of Reports.	Abbreviations	Name of Court.	Date of Reports.	Volume of English Common Law Reports.
1	Adolphus Ellis (N. S.)...	Q. B. or	Queen's Bench.	1841	41
2	or Queen's Bench.......	A.&E. (N.S.)	......do... ..	1841-2	42
3	..........do............	....do....	......do......	1842-3	43
4	..........do............	....do....	......do......	1843	45
5	..........do............	....do....	......do......	1843-4	48
6	..........do............	....do....	......do......	1844-5	51
7	..........do............	....do....	......do :....	1845	53
8	..........do............	....do....	......eo......	1846	55
9	..........do............	....do....	......do......	1846-7	58
10	..........do........	....do....	......do......	1847	59
11	....do............	....do....	......do......	1847-8	63
12	....do............	....do....	.....do......	1848	64
13	..........do............	....do....	......do......	1848-9	66
14	..........do............	....do....	......do......	1849	68
15	..........do........	....do....	... ..do......	1850	69
16	..........do............	....do....	......do......	1851	71
17	..........do............	....do....	......do......	1852	79
18	..........do............	....do....	......do......	1852	83
1	Barnewall & Adolphus..	B. & Ad.	King's Bench.	1830-1	20
2	..........do............	....do....	......do......	1831	22
3	..........do'............	....do....	......do......	1832	23
4	..........do............	....do....	......do......	1832-3	24
5	..........do............	....do....	......do......	1833-4	27
3	Barnewall & Alderson...	B. & A.	......do......	1819-20	5
4	..........do............	....do....	.....do......	1820-1	6
5	..........do............	....do....	......do......	1821-2	7
1	Barnewall & Cresswell..	B. & C.	......do......	1822-3	8
2	..........do............	....do....	......do	1823-4	9
3,4	..........do............	... do....	......do......	1824-5	10
5	..........do............	...do....	......do......	1825-6	11
6	..........do............	...do....	......do......	1826-7	13
7	..........do............	....do....	......do......	1827	14
8	..........do............	....do....	......do......	1828	15
9	..........do............	...do....	......do......	1829	17
10	..........do............	....do....	.. ..do......	1829-30	21
1	Best & Smith...........	B. & S.	Queen's Bench.	1861	101
2	.....do................	....do....	......do......	1862	110
3	......do	....do....	......do......	1862-3	113
4	......do................	....do....	......do......	1863-4	116
1	Bingham	Bing.	Common Pleas.	1822-4	8
2	....do.................	....do....	......do......	1824-5	9
3	....do.................	....do....	......do......	1825	11
4	....do.................	....do....	.. ..do......	1826-7-8	13
5	....do.................	....do....	......do......	1828-9	15
6	....do.................	....do....	......do......	1829-30	19
7	....do.................	....do....	......do......	1830-1	20
8	....do...............	....do....	......do......	1831-2	21
9	....do.................	...do....	......do......	1832-3	23
10	....do.................	... do....	......do......	1833-4	25
1	Bingham's New Cases...	Bing. N. C.	......do.. ...	1834-5	27

English Common Law Reports—continued.

Vol. of original Reports.	Title of Reports.	Abbreviations	Name of Court.	Date of Reports.	Volume of English Common Law Reports.
2	Bingham's New Cases ..	Bing, N. C.	Common Pleas.	1835–6	29
3	..........do..........	....do....	......do......	1836–7	32
4	..........do..........	....do....	......do......	1837–8	33
5	..........do..........	....do....	......do......	1838–9	35
6	..........do..........	....do....	......do......	1839–40	37
1	Broderip and Bingham..	B. & B.	......do......	1819–20	5
2	..........do..........	....do....	......do......	1820–1	6
3	..........do..........	....do....	......do......	1821–2	7
1	Carrington and Kirwan..	C. & K.	Nisi Prius.	1844	47
2	..........do..........	....do....	......do......	1844–9	61
	Carrington & Marshman.	C. & M.	......do......	1840–1–2	41
1, 2	Carrington and Payne...	C. & P.	......do......	1825–7	12
3	..........do..........	....do....	......do......	1827–9	14
4	..........do..........	....do....	......do......	1829–31	19
5	..........do..........	....do....	......do......	1831–3	24
6	..........do..........	....do....	......do......	1833–5	25
7	..........do..........	....do....	......do......	1835–7	32
8	..........do..........	....do....	......do......	1837–9	34
9	..........do..........	....do....	......do......	1839–41	38
1, 2	Chitty..................	Chit.	King's Bench.	1819	18
1	Com. B'ch, M., Gr. & Scott	C. B. or	Common Pleas.	1845	50
2	..........do...... do ...	Com. B.	......do......	1845–6	52
3	..........do...... do ...	....do....	......do......	1846–7	54
4	..........do...... do ...	....do....	......do......	1847	56
5	..........do...... do ...	....do....	......do......	1847–8	57
6	..........do...... do ...	....do....	......do......	1848	60
7	..........do...... do ...	....do....	......do......	1849	62
8	..........do...... do ...	....do....	......do......	1849	65
9	..........do...... do ...	....do....	......do......	1850	67
10	..........do.. J. Scott, 1	....do....	......do......	1851	70
11	..........do...... do 2	....do....	......do......	1852	73
12	..........do...... do 3	....do....	......do......	1853	74
13	..........do...... do 4	....do....	......do......	1853	76
14	..........do...... do 5	....do....	......do......	1854	78
15	..........do...... do 6	....do....	......do......	1854	80
16	..........do...... do 7	....do....	......do......	1855	81
17	..........do...... do 8	....do....	......do......	1856	84
18	..........do...... do 9	....do....	......do......	1856	86
1	..........do (N. S.) do ...	... do N. S.	......do......	1856–7	87
2	..........do...... do ...	....do..do	......do......	1857	89
3	..........do...... do ...	....do..do	......do......	1857–8	91
4	..........do...... do ...	....do..do	......do......	1858	93
5	..........do...... do ...	....do..do	......do......	1859	94
6	..........do...... do ...	....do..do	......do......	1859	95
7	..........do...... do ...	....do..do	......do......	1860	97
8	..........do...... do ...	....do..do	......do......	1860	98
9	..........do...... do ...	....do..do	......do......	1860–1	99
10	..........do...... do ...	....do..do	......do......	1861	100
11	..........do...... do ...	....do..do	......do......	1861–2	103
12	..........do...... do ...	....do..do	......do......	1862	104

English Common Law Reports—continued.

Vol. of original Reports.	Title of Reports.	Abbreviations	Name of Court.	Date of Reports.	Volume of English Common Law Reports.
13	Common Bench, J. Scott.	Com.B.,N.S.	Common Pleas.	1862–3	106
14	..........do...... do ...	....do..do	......do......	1863	108
15	..........do...... do ...	....do..do	......do......	1863	109
16	..........do...... do ...	....do..do	......do......	1864	111
17	..........do...... do ...	....do..do	......do.....	1864	112
18	..........do...... do ...	....do..do	......do......	1864–5	114
19	..........do...... do ...	....do..do	......do.. ...	1865	115
20	..........do...... do ...	....do..do	......do......	1865	117
	Deacon	Deac.	B'krupt'y Cases.	1835–6	38
3, 4	Douglas	Doug.	King's Bench.	1781–5	26
1–8	Dowling and Ryland	D. & R.	......do......	1822–6	16
9	..........do............	....do.....	......do......	1826–7	22
1	..........do.......	D. & R. N. P.	......do......	1822–3	16
1	*Ellis and Blackburn ...	E. & B.	Queen's Bench.	1852–3	72
2	..........do............	....do.....	......do......	1853	75
3	..........do............	....do.....	.....do......	1854	77
4	..........do............	....do.....	......do......	1854–5	82
5	..........do............	....do.....	......do......	1856	85
6	..........do............	....do.....	......do......	1856	88
7	..........do............	....do.....	......do......	1857	90
8	..........do......	....do.....	......do......	1857–8	92
	Ellis, Blackurn and Ellis,	E., B. & E.	......do......	1858–9	96
1	Ellis and Ellis	E. & E.	......do......	1858–9	102
2	..........do............	....do.....	......do......	1859–60	105
3	..........do............	....do.....	......do......	1860	107
	Gow	Gow.	......do......	1818–19	5
	Holt..................	Holt.	......do......	1815–17	3
1	Manning and Granger...	M. & G.	Common Pleas.	1840	39
2	..........do............	....do.....	......do......	1840–1	40
3	..........do	....do.....	......do......	1841–2	42
4	..........do............	....do.....	......do......	1842	43
5	..........do............	....do.....	......do......	1843	44
6	..........do............	....do.....	......do......	1843–4	46
7	..........do............	....do.....	......do......	1844	49
1, 2	Manning and Ryland....	M. & R.	King's Bench.	1837–8	17
1, 2	Marshall...........	Marsh.	C. P. and Exch.	1813–16	4
	Moody and Malkin......	Moody & M.	Nisi Prius.	1827–30	22
1, 2, 3	J. B. Moore	Moore.	C. P. and Exch.	1817–19	4
4, 5	..........do............	...do.....	......do......	1819–21	16
6–10	..........do............	...do.....	......do......	1821–5	17
11, 12	..........do............	...do.....	......do......	1825–7	22
1, 2	Moore and Payne	M. & P.	......do......	1827–9	17
1, 2	Moore and Scott........	M. & S.	......do......	1831–3	28
3, 4	..........do	...do.....	......do......	1833–4	30
1, 2, 3	Nevile and Manning....	N. & M.	King's Bench.	1832–4	28
4	..........do............	....do.....	......do......	1834–5	30
5, 6	..........do........ ...	....do.....	......do......	1835–6	36
1	Nevile and Perry	N. & P.	King's B. & Exc.	1836–7	36
	Ryan and Moodie.......	R. & M.	Nisi Prius.	1823–6	21
2	Scott	Scott.	C. P. and Exch.	1835–6	30

English Common Law Reports—continued.

No. of original Reports.	Title of Reports.	Abbreviations	Name of Court.	Date of Reports.	Volume of English Common Law Reports.
3, 4	Scott..................	Scott.....	C. P. and Exch.	1836–7	36
1	Starkie..........	Stark.....	Nisi Prius.	1814–16	2
2, 3	....do.................	....do.....	N.P.K.BandC.P	1820–22	3
5, 6	Taunton........	Taunt.....	Common Pleas.	1813–16	1
7	....do.................	....do.....	.......do......	1816–17	2
8	....do...	....do.....	C. P. and Exch.	1817–19	4

ENGLISH ECCLESIASTICAL REPORTS. Reports of Cases argued and determined in the English Ecclesiastical Courts. Edited by Edward D. Ingraham. 7 vols. Philadelphia. 1831–45.

Vol. 1. Phillimore. 3 vols. 1809–21.
Vol. 2. Adams. 3 vols. 1822–26.
Vol. 3. Haggard, Vol. 1. Ferguson's Consistory Reports.
Vol. 4. Haggard, Vol. 2. Haggard's Consistory Reports, Vols. 1 and 2.
Vol. 5. Haggard, Vol. 3. Lee, Vol. 1.
Vol. 6. Lee, Vol. 2. Curteis, Vol. 1.
Vol. 7. Curteis, Vols. 2 and 3.

ENGLISH EXCHEQUER REPORTS. Reports of Cases argued and determined in the Court of Exchequer at Law and in Equity, and in the Exchequer Chamber, in Equity and in Error. Edited by Francis J. Troubat. 6 vols. Philadelphia. 1835.

Vol. 1. Price, Vols. 1, 2 and 3.
Vol. 2. Price, Vols. 4, 5 and 6.
Vol. 3. Price, Vols. 7 and 8.
Vol. 4. Price, Vols. 9 and 10.
Vol. 5. Price, Vols. 11 and 12.
Vol. 6. Price, Vol. 13, and Part III. of Vol. 10.

"ENGLISH LAW REPORTS." New Series, under the supervision of the Council of Reporting. See "Law Reports."

ENGLISH LAW AND EQUITY REPORTS. Containing Reports of Cases in the House of Lords, Privy Council, Courts of Equity and Common Law; and in the Admiralty and Ecclesiastical Courts; including also Cases in Bankruptcy and Crown Cases reserved. Edited by Edmund H. Bennett and Chauncey Smith. 40 vols. Boston. 1851–58.

English Railway and Canal Cases. Cases relating to Railways and Canals argued and adjudged in the Courts of Law and Equity: 1835 to 1852. Henry Illtid Nichol, Thomas Hare, and John Monson Carrow. From the London Edition. Edited by Chauncey Smith and Samuel W. Bates. 6 vols. Boston. 1854.

Espinasse (Isaac.) Reports of Cases argued and ruled at Nisi Prius, in the Courts of King's Bench and Common Pleas, from Easter Term, 33 Geo. III. (1793) to Trinity Term, 47 Geo. III. (1807.) A New Edition, by Thomas Day. 6 vols. Hartford and New York. 1818–25.

Exchequer Reports. Reports of Cases argued and determined in the Courts of Exchequer and Exchequer Chamber, from Trinity Term, 10 Vict., to Hilary Vacation, 19 Vict., both inclusive. By W. N. Welsby, E. F. Hurlstone and J. Gordon. J. I. Clark Hare, and H. B. Wallace, Editors. 11 vols. Philadelphia. 1849–57.

Fairfield (John.) Reports of Cases argued and determined in the Supreme Judicial Court of the State of Maine. 3 vols. Hallowell. 1835–1837. (Maine Reports, Vols. 10–12.)

Falconer (Thomas) and Fitzherbert (Edward H.) Cases of Controverted Elections determined in Committees of the House of Commons, in the Second Parliament of the reign of Queen Victoria. London. 1839. "Election Cases. 1836–1838."

Ferguson (James.) Reports of some Recent Decisions by the Consistorial Court of Scotland, in Actions of Divorce, Concluding for dissolution of marriages celebrated under the English Law. Philadelphia. 1832. (English Ecclesiastical Reports, Vol. 3.)

Finch (Thomas.) Precedents in Chancery; being a Collection of Cases argued and adjudged in the High Court of Chancery, from the year 1689 to 1722. 2d Ed. Dublin. 1792.

Finch (Sir Heneage.) Reports of Cases decreed in the High Court of Chancery, during the time Sir Heneage Finch, afterwards Earl of Nottingham, was Lord Chancellor. Folio. In the Savoy. 1725.

Fitzgibbon (John.) The Reports of several Cases argued and adjudged in the Court of King's Bench at Westminister; with some special Cases in the Courts of Chancery, Common Pleas and Exchequer. In the 1, 2, 3, 4 and 5 years of his present Majesty, King George II. Folio. In the Savoy. 1732.

FLORIDA.
Branch's Reports. (1 Fla.) 1846.
Archer's Reports. (2 Fla.) 1847.
Hogue's Reports. (3–5 Fla.) 1848–1851.
Papy's Reports. (6–8 Fla.) 1852–1859.
Galbraith's Reports. (9–11 Fla.) 1859–1867.
Galbraith and Meek's Reports. (12 Fla.) 1867–1869.

FOGG (George G.) Reports of Cases argued and determined in the Supreme Judicial Court of New Hampshire. 6 vols. Concord 1857–1859. (New Hampshire Reports, Vols. 32–37.)

FONBLANQUE (J. W. M.) Reports of Cases adjudicated in the several Courts of the Commissioners in Bankruptcy, under the Bankrupt Laws Consolidation Act, 1849. London and Dublin. 1857. "Fonblanque's Bankruptcy Cases. 1849–1852."

FORREST. Cases argued and determined in the Court of Exchequer, in 41 Geo. III. 1800–01. [No Title-page or Index.]

FOSTER (William L.) Reports of Cases argued and determined in the Superior Court of Judicature of New Hampshire. 12 vols. Concord and Boston. 1852–1857. (New Hampshire Reports, Vols. 19, 21–31.)

FOSTER (Sir Michael). A Report of some Proceedings on the Commission for the Trial of the Rebels in the year 1746, in the County of Surry; and of other Crown Cases: to which are added Discourses upon a few branches of the Crown Law. 3d Ed. London. 1792.

FOSTER (T. Campbell) and FINLASON (W. F.) Reports of Cases decided at Nisi Prius and at the Crown Side on Circuit; with Select Decisions at Chambers. From Hilary Vacation, 1856, to Hilary Vacation, 1867. 4 vols. London and Dublin. 1860–67.

FRASER (Simon). Reports of the Proceedings before select Committees of the House of Commons, in certain Cases of Controverted Elections; heard and determined during the First and Second Sessions of the Seventeenth Parliament of Great Britain. 2 vols. London. 1791–1793. "Election Cases, 1790–1792."

FREEMAN (John D.) Reports of Cases decided in the Superior Court of Chancery of the State of Mississippi. Containing a series of Cases decided between December Term, 1839, and July Term, 1843. Cincinnati. 1844.

FREEMAN (Hon. Richard). Reports of Cases argued and determined in the Courts of King's Bench and Common Pleas, from 1670 to 1704. 2d Ed. London and Dublin. 1826.

Reports of Cases argued and determined in the High Court of Chancery, principally between the years 1660 and 1706. 2d Ed. by John Ekyn Hovenden. London and Dublin. 1823.

FREEMAN (Richard). Reports of Cases argued and adjudged in the Courts of King's Bench and Common Pleas, from 1670 to 1683. Folio. In the Savoy. 1742.

FRENCH (Benjamin B.) Reports of Cases argued and determined in the Superior Court of Judicature of the State of New Hampshire. From February Term, 1832, to July Term, 1834, both inclusive. Newport, N. H. 1835. (New Hampshire Reports, Vol. 6.)

FREEMAN (William). Trial of William Freeman for the murder of John G. Van Nest, including the evidence and arguments of Counsel with the Decision of the Supreme Court granting a New Trial, and an account of the death of the prisoner and of the *post mortem* examination by Amariah Brigham, M. D., and others. Reported by Benjamin F. Hall. Auburn. 1848.

FREEMAN (Norman L.) Reports of Cases at Law and in Chancery, argued and determined in the Supreme Court of Illinois, from January Term, 1863, to January Term, 1870. 24 vols. Chicago and Springfield. 1863–1871. (Illinois Reports, Vols. 31–54.)

GALE (Charles James) and DAVISON (Henry). Reports of Cases argued and determined in the Court of Queen's Bench, and upon Writs of Error from that Court to the Exchequer Chamber, from Easter Term, 1841, to Easter Term, 1843. 3 vols. London and Dublin. 1842–3.

GALBRAITH (John B.) Reports of Cases argued and adjudged in the Supreme Court of Florida, at Terms held in 1860–1867. Tallahassee. 1861–1867. (Florida Reports, Vols. 9–11.)

GALBRAITH (John B.) and MEEK (A. R.) Reports of Cases argued and adjudged in the Supreme Court of Florida at Terms held in 1867–1869. Tallahassee. 1869. (Florida Reports, Vol. 12.)

GALLISON (John). Reports of Cases argued and determined in the Circuit Court of the United States for the First Circuit. 2 vols. Second Edition. Boston. 1845.

GARDENHIRE (Jas. B.) Reports of Cases argued and decided in the Supreme Court of the State of Missouri. 2 vols. Jefferson City. 1852. (Missouri Reports, Vols. 14–15.)

GEORGIA.
Dudley's Reports, 1 vol., 1821–1833.
Georgia Decisions, 1 vol., 1842–1843.
Kelly's Reports (1–3 Ga.), 1846–1847.
Kelly and Cobb's Reports (4–5 Ga.), 1848.
Cobb's Reports (6–20 Ga.), 1849–1857.
Martin's Reports (21–30 Ga.), 1858–1862.
Lester's Reports (31–33 Ga.), 1860–1861.
Bleckly's Reports (34–35 Ga.), 1864–1866.
Hammond's Reports (36–40 Ga.), 1867–1870.

GEORGIA DECISIONS. Decisions of the Superior Courts of the State of Georgia. Part 1. Containing the Decisions Rendered during the year 1842. Augusta. 1843.

GEORGE (James Z.) Reports of Cases argued and determined in the High Court of Errors and Appeals, for the State of Mississippi. Containing the Cases determined from December Term, 1855, to April Term, 1863. 10 vols. Philadelphia. 1857–1867. (Mississippi Reports, Vols. 30–39.)

GIBBS (George C.) Reports of Cases argued and determined in Supreme Court of the State of Michigan. 3 vols. Detroit and Lansing. 1854–1857. (Michigan Reports, Vols. 2–4.)

GIFFARD (J. W. DeLongueville.) Reports of Cases adjudged in the High Court of Chancery, by the Vice-Chancellor Sir John Stuart. From 1858–65. In 5 vols. Vols. 1, 2 and 5. London and Dublin. 1860–71.

GILL (Richard W.) Reports of Cases argued and determined in the Court of Appeals of Maryland. Containing the Cases from 1843 to 1851. 9 vols. Annapolis. 1846–1852.

GILL (Richard W) and JOHNSON (John.) Reports of Cases argued and determined in the Court of Appeals of Maryland. Containing the Cases from 1829–1842. 12 vols. Baltimore and Annapolis. 1830–1845.

GILMAN (Charles.) Reports of Cases argued and determined in the Supreme Court of the State of Illinois. 5 vols. Quincy, Galena, Chicago, and Springfield. 1846–1849. (Illinois Reports, Vols. 6–10.)

GILMER (Francis W.) Reports of Cases decided in the Court of Appeals of Virginia, from April 10th, 1820, to June 28th, 1821. Richmond. 1821.

GILPIN (Henry D.) Reports of Cases adjudged in the District Court of the United States for the Eastern District of Pennsylvania. Philadelphia. 1837.

GLANVILLE (John.) Reports of Certain Cases determined and adjudged by the Commons in Parliament in the Twenty-first and Twenty-second years of the Reign of King James the First. London. 1775. "Election Cases, 1623–1624."

GLENN (S. F.) Reports of Cases argued and determined in the Supreme Court of Louisiana. For the years 1861–1866. 3 vols. New Orleans 1866–1867. (Louisana Annual Reports, Vols. 16–18.)

GLYN (Thomas C.) and JAMESON (Robert S.) Cases in Bankruptcy. Containing Reports of Cases decided by Lord Chancellor Eldon and by Vice Chancellor Sir John Leach, from Michaelmas Term, 1821, to Easter Term, 1828. 2 vols. London. 1824–1828.

GODBOLT'S REPORTS. Reports of Certain Cases, arising in the several Courts of Record at Westminster; in the Raignes of Q. Elizabeth, K. James, and the late King Charles. London. 1752.

GOLDSBRROUGH (J.) Reports of Choice Cases, in all the Courts at Westminster, in the later years of the Reign of Queen Elizabeth. London. 1653.

GOW (NIEL.) Reports of Cases argued and ruled at Nisi Prius, in the Court of Common Pleas, by the Lord Chief Justice Dallas, and on the Oxford Circuit; Lent Assizes, 1818. Vol. 1, Pt. I. Philadelphia. 18[illegible]2. (Eng. Com. Law Reps., Vol. 5.)

GRANT (BENJAMIN). Reports of Cases argued and adjudged in the Supreme Court of Pennsylvania. 3 vols. Philadelphia. 1859–1864.

GRATTAN (Peachy R.) Reports of cases decided in the Supreme Court of Appeals and the General Court of Virginia. 20 vols. From 1844 to 1871. Richmond. 1845–1871.

GRAY (Horace.) Reports of Cases argued and determined in the Supreme Judicial Court of Massachusetts. 16 vols. Boston. 1855–1871.

GREEN (Charles Ewing.) Reports of Cases argued and determined in the Court of Chancery, the Prerogative Court, and on Appeal, in the Court of Errors and Appeals, of the State of New Jersey. 6 vols. Trenton. 1867–1871. (New Jersey Equity Reports, Vols. 16–21.)

GREEN (James S.) Reports of Cases argued and adjudicated in the Supreme Court of Judicature of New Jersey. 1831-1836. 3 vols. Trenton and Woodbury. 1833–1838.

GREEN (Henry W.) Reports of Cases determined in the Court

of Chancery of New Jersey. 3 vols. Elizabethtown. 1842–1846.

GREENE (George.) Reports of Cases in Law and Equity determined in the Supreme Court of Iowa. 4 vols. Dubuque, Iowa. 1849–1858.

GREENLEAF (Simon.) Reports of Cases argued and determined in the Supreme Judicial Court of Maine. 9 vols. Hallowell and Portland. 1822–1835. (Maine Reports, Vols. 1–9.)

GRISWOLD (Hiram.) Reports of Cases argued and determined in the Supreme Court of the State of Ohio, in Bank. 6 vols. Columbus. 1846–1851. (Ohio Reports, Vols. 14–19.)

HADLEY (Amos.) Reports of Cases argued and determined in the Supreme Judicial Court of New Hampshire. 4 vols. Concord. 1866–1871. (New Hampshire Reports, Vols. 45–48.)

HAGGARD (John.) Reports of Cases argued and determined in the High Court of Admiralty, during the time of the Right Hon. Lord Stowel. Edited by George Minot. 2 vols. 1822–1838. Boston, 1853. (English Admiralty Reports, Vols. 7 and 8.)

Reports of Cases argued and determined in the Ecclesiastical Courts at Doctors' Commons; and in the High Court of Delegates, Containing the Cases from Michaelmas Term, 1827, to Hilary Term, 1832. 3 vols. Philadelphia. 1832–1835. (English Ecclesiastical Reports, Vols. 3, 4 and 5.)

Reports of Cases argued and determined in the Consistory Court of London; containing the Judgments of the Right Hon. Sir William Scott. 2 vols. Philadelphia. 1832. (English Ecclesiastical Reports, Vol. 4.)

HALE (J. E.) Reports of Cases determined in the Supreme Court of the State of California. 5 vols. San Francisco. 1868–1870. (California Reports, Vols. 33–37.)

HALL (Jona. Prescott). Reports of Cases argued and determined in the Superior Court of the City of New York. 2 vols. New York. 1831–1833.

HALL (Frederick James) and TWELLS (Philip). Reports of Cases argued and determined in the High Court of Chancery, during the time of Lord Chancellor Cottenham. 1849–50, 12th–14th Vict. 2 vols. London and Dublin. 1850–51.

HALSTED (George B.) Reports of Cases determined in the Court of Chancery and in the Prerogative Court, and, on Appeal, in the Court of Errors and Appeals of the State of New Jersey. 4 vols. Elizabethtown and Newark, N. J. 1849–1854.

HALSTED (William, Jr.) Reports of Cases argued and determined in the Supreme Court of Judicature of the State of New Jersey. 7 vols. Trenton. 1822–1831.

HAMMOND (N. J.) Reports of Cases in Law and Equity argued and determined in the Supreme Court of Georgia, at Milledgeville, from June Term, 1867, to June Term, 1870. 5 vols. Macon, Ga. 1868–1871. (Georgia Reports, Vols. 36–40.)

HAMMOND (Charles). Cases decided in the Supreme Court of Ohio, upon the Circuit, and at the Special Sessions in Columbus, December, 1823–1839. Second Edition. 9 vols. Cincinnati and Columbus. 1833–1840. (Ohio Reports, Vols. 1–9.)

HAND (Samuel). Reports of Cases argued and determined in the Court of Appeals of the State of New York. 6 vols. New York and Albany. 1869–1872. (New York Reports, Vols. 40–45.)

HANWAY'S CASE. Report of the Trial of Castine Hanway for Treason, in the Resistance of the execution of the Fugitive Slave Law of September, 1859. Before Judges Grier and Kane, in the Circuit Court of the United States for the Eastern District of Pennsylvania, held at Philadelphia in November and December, 1851. Philadelphia. 1852.

HANDY (R. D. and J. H.) Reports of Cases argued and adjudged in the Superior Court of Cincinnati, in 1854–1855. 2 vols. in one. Cincinnati. 1855.

HARDIN (Martin D.) Reports of Cases argued and adjudged in the Court of Appeals of Kentucky, from Spring Term, 1805, to Spring Term, 1808, inclusive. Frankfort, Ky., 1810.

HARDRESS (Sir Thomas.) Reports of Cases adjudged in the Court of Exchequer, in the years 1655, 1656, 1657, 1658, 1659, 1660. And from thence continued to the 21st year of his late Majesty, King Charles II. 2d Ed. Dublin. 1792.

HARE (Thomas.) Reports of Cases adjudged in the High Court of Chancery, before the Right Hon. Sir James Wigram, Knt., Vice Chancellor. 1841–1853. 9 vols. New York and Albany. 1851–1856. (English Chancery Reports, Vols. 23, 27, 30–32, 41.)

HARMON (John B.) Reports of Cases determined in the Supreme Court of the State of California. 3 vols. San Francisco. 1860–1861. (California Reports, Vols. 13–15.)

HARPER (William). Reports of Cases determined in the Constitutional Court of South Carolina. 3d. Ed. Charleston, S. C. 1861.

HARRINGTON (Samuel M.) Reports of Cases argued and adjudged in the Superior Court and Court of Errors and Appeals of the State of Delaware, from the organization of those courts under the amended Constitution; with references to some of the Earlier cases. 5 vols. Dover. 1837–1856.

HARRINGTON (E. Burke.) Reports of Cases determined in the Court of Chancery of the State of Michigan. Detroit. 1845.

HARRIS (George W.) Pennsylvania State Reports. Reports of Cases adjudged by the Supreme Court of Pennsylvania. 12 vols. Lancaster and Philadelphia. 1850–1869. (Pennsylvania State Reports, Vols. 13–24.

HARRIS (Thomas, Jr.) and M'HENRY (John.) Maryland Reports, being a series of the most important Law Cases argued and determined in the Provincial Court and Court of Appeals of the then Province of Maryland, from the year 1700 down to the American Revolution. 4 vols. New York and Philadelphia. 1809–1840.

HARRIS (Thomas) and JOHNSON (Reverdy.) Reports of Cases argued and determined in the General Court and Court of Appeals of the State of Maryland, from 1800–1826, inclusive. 7 vols. Annapolis. 1821–1827.

HARRIS (Thomas) and GILL (Richard W.) Reports of Cases argued and determined in the Court of Appeals of Maryland in 1826, 1827, 1828 and 1829. 2 vols. Annapolis. 1828–1829.

HARRISON (Josiah.) Reports of Cases decided in the Supreme Court of Judicature of New Jersey, from 1837 to 1842. 4 vols. Camden. 1839–1843.

HARRISON (Benjamin.) Reports of Cases argued and determined in the Supreme Court of Judicature of Indiana. 10 vols. Indianapolis. 1861–1869. (Indiana Reports, Vols. 15–17 and 23–29.)

HARRISON (Octavian B. C.) and RUTHERFORD (Henry.) Reports of Cases argued and determined in the Court of Common Pleas, and the Court of Exchequer Chamber on

Appeal from the Court of Common Pleas. 27 Vict. 1865–6. London and Dublin. 1868.

HARTLEY (Oliver C.) Reports of Cases argued and decided in the Supreme Court of Texas. 7 vols. Galveston. 1852–1853. (Texas Reports, Vols. 4–10.)

HARTLEY (O. C.) and HARTLEY (R. K.) Reports of Cases argued and decided in the SUPREME Court of Texas. 11 vols. Galveston. 1854–1859. (Texas Reports, Vols. 11–21.)

HAWKINS (J.) Reports of Cases argued and determined in the Supreme Court of Louisiana. For the years 1867–1869. 3 vols. New Orleans. 1868–1869. (Louisiana Annual Reports, Vols. 19–21.)

HAWKS (Francis L.) Reports of Cases argued and adjudged in the Supreme Court of North Carolina, from 1820 to 1826. 4 vols. Raleigh. 1843–1845.

HAY (Sir George) and MARRIOTT (Sir James). Decisions in the High Court of Admiralty during the time of. Edited by George Minot. Volume 1. Michaelmas Term, 1776, to Hilary Term, 1779. Boston. 1853. (English Admiralty Reports, Vol. 4.)

HAYWOOD (John). Reports of Cases adjudged in the Superior Courts of Law and Equity of the State of North Carolina, from the year 1789 to the year 1806. 2 vols. Second Edition, by William H. Battle. Raleigh. 1832–1843.

HAYWOOD (John). Reports of Cases ruled and decided by the Supreme Court of Errors and Appeals, for the State of Tennessee. Vols. 4 and 5. Nashville, Tenn. 1818.

The Same. New Ed. Vols. 3–5 in one. With Notes and References. By Melville M. Bigelow. New York. 1870.

HEAD (John W.) Reports of Cases argued and determined in the Supreme Court of Tennessee, from 1856 to 1860. 3 vols. Nashville. 1860–1866.

HEATH (Solyman). Reports of Cases in Law and Equity determined by the Supreme Judicial Court of Maine. 5 vols. Hallowell. 1855–1856. (Maine Reports, Vols. 36–40.)

HEISKELL (Joseph B.) Reports of Cases argued and determined in the Supreme Court of Tennessee. For the years 1870–1871. 2 vols. Nashville. 1870–1871.

HELM (Alfred.) Reports of Cases determined in the Supreme Court of the State of Nevada, from 1866 to 1870, both inclusive. 5 vols. San Francisco. 1867–1871. (Nevada Reports, Vols. 2–6.)

HEMPSTEAD (Samuel H.) Reports of Cases argued and determined in the United States Superior Court for the Territory of Arkansas, from 1820 to 1836; and in the United States District Court for the District of Arkansas, from 1836 to 1849; and in the United States Circuit Court for the District of Arkansas, in the Ninth Circuit, from 1839 to 1856. Boston. 1856.

HENING (William W.) and MUNFORD (William.) Reports of Cases argued and determined in the Supreme Court of Appeals of Virginia; with select cases, relating chiefly to points of Practice, decided by the Superior Court of Chancery for the Richmond District. Second Edition. 4 vols. Flatbush, N. Y. and New York. 1809–1811.

HEPBURN (H. P.) Reports of Cases argued and determined in the Supreme Court of the State of California, in the year 1852. 3 vols. Philadelphia and San Francisco. 1854–1856. (California Reports, Vols. 2–4.)

HETLEY (Sir Thomas.) Reports and Cases taken in the third, fourth, fifth, sixth and seventh years of the late King Charles. As they were argued by most of the King's Sergeants at the Common Pleas Barre. London. 1657.

HILL (Nicholas.) Reports of Cases argued and determined in the Supreme Court of the State of New York. 7 vols. Albany and New York. 1845–1847.

HILL (W. R.) Reports of Cases at law argued and determined in the Court of Appeals of South Carolina. 3 vols. in 2. Charleston, S. C. 1857.

Reports of Cases in Chancery, argued and determined in the Court of Appeals of South Carolina; from January, 1833, to May, 1837, both inclusive. 2 vols. Columbia, S. C. 1834–1837.

HILL and DENIO. Reports of Cases argued and determined in the late Supreme Court of the State of New York. Supplement to Hill and Denio. [By T. M. Lalor. Albany. 1857.

HILLYER (Curtis J.) Reports of Cases determined in the Supreme Court of the State of California. 3 vols. San Francisco. 1863–1864. (California Reports, Vols. 20–22.)

HILTON (Henry.) Reports of Cases argued and determined in the Court of Common Pleas for the City and County of New York. 2 vols. New York and Albany. 1859–1860.

HOBART (Sir Henry.) Reports of. 1st Am., from 5th Eng. Ed. By John M. Williams. Boston. 1829.

HOFFMAN (Murray.) Reports of Cases argued and determined

in the Court of Chancery of the State of New York, before the Assistant Vice Chancellor of the First Circuit Vol. 1. New York. 1841.

HOGUE (David P.) Reports of Cases argued and adjudged in the Supreme Court of Florida, from 1849 to 1852. Vols. 2, 3 and 4. Tallahasse. 1849–1852. (Florida Reports, Vols. 3–5.)

HOLLINSHEAD (William.) Michigan Reports, Vol. 1. See OFFICER.

HOLT (Francis Ludlow.) Reports of Cases ruled and determined at Nisi Prius, in the Court of Common Pleas, and on the Northern Circuit; from the Sittings after Trinity Term, 55 Geo. III. (1815,) to the Sittings after Michaelmas Term, 58 Geo. III., (1817,) both inclusive. Vol. 1. Philadelphia. 1836. (Eng. Com. Law Reps, Vol. 3.)

HOLT (Sir John.) A Report of all the Cases determined by Sir John Holt, Knt., from 1688 to 1710, during which time he was Lord Chief Justice of England. Folio. In the Savoy. 1738.

HOOKER (John.) Connecticut Reports; containing Cases argued and determined in the Supreme Court of Errors of the State of Connecticut. 12 vols. Hartford. 1858–1871. (Connecticut Reports, Vols. 25–36.)

HOPKINS (Samuel M.) Reports of Cases argued and determined in the Court of Chancery of the State of New York. Vol. 1. New York. 1827.

HOPKINSON (Francis.) The Pennsylvania State Trials, containing the impeachment, trial and acquittal of Francis Hopkinson and John Nicholson, Esquires, the former being Judge of the Court of Admiralty, and the latter the Comptroller General of the Commonwealth of Pennsylvania. Vol. 1. Philadelphia. 1794.

HORWOOD. (See YEAR BOOKS OF EDW. I.)

HOUSE OF LORDS CASES on Appeals and Writs of Error, Claims of Peerage, and Divorces, during the Sessions of 1847–1866. By Charles Clark and W. Finnelly. 11 vols. Boston. 1870–1.

HOUSE OF LORDS REPORTS.

Shower. 1 vol., folio. 1694–1699.
Colles. 1 vol. 1697–1714.
Brown, by Tomlins. 8 vols. 1702–1800.
Dow. 6 vols. 1812–1818.
Bligh. 3 vols. 1819–1821, and Part 1 of Vol. 4.
Bligh. New Series. 10 vols. 1827–1837, and Parts and 3 of Vol. 11.

Dow and Clark. 2 vols. 1827–1832.
House of Lords Cases. 11 vols. 1847–1866.

HOUSTON (John W.) Reports of Cases decided in the Superior Court, and the Court of Errors and Appeals, of the State of Delaware. Volume 1. Philadelphia. 1866.

HOWARD (Volney E.) Reports of Cases argued and determined in the High Court of Errors and Appeals of the State of Mississippi. 7 vols. Philadelphia and Cincinnati. 1839–1844. (Mississippi Reports, Vols. 2–8.)

HOWARD (Benjamin C.) Reports of Cases argued and adjudged in the Supreme Court of the United States, from January Term, 1843, to December Term, 1860. 24 vols. Washington, D. C. 1861.

HOWARD (Nathan). Cases in the Court of Appeals of the State of New York. Vol. 1. New York. 1855.

Reports of Cases argued and determined in the Supreme Court, at Special Term, with the Points of Practice Decided. Second Edition. 41 vols. Albany and New York. 1851–1871.

HOWELL (T. B.) A Complete Collection of State Trials and Proceedings for High Treason and other Crimes and Misdemeanors from the Earliest period to the present Time. Compiled by T. B. Howell to the year 1783, and from that to the present time by Thomas Jones Howell. The whole comprising the period from the 9th year of the Reign of King Henry the Second, 1163, to the 1st year of the Reign of King George the Fourth, 1820. 34 vols. London and Dublin. 1809–26.

HUBBARD (Wales.) Reports of Cases in Law and Equity determined by the Supreme Judicial Court of Maine. 7 vols. Hallowell, 1859–1866. (Maine Reports, Vols. 45–51.)

HUBBELL (Levi.) Trial of Impeachment of Levi Hubbell, Judge of the Second Judicial Circuit, by the Senate of the State of Wisconsin. June, 1853. Reported by T. C. Leland. Madison. 1853.

HUGHES (James.) Report of Causes determined by the late Supreme Court for the District of Kentucky, and by the Court of Appeals; in which the Titles to Land were in dispute. 4to, Lexington. 1803.

HUMPHREYS (West H.) Reports of Cases argued and determined in the Supreme Court of Tennessee, from 1839 to 1851. 11 vols. Nashville. 1841–1851.

HURLSTONE (E. T.) and COLTMAN (F. J.) Reports of Cases argued and determined in the Courts of Exchequer and

Exchequer Chamber, from Easter Term 25 Vict., to Trinity Vacation, 29 Vict., both inclusive. 3 vols. Samuel Dickson and James Parsons, Editors. Philadelphia. 1865–69.

HURLSTONE, (E. T.) and NORMAN (J. P.) Reports of Cases argued and determined in the Courts of Exchequer and Exchequer Chamber, from Easter Term, 19 Vict. to Hilary Vacation, 25 Vict., both inclusive. J. J. Clark Hare and Henry Wharton, Editors. 7 vols. Philadelphia. 1860–64.

HUTTON (Sir Richard.) The Reports of that Reverend and Learned Judge, Sir Richard Hutton, Knight; sometime one of the Judges of the Common Pleas; containing many choice Cases, Judgments and Resolutions, in points of Law, in the several Reigns of King James and King Charles. Second Edition. Folio. London. 1682.

ILLINOIS.

Breese's Reports. (1 Ill.) 1819–1830.
Scammon's Reports. (2–5 Ill.) 1832–1843.
Gilman's Reports. (6–10 Ill.) 1844–1848.
Peck's Reports. (11–30 Ill.) 1849–1863.
Freeman's Reports. (31–54 Ill.) 1863–1872.

INDIANA.

Blackford's Reports. 8 vols. 1817–1847.
Smith's Reports. 1 vol. 1848–1849.
Indiana Reports. 1848–1870.
Carter (1–2.)
Porter (3–7.)
Tanner (8–14.)
Harrison (15–17.)
Kerr (18–22.)
Harrison (23–29.)
Black (30–33.)

INDIANA TREASON TRIALS. The Trials for Treason at Indianapolis, disclosing the plans for establishing a North Western Confederacy. Edited by Benn Pitman. Cincinnati. 1865.

IOWA.

Morris' Reports. 1 vol. 1839–1845.
G. Greene's Reports. 4 vols. 1847–1852.
Iowa Reports. 1855–1870.
Clarke (1–8).
Withrow (9–21).
Stiles (22–30).

IREDELL (James). Reports of Cases at Law argued and determined in the Supreme Court of North Carolina, from June Term, 1840, to August Term, 1852, both inclusive. 13 vols. Raleigh. 1841–1852.

Reports of Cases in Equity argued and determined in the Supreme Court of North Carolina. 1840–1852. 8 vols. Raleigh. 1841–1852.

IRISH TERM REPORTS: or, Reports of Cases determined in the King's Courts, Dublin, from Easter Term, 34 Geo. III., to Hilary Term, 35 Geo. III., inclusive. By William Ridgeway, William Lapp, and John Schoales. Vol. 1. Dublin. 1796.

JACOB (Edward). Reports of Cases decided in the High Court of Chancery in England, during the time of Lord Chancellor Eldon, 1821, 1822. Philadelphia. 1839. (Eng. Chancery Reports, Vol. 4.)

JACOB (Edward) and WALKER (John). Reports of Cases argued and determined in the High Court of Chancery, during the time of Chancellor Eldon, 1819, 1820, 1821. 1st Am. from 1st London Edition. 2 vols. New York. 1822–27.

JEBB (Robert). Cases, chiefly relating to the Criminal and Presentment Law, reserved for consideration, and decided by the Twelve Judges of Ireland, from May, 1822, to November, 1840. First American Edition. Philadelphia. 1842. (British Crown Cases, Vol. 3.)

JEBB (Robert) and SYMES (Arthur R.) Reports of Cases argued and determined in the Courts of Queen's Bench and Exchequer Chamber in Ireland, from Hilary Term, 1 Vict., to Trinity Term, 4 Vict., inclusive. 2 vols. Dublin and London. 1840–42.

JENNISON (William). Reports of Cases heard and decided in the Supreme Court of Michigan, from November 11, 1865, to July, 12, 1869. 5 vols. Detroit. 1867–1869. (Michigan Reports, Vols. 14–18.)

JEFFERSON (Thomas). Reports of Cases determined in the General Court of Virginia, from 1730 to 1740; and from 1768 to 1762. Charlottesville. 1829.

JENKINS. Eight Centuries of Reports: or Eight Hundred Cases Solemnly adjudged in the Exchequer Chamber, or upon Writs of Error. Published originally in Latin and French by Judge Jenkins. Folio. In the Savoy. 1734.

JOHNSON (John). Reports of Cases decided in the High Court of Chancery of Maryland. Containing the Cases from 1847 to 1854. 4 vols. Baltimore. 1851–1854. "Maryland Chancery Decisions."

JOHNSON (William). Reports of Cases argued and determined in the Supreme Court of Judicature and in the Court for the Trial of Impeachments and the Correction of Errors in the State of New York. 20 vols. Philadelphia. 1836.

JOHNSON (William). Reports of Cases adjudged in the Supreme Court of Judicature of New York, from January Term, 1799, to January Term, 1803. Together with Cases determined in the Court for the Correction of Errors during that Period. 3 vols. New York. 1808–1812.

The Same. Second Edition: with many Additional Cases, etc. 3 vols. New York and Albany. 1840–1849.

JOHNSON (William). Reports of Cases adjudged in the Court of Chancery of New York. 7 vols. Containing the Cases from March, 1814, to July, 1823. Philiadelphia. 1834–1836.

JOHNSON (Andrew). Proceedings in the Trial of Andrew Johnson, President of the United States, before the United States Senate, on Articles of Impeachment exhibited by the House of Representatives. Washington. 1868.

JOHNSON (Henry Robert Vaughan). Reports of Cases adjudged in the High Court of Chancery, before Sir William Page Wood, Knt., Vice Chancellor. 1858, 1859, 1860. London and Dublin. 1860.

JONES (Hamilton C.) Reports of Cases at Law argued and determined in the Supreme Court of North Carolina, from December Term, 1853, to June Term, 1862. 8 vols. Raleigh and Salisbury. 1854–1862.

Reports of Cases in Equity argued and determined in the Supreme Court of North Carolina, from December Term, 1853, to June Term, 1863. 6 vols. Raleigh and Salisbury. 1855–1863.

JONES (Horatio M.) Reports of Cases argued and determined in the Supreme Court of Missouri. 9 vols. St Louis. 1856–1861. (Missouri Reports, Vols. 22–30.)

JONES (Sir Thomas). Reports of several special Cases adjudged in the Courts of King's Bench and Common Pleas at Westminster, in the Reign of King Charles II. Folio. In the Savoy. 1729.

JONES (Thomas G.) Reports of Cases argued and determined in

the Supreme Court of Alabama, from January Term, 1869, to June Term, 1871. 3 vols. Montgomery, Alabama. 1870–1871. (Alabama Reports, Vols. 43–45.)

JONES (Sir William.) Les Reports de Sir William Jones, Chevalier. Jades un des Justices del' Banck le Roy. Et devant un des Justices del' Court de Common Banck. Et devant Capital Justice d'Ireland. Folio. London. 1675.

JONES (J. Pringle.) Pennsylvania State Reports, containing Cases adjudged in the Supreme Court from May Term, 1849, to December Term, 1849. 2 vols. Philadelphia. 1850–1853. (Pensylvania State Reports, Vols. 11, 12.)

KANSAS.

Bank's Reports (1–5 Kansas.) Vols. 2–5. 1863–1869.
McCahon's Reports. 1870.

KANSAS IMPEACHMENT CASE. Proceedings in the Cases of the Impeachment of Charles Robinson, Governor; John W. Robinson, Secretary of State; George S. Hillyer, Auditor of State, of Kansas. Lawrence. 1862.

KAY (Edward E.) Reports of Cases adjudged in the High Court of Chancery, before Sir William Page Wood, Knt., Vice Chancellor. 1853–1854. London and Dublin. 1854.

KAY (Edward E.) and JOHNSON (Henry R. Vaughan.) Reports of Cases adjudged in the High Court of Chancery, before Sir William Page Wood, Knt., Vice Chancellor. 1854–58. 4 vols. London and Dublin. 1855–59.

KEBLE (Jos.) Reports in the Court of King's Bench at Westminster, from the XII to the XXX Year of the Reign of our late Sovereign Lord King Charles II. 3 vols. Folio. London. 1685.

KEEN (Benjamin.) Reports of Cases in Chancery argued and determined in the Rolls Court during the time of Lord Langdale, Master of Rolls. 2 vols. 1836–39. London. 1837–39.

The Same. Notes and References by John A. Dunlap. New York and Albany. 1844. (English Chancery Reports, Vol. 15.)

KEILWEY (Robert.) Reports d'ascems Cases (Qui ont evenus aux temps dy Roy Henry le Septieme de tres hereuse memoire, et du tres illustre Roy Henry le huitiesme, etne sont comprises deins les livres des Terms et Ans demesnes les Roys.) Seliges hors des papieres de Robert Keilway, Esq. Par Jean Croke. Small Folio. London. 1688.

KELLY (James M.) Reports of Cases in Law and Equity argued and determined in the Supreme Court of the State of Georgia, in the year 1846. 3 vols. New York and Savannah. 1847–1848. (Georgia Reports, Vols. 1–3.)

KELLY (James M.) and COBB (Thos. R. R.) Reports of Cases in Law and Equity argued and determined in the Supreme Court of the State of Georgia, from Savannah Term to Milledgeville Term, 1848, inclusive; being a continuation of Kelly's Reports. 2 vols. Athens. 1848–1849. (Georgia Reports, Vols. 4–5.)

KELYNG (Sir John.) A Report of Divers Cases in Pleas of the Crown, adjudged and determined in the reign of the late King Charles II. With Directions for Justices of the Peace and others. Folio. London. 1708.

KELYNGE (William.) A Report of Cases in Chancery, the King's Bench, etc. In the fourth, fifth, sixth, seventh and eighth years of his late Majesty King George the Second. Folio. London. 1764.

KENTUCKY.
Sneed's Reports, or Kentucky Decisions. 1801–1805.
Hardin's Reports. 1805–1808.
Bibb's Reports. 4 vols. 1808–1817.
Marshall's (A. K.) Reports. 3 vols. in 2. 1817–1821.
Littell's Reports. 5 vols. 1822–1824.
Littell's Select Cases. 1 vol. 1795–1821.
Monroe's (T. B.) Reports. 7 vols. in 6. 1824–1828.
Marshall's (J. J.) Reports. 7 vols. 1829–1832.
Dana's Reports. 9 vols. in 5. 1833–1840.
Monroe's (B.) Reports. 18 vols. 1840–1858.
Metcalfe's Reports. 4 vols. 1859–1863.
Duval's Reports, Vol. 1. 1863–1864.
Bush's Reports. 7 vols. 1866–1870.

KENYON (Lloyd, Lord.) Notes of Cases argued and adjudged in the Court of King's Bench, and of some determined in the other High Courts. 1753–59. 2 vols. London. 1819–25.

KERNAN (Francis.) Reports of Cases argued and determined in the Court of Appeals of the State of New York; with Note References, and an Index. 4 vols. New York and Albany. 1855–1857. (New York Reports, Vols. 11–14.)

KERR (Michael C.) Reports of Cases argued and determined in the Supreme Court of Judicature, of the State of Indiana. Containing the Cases from May Term, 1862 to May Term, 1864, inclusive. 5 vols. Indianapolis. 1863–1864. (Indiana Reports, Vols. 18–22.)

KEYES (Emerson W.) Reports of Cases argued and determined in the Court of Appeals of the State of New York; with Notes, References, and an Index. 4 vols. Albany. 1867–1869.

KING (William W.) Reports of Cases argued and determined in the Supreme Court of Louisiana. For the years 1850–1851. 2 vols. New Orleans. 1851–1852. (Louisiana Annual Reports, Vols. 5–6.)

KNAPP (Jerome Wm.) Reports of Cases argued and determined before the Committee of His Majesty's most Honorable Privy Council, appointed to hear Appeals and Petitions. 1829–36. 3 vols. London. 1831–37.

KNAPP (Jerome William) and OMBLER (Edward). Cases of Controverted Elections in the Twelfth Parliament of the United Kingdom, being the Second Parliament since the passing of Acts for the amendment of the Representation of the People. London, Dublin, and Edinburgh. 1837. "Election Cases, 1834–1835."

KNOWLES (John P.) Reports of Cases argued and determined in the Supreme Court of Rhode Island. Providence. 1856. (Rhode Island Reports, Vol. 3.)

LANE (Richard). Reports in the Court of Exchequer, beginning in the third and ending in the ninth year of the raign of the late King James. Folio. London. 1657.

LALOR (T. M.) Supplement to Hill's and Denio's Reports. See HILL and DENIO.

LANSING (Abraham). Reports of Cases argued and determined in the Supreme Court of the State of New York. 3 vols. New York and Albany. 1870–71.

LATCH (Jean). Plusiers tres-bons Cases Come ils estoyent adjudges es trois premiers ans du Raign du feu Roy Charles le Premier, en la Court de Bank le Roy, non encore publices par aucun autre. Folio. London. 1661.

LAW REPORTS (The). Philadelphia. 1867–71.
Queen's Bench. Vols. 1–5.
Common Pleas. Vols. 1–5.
Court of Exchequer. Vols. 1–5.

Equity Cases. Vols. 1–10.
Courts of Admiralty and
Ecclesiastical Courts. Vols. 1–2.
Chancery Appeal Cases. Vols. 1–5.
Courts of Probate and Divorce. Vol. 1.
Privy Council Appeal Cases. Vol. 1.
House of Lords Appeal Cases. Vols. 1–3.

LAWRENCE (William). Reports of Cases argued and determined in the Supreme Court of the State of Ohio, in Bank. Columbus. 1852. (Ohio Reports, Vol. 20.)

LEACH (Thomas). Cases in Crown Law, determined by the Twelve Judges, by the Court of King's Bench, and by Commissioners of Oyer and Terminer and General Gaol Delivery, from the Fourth year of George the Second to the Twenty-Ninth year of George the Third. Dublin. 1789.

LEE (Sir George.) Reports of Cases argued and determined in the Arches and Prerogative Courts of Canterbury, and in the High Court of Delegates; containing the Judgments of the Right Honorable Sir George Lee. By Joseph Phillimore, LL.D. Containing the Cases from Hilary Term, 1752, to Michaelmas Term, 1758, inclusive. Philadelphia. 1835–1841. (English Ecclesiastical Reports, Vols. 5 and 6.)

LEE (Harvey.) Reports of Cases argued and determined in the Supreme Court of the State of California, during January and April Terms, 1858. 4 vols. San Francisco and Sacramento. 1858–1860. (California Reports, Vols. 9–12.)

LEGAL OBSERVER (New York.) The New York Legal Observer, Containing Reports of Cases decided in the Courts of Equity and Common Law, and important decisions in the English Courts; etc. Edited by Samuel Owen. From October, 1842, to October, 1854. Vols. 1–12, inclusive. New York. 1843–1854.

LEGAL OBSERVER, (The,) or Journal of Jurisprudence. Published Weekly. November, 1830, to October, 1853, inclusive. 46 vols. With 8 vols. of Digests, Monthly Records, etc. London, Edinburg and Dublin. 1831–1853.

LEIGH (Benjamin Watkins.) Reports of Cases argued and determined in the Court of Appeals and in the General Court of Virginia. 12 vols. Richmond. 1830–1844.

LEONARD (William.) Reports and Cases of Law, argued and adjudged in the Courts of Law, at Westminister, in the time of the late Queen Elizabeth, from the 18th to the 33d year of her reign. London. 1658.

LESTER (Geo. N.) Reports of Cases in Law and Equity, argued and determined in the Supreme Court of Georgia. From August Term, 1860, to June Term, 1861. 2 vols. Macon, Georgia. 1869–1871. (Georgia Reports, Vols. 31–32.)

LEVINZ (Sir Creswell.) Les Reports de Sir Creswell Levins, jades un del Justices del Common Bank; en trais parts: Commencant en le 12 An de Roy Charles I. et fini en le 8 An de son Majesty William III. 3 vols. Folio. London. 1702.

LEWIS (J. F.) Report of Cases determined in the Supreme Court of the State of Nevada, Reported by the Judges of the Court during the year 1865. Sacramento. 1866. (Nevada State Reports, Vol. 1.)

LEY (Sir James.) Report of Divers Resolutions in Law, arising upon Cases in the Court of Wards, and other Courts at Westminster, in the reigns of the late Kings, King James and King Charles. Folio. London. 1659.

LITTELL (William). Reports of Cases at Common Law and in Chancery, decided in the Court of Appeals of the Commonwealth of Kentucky. 6 vols. Frankfort. 1823–1824.

(Vol. 6 is entitled, "Cases selected from the Decisions of the Court of Appeals of Kentucky, not heretofore reported." It is usually cited as, "Littell's Select Cases.")

LITTLETON (Edw.) Les Reports des tres honorable Edw. Seigneur Littleton, Baron de Mounslow, Custos de la Grand Seale d'Angliterre, et de ses Majesty pluis honorable Privy Council, en le Courts del Common Banck et Exchequer, en le 2, 3, 4, 5, 6, 7, ans del Reign de Roy Charles le 1. Folio. London. 1683.

LLOYD & GOOLD. Cases argued and determined in the High Court of Chancery, in Ireland, during the time of Lord Chancellor Sugden. Philadelphia. 1838. (English Chancery Reports, Vol. 10.)

LLOYD (J. H.) and WELSBY (W. N.) Reports of Cases relating to Commerce, Manufactures, etc., etc., determined in the Courts of Common Law, 1829 and 1830. Parts 1, 2 and 3. London.

LOCKWOOD (Ralph). An Analytical and Practical Synopsis of all the Cases argued and reversed in Law and Equity, in the Court for the Correction of Errors of the State of New York, from 1799 to 1847, with the names of the Cases and a table of the Titles, etc. New York and Albany. 1848.

LOFFT (Capel). Reports of Cases adjudged in the Court of King's Bench, from Easter Term, 12 Geo. 3, to Michaelmas Term, 14 Geo. 3, (both inclusive.) With some select cases in the Court of Chancery and of the Common Pleas, which are within the same period. To which is added, the Case of General Warrants, and a Collection of Maxims. Dublin. 1790.

LOUISIANA.

Martin's Reports. N. S. 8 vols. 1823–1830. New Edition, with Notes.

Martin's Reports. Both Series. Condensed by Harrison. 20 vols. in 4. 1809–1830.

Lousiana Reports. New Edition. 19 vols. in 10. 1830–1841.

Miller (1–6.)

Curry (6–19.)

Robinson's Reports. 1841–1846.

Lousiana Annual Reports. 1846–1869.

Robinson. (Vols. 1–4.)

King. (Vols. 5–6.)

Randolph. (Vols. 8–11.)

Ogden. (Vols. 12–15.)

Glenn. (Vols. 16–18.)

Hawkins. (Vols. 19–21.)

LOWNDES (John James.) Reports of Cases argued and determined in the Queen's Bench Practice Court; with Points of Practice and Pleading Decided in the Courts of Common Pleas and Exchequer; from Hilary Term, 1850, to Michaelmas Term, 1851. 2 vols. London and Dublin. 1851–2.

LOWNDES and MAXWELL. Cases argued and determined in the Bail Court. Vol. 1. 1852–54. "Bail Court Cases. 1852–1854." [No Title page or Index.]

LOWNDES (John James), MAXWELL (Peter Benson) and POLLOCK (Charles Edward.) Reports of Cases argued and determined in the Queen's Bench Practice Court; with Points of Practice and Pleading decided in the Courts of Common Pleas and Exchequer; from Hilary Term, 1850, to Michaelmas Term, 1851. 2 vols. London and Dublin. 1851–1852.

LUDDEN (Timothy.) Reports of Cases in Law and Equity, determined in the Supreme Judicial Court of Maine. 2 vols. Lewiston. 1858–1859. (Maine Reports, Vols. 43–44.)

LUDERS (Alexander.) Reports of the Proceedings in Committees of the House of Commons upon Controverted Elections, heard and determined during the present Parliament. 3 vols. London. 1785–1790.

LUTWYCHE (Sir Edward.) Un livre des Entries; Contenant auxi un Report des Resolutions del Court Sur diverse Exceptions Prises as Pleadings, et sur auters Matters en Ley. 2 vols. Folio. London. 1704.

MADDOCK (Henry.) Reports of Cases argued and determined in the Court of the Vice Chancellor of England, during the time of the Right Hon. Sir Thomas Plumer, Knt. First American Edition. 6 vols. Philadelphia. 1829.

MAGRUDER (A. C.) Maryland Reports, containing Cases adjudged in the Court of Appeals of that State from December Term, 1851, to December Term, 1852, inclusive. 2 vols. Annapolis. 1852–1853. (Maryland Reports, Vols. 1–2.)

MAINE.

Maine Reports. 58 vols. 1820–1870.

Greenleaf (1–9.) 1820–1832.
Fairfield's (10–12.) 1833–1835.
Shepley (13–18.) 1836–1841.
Appleton's (19–20.) 1841.
Shepley (21–30.) 1842–1849.
Redington (31–45.) 1849–1853.
Heath (36–40.) 1853–1855.
Adams (41–42.) 1856.
Ludden (43–44.) 1857–1858.
Hubbard (45–51.) 1858–1864.
Virgin (52–58.) 1860–1870.

MANNING (Randolph.) Reports of Cases argued and determined in the Supreme Court of the State of Michigan. Vol. 1. Pontiac, Mich. 1852. (Michigan Reports, Vol. 1.)

MANNING (James) and GRANGER (F. C.) Reports of Cases argued and determined in the Court of Common Pleas. Containing the Cases from Easter Term, 1840, to Easter Term, 1845. 7 vols. Philadelphia. 1842–46. (Eng. Com. Law Reps., Vols. 39, 40, 42–44, 46, 49.)

MANNING (James,) GRANGER (T. C.) and SCOTT (John.) Common Bench Reports. Cases argued and determined in the Court of Common Pleas from Hilary Term and Vacation, 1845, to Michaelmas Term and Vacation, 1849. 8 vols. Philadelphia. 1846–1853. (English Common Law Reports, Vols. 50, 52, 54, 56, 57, 60, 62, 65.)

MANNING (J.) and RYLAND (A.) Reports of Cases argued and determined in the Court of King's Bench. Containing the Cases from Michaelmas Term, 1827, to Trinity Term, 1828. 2 vols. Philadelphia. 1830. (English Common Law Reports, Vol. 17.)

MANNING (J.) and RYLAND (Archer.) Reports of Cases argued and determined in the Court of King's Bench from Michaelmas Term, 8 Geo. IV, to Easter Term, 11 Geo. IV. 5 vols. London and Dublin. 1828–1837.

MARCH (John). Reports, or New Cases; taken in the 15, 16, 17 and 18 years of King Charles the First. Second Edition. Small 4to. London. 1675.

Some New Cases of the years and time of King Hen. 8, Edw. 6, and Qu. Mary; written out of the Great Abridgment, composed by Sir Robert Brook, Knight, etc., there dispersed in the Titles, but here collected under years. 16mo. London. 1651.

MARSHALL'S (John) Decisions. Reports of Cases decided by the Honourable John Marshall in the Circuit Court of the United States for the District of Virginia and North Carolina, from 1802 to 1833, inclusive. Edited by John W. Brockenbrough. 2 vols. Philadelphia and Pittsburgh. 1837.

MARSHALL (Charles). Reports of Cases argued and determined in the Court of Common Pleas. Containing the Cases from Michaelmas Term, 1813, to Trinity Term, 1816. 2 vols. Philadelphia. 1836. (Eng. Com. Law Reps., Vol. 4).

MARSHALL (A. K.) Decisions of the Court of Appeals of Kentucky, commencing with the fall term, 1817, and ending with the fall term, 1821. 3 vols. in 2. 2d edition. Cincinnati. 1848.

MARSHALL (J. J.) Reports of Cases at Law and in Equity, argued and decided in the Court of Appeals of the Commonwealth of Kentucky. 7 vols. Containing the Cases determined between the 15th of January, 1829, and the 5th of November, 1832, inclusive. Frankfort. 1831–1834.

MARTIN (B. Y.) Reports of Cases in Law and Equity argued and determined in the Supreme Court of Georgia, 1857–1860. 10 vols. Columbus, Georgia. 1857–1860. (Georgia Reports, Vols. 21–29).

MARTIN (Francois-Xavier). Louisiana Term Reports, or Cases argued and determined in the Supreme Court of that State. New Series. 8 vols. New Orleans. 1824–1830.

MARTIN'S CONDENSED. Condensed Reports of Cases in the Superior Court of the Territory of Orleans, and in the Supreme Court of Louisiana; Containing the Decisions of those Courts from the Autumn Term, 1809, to the March Term, 1830. 20 vols. in 4. Edited by J. Burton Harrison. New Orleans. 1839–1841.

MARTIN (Francis Xavier). North Carolina Reports, embracing "Notes of a few decisions in the Superior Courts of the State of North Carolina, and in the Circuit Court of the United States for the District of North Carolina." Also, "Reports of Cases Adjudged in the Superior Courts of Law and Equity, Court of Conference and Federal Court for the State of North Carolina, from the year 1797 to 1806." By John Haywood. Second Edition. By William H. Battle, Esq. Raleigh. 1843.

MARTIN (John H.) and YERGER (Geo. S.) Reports of Cases argued and determined in the Supreme Court of Tennessee. Tennessee Reports, Cooper's Edition, Vol. 4. St. Louis. 1871.

MARYLAND CHANCERY DECISIONS. Reports of Cases decided in the High Court of Chancery of Maryland. Hon. John Johnson, Chancellor. 4 Vols. Containing cases from 1847 to 1854. Baltimore. 1851–1854.

MARYLAND.

Harris & McHenry's Reports. 4 vols. 1700–1799.
Harris & Johnson's Reports. 7 vols. 1800–1826.
Harris & Gill's Reports. 2 vols. 1826–1829.
Gill and Johnson's Reports. 12 vols. 1829–1843.
Gill's Reports. 9 vols. 1843–1851.
Maryland Reports. 33 vols. 1851–1870.
  Magruder. (Vols. 1–2.)
  Miller. (Vols. 3–18.)
  Brewer. (Vols. 19–26.)
  Stockett. (Vols. 27–33.)
Bland's Chancery Reports. 3 vols. 1811–1832.
Maryland Chancery Decisions (Johnson.) 4 vols. 1847–1854.

MASON (William P.) Reports of Cases argued and determined in the Circuit Court of the United States for the First Circuit. 5 vols. Containing the Cases determined in the years 1816 to 1830. Boston. 1831.

MASSACHUSETTS.

Quincy's Reports. 1 vol. 1761–1772.
Massachusett's Reports. 1804–1822.
  Williams. (Vol. 1.)
  Tyng. (2–17.)

Pickering's Reports. 24 vols. 1822–1840.
Metcalf's Reports. 13 vols. 1840–1847.
Cushing's Reports. 12 vols. 1848–1853.
Gray's Reports. 16 vols. 1854–1860.
Allen's Reports. 14 vols. 1861–1867.
Massachusetts Reports. 8 vols. 1867–1869.
Browne. (Vols. 97–104.)

MATSON (William N.) Connecticut Reports, containing Cases argued and determined in the Supreme Court of Errors. 3 vols. Hartford. 1854–1857. (Connecticut Reports, Vols. 22–24.)

MAULE (George) and SELWYN (William.) Reports of Cases argued and determined in the Court of King's Bench Edited by Theron Metcalf. 6 vols. in 2. Boston. 1832.

MAYNARD. (See YEAR BOOKS, Pt. 1.)

McALLISTER (Cutler.) Reports of Cases argued and determined in the Circuit Court of the United States for the District of California. New York. 1859.

McCAHON (James). Reports of Cases determined in the Supreme Court of the Territory of Kansas. Together with an important Case determined in the District Court of the First Judicial District of said Territory, etc., etc. With Preface, Table of Cases, Notes, and Index. Chicago. 1870.

McCLELLAND (Thomas). Reports of Cases argued and determined in the Courts of Exchequer and Exchequer Chamber, at Law, in Equity, and in Error, from Hilary Term, 4 and 5 Geo. IV., to Michaelmas Term, 5 Geo. IV., both inclusive. London and Dublin. 1825.

McCLELLAND (Thomas) and YOUNGE (Edward). Reports of Cases argued and determined in the Courts of Exchequer and Exchequer Chamber, at Law, in Equity, and in Error, from Hilary Term, 5 and 6 Geo. IV., to Michaelmas Term, 6 Geo. V., both inclusive. J. I. Clark Hare, Editor. Vol. 1. Philadelphia. 1853.

McCLELLAND (Thomas). Reports of Cases argued and determined in the Court of Exchequer and Exchequer Chamber, at Law, in Equity, and in Error. Containing Cases from Hilary Term, 4 and 5 Geo. IV., to Michaelmas Term, 5 Geo. IV., both inclusive. 1 vol. Philadelphia. 1835. (English Exchequer Reports, Vol. 6.)

McCARTER (Thomas N.) Reports of Cases argued and determined in the Court of Chancery and in the Prerogative Court of the State of New Jersey. 2 vols. Trenton. 1865–1867. (New Jersey Equity Reports, Vols. 14, 15.)

McCook (George W.) Reports of Cases argued and determined in the Supreme Court of Ohio. 1 vol. Columbus. 1853. (Ohio State Reports, Vol. 1.)

McCord (D. J.) Chancery Cases argued and determined in the Court of Appeals of South Carolina, from January, 1825, to May, 1826, both inclusive. Vol. 1. Charleston, S. C. 1857.

Reports of Cases determined in the Constitutional Court of South Carolina. 4 vols. in 2 Charleston. 1853.

McCorkle (J. M.) North Carolina Reports. Cases argued and determined in the Supreme Court of North Carolina, January and June Terms, 1871. Raleigh. 1871. (North Carolina Reports, Vol. 65.)

McLean (John.) Reports of Cases argued and decided in the Circuit Court of the United States for the Seventh Circuit. 6 vols. Cincinnati. 1840–1856.

McMullan (J. J.) Cases at Law argued and determined in the Court of Appeals of South Carolina. 2 vols. From November, 1840, to May, 1842, both inclusive. To which are added Cases omitted by former Reporters, from 1835–1840. Columbia, S. C. 1841–1843.

McMullan (J. J.) Equity Cases argued and determined in the Court of Appeals of South Carolina. Vol. 1. From November, 1840, to May, 1842, inclusive. To which are added Cases omitted by former Reporters, from 1827 to 1837. Columbia, S. C. 1842.

McNaghten (Stewart) and Gordon (Alexander.) Report of Cases argued and determined in the High Court of Chancery during the time of Lord Chancellor Cottenham. 1849–51. 3 vols. London. 1850–2.

Meddaugh (Elijah W.) Michigan Reports. Reports of Cases heard and decided in the Supreme Court of Michigan from October 18th, 1864, to November 11th, 1865. Detroit. 1866. (Michigan Reports, Vol. 13.)

Meeson (R.) and Welsby (W. N.) Reports of Cases argued and determined in the Courts of Exchequer and Exchequer Chamber, from Hilary Term, 6 Will. IV., to Easter Term, 10 Vict., both inclusive. J. I. Clark Hare and H. B. Wallace, Editors. 17 vols. 1847–50.

Meigs (Returu J.) Reports of Cases argued and determined in the Supreme Court of Tennessee, during the years 1838–1839. Nashville. 1838.

Merivale (J. H.) Reports of Cases argued and determined in the High Court of Chancery. 1815–1817. 3 vols. 1st Am. from last London Edition. New York. 1825.

METCALFE (James P.) Reports of Selected Civil and Criminal Cases decided in the Court of Appeals of Kentucky. 4 vols. Containing Cases decided from 1858 to 1863. Frankfort. 1859–1864.

METCALF (Theron.) Reports of Cases argued and determined in the Supreme Judicial Court of Massachsetts. 13 vols. Boston. 1847–1851.

MICHIGAN.

Harrington's Chancery Reports. 1 vol. 1838–1842.
Walker's Chancery Reports. 1 vol. 1842–1845.
Douglass' Reports. 2 vols. 1843–1847.
Michigan Reports. 20 vols. 1847–1871.
Manning (Vol. 1).
Gibbs (Vols. 2–4).
Cooley (Vols. 5–12).
Meddaugh (Vol. 13).
Jennison (Vols. 14–18).
Clarke (Vols. 18–20).

MILLER (Oliver). Maryland Reports, containing Cases argued and determined in the Court of Appeals of Maryland. Containing the Cases from December Term, 1852, to June Term, 1862, inclusive. 16 vols. Annapolis. 1853 –1862. (Maryland Reports, Vols. 3–18.)

MILLER (Branch W.) Reports of Cases argued and determined in the Supreme Court of the State of Louisiana. 3 vols. New Orleans. 1854. (Louisiana Reports, Vols. 1–3.)

MILES (John). Reports of Cases determined in the District Court for the City and County of Philadephia. Containing the Cases from March, 1835, to 1841. 2 vols. Philadelphia. 1836–1842.

MILLS' CONSTITUTIONAL. Reports of Judicial Decisions in Constitutional Court of South Carolina, held in Charleston and Columbia, in 1817, 1818. A New Edition. 2 vols. in 1. Charleston. 1837.

MINOR (Henry). Reports argued and determined in the Supreme Court of Alabama, from May, 1820, to July, 1826. New York. 1829.

MINNESOTA.

Minnesota Reports. 15 vols. 1851–1870.
Vol. 1 Containing the Reports of Hollinshead, Atwater, Brisbin, Ames and Officer. (1851–1858.)
Officer. (Vols. 2–9.) (1858–1864.)
Spencer. (Vols. 10–15.) (1865–1870.)

MISSISSIPPI.

Mississippi Reports. 41 vols. 1818–1867.

Walker. (Vol. 1.)
Howard. (Vols. 2–8.)
Smedes & Marshall. (Vols. 9–22.)
Cushman. (Vols. 23–29.)
George. (Vols. 30–39.)
Reynolds. (Vols. 40–41.)

MISSOURI.

Missouri Reports. 47 vols. 1821–1871.
Bay, (Vols. 1–3.)
Napton, (Vol. 4.)
Bay, (Vols. 5–8.)
Stringfellow, (Vols. 9–11.)
Robards, (Vols. 12–13.)
Gardenhire, (Vols. 14–15.)
Bennett, (Vols. 16–21.)
Jones, (Vols. 22–30.)
Vol. 31, by Authority.
Whittlesey, (Vols. 32–41.)
Post, (Vols. 42–47.)

MODERN REPORTS; or Select Cases adjudged in the Courts of King's Bench, Chancery, Common Pleas and Exchequer, from the Restoration of Charles II. to the End of the Reign of William III. 5th Ed. 12 vols. London and Dublin. 1793–6.

MOLLOY. Condensed Reports of Cases decided in the High Court of Chancery in Ireland. Edited by E. D. Ingraham, Esq. Containing the Cases decided by Sir Anthony Hart, Lord Chancellor, and Sir William McMahon, Master of the Rules. Vols. 1 and 2. Philadelphia. 1840. (English Chancery Reports, vol. 12.)

MONROE (Thomas B.) Reports of Cases at Common Law and in Equity, argued and decided in the Court of Appeals of the Commonwealth of Kentucky. Containing the Cases determined from the Fall Term, 1824, to April, 1828. 7 vols. in 6. Frankfort. 1825–1830.

MONROE (Ben.) Reports of Cases at Common Law and in Equity decided in the Court of Appeals of Kentucky. Containing the Cases from the Fall Term, 1840, to Winter Term, 1857. 18 vols. Cincinnati and Frankfort. 1854–1858.

MONTAGU (Basil.) Reports of Cases in Bankruptcy decided by the Lord Chancellors Lyndhurst and Brougham, the Vice Chancellor Sir Lancelot Shadwell, and the Court of Review. London, Dublin and Edinburgh. 1832.

MONTAGU (Basil), and BLIGH (Richard.) Reports of Cases in Bankruptcy, decided by the Lord Chancellor Brougham, the Vice Chancellor Sir Lancelot Shadwell, and the Court of Review. London, Dublin and Edinburgh. 1835.

MONTAGU (Basil and CHITTY (Edward.) Reports of Cases in Bankruptcy, decided by the Lord Chancellor Cottenham and the Court of Review. London and Dublin. 1840.

MONTAGU (Basil) and AYRTON (Scrope). Reports of Cases in Bankruptcy decided by the Lord Chancellor Brougham, the Court of Review and Subdivision Courts. 3 vols. 1833–1838. London, Dublin and Edinburgh. 1834–1839.

MONTAGU (Basil) and MACARTHUR (John). Reports of Cases in Bankruptcy decided by the Lord Chancellor and Vice Chancellor. London, Dublin and Edinburgh. 1830.

MONTAGU (Basil), DEACON (Edward E.) and DE GEX (John). Reports of Cases in Bankruptcy argued and determined in the Court of Review and on Appeal before the Lord Chancellor. 3 vols. London. 1842.

MOODY (William) and MALKIN (Benjamin Heath). Reports of Cases argued and ruled at Nisi Prius, in the Courts of King's Bench and Common Pleas, and on the Western and Oxford Circuits; from the Sittings after Michaelmas Term, 1827, to the Sittings after Trinity Term, 1830, inclusive. 1 vol. Philadelphia. 1833. (Eng. Com. Law Reps., vol. 22).

MOODY (William) and ROBINSON (Frederic). Reports of Cases determined at Nisi Prius, in the Courts of King's Bench, Common Pleas, and Exchequer, and on the Northern and Western Circuits, from the Sittings after Michaelmas Term, 1 Will. IV. (1830), to the Sittings after Hilary Term, 7 Vict. (1844), inclusive. 2 vols. London. 1837–44.

MOODY (William). Crown Cases Reserved for Consideration, and decided by the Judges of England, from the year 1824 to the year 1837. 2 vols. Philadelphia. 1839–1853. (British Crown Cases, Vols. 2 and 4.)

MOORE (John Bayly). Reports of Cases argued and determined in the Courts of Common Pleas and Exchequer Chamber. Containing the Cases from Hilary Term, 57 Geo. III., to Trinity Term, 8 Geo. IV., inclusive. 12 vols. London. 1818–31.

The Same. 12 vols. Philadelphia. 1833–1836. (English Common Law Reports, Vols. 4, 16, 17, 22.)

MOORE (Sir Fra.) Cases Collect et Report per Sir Fra. Moore,

Chevalier, Sergeant del Ley. Imprime et Publie per l'Original jadis remainent en les maines de Sir Gefrey Palmer, Chevalier et Bar., Attorney-General a son Tres-Excellent Majesty le Roy Charles le Second. Le Second Edition. Folio. London. 1688.

MOORE (George F.) and WALKER (Richard S.) Report of Cases argued and decided in the Supreme Court of the State of Texas, from Austin Term, 1858, to Galveston Term, 1860. 3 vols. Philadelphia. 1860–1861. (Texas Reports, Vols. 22–24.)

MOORE (John Bayly) and PAYNE (Joseph.) Reports of Cases argued and determined in the Court of Common Pleas and Exchequer Chamber, from Michaelmas Term, 8 Geo. IV. (1827), to Trinity Term, 1 Will. IV. (1831), both inclusive, 5 vols. London and Dublin. 1828–32.

MOORE (John Bayly) and PAYNE (Joseph.) Reports of Cases argued and determined in the Courts of Common Pleas and Exchequer Chamber. Containing the Cases from Michaelmas Term, 1827, to Hilary Term, 1829. 5 vols. London. 1828–32.

MOORE (John Bayly), PAYNE (Joseph) and SCOTT (John.) Reports of Cases argued and determined in the Court of Common Pleas, and Exchequer Chamber during the 2d, 3d and 4th William IV., 1831–4. 4 vols. Philadelphia. 1836–38. (Eng. Common Law Reports, Vols. 28, 30.)

MORRIS (Wm. Governeur.) Reports of Cases argued and determined in the Supreme Court of the State of California, in the year 1855. Sacramento. 1857. (California Reports, Vol. 5.)

MORRIS (Eastin.) Reports of Cases argued and determined in the Supreme Court of Iowa. Iowa City. 1847. (Iowa Reports, Vol. 1.)

MOSELY (William.) Reports of Cases argued and determined in the High Court of Chancery, during the time of the late Lord Chancellor King. Dublin. 1793.

MUMFORD (William.) Reports of Cases argued and determined in the Supreme Court of Appeals of Virginia. 6 vols. New York and Richmond. 1812–1821.

MURPHEY (A. D.) Reports of Cases argued and adjudged in the Supreme Court of North Carolina, from the year 1804 to the year 1819, inclusive. 3 vols. Raleigh. 1822–1845.

MYLNE (W.) and CRAIG (R. D.) Reports of Cases argued and determined in the High Court of Chancery during the time of Lord Chancellor Cottenham, with a few of the time of the Lord Commissioners, and of Sir C. C. Pepys, Master of the Rolls. 1835–41. 5 vols. London. 1837–48.

The Same. Vol. 5. London. 1848.

The Same. Vols. 1–4. New York and Albany. 1842–1848. (English Chancery Reports, Vols. 13, 14, 18.)

MYLNE (James Wm.) and KEEN (Benjamin). Reports of Cases argued and determined in the High Court of Chancery, during the time of Lord Chancellor Brougham and Sir John Leach, Master of the Rolls. 1832–35. 3 vols. London. 1834–7.

The Same. Vols. 1–3. London. 1834–38. (English Chancery Reports, Vols. 6, 7, 9, 10.)

NAPTON (W. B.) Reports of Cases argued and decided in the Supreme Court of the State of Missouri, from 1835 to 1837. Fayette, Missouri. 1837. (Missouri Reports, Vol. 4.)

NEBRASKA.

Woolworth (Vol. 1.)

NELSON (W.) Reports of Special Cases argued and decreed in the Court of Chancery, in the Reigns of King Charles I., King Charles II., and King William III. London. 1717.

NEVADA.

Nevada Reports. 6 vols. 1865–1870.

Lewis (Vol. 1.)

Helm (Vols. 2–6.)

NEVILE (S.) and MANNING (W. M.) Reports of Cases argued and determined in the Court of King's Bench. Containing the Cases from Michaelmas Term, 1832, to Trinity Term, 1836. 6 vols. Philadelphia. 1836–40. (Eng. Com. Law Reps., Vols. 28, 30, 36.)

NEVILE (Sandford) and PERRY (Thomas Erskine). Reports of Cases argued and determined in the Court of Queen's Bench, and upon Writs of Error from that Court to the Exchequer Chamber, from Trinity Term, 1837, to Trinity Term, 1838. 3 vols. London and Dublin. 1838–9.

Reports of Cases argued and determined in the Court of King's Bench, and Exchequer Chamber. Containing the Cases in Michaelmas Term, 1836, and Hilary and Easter Terms, 1837. Philadelphia. 1840. (Eng. Com. Law Reps., Vol. 36.)

NEWBERRY (John S.) Reports of Admiralty Cases argued and adjudged in the District Courts of the United States for the District of Michigan, etc., from 1842 to 1857. Vol. 1. New York and Albany. 1857.

NEW HAMPSHIRE.

New Hampshire Reports. 48 vols. 1816–1870.
Adams, (Vol. 1.)
Richardson & Woodbury, (Vol. 2.)
French, (Vol. 6.)
Foster, (Vol. 19.)
Chandler, (Vol. 20.)
Foster, (Vols. 21–31.)
Fogg, (Vols. 32–37.)
Chandler, (Vols. 38–44.)
Hadley, (Vols. 45–48.)

NEW JERSEY.

Law.

Coxe's Reports, 1 vol. 1790–1795. (1 N. J.)
Remington's Reports, 1 vol. 1806–1813. (2 and 3 N. J.)
Southard's Reports, 2 vols. 1816–1820 (4 and 5 N. J.)
Halsted's Reports, 7 vols. 1821–1831. (6–12 N. J.)
Green's Reports, 3 vols. 1831–1836. (13–15 N. J.)
Harrison's Reports, 4 vols. 1837–1842. (16–19 N. J.)
Spencer's Reports, 1 vol. 1842–1845. (20 N. J.)
Zabriskie's Reports, 4 vols. 1847–1855. (21–24 N. J.)
Dutcher's Reports, 5 vols. 1855–1863. (25–29 N. J.)
Vroom's Reports, 5 vols. 1863–1870. (30–34 N. J.)

Chancery.

Saxton's Reports, 1 vol. 1830–1832. (1 N. J. Eq.)
Green's Reports, 3 vols. 1838–1846. (2–4 N. J. Eq.)
Halsted's Reports, 4 vols. 1845–1852. (5–8 N. J. Eq.)
Stockton's Reports, 3 vols. 1852–1859. (9–11 N. J. Eq.)
Beasley's Reports, 2 vols. 1859–1862. (12, 13 N. J. Eq.)
McCarter's Reports, 2 vols. 1862–1864. (14, 15 N. J. Eq.)
Green's Reports, 6 vols. 1864–1870. (16–20 N. J. Eq.)

NEW YORK.

Law.

Coleman & Caines' Cases, 1 vol. 1794–1805.
Johnson's Cases, 3 vols. 1799–1803.
Lockwood's Reversed Cases, 1 vol. 1799–1847.
Caines' Reports, 3 vols. 1803–1805.
Caines' Cases, 2 vols. 1804–1805.
Johnson's Reports, 20 vols. 1806–1823.
Anthon's Nisi Prius Cases, 1 vol. 1808–1818.
Yates' Select Cases, 1 vol. 1811.

Cowen's Reports, 9 vols. 1823–1828.
Wendell's Reports, 26 vols. 1828–1841.
Hill's Reports, 7 vols. 1841–1845.
Denio's Reports, 5 vols. 1845–1848.
Lalor's Supplement to Hill & Denio's Reports, 1 vol. 1842–1844.
Barbour's Supreme Court Reports, 54 vols. 1847–1869.
Lansing's Supreme Court Reports, 3 vols. 1869–1871.

Court of Appeals.

Howard's Cases, 1 vol. 1847–1848.
Keyes' Reports, 4 vols. 1864–1869.
New York Reports, 45 vols.
Comstock. (Vols. 1–4.) 1847–1851.
Selden. (Vols. 5–10.) 1851–1860.
Kernan. (Vols. 11–14). 1854–1857.
Smith. (Vols. 15–27). 1857–1864.
Tiffany. (Vols. 28–39). 1864–1868.
Hand. (Vols. 39–45). 1864–1870.

Superior Court.

Hall's Reports, 2 vols. 1828–1829.
Sandford's Reports, 5 vols. 1847–1852.
Duer's Reports, 6 vols. 1852–1856.
Bosworth's Reports, 10 vols. 1856–1864.
Robinson's Reports, 7 vols. 1863–1868.
Sweeny's Reports, 2 vols. 1869–1870.

Practice and Code Reports.

Howard's Practice Reports, 4 vols. 1844–1871.
Abbott's Practice Reports, 19 vols. 1854–1865.
Abbott's Practice, New Series, 10 vols. 1865–1871.
Code Reporter, 3 vols. in 2. 1848–1851.
Code Reporter, New Series, 1 vol. 1851.

Common Pleas.

Smith's Reports, 4 vols. 1850–1854.
Hilton's Reports, 2 vols. 1855–1860.
Daly's Reports, 2 vols. 1859–1869.

Chancery.

Johnson's Chancery Reports, 7 vols. 1814–1823.
Hopkins' Reports, 1 vol. 1823–1826.
Paige's Reports, 11 vols. 1828–1845.
Barbour's Chancery Reports, 3 vols. 1845–1848.
Edwards' Reports, 4 vols. 1831–1850.
Hoffman's Reports, 1 vol. 1839–1840.
Clark's Reports, 1 vol. 1839–1841.
Sandford's Chancery Reports. 1843–1847.

Criminal.

Parker's Criminal Reports, 6 vols. 1839–1867.
Wheeler's Criminal Cases, 3 vols. 1776–1824.

Probate.

Bradford's Reports, 4 vols. 1849–1857.
Redfield's Reports, 1 vol. 1857–1864.

NEW YORK LEGAL OBSERVER. Containing Reports of Cases decided in the Courts of Equity and Common Law, and important Decisions in the English Courts; also articles on Legal Subjects, Practical Points of general interest Remarkable, Trials, Sketches of the Bench and Bar, Anecdotes, etc., etc., with Table of Cases, a General Index and a Digest of the Reports. Edited by Samuel Owen. Vols. 1–12. October, 1842, to October, 1854. New York. 1843–1854.

NORTH CAROLINA.

Law.

Haywood's Reports, Vol. 1. 1789–1798.
Martin's Reports and Haywood's Reports, (Vol. 2.) } 2 vols in 1. 1797–1806.
Taylor's Reports, Conference Reports, } 2 vols. in 1. { 1799–1802. 1800–1804.
Murphey's Reports, 3 vols. 1804–1819.
Hawks' Reports, 4 vols. 1820–1826.
Devereux's Reports, 4 vols. 1826–1834.
Devereux & Battle's Reports, 4 vols in 3. 1834–1839.
Iredell's Reports, 13 vols. 1840–1852.
Busbee's Reports, 1 vol. 1852–1853.
Jones' Reports, 8 vols. 1853–1862.
Winston's Reports, 1 vol. 1863–1864.

Equity.

Devereux's Equity Reports, 2 vols. 1828–1834.
Devereux & Battle's Equity Reports, 2 vols. 1834–1840.
Iredell's Equity Reports, 8 vols. 1840–1852.
Busbee's Equity Reports, 1 vol. 1852–1853.
Jones's Equity Reports, 6 vols. 1853–1860.
Winston's Reports, 1 vol. 1864.

Law and Equity.

North Carolina Reports, 3 vols. 1868–1871.
Phillips, (Vols. 63–64.) 1868–1870.
McCorkle, (Vol. 65.) 1871.

NOTT (Henry Junius) and MCCORD (David James.) Reports of Cases determined in the Constitutional Court of South Carolina. Containing the decisions from November

Term, 1817, to November Term, 1820, inclusive. 2d Edition. 2 vols. Charleston. 1842.

NOTT (Charles C.) and HUNTINGTON (Samuel H.) Cases decided in the Court of Claims of the United States, from October Term, 1863, to January Term, 1869, inclusive. Vols. 1–5. Washington, D. C. 1867.

OFFICER (Harvey.) Reports of Cases argued and determined in the Supreme Court of the Territory of Minnesota from the organization of the territority until its admission into the Union, in 1858. 9 vols. Vol. 1 containing the Reports of William Hollinshead, Isaac Atwater, John B. Brisbin, Michael E. Ames, and Harvey Officer. Vols. 2–9 containing the Reports of Harvey Officer. Saint Paul. 1858–1865. (Minnesota Reports, Vols. 1–9.)

OHIO.

Tappan's Reports, 1 vol. 1816–1819.

Ohio Reports, 20 vols.

Hammond, (Vols. 1–9.) 1821–1839.

Wilcox, (Vol. 10.) 1840–1841.

Stanton, (Vols. 11–13.) 1841–1844.

Griswold, (Vols. 14–19.) 1845–1850.

Lawrence, (Vol. 20.) 1851.

Ohio State Reports, 19 vols.

McCook, (Vol. 1.) 1852.

Warden, (Vols. 2–4.) 1853–1855.

Critchfield, (Vols. 5–20.) 1855–1870.

Handy's Cincinnati Superior Court Reports, 2 vols. in 1. 1854–1862.

Disney's Cincinnati Superior Court Reports, 2 vols. 1854–1860.

OGDEN (A. N.) Reports af Cases argued and determined in the Supreme Court of Louisiana. For the years 1857–1860. 4 vols. New Orleans. 1858–1861. (Louisiana Reports, Vols. 12–15.)

OLCOTT (Edward R). Reports of Cases argued and determined in the District Court of the United States for the Southern District of New York. New York. 1857.

O'MALLEY (Edward Loughlin) and HARCASTLE (Henry). Reports of Decisions of the Judges for the Trial of Election Petitions in England and Ireland, pursuant to the Parliamentary Elections Act, 1868. Vol. 1. London. 1870.

OREGON.

Oregon Reports.

Wilson (Vols. 1–2.) 1853–1869.

ORMOND (J. J.) Reports of Cases argued and determined in the Supreme Court of Alabama, during the January and June Terms, 1848, and January Term, 1849. 3 vols. Tuscaloosa. 1849. (Alabama Reports, Vols. 13–15.)

OVERTON (John). Tennessee Reports ; or Cases ruled and adjudged in the Superior Courts of Law and Equity, and Federal Courts for the State of Tennessee. Vols. 1 and 2. Tennessee Reports, Cooper's Edition, Vol. 1. St. Louis. 1870.

OWEN (Thomas). The Reports of that late Reverend and Learned Judge, Thomas Owen, Esquire ; One of the Justices of the Common Pleas. Folio. London. 1656.

PAIGE (Alonzo C.) Reports of Cases argued and determined in the Court of Chancery of the State of New York. 11 vols. New York and Albany. 1830–1848.

PALMER (Sir Gefrey). Les Reports de Sir Gefrey Palmer, Chevalier et Baronet ; Attorney General a son tres-excellent Majesty le Roy Charles le Second. London. 1688.

PAINE (Elijah.) Report of Cases argued and determined in the Circuit Court of the United States for the Second Circuit, comprising the Districts of New York, Connecticut and Vermont. 2 vols. New York and Albany. 1827–1860.

PAPY (Marius D.) Reports of Cases argued and adjudged in the Supreme Court of Florida, at Terms held from 1855 to 1858. 3 vols. Tallahassee. 1856–1858. (Florida Reports, Vols. 6–8.)

PARKER (Sir Thomas.) Reports of Cases concerning the Revenue, argued and determined in the Court of Exchequer, from Easter Term, 1743, to Hilary Term, 1767. Dublin. 1791.

PARKER (Amasa J.) Reports of Decisions in Criminal Cases, made at Term, at Chambers, and in the Courts of Oyer and Terminer of the State of New York. 6 vols. Albany and New York. 1855–1868.

PASCHAL (George W.) Reports of Cases argued and decided in the Supreme Court of the State of Texas, during the conclusion of the Tyler Session, 1860, and the whole of Austin Session, 1860. Washington, D. C. 1869. (Texas Reports, Supplement to Vol. 25.)

Reports of Cases argued and decided in the Supreme Court of the State of Texas during Austin Session, 1866. Washington, D. C., 1869. (Texas Reports, Vol. 28.)

PATTON, JR. (John M.) and HEATH (Roscoe B.) Reports of Causes decided in the Special Court of Appeals of Virginia, held at Richmond; and a general index to Grattan's Reports, from the 2d to the 11th Volume, inclusive. Richmond, Va. 1856–1857.

PEAKE (Thomas.) Cases determined at Nisi Prius, in the Court of King's Bench. From the Sittings after Easter Term, 30 Geo. III., to the Sittings after Michaelmas Term, 35 Geo. III., both inclusive. Dublin. 1795.

PECK (Jacob.) Reports of Cases argued and adjudged in the Supreme Court of Errors and Appeals of the State of Tennessee, commencing September Term, 1822, and ending with May Term, 1822. By Jacob Peck, one of the Judges. Knoxville, Tenn. 1824.

Reports of Cases argued and adjudged in the Supreme Court of Errors and Appeals of the State of Tennessee, from September Term, 1822, to May Term, 1824. Tennessee Reports. Cooper's Edition, Vol 4. St. Louis. 1871.

PECK (E.) Reports of Cases determined in the Supreme Court of the State of Illinois, from November Term, 1849, to January Term, 1863. 20 vols. Springfield and Chicago. 1854–1860. (Illinois Reports, Vols. 11–30.)

PECK (James H.) Report of the Trial of James H. Peck, Judge of the United States District Court for the District of Missouri, before the Senate of the United States, on an Impeachment preferred by the House of Representatives against him for High Misdemeanor in office. By Arthur J. Stansbury. Boston. 1833.

PECKWELL (Robert Henry.) Cases of Controverted Elections in the Second Parliament of the United Kingdom: begun and holden August 31, 1802. 2 vols. London. 1805–1806.

PENNSYLVANIA.

Dallas's Reports. 4 vols. 1754–1806.
Addison's Reports. 1 vol. 1791–1799.
Yeates's Reports. 4 vols. 1791–1798.
Binney's Reports. 6 vols. 1799–1814.
Browne's Reports. 2 vols. 1806–1814.
Ashmead's Reports. In 2 vols. Vol. 2. 1831–1841.
Sergeant & Rawle's Reports. 17 vols. 1818–1829.
Rawle's Reports. 5 vols. 1828–1835.
Penrose & Watts's Pennsylvania Reports. 3 vols. 1829–1832.
Watts's Reports. 10 vols. 1832–1840.
Miles's Reports. 2 vols. 1835–1840.
Wharton's Reports. 6 vols. 1835–1841.

Watts & Sergeant's Reports. 9 vols. 1841–1844.
Brightly's Nisi Prius Reports. 1 vol. 1809–1851.
Grant's Cases. 3 vols. 1852–1863.
Philadelphia Reports, Common Pleas. 5 vols. 1850–1864.
Pennsylvania State Reports. 66 vols. 1844–1871.
Barr (Vols. 1–10). 1844–1849.
Jones (Vols. 11–12). 1849.
Harris (Vols. 13–24). 1849–1855.
Casey (Vols. 25–36). 1854–1860.
Wright (Vols. 37–50). 1860–1865.
Smith (Vols. 51–66). 1865–1871.

PENNSYLVANIA STATE TRIALS; containing the Impeachment, Trial, and Acquittal of Francis Hopkinson, and John Nicholson, Esquires. The former being Judge of the Court of Admiralty, and the latter the Comptroller General of the Commonwealth of Pennsylvania. Vol. 1. Philadelphia. 1794.

PENNINGTON (William Sanford). Reports of Cases argued and determined in the Supreme Court of Judicature of the State of New Jersey; from May Term, 1806, to September, 1813, inclusive. Second Edition. Camden, N. J. 1835.

PENROSE (Charles B.), WATTS (Frederick) and RAWLE, Jun. (William). Reports of Cases adjudged in the Supreme Court of Pennsylvania. 3 vols. Harrisburg and Carlisle. 1830–1833.

PERRY (Thomas Erskine) and DAVISON (Henry). Reports of Cases argued and determined in the Court of Queen's Bench, and upon Writs of Error from that Court to the Exchequer Chamber, from Michaelmas Term, 2d Vict., to Hilary Term, 4 Vict. London and Dublin. 1839–42.

PERRY (Henry James) and KNAPP (Jerome William). Cases of Controverted Elections in the Eleventh Parliament of the United Kingdom, being the first Parliament since the passing of the Acts for the Amendment of the Representation of the People. London. 1833.

PETERS (Richard.) Admiralty Decisions in the District Court of the United States, for the Pennsylvania District, by the Hon. Richard Peters; comprising also some decisions in the same Court by the late Francis Hopkinson, Esq. To which are added Cases determined in other Districts of the United States. 2 vols. Philadelphia. 1807.

PETERS (Richard.) Reports of Cases argued and adjudged in the Supreme Court of the United States, from January

Term, 1828, to January Term, 1842. 16 vols. Philadelphia and New York. 1829–1851.

PETERS (Richard.) Reports of Cases argued and determined in the Circuit Court of the United States, for the Third Circuit. Vol. 1. Philadelphia. 1819.

PHILADELPHIA REPORTS; or, Legal Intelligencer condensed; containing the decisions published in the Legal Intelligencer, from 1850 to 1864, inclusive. By Henry E. Wallace, Esq. 2d Edition. 5 vols. Philadelphia. 1860–1867.

PHILLIMORE (Joseph.) Reports of Cases argued and determined in the Ecclesiastical Courts at Doctor's Commons, and in the High Court of Delegates, from Hilary Term, 1809, to Michaelmas Term, 1831, inclusive. 3 vols. London and Dublin. 1818–27.

PHILLIMORE (Joseph.) Reports of Cases argued and determined in the Ecclesiastical Courts at Doctor's Commons, and in the High Court of Delegates. 3 vols. Containing Cases from Hilary Term, 1809, to Michaelmas Term, 1821, inclusive. Philadelphia. 1831. (English Ecclesiastical Reports, Vol. 1.)

PHILLIPS (T. J.) Reports of Cases argued and determined in the High Court of Chancery. 1841–1849. With Notes and References by John A. Dunlap. 2 vols. New York and Albany. 1848–1850. (Eng. Chancery Reports, Vols. 19 and 22.)

PHILLIPS (S. F.) North Carolina Reports. Cases argued and determined in the Supreme Court of North Carolina, from June Term, 1868, to June Term, 1870. 2 vols. Raleigh. 1869–1870. (North Carolina Reports, Vols. 63–64.)

PICKERING (Octavius.) Reports of Cases argued and determined in the Supreme Judicial Court of Massachusetts. 24 vols. 2d Edition, with Notes and References. Boston. 1833–1848.

PIKE (Albert.) Reports of Cases argued and determined in the Supreme Court of the State of Arkansas, in Law and Equity. 5 vols. Little Rock. 1840–1845. (Arkansas Reports, Vols. 1–5.)

PLOWDEN (Edmund.) The Commentaries or Reports of. 2 vols. Dublin. 1792.

POLLEXFEN (Sr. Hen.) The Arguments and Reports of Sr. Hen. Pollexfen, Kt., late Lord Chief Justice of the Court of Common Pleas, in some special cases, by him argued during the time of his Practice at the Bar. Together with divers Decrees in the High Court of Chancery, upon the Limitations of Trusts of Terms for years. Folio. London. 1702.

POPHAM (Sir John.) Reports and Cases collected by the learned Sir John Popham, Knight, late Lord Chief Justice of England Folio. London. 1656.

PORTER (David.) A Report of the Trial of Commodore David Porter, of the Navy of the United States, before a General Court Martial, held at Washington in July, 1825. Washington City. 1825.

PORTER (Albert G.) Reports of Cases argued and determined in the Supreme Court of Judicature of the State of Indiana, being an official continuation of Blackford's Reports. 5 vols. Indianapolis. 1853–1856. (Indiana Reports, Vols. 3–7.)

PORTER (Benjamin F.) Reports of Cases argued and adjudged in the Supreme Court of Alabama, from June Term, 1834, to June Term, 1839, inclusive. 9 vols. Tuscaloosa. 1835–1840.

POST (Truman A.) Reports of Cases argued and determined in the Supreme Court of the State of Missouri. 6 vols. St. Louis. 1869–1871. (Missouri Reports, Vols. 42–47.)

PRICE (George). Reports of Cases argued and determined in the Court of Exchequer at Law and in Equity, and in the Exchequer Chamber, in Equity and in Error. Edited by Francis J. Troubat, Esq. Containing the Cases Reported by George Price. Philadelphia. 1835. (English Exchequer Reports, Vols. 1–6.)

PROBATE AND DIVORCE CASES. The Law Reports. Courts of Probate and Divorce. Reported by T. H. Tristram, D. C. L., Advocate, Richard Searle, Barrister-at-Law, and John G. Middleton, LL. D., Advocate. Edited by James Redfoord Bulwer, Q. C. Vol. 1. From Michaelmas Term, 1865, to Trinity Term, 1869, both inclusive. Philadelphia. 1870.

QUEEN'S BENCH. See ADOLPHUS & ELLIS, N. S.

QUEEN'S BENCH. The Law Reports. Court of Queen's Bench. Reported by William Mills and Henry Holroyd, Barrister at Law. And in the Bail Court by E. A. C. Schalch, Barrister at Law. Edited by James Redfoord Bulwer, Q. C. From Michaelmas Term, 1865, to Trinity Term, 1870, both inclusive. 5 vols. Philadelphia. 1867–1871.

QUINCY (Josiah). Reports of Cases argued and adjudged in the Superior Court of Judicature of the Province of Massachusetts Bay, between 1761 and 1772. By Josiah Quincy, Junior. Printed from his original manuscripts in the possession of his son, Josiah Quincy, and Edited by his great grand-son, Samuel M. Quincy. Boston. 1865.

RAILWAY CASES. American Cases relating to the Law of Railways, decided in the Supreme Court of the United States, and in the Courts of the several States. With Notes by Chauncey Smith and Samuel W. Bates, Counsellors at Law. 2 vols. Boston. 1854–1856.

RAILWAY CASES. See ENGLISH RAILWAY AND CANAL CASES.

RANDOLPH (Peyton). Reports of Cases argued and determined in the Court of Appeals of Virginia. 6 vols. Richmond. 1823–1829.

RANDOLPH (W. M.) Reports of Cases argued and determined in the Supreme Court of Louisiana. For the years 1853–1856. 4 vols. New Orleans. 1854–1857. (Louisiana Reports, Vols. 8–11.)

RAWLE Jr. (William). Reports of Cases adjudged in the Supreme Court of Pennsylvania. 5 vols. Philadelphia. 1829–1836.

RAYMOND (Robert, Lord). Reports of Cases argued and adjudged in the Courts of King's Bench and Common Pleas, in Reigns of the late King William, Queen Anne, King George the First, and King George the Second. 3 vols. Dublin. 1792.

RAYMOND (Sir T.) Reports of Divers Special Cases, adjudged in the Courts of King's Bench, Common Pleas and Exchequer, in the Reign of King Charles II. 3d Edition. Dublin. 1793.

REDFIELD (Amasa A.) Reports of Cases argued and determined in the Surrogates' Courts of the State of New York. Vol. 1. New York. 1864.

REDINGTON (Asa.) Reports of Cases in Law and Equity, determined by the Supreme Judicial Court of Maine. 5 vols. Hallowell. 1851–1854. (Maine Reports, Vols. 31–35.)

REPERTORIUM JURIDICUM. A General Index to all the Cases and Pleadings in Law and Equity, contained in all Reports, Year Books, etc., hitherto published. In two parts. By T. E. Tomlins, of the Inner Temple, Barrister at Law. Dublin. 1788.

REPORTS IN CHANCERY. Cases argued and determined in the High Court of Chancery in Ireland. 1827.

REPORTS IN CHANCERY. Reports of Cases taken and adjudged in the Court of Chancery, in the Reign of King Charles I., Charles II., William III., and Queen Anne. Being Special Cases. Three Vols. in one. In the Savoy. 1736.

REYNOLDS (R. O.) Reports of Cases argued and determined in the High Court of Errors and Appeals for the State of Mississippi. 2 vols. New York. 1867. (Mississippi Reports, Vols. 40–41.)

RHODE ISLAND.

Rhode Island Reports, 8 vols. 1828–1867.

Angell. (Vol 1.)

Durfee. (Vol. 2.)

Knowles. (Vol. 3.)

Ames. (Vols. 4–7.)

Ames, Knowles & Bradley. (Vol. 8.)

RICE (William). Reports of Cases at Law, argued and determined in the Court of Appeals and Court of Errors of South Carolina, from December, 1838, to May, 1839, both inclusive. Charleston. 1839.

Reports of Cases in Chancery, argued and determined in the Court of Appeals and Court of Errors of South Carolina, from December, 1838, to May, 1839, both inclusive. Charleston. 1839.

RICHARDSON (J. S. G.) Reports of Cases at Law, argued and determined in the Court of Appeals and Court of Errors of South Carolina. From December, 1844, to May, 1868, both inclusive. 15 vols. Columbia, S. C. 1845–1869.

Reports of Cases in Equity, argued and determined in the Court of Appeals in Equity and Court of Errors of South Carolina. From December, 1844, to May, 1868, both inclusive. 14 vols. Columbia, S. C. 1845–1869.

Reports of Cases in Chancery, argued and determined in the Court of Appeals of South Carolina, from May Term, 1831, to May Term, 1832, both inclusive. Charleston, S. C. 1853.

RICHARDSON (William M.) and WOODBURY (Levi). Reports of Cases argued and determined in the Superior Court of Judicature for the State of New Hampshire, between February, 1819, and May, 1823, inclusive. Concord. 1824. (New Hampshire Reports, Vol. 2.)

RIDGEWAY (William). Reports of Cases argued and determined in the King's Bench and Chancery, during the time in which Lord Hardwicke presided in those Courts. Dublin. 1794.

RIDGEWAY (William), LAPP (William) and SCHOALES (John). See IRISH TERM REPORTS.

RILEY'S LAW CASES. Reports of Law Cases, determined in the Court of Appeals of South Carolina, January Term, 1836, April Term, 1836, and February Term, 1837. Charleston. 1839.

RILEY'S CHANCERY CASES. Chancery Cases determined in the Court of Appeals of South Carolina, April Term, 1836, and February Term, 1837. Charleston. 1839.

ROBARDS (Wm. A.) Reports of Cases argued and decided in the Supreme Court of the State of Missouri. 2 vols. Jefferson City. 1849–1850. (Missouri Reports, Vols. 12–13.)

ROBARDS (Charles L.) and JACKSON (A. M.) Reports of Cases argued and decided in the Supreme Court of the State of Texas, from Austin Session, 1861, to Galveston Session, 1865, both inclusive. 2 vols. Austin, 1867. (Texas Reports, Vols. 26–27.)

ROBERTSON (Anthony L.) Reports of Cases argued and determined in the Superior Court of the City of New York. 7 vols. Albany. 1867–1869.

ROBINSON (Merritt M.) Reports of Cases argued and determined in the Supreme Court of Louisiana. 12 vols. New Orleans. 1842–1846.

Reports of Cases argued and determined in the Supreme Court of Louisiana. From the reorganization of the Court under the Constitution of 1845, to the year 1850. 4 vols. New Orleans. 1847–1850. (Louisiana Annual Reports, Vols. 1–4.)

ROBB (James B.) A Collection of Patent Cases, decided in the Supreme and Circuit Courts of the United States, from their organization to the year 1850. 2 vols. Boston. 1854.

ROBINSON (Conway). Reports of Cases decided in the Supreme Court of Appeals and in the General Court of Virginia. From April 1, 1842, to April 1, 1844. 2 vols. Richmond. 1843–1844.

ROBINSON (Tod). Reports of Cases determined in the Supreme Court of the State of California, at the July and October Terms, 1869. San Francisco. 1870. (California Reports, Vol. 38.)

ROLLE (Henry). Les Reports de Henry Rolle Serjeant del Ley, de divers Cases en le Court del Banke le Roy, En le temps del reign de Roy Jacques. Folio. 2 vols. London. 1675–1676.

ROOT (Jesse). Reports of Cases adjudged in the Superior Court and Supreme Court of Errors, from July, A. D. 1789, to January, A. D. 1798; with a variety of Cases anterior to that period. Prefaced with observations upon the Government and Laws of Connecticut. 2 vols. Hartford. 1798–1802.

ROSE (George.) Cases in Bankruptcy. Containing Reports of Cases decided by Lord Chancellor Eldon from Easter Term, 1810, to the Sittings after Trinity Term, 1816, inclusive, and Cotemporaneous Cases in other courts. Second Edition. London. 1821.

RUSSELL (James.) Reports of Cases argued and determined in the High Court of Chancery, during the time of Lord Chancellor Eldon. Vol. 1. 1826. New York. 1828.

The Same. 5 vols. 1827.

The Same. Vols. 2–4. Philadelphia. 1832. (English Chancery Reports, Vol. 3.)

RUSSELL (James) and MYLNE (J. W.) Reports of Cases argued and determined in the High Court of Chancery during the time of Lord Chancellor Lyndhurst. 1829–31. 2 vols. London. 1832–37.

The Same. Philadelphia. 1833, 1842. (English Chancery Reports, Vols. 4, 13.)

RUSSELL (William Oldnall) and RYAN (Edward.) Crown Cases Reserved for consideration, and decided by the Twelve Judges of England, from 1799 to 1824. With References to the English Common Law Reports. 1 vol. Philadelphia. 1839. (British Crown Cases, Vol. 1.)

RYAN (Edward) and MOODY (William.) Reports of Cases determined at Nisi Prius, in the Courts of King's Bench and Common Pleas, and on the Oxford and Western Circuits, from the Sittings after Michaelmas Term, 1823, to the Sittings after Trinity Term, 1826, inclusive. Philadelphia. 1832. (Eng. Com. Law Reps., Vol. 21.)

SALKELD (William.) Reports of Cases adjudged in the Court of King's Bench; with some special Cases in the Court of Chancery, Common Pleas and Exchequer. 2 vols. 6th Ed. Dublin. 1791.

SANDFORD (Lewis H.) Reports of Cases argued and determined in the Court of Chancery of the State of New York, before the Hon. Lewis H. Sandford, Assistant Vice-Chancellor of the First Circuit. 4 vols. New York and Albany. 1846–1850.

Reports of Cases argued and determined in the Superior Court of the City of New York. 5 vols. New York and Albany. 1849–1853.

SAUNDERS (Sir Edward, Knt) Reports of, of several Pleadings and Cases in the Court of King's Bench, in the time of the reign of King Charles the Second. Edited by John Williams. 5th Am. from the last London Edition. By John Patteson and Edward Vaughan Williams. 2 vols. New York. 1833.

SAUNDERS (Thomas William) and COLE (Henry Thomas.) Bail Court Reports. Containing the Cases from Hilary Term, 9 Vict., to Michaelmas Term, 12 Vict. London. 1847–9.

SAVILE (Sir John). Les Reports de Sir John Savile, Chevalier, Nadgairis Baron de l'Exchequer, de divers special cases cybien en le Court de Common Bank come l'Exchequer en le temps de Royne Elizabeth. Folio. London. 1688.

SAXTON (N.) Reports of Cases decided in the Court of Chancery of the State of New Jersey. Elizabethtown. 1836.

SAYER (Joseph). Reports of Cases adjudged in the Court of King's Bench, beginning Michaelmas Term, 25 Geo. 2, ending Trinity Term, 29 and 30 Geo. 2. Folio. London. 1775.

SCAMMON (J. Young). Reports of Cases argued and determined in the Supreme Court of the State of Illinois. Second Edition. 4 vols. Philadelphia, Boston, Chicago and Galena. 1841–1844. (Illinois Reports, Vols. 2–5.)

SCHOALES (John) and LEFROY (Thomas). Reports of Cases argued and determined in the High Court of Chancery in Ireland, during the time of Lord Redesdale, from Easter Term, 1802, to the period of Lord Redesdale's resignation of the Great Seal. London. 1806–21.

SCOTT (John). Cases in the Court of Common Pleas and Exchequer Chamber, from Michaelmas Term, 5 Will. IV., to Hilary Term, 3 Vict. 8 vols. London and Dublin. 1835–41.

New Reports in the Court of Common Pleas and Exchequer Chamber, from Easter Term, 3 Vict., to Michaelmas Term, 8 Vict. 8 vols. London. 1841–45.

Reports of Cases argued and determined in the Court of Common Pleas and Exchequer Chamber, during the years 1835–7. Philadelphia. 1838, 1840. (Eng. Com. Law Reps., Vols. 30, 36.)

SELDEN (Henry R.) Reports of Cases argued and determined in the Court of Appeals of the State of New York. 6 vols. Albany. 1853. (New York Reports, Vols 5–10.)

SELECT CASES IN CHANCERY. Select Cases argued and adjudged in the High Court of Chancery, before the late Lords' Commissioners of the Great Seal, and the late Lord Chancellor King. From 1724 to 1733. Folio. In the Savoy. 1740.

SELECT EQUITY CASES. Select Cases in Equity argued and determined in the Court of Common Pleas of the First Judicial District of Pennsylvania, from 1841 to 1850. Reported by A. V. Parsons, One of the Judges of the Court. Vol. 1. Philadelphia. 1859.

SERGEANT (Thomas) and RAWLE (William, Jun.) Reports of Cases adjudged in the Supreme Court of Pennsylvania. 17 vols. Philadelphia. 1818–1829.

SESSIONS CASES, Adjudged in the Court of King's Bench, Chiefly touching Settlements, from the latter end of Queen Anne's Reign to the Present Time. 2d Ed. 2 vols. London. 1760.

SHAW (G. B.) Reports of Cases argued and determined in the Supreme Court of the State of Vermont. 2 vols. Burlington. 1839–1840. (Vermont Reports, Vols. 10–11.)

SHAW (W. G.) Reports of Cases argued and determined in the Supreme Court of the State of Vermont. 6 vols. Rutland. 1859–1864. (Vermont Reports, Vols. 30–35.)

SHEPHERD (J. W.) Reports of Cases argued and determined in the Supreme Court of Alabama, from January Term, 1851, to January Term, 1868. 21 vols. Montgomery, Ala. 1852–1869. (Alabama Reports, Vols. 19–21, 24–41.)

SHEPLEY (John). Reports of Cases in Law and Equity determined by the Supreme Judicial Court of Maine. 17 vols. Hallowell. 1838–1851. (Maine Reports, Vols. 13–18, 20–30.)

SHIPPEN (Edward), YEATES (Jasper) and SMITH (Thomas). Report of the Trial and Acquittal of Edward Shippen, Esquire, Chief Justice, and Jasper Yeates and Thomas Smith, Esquires, Assistant Justices, of the Supreme Court of Pennsylvania, on an impeachment, before the Senate of the Commonwealth, January, 1805. By William Hamilton. Lancaster. "Trial of the Judges."

SHOWER (Sir Bartholomew). Reports of Cases adjudged in the Court of King's Bench, during the Reigns of Charles II., James II., and William III. 2 vols. 2d Ed. By Thomas Leach. London. 1794.

SHOWER (Sir Bartholomew.) Cases in Parlaiment resolved and adjudged upon Petitions, and Writs of Error. Folio. In the Savoy. 1740.

Reports of Cases adjudged in the Court of Kings Bench, during the reigns of Charles the Second, James the Second and William the Third. 2 vols. London. 1794.

SIDERFIN (Tho.) Les Reports des divers special Cases argue et adjudgee an le Court del Bank le Roy et Auxy en le Co. Ba. et L'Exchequer en les premier dix-ans apres le Restauration del son Tres-Excellent Majesty Le Roy Charles le II. Folio. 2 Editions. 1683 and 1714.

SIMONS (Nicholas.) Reports of Cases decided in the High Court of Chancery, by the Right Hon. Sir Lancelot Shadwell, Vice Chancellor of England, and the Right Hon. Sir Richard Torin Kindersley, Vice Chancellor. Vol. 17. Containing Cases in 1849, 1850 and 1852. London and Dublin. 1854.

SIMONS (Nicholas.) Reports of Cases decided in the High Court of Chancery, by the Right Hon. Sir John Leach and the Right Hon. Sir Anthony Hart, Vice Chancellors of England, from 1826 to 1840. 10 vols. London. 1829 –1842.

The Same. Vols. 1–17. (English Chancery Reports, Vols. 2, 5–7, 9–11, 16, 34–39, 42.)

New Series. Reports of Cases decided in the High Court of Chancery in 1851 and 1852, by the Right Hon. Lord Cranworth and Sir Richard Torin Kindersley, Vice Chancellors. With some Cases Reported by C. Stewart Drewry, Esq. Vol. 2. London and Dublin. 1852.

The Same. Vols. 1 and 2. New York and Albany. 1856–1857. (English Chancery Reports, Vols. 40, 42.)

SIMONS (Nicholas) and STUART (John.) Reports of Cases decided in the High Court of Chancery, by the Right Hon. Sir John Leach, Vice Chancellor of England, from 1822–26. 2 vols. London. 1824–7.

The Same. Philadelphia. 1831. (Eng. Chancery Reports, Vol. 1.)

SKINNER (Robert.) Reports of Cases adjudged in the Court of King's Bench, from the Thirty-third Year of King Charles the Second, to the Ninth Year of King William the Third, with some Arguments in Special Cases. Folio. In the Savoy. 1728.

SLADE (William.) Reports of Cases argued and determined in the Supreme Court of the State of Vermont. Burlington. 1844. (Vermont Reports, Vol. 15.)

SMALE (John) and GIFFARD (J. W. De Longueville.) Reports of Cases Adjudged in the High Court of Chancery, by the Vice-Chancellor Sir John Stuart, from 1852 to 1857. 3 vols. London and Dublin. 1855–8.

SMEDES (W. C.) and MARSHALL (T. A.) Reports of Cases argued and determined in the High Court of Errors and Appeals for the State of Mississippi. 14 vols. Boston. 1844–1857. (Mississippi Reports, Vols. 9–22.)

Reports of Cases argued and determined in the Superior Court of Chancery of the State of Mississippi. Boston. 1844.

SMITH (John Prince). Reports of Cases argued and determined in the Court of King's Bench, together with some Cases in the High Court of Chancery, from Michaelmas Term, 44 Geo. III. (1803), to Trinity Term, 46 Geo. III. (1806). 3 vols. 2d Ed. London. 1806–7.

SMITH (Abram D.) Reports of Cases argued and determined in the Supreme Court of the State of Wisconsin, from June Term, 1853, to July Term, 1860, both inclusive. 11 vols. Milwaukee and Madison, Wis. 1854–1861. (Wisconsin Reports, Vols. 1–11.)

SMITH (Thomas L.) Reports of Cases in the Supreme Court of the State of Indiana. New Albany. 1850.

SMITH (P. Frazer). Pennsylvania State Reports. Comprising Cases adjudged in the Supreme Court of Pennsylvania. 16 vols. Philadelphia. 1867–1871. (Pennsylvania State Reports, Vols. 51–66.)

SMITH (E. Delafield). Reports of Cases argued and determined in the Court of Common Pleas for the City and County of New York. 4 vols. New York. 1855–1859.

SMITH (E. Peshine). Reports of Cases argued and determined in the Court of Appeals of the State of New York. 13 vols. New York and Albany. 1858–1865. (New York Reports, Vols. 15–27.)

SNEED (John L. T.) Reports of the Cases argued and determined in the Supreme Court of Tennessee, during the years 1853–1858. 5 vols. Nashville. 1855–1859.

SNEED'S KENTUCKY DECISIONS. Decisions of the Court of Appeals of the State of Kentucky, from March 1, 1801, to January 18, 1805, inclusive. Edited by Harvey Myers. Cincinnati. 1869.

SOUTHARD (Samuel L.) Reports of Cases argued and determined in the Supreme Court of Judicature of the State of New Jersey. 2 vols. Trenton. 1819–1820.

SOUTH CAROLINA.

Law.

Bay's Reports, 2 vols. 1783–1804.
Brevard's Reports, 3 vols. in 2. 1794–1816.
Treadway's Constitutional Court Reports, 2 vols. 1812–1816.
Mill's Constitutional Court Reports. 1817–1818.
Nott & McCord's Reports, 2 vols. 1817–1820.
McCord's Reports, 4 vols. in 2. 1820–1828.
Harper's Reports. 1823–1824.
Bailey's Reports, 2 vols. 1828–1832.
Hill's Reports, 3 vols. in 2. 1833–1837.
Riley's Reports (Law and Equity.) 1836–1837.
Dudley's Reports. 1837–1838.
Rice's Reports. 1838–1839.
Cheves' Reports. 1839–1840.
McMullan Reports, 2 vols. 1835–1842.
Spear's Reports, 2 vols. 1843–1844.
Richardson's Reports, (Vols. 1–4.) 1844–1847.
Strobhart's Reports, 5 vols. 1846–1850.
Richardson's Reports, (Vols. 5–12.) 1850–1860.
Richardson's Reports, (Vol. 13, Law; and Vol. 12, Equity.) 1860–1866.
Richardson's Reports, (Vols. 14–15.) 1866–1868.

Chancery.

Dessaussure's Reports, 4 vols. in 2. 1785–1813.
Harper's Reports. 1824.
McCord's Chancery Reports, 2 vols. in 1. 1825–1827.
Bailey's Chancery Reports. 1830–1831.
Richardson's Chancery Cases. 1831–1832.
Hill's Chancery Reports, 2 vols. 1833–1838.
Riley's Chancery Reports. 1836–1837.
Dudley's Equity Reports. 1837–1838.
Rice's Chancery Reports. 1838–1839.
Cheves' Chancery Reports. 1839–1840.
McMullan's Chancery Reports, 1840–1842.
Spear's Equity Reports, 1842–1844.
Richardson's Equity Reports, (Vols. 1–2.) 1844–1846.
Strobhart's Equity Reports. 1846–1850.
Richardson's Equity Reports, Vols 3–14. 1850–1868.

SPEARS (R. H.) Reports of Cases at Law argued and determined in the Court of Appeals and Court of Errors of South Carolina. From November, 1842, to May, 1844, both inclusive. 2 vols. Columbia, S. C. 1843–1844.

SPECIAL TRIALS.
- Addison.
- Bashford vs. Barstow.
- Burr (Aaron).
- Chase (Samuel).
- Conspiracy Trial.
- D'Hauteville Case.
- Freeman (William).
- Hanway's Case.
- Hubbell (Levi).
- Indiana Treason Trials.
- Johnson (Andrew).
- Judges, The (Shippen, Yeates and Smith).
- Peck (Judge James H.)
- Pennsylvania State Trials.
- Porter (Commodore David).
- Remarkable Trials.
- Surratt (John H.)
- Vallandigham (Clement L.)

SPEERS (R. H.) Equity Cases argued and determined in the Court of Appeals of South Carolina, from November, 1842, to May, 1844, both inclusive. Vol. 1. Columbia, S. C. 1844.

SPENCER (William A.) Reports of Cases argued and determined in the Supreme Court of Minnesota. 6 vols. Chicago and Saint Paul. 1866–1871. (Minnesota Reports, Vols. 10–15.)

SPENCER'S REPORTS. Supreme Court of New Jersey. November Term, 1842, to October Term, 1846. Four Parts in One Vol. Camden, N. J., and Princeton, N. J. 1844–1847.

SPOONER (Philip L.) Reports of Cases argued and determined in the Supreme Court of the State of Wisconsin. Containing the Cases determined from January Term, 1860, to June Term, 1862. 4 vols. Madison, Wis. 1861–1864. (Wisconsin Reports, Vols. 12–15).

SPRAGUE'S DECISIONS. Decisions of Hon. Peleg Sprague, in Admiralty and Maritime Causes in the District Court of the United States for the District of Massachusetts. 1841–1864. 2 vols. Philadelphia. 1861–1868.

STANTON (Edwin M.) Reports of Cases argued and determined in the Supreme Court of the State of Ohio, in Bank. 3 vols. Columbus. 1843–1845. (Ohio Reports, Vols. 11–13.)

STARKIE (Thomas.) Reports of Cases determined at Nisi Prius, in the Courts of King's Bench and Common Pleas, and on the Circuit, from the Sittings after Michaelmas Term, 55 Geo. III. (1814), to the Sittings after Michaelmas Term, 60 Geo. III. (1819.) 2 vols. London. 1817–20.

The Same. 2 vols. Philadelphia. 1836. (Eng. Com. Law Reps., Vols. 2 and 3.)

STEWART (George N.) Reports of Cases argued and determined in the Supreme Court of Alabama, embracing the decisions made in the years 1827–1830, and in January Term, 1831, at Law and in Equity. 3 vols. Tuscaloosa. 1830–1835.

STEWART (George N.) and PORTER (Benjamin F.) Reports of Cases at Law and in Equity argued and determined in the Supreme Court of Alabama. 5 vols. Tuscaloosa. 1836–1837.

STILES (Edward H.) Reports of Cases in Law and Equity determined in the Supreme Court of the State of Iowa. 9 vols. Ottumwa. 1867–1872. (Iowa Reports, Vols. 22–30.)

STOCKETT (J. Schaaff). Reports of Cases argued and determined in the Court of Appeals of Maryland. Containing the Cases from April Term, 1867, to October Term, 1870, both inclusive. 7 vols. Baltimore. 1869–1871. (Maryland Reports, Vols. 27–33.)

STOCKTON (John P.) Reports of Cases determined in the Court of Chancery, and on Appeal, in the Court of Errors and Appeals, of the State of New Jersey. 3 vols. Trenton. 1856–1860.

STORY (William W.) Reports of Cases argued and determined in the Circuit Court of the United States for the First Circuit. 3 vols. Boston. 1842–1847.

STRANGE (Sir John). Reports of adjudged Cases in the Courts of Chancery, King's Bench, Common Pleas and Exchequer, from Trinity Term, 2d Geo. I., to Trinity Term, 21 Geo. II. 2d Ed. 2 vols. London. 1782.

STRINGFELLOW (B. F.) Reports of Cases argued and decided in the Supreme Court of the State of Missouri. 3 vols. Jefferson City. 1848–1851. (Missouri Reports, Vols. 9–11.)

STROBHART (James A.) Reports of Cases argued and determined in the Court of Appeals and Court of Errors of South Carolina, on Appeals from the Courts of Law. 5 vols. Charleston. 1847–1851.

Reports of Cases in Equity argued and determined in the Court of Appeals and in the Court of Errors of South

Carolina, from November, 1846, to May Term, 1850. 4 vols. Charleston, S. C. 1848-1851.

STYLE (William). Narrationes Modernae, or Modern Reports begun in the now Upper Bench Court at Westminster, in the beginning of Hilary Term, 21 Caroli., and continued to the end of Michaelmas Term, 1655, as well on the Criminall, as on the Pleas Side. Most of which time the Lord Chief Justice Roll gave the rule there. Folio. London. 1658.

SUMNER (Charles). Reports of Cases argued and determined in the Circuit Court of the United States for the First Circuit. 3 vols. Boston. 1836-1841.

SURRATT (John H.) Trial of John H. Surratt in the Criminal Court for the District of Columbia, Hon. George P. Fisher. 2 vols. Washington. 1867.

SWABEY (M. C. Merttins) and Tristram (Thomas Hutchinson.) Reports of Cases decided in the Court of Probate and in the Court for Divorce and Matrimonial Causes, from Hil. T., 1858, to Mich. T., 1864. 3 vols. London and Dublin. 1860-5.

The Same. 1865-6. Vol. 4. London and Dublin. 1871.

SWAN (WILLIAM G.) Reports of the Cases argued and determined in the Spreme Court of Tennessee, during the years 1851-1853. 2 vols. Nashville. 1853-1854.

SWANSTON (Clement Tredway.) Reports of Cases argued and determined in the High Court of Chancery, during the Time of Lord Chancellor Eldon. From the Commencement of the Sittings before Hilary Term, 1818, the end of the Sittings after Michaelmas Term, 1819. 3 vols. New York. 1828.

SWEENY (James M.) Reports of Cases argued and determined in the Superior Court of the City of New York. 2 vols. New York and Albany. 1871.

TAMLYN (John). Condensed Reports of Cases decided in the High Court of Chancery, by Right Hon. Sir John John Leach. Philadelphia. 1833. (English Chancery Reports, Vol. 5).

TANEY'S Circuit Court Decisions. (See CAMPBELL, J. M.)

TANNER (Gordon). Reports of Cases argued and determined in the Supreme Court of Judicature of the State of Indiana. Containing the Cases decided from November Term, 1856, to May Term, 1860, inclusive. 7 vols.

Cincinnati and Indianpolis. 1857–1861. (Indiana Reports, Vols. 8–14).

TAPPAN (Benjamin). Cases decided in the Courts of Common Pleas, in the Fifth Circuit of the State of Ohio; commencing with May Term, 1816. To which is added the opinion of Judge McLean in the case of Lauderback vs. Moore. Steubenville. 1831.

TAUNTON (William Pyle.) Reports of Cases argued and determined in the Court of Common Pleas, and other Courts, from Michaelmas Term, 48 Geo. III. (1807), to Easter Term, 53 Geo. III. (1809), both inclusive. 2d Ed. 4 vols. London and Philadelphia. 1815–50.

Reports of Cases argued and determined in the Court of Common Pleas and other Courts, from Trinity Term, 53 Geo. III., (1813), to Trinity Term, 58 Geo. III. (1817). Vols. 5–8. Philadelphia. 1834–36. (Eng. Com. Law Reps., Vols. 1, 2 and 4.)

TAYLOR (J. L.) North Carolina Reports, embracing the "Carolina Law Repository," containing "Opinions of American jurists, and Reports of Cases adjudged in the Supreme Court of North Carolina." Vols. 1 and 2. Also, "North Carolina Term Reports," or "Cases adjudged in the Supreme Court of North Carolina, from July Term, 1816, to January Term, 1818, inclusive." Second Edition. By William H. Battle, Esq. Raleigh. 1844.

North Carolina Reports, embracing "Cases determined in the Superior Courts of Law and Equity of the State of North Carolina." By John Louis Taylor; also, "Reports of Cases ruled and determined by the Court of Conference of North Carolina." By Duncan Cameron and William Norwood, of Hillsborough. Second Edition. By William H. Battle, Esq., Raleigh. 1844.

TENNESSEE.

Overton's Tennessee Reports, 2 vols. in 1. 1791–1815.
Cook's Reports. 1811–1814.
Haywood's Reports, 3 vols. in 1. 1816–1818.
Peck's Reports. } 2 vols. in 1. { 1822–1824.
Martin & Yerger's Reports. } 2 vols. in 1. { 1825–1828.
Yerger's Reports, 10 vols. 1832–1837.
Meigs' Reports. 1838–1839.
Humphrey's Reports, 11 vols. 1839–1851.
Swan's Reports, 2 vols. 1851–1853.
Sneed's Reports, 5 vols. 1853–1858.
Head's Reports, 3 vols. 1859–1860.
Coldwell's Reports, 6 vols. 1860–1869.
Heiskell's Tennessee Reports, 2 vols. 1870–1871.

TERM REPORTS. See DURNFORD & EAST.

TEXAS.

Texas Reports, 32 vols. 1846–1866.
Webb & Duval, (Vols. 1–3.)
Hartley (O. C.), (Vols. 4–10.)
Hartley (O. C. & R. K.), (Vols. 11–21.)
Moore & Walker, (Vols. 22–24.)
Walker, (Vol. 25.)
Paschal, (Supplement to Vol. 25.)
Robards & Jackson, (Vols. 26, 27.)
Paschal, (Vol. 28.)
Wheelock, (Vol. 32.)

TIFFANY (Joel.) Reports of Cases argued and determined in the Court of Appeals of the State of New York. 12 vols. Albany. 1865–1869. (New York Reports, Vols. 28–39.)

THOMPSON (R. Aug.) Reports of Cases determined in the Supreme Court of the State of California at the January, April and July Terms, 1870. San Francisco. 1871. (California Reports, Vol. 39.)

TOMLINS (T. E.) See REPERTORIUM JURIDICUM.

TOTHILL (Will.) Transactions of the High Court of Chancery both by Practice and Precedent, with the Fees thereunto belonging, and all Special Orders in extraordinary cases which are to be found in the Register's Office, as as they are quoted by terms, years and books. 16mo. 1649.

TREADWAY. Reports of Judicial Decisions in the Constitutional Court of the State of South Carolina; held at Charleston and Columbia, during the years 1812 to 1816. To which is added two cases determined in the Court of Equity in the year 1822. In two volumes. Charleston. 1823.

TUCKER (Gideon J.) Reports of Cases argued and determined in the Surrogate's Court of the County of New York. Vol. 1. New York and Albany. 1870.

TURNER (G. J.) and RUSSELL (J.) Reports of Cases determined in the High Court of Chancery during the time of Lord Chancellor Eldon. Philadelphia. 1840. (English Chancery Reports, Vol. 11.)

TUTTLE (Charles A.) Reports of Cases determined in the Supreme Court of the State of California. 10 vols. San Francisco. 1864–1867. (California Reports, Vols. 23–32.)

TYLER (Royall). Reports of Cases argued and determined in the Supreme Court of Judicature of the State of Vermont. Commencing with the Nineteenth Century. 2 vols. New York. 1809–1810.

TYNG (Dudley Atkyns). Reports of Cases argued and determined in the Supreme Judicial Court of the Commonwealth of Massachusetts, from March Term, 1806, to March Term, 1822. 16 vols. Boston. 1823–1833. (Massachusetts Reports, Vols. 2–17).

TYRWHITT (Robert Philip). Reports of Cases argued and determined in the Courts of Exchequer and Exchequer Chamber, from Michaelmas Term, 1 Will. IV. (1830), to Trinity Term, 5 Will. IV. (1835), both inclusive. London. 1832–7.

TYRWHITT (Robert Philip) and GRANGER (Thomas Colpitts) Reports of Cases argued and determined in the Courts of Exchequer and Exchequer Chamber, from Michaelmas Term, 6 Will. IV. (1835), to Trinity Term, 6 Will. IV. (1836), both inclusive. London. 1837.

VALLANDIGHAM (Clement L.) The Trial of, by a Military Commission, and the Proceedings under his application for a writ of Habeas Corpus in the Circuit Court of the United States for the Southern District of Ohio. Cincinnati. 1863.

VAN NESS (William P.) Reports of Two Cases determined in the Prize Court for the New York District. New York. 1814.

VAUGHAN (Sir John). The Reports and Arguments of that Learned Judge, Sir John Vaughan, Kt., late Lord Chief Justice of the Court of Common Pleas, being all of them special cases; and many wherein he pronounced the Resolution of the whole court of Common Pleas, at the time he was Chief Justice there. Folio. London. 1706.

VEAZEY (Wheelock G.) Reports of Cases argued and determined in the Supreme Court of the State of Vermont. 8 vols. Rutland and Montpelier. 1865–1871. (Vermont Reports, Vols. 36–43.)

VENTRIS (Sir Peyton). The First Part of the Reports of Sir Peyton Ventris, Kt., late one of the Justices of the Common Pleas: Containing select cases Adjudged in the Court of King's Bench, in the Reign of K. Charles II. With three learned arguments, one in the King's Bench, by Sir Francis North, when *Attorney General;* and two in the Exchequer, by Sir Matthew Hale when

Lord Chief Baron. The Second Part : Containing Select Cases adjudged in the Court of Common Pleas in the Reigns of K. Charles II. and K. James II., and in the three first years of the Reign of K. William and Q. Mary ; also Several Cases and the Pleadings thereon in the Exchequer Chamber upon Writs of Error from the King's Bench, together with many remarkable and curious Cases in the Court of Chancery. Both Parts bound in one volume. Folio. London. 1701.

VERNON (Thomas). Cases argued and adjudged in the High Court of Chancery. 1st Am., from the 3d London Edition. 2 vols. Brookfield, Mass. 1829.

VERMONT.

D. Chipman's Reports, 2 vols. in 1. 1789–1825.
Tyler's Reports, 2 vols. 1801–1803.
Brayton's Reports. 1815–1819.
Aiken's Reports, 2 vols. 1826–1827.
Vermont Reports, 43 vols. 1826–1871.
Vols. 1–9, by the Judges of the Court.
Shaw, (Vols. 10–11).
Weston, (Vols. 12–14).
Slade, (Vol. 15).
Washburn, (Vols. 16–23.)
Deane, (Vols. 24–26).
Williams, (Vols. 27–29).
Shaw, (Vols. 30–35).
Veazey, (Vols. 36–43).

VESEY (Francis, Sen.) Reports of Cases argued and determined in the High Court of Chancery, in the time of Lord Chancellor Hardwicke, from the year 1746–7 to 1755. 2 vols. By Robert Bell. 1st Am., from the last London Edition. Philadelphia, 1831.

VESEY (FRANCIS, Jr.) Reports of Cases argued and determined in the High Court Chancery. 1st. Am. from the 3d. London Edition. 20 vols. Philadelphia. 1821–2.

A Supplement to the Reports of. By John Ekyn Hovenden. 2 vols. Philadelphia. 1828.

Vesey (Francis), and Beames (John). Reports of Cases argued and determined in the High Court of Chancery, in the time of Lord Chancellor Eldon. 1st. Am. from the 2d London Edition. 3 vols. Philadelphia. 1822.

VIRGIN (Wm. Wirt.) Reports of Cases in Law and Equity determined by the Supreme Judicial Court of Maine. 7 vols. Hallowell and Portland. 1866–1870. (Maine Reports, Vols. 52–58.)

VIRGINIA—

Jefferson's Reports { 1730–1740. 1768–1772.

Wythe's Chancery Reports, 1788–1799.

Washington's Reports, 2 vols. 1790–1796.

Virginia Cases, 2 vols. 1789–1826.

Call's Reports, 6 vols. 1790–1825.

Henning & Munford's Reports, 4 vols. 1806–1809.

Munford's Reports, 6 vols. 1810–1820.

Gilmer's Reports, 6 vols. 1820—1821.

Randolph's Reports. 1821–1828.

Leigh's Reports, 12 vols. 1829–1841.

Robinson's Reports, 2 vols. 1842–1844.

Grattan's Reports, 20 vols. 1844–1871.

Patton, Jr., & Heaths Reports, (Special Court of Appeals), 2 vols. 1855–1857.

VIRGINIA CASES. Vol. 1. A collection of Cases decided by the General Court of Virginia, chiefly relating to the Penal Laws of the Commonwealth. Commencing in the year 1789, and ending in 1814. Copied from the Records of said Court, with explanatory notes, by Judges Brockenbrough and Holmes. Philadelphia. 1815.

Vol. 2, Virginia Cases, or Decisions of the General Court of Virginia, chiefly on the Criminal Law of the Commonwealth, commencing June Term, 1815, and ending June Term, 1826. With an Index to both vols. By William Brockenbrough, one of the Judges of that Court. Richmond. 1826.

VROOM (Peter D.) Reports of Cases argued and determined in the Supreme Court and the court of Errors and Appeals of the State of New Jersey. 5 vols. Trenton. 1866–1871. New Jersey Reports, Vols. 30–34.

WALKER (Henry N.) Reports of Cases argued and determined in the Court of Chancery of the State of Michigan. Detroit. 1845.

WALKER (R. J.) Reports of Cases adjudged in the Supreme Court of Mississippi. Natchez. 1834.

WALKER (Richard S.) Reports of Cases argued aud decided in the Supreme Court of the State of Texas, during part of the Galveston Session, and the Tyler Session, 1860. Austin. 1867. (Texas Reports, Vol. 25.)

WALLACE (John B.) Reports of Cases adjudged in the Circuit Court of the United States for the Third Circuit. Second Edition. Philadelphia. 1838.

WALLACE (John William). Cases in the Circuit Court of the United States for the Third Circuit, with an Appendix. 2 vols. Philadelphia. 1849.

WALLACE (John William). Cases argued and adjudged in the Supreme Court of the United States, from December Term, 1863, to December Term, 1870. 11 vols. Washington, D. C. 1864–1871.

WARDEN (Robert B.) Reports of Cases argued and determined in the Supreme Court of Ohio. New Series. 3 vols. Cincinnati. 1855–1856. (Ohio State Reports, Vols. 2–4.)

WARE (Ashur). Reports of Cases argued and determined in the District Court of the United States, for the District of Maine. 1822–1839. Second Edition, with Cases in 1854–1855. Boston. 1856.

WASHBURNE (Peter T.) Reports of Cases argued and determined in the Supreme Court of the State of Vermont. New Series. 8 vols. Woodstock. 1845–1852. (Vermont Reports, Vols. 16–23.)

WASHINGTON (Bushrod). Reports of Cases determined in the Circuit Court of the United States for the Third Circuit, comprising the Districts of Pennsylvania and New Jersey; commencing at April Term, 1803. Second Edition. 4 vols. Philadelphia. 1852–1853.

Reports of Cases argued and determined in the Court of Appeals of Virginia. Second Edition. 2 vols. Philadelphia. 1823.

WATTS (Frederick). Reports of Cases argued and determined in the Supreme Court of Pennsylvania, from May, 1832, to September, 1840. 10 vols. Philadelphia. 1834–1841.

WATTS (Frederick) and SERGEANT (Henry J.) Reports of Cases adjudged in the Supreme Court of Pennsylvania. Containing the cases decided from May Term, 1841, to May Term, 1845. 9 vols. Philadelphia and Pittsburg. 1842–1846.

WEBB (James.) and DUVAL (Thomas H.) Reports of Cases argued and decided in the Supreme Court of the State of Texas, from December Term, 1846, to December Term, 1848, inclusive. 3 vols. Galveston and Austin. 1848–1851. (Texas Reports, Vols. 1–3.)

WELSBY (W. N.), HURLSTONE (E. T.) and GORDON (J.) The Exchequer Reports. Reports of Cases argued and determined in the Courts of Exchequer and Exchequer Chamber, from Trinity Term, 10 Vict., to Easter Term,

17 Vict., both inclusive. 9 vols. Philadelphia. 1849–1850. (Exchequer Reports, Vols. 1-9.)

WENDELL (John L.) Reports of Cases argued and determined by the Supreme Court of Judicature and in the Court for the Trial of Impeachments and the Correction of Errors of the State of New York. 26 vols. Albany and New York. 1829–1842.

WEST (Martin John). Reports of Cases argued and determined in the High Court of Chancery, from 1736 to July, 1739. Vol. 1. London. 1827.

WESTON (William). Reports of Cases argued and determined in the Supreme Court of the State of Vermont. Third Series. 3 vols. Burlington. 1841–1843. (Vermont Reports, Vols. 12–14.)

WEST VIRGINIA.

Hagan's Reports, of the Supreme Court of Appeals. 1863–1869. 3 vols. Morgantown, Va. 1866–69.

WHARTON (Thomas I.) Reports of Cases adjudged in the Supreme Court of Pennsylvania in the Eastern District. Containing the Cases decided from December Term, 1835, to March Term, 1841, both inclusive. 6 vols. Philadelphia. 1836.

WHEATON (Henry). Reports of Cases argued and adjudged in the Supreme Court of the United States, from February Term, 1816, to January Term, 1827. New York. 1827.

WHEELER (Jacob D.) Reports of Criminal Law Cases, with Notes and References, containing, also, a view of the Criminal Laws of the United States. 3 vols. Albany and New York. 1825–1851.

WHITTLESEY (Chas. C.) Reports of Cases argued and determined in the Supreme Court of the State of Missouri. 10 vols. St. Louis. 1863–1868. (Missouri Reports, Vols. 32–41.)

WIGHTWICK (John). Reports of Cases argued and determined in the Court of Exchequer. From the Sittings after Hilary Term, 50 Geo. III. (1810), to the Sittings after Easter Term, 51 Geo. III. (1811). Philadelphia. 1835. (English Exchequer Reports, Vol. 6.)

WILLES (Lord Chief Justice). Reports of adjudged Cases in the Court of Common Pleas, during the time Lord Chief Justice Willes presided in that Court. By Charles Durnford. Philadelphia. 1802.

WILLIAMS (William Peere). Reports of Cases argued and determined in the High Court of Chancery, and of some

Special Cases Adjudged in the Court of King's Bench. 1st Am., from the last London Edition. 3 vols. Philadelphia. 1823–4.

WILLIAMS (John Griffith). Cases in Equity during the time of the late Lord Chancellor Talbot. Dublin. 1793.

WILLIAMS (Ephraim). Reports of Cases argued and determined in the Supreme Judicial Court of the Commonwealth of Massachusetts. From September, 1804, to June, 1805, both inclusive. Third Edition. Exeter, N. H. 1821. (Massachusetts Reports, Vol. 1.)

WILLIAMS (Charles L.) Reports of Cases argued and determined in the Supreme Court of the State of Vermont. 3 vols. Rutland. 1856–1858. (Vermont Reports, Vols. 27–29.)

WILCOX (P. B.) Reports of Cases argued and determined in the Supreme Court of Ohio in Bank. Columbus. 1842. (Ohio Reports, Vol. 10.)

WILMOT (Sir John Eardley). Notes of Opinions and Judgments delivered in different Courts by the Right Honorable Sir John Eardley Wilmot, Knt., late Lord Chief Justice of the Court of Common Pleas, and one of his Majesty's most Honorable Privy Council. 4to. 1802.

WILSON (George.) Reports of the Cases argued and adjudged in the King's Courts at Westminister, from 1743 to 1774. In three parts. 3d. Ed. 3 vols. Dublin. 1784.

WILSON. Cases in the Exchequer. Vol. 1, Pt. 1. 1805–17. [No title page.]

WILSON (John). Cases in Chancery. 1818 and 1819. Vol. 1 in three parts, and Vol. 2, Part 1. [No title page.]

WILSON (Jos. G.) Reports of Cases argued and determined in the Supreme Court of the Territory of Oregon, and of the State of Oregon. 2 vols. New York. 1862–1869.

WINSTON. Cases at Law argued and determined in the Supreme Court of North Carolina, during June Term of the years 1863 and 1864. [No title page.]

Cases at law decided at the Extra Term, commencing on the 26th of October, 1864. Cases in Equity argued and determined in the Supreme Court of North Carolina, Juue and December Terms, 1864. [No title page.]

WINCH (Sir Humphrey.) Reports of that Reverend and Learned Judge, Sir Humphrey Winch, Knight; Sometime one of the Judges of the Court of Common Pleas. Containing many choice cases, and excellent matters touching Declarations, Pleadings, Demurrers, Judgments, and

Resolutions, in Points of Law, in the four last years of the Raign of King James. 4to. London. 1657.

WISCONSIN.

Burnett's Reports. 1842.

Chandler's Reports. 4 vols. 1849–1852.

Wisconsin Reports. 26 vols. 1853–1870.

Smith (Vols. 1–11). 1853–1860.

Spooner (Vols. 12–15). 1861–1862.

Conover (Vols. 16–26). 1862–1870.

WYTHE (George). Decisions of Cases in Virginia by the High Court of Chancery, with remarks upon Decrees, by the Court of Appeals, reversing some of those Decisions. Richmond. 1852.

WITHROW (Thos. F.) Reports of Cases in Law and Equity, determined in the Supreme Court of the State of Iowa. 13 vols. Des Moines and Chicago. 1860–1868. (Iowa Reports, Vols. 9–21.)

WOLFERSTAN (F. S. P.) and BRISTOWE (S. B.) Reports of the Decisions of Election Committees during the Eighteenth Parliament of the United Kingdom. 1859–1864. 12mo. London. 1865.

WOLFERSTAN (F. S. P.) and DEW (Edward L'Estrange). Reports of the Decisions of Committees of the House of Commons in the Trial of Controverted Elections, during the Seventeenth Parliament of the United Kingdom. Vol. 1. 1857. 12mo. London. 1859.

WOODBURY (Charles L.) and MINOT (George). Reports of Cases argued and determined in the Circuit Court of the United States for the First Circuit. 3 vols. Boston. 1847–1852.

WOOLWORTH (James M.) Reports of Cases in the Supreme Court of Nebraska. Chicago. 1871. (Nebraska Reports, Vol. 1.)

WRIGHT (Robert E.) Pennsylvania State Reports. Comprising Cases adjudged in the Supreme Court of Pennsylvania. Containing Cases decided from May Term, 1860, to May Term, 1865, both inclusive. 14 vols. Philadelphia. 1861–1866. (Pennsylvania State Reports, Vols. 37–50.)

WRIGHT (John C.) Reports of Cases at Law and in Chancery decided by the Supreme Court of Ohio, during the years 1831 to 1834. Columbus, Ohio. 1835.

YATES (John V. N.) Select Cases adjudged in the Courts of the State cf New York. Vol. 1. New York. 1811.

YATES (Jasper). Reports of Cases adjudged in the Supreme Court of Pennsylvania; with some select cases at Nisi Prius, and in the Circuit Courts. 4 vols. Philadelphia. 1817–1819.

YEAR BOOKS of the Reign of Edward the First during his 30th, 31st, 32d and 33d years. Edited and Translated by Alfred J. Horwood. Vols. 1 and 2. London. 1863–1864.

YEAR BOOKS. Folio. Eleven Parts, in ten vols. London. 1678–1680.

Part 1. Maynard. Edward I. and II.
Part 2. 1–10, Edward III.
Part 3. 17–39, Edward III.
Part 4. 40–50, Edward III.
Part 5. Liber Assisarum, 1–51, Edward III.
Part 6. 1–14, Henry IV. 1–9, Henry V.
Part 7. 1–20, Henry VI.
Part 8. 22–39, Henry VI.
Parts 9 and 10. 1–22, Edward IV. Long Quinto, 5 Edward IV.
Part 11. Edward V., Richard III., Henry VII., Henry VIII.

YELVERTON (Sir Henry). The Reports of Sir Henry Yelverton, Knight and Baronet, late one of the Justices of the Court of Common Pleas, of divers special Cases in the Court of King's Bench, as well in the latter end of the Reign of Q. Elizabeth, as in the first Ten Years of K. James. 4th Edition. Dublin. 1792.

YERGER (Geo. S.) Reports of Cases argued and determined in the Supreme Court of Tennessee. 10 vols. Nashville. 1832–1838.

YOUNGE (Edward). Reports of Cases argued and determined in the Court of Exchequer in Equity; from Trinity Term, 11 Geo. IV., to Michaelmas Term, 2 Will. IV., both inclusive. Vol. 1. London and Dublin. 1833.

YOUNGE (Edward) and COLLYER (John). Reports of Cases argued and determined in the Court of Exchequer in Equity; from Trinity Term, 4 Will. IV., to Trinity Vacation, 4 and 5 Vict., both inclusive. 4 vols. London and Dublin. 1836–46.

YOUNGE (Edward) and JERVIS (JOHN.) Reports of Cases argued and determined in the Courts of Exchequer and Exchequer Chamber, at Law, in Equity, and in Error, from Michaelmas Term, 7 Geo. IV., to Hilary Term, 10 & 11

Geo. IV., both inclusive. J. I. Clark Hare and H. B. Wallace, Editors. 3 vols. Philadelphia. 1852–3.

ZABRISKIE (A. O.) Reports of Cases argued and determined in the Supreme Court and the Court of Errors and Appeals of the State of New Jersey, from July Term, 1847, to March Term, 1855, inclusive. 4 vols. New Brunswick and Trenton. 1849–1856.

CHRONOLOGICAL LIST OF BRITISH LAW REPORTS.

ENGLISH.

REPORTERS.	Date of last Edition.	No. of Vols.	Size.	Period.
HOUSE OF LORDS.				
Shower	1740	1	folio.	1694 to 1699
Colles	1789	1	8vo.	1697 to 1714
Brown, by Tomlins	1803	8	roy. 8vo.	1702 to 1800
Dow	....	6	roy. 8vo.	1812 to 1818
Bligh and Part 1 of Vol. IV.	....	3	roy. 8vo.	1819 to 1821
Bligh. *New Series* and Parts 1, 2 and 3, Vol. XI.	....	10	roy. 8vo.	1827 to 1837
Dow and Clark	....	2	roy. 8vo.	1827 to 1832
Clark and Finnelly	....	12	roy. 8vo.	1831 to 1846
Maclean and Robinson	....	1	roy. 8vo.	1839
West	....	1	roy. 8vo.	1839 to 1841
House of Lord's Cases (Clark)	....	11	roy. 8vo.	1847 to 1865
PRIVY COUNCIL.				
Acton and Part 1, Vol. II.	....	1	roy. 8vo.	1809 to 1811
Knapp	....	3	roy. 8vo.	1829 to 1836
Moore	....	15	roy. 8vo.	1836 to 1861
Moore. *New Series*	....	7	roy. 8vo.	1862 to 1871
Moore. The Gorham case	....	1	roy. 8vo.	1850
Moore. East India Appeals	....	13	roy. 8vo.	1836 to 1871
CHANCERY.				
Cary	1820	1	12mo.	1557 to 1604
Choice Cases in Chancery	1672	1	12mo.	1557 to 1606
Tothill	1820	1	12mo.	1559 to 1646
Dickens	1803	2	roy. 8vo.	1559 to 1798
Reports in Chancery	1736	1	folio.	1615 to 1712
Nelson	1717	1	8vo.	1625 to 1693
Equity Cases Abridged	1739–69	2	folio.	
Cases in Chancery	1835	1	folio.	1660 to 1688

Chronological List, English Reports—continued.

Reporters.	Date of last Edition.	No. of Vols.	Size.	Period.
CHANCERY—continued.				
Freeman	1823	1	roy. 8vo.	1660 to 1706
Finch (Sir H.)	1725	1	folio.	1673 to 1681
Vernon	1828	2	roy. 8vo.	1681 to 1720
Finch's Precedents	1786	1	roy. 8vo.	1689 to 1723
Peere Williams	1826	3	roy. 8vo.	1695 to 1736
Gilbert	1742	1	folio.	1705 to 1727
Select Cases temp. King	1850	1	roy. 8vo.	1724 to 1734
Moseley	1803	1	8vo.	1726 to 1731
Kelynge (W.)	1764	1	folio	1731 to 1736
Talbot, Cases temp	1793	1	8vo.	1734 to 1738
West	1827	1	roy. 8vo.	1736 to 1739
Atkyns	1794	3	roy. 8vo.	1736 to 1755
Ambler	1828	2	roy. 8vo.	1737 to 1784
Barnardiston	1742	1	folio.	1740 to 1741
Ridgeway temp. Hardwicke	1794	1	roy. 8vo.	1744 to 1746
Vesey, Sen., and Belt's Suppl't.	1818–25	3	roy. 8vo.	1747 to 1756
Eden	1827	2	roy. 8vo.	1757 to 1767
Brown, by Eden	1819	4	roy. 8vo.	1778 to 1794
Brown, by Belt	1820	4	roy. 8vo.	1778 to 1794
Cox	1816	2	roy. 8vo.	1783 to 1796
Vesey, Jun., with Index, and Hovenden's Supplement	1827	22	roy. 8vo.	1789 to 1816
Vesey and Beames	1818	3	roy. 8vo.	1812 to 1814
Cooper	1815	1	roy. 8vo.	1815
Merivale	....	3	roy. 8vo.	1815 to 1817
Swanston	....	3	roy. 8vo.	1818 to 1819
Wilson. 4 parts	....	1	roy. 8vo.	1818 to 1819
Jacob and Walker	....	2	roy. 8vo.	1819 to 1821
Jacob	....	1	roy. 8vo.	1821 to 1822
Turner and Russell	....	1	roy. 8vo.	1822 to 1824
Russell	....	5	roy. 8vo.	1826 to 1829
Only 2 parts 5th vol. publ'd.				
Russell and Mylne	....	2	roy. 8vo.	1829 to 1831
Mylne and Keen	....	3	roy. 8vo.	1833 to 1835
Mylne and Craig	....	5	roy. 8vo.	1836 to 1840
Craig and Phillips	....	1	roy. 8vo.	1841
Phillips	....	2	roy. 8vo.	1841 to 1849
Hall and Twells	....	2	roy. 8vo.	1848 to 1850
Macnaghten and Gordon	....	3	roy. 8vo.	1849 to 1851
De Gex, Macnaghten and Gordon	....	8	roy. 8vo.	1851 to 1857
De Gex and Jones	....	4	roy. 8vo.	1857 to 1860
De Gex, Fisher and Jones	....	4	roy. 8vo.	1860 to 1862
De Gex, Jones and Smith	....	3	roy. 8vo.	1863 to 1865
ROLLS COURT.				
Tamlyn	....	1	roy. 8vo.	1829 to 1830
Keen	....	2	roy. 8vo.	1836 to 1838
Beavan, with Index	....	36	roy. 8vo.	1838 to 1866

Chronological List, English Reports—continued.

Reporters.		Date of last Ed.	No. of Vols.	Size.	Period.
VICE-CHANCELLOR'S COURT.					
Maddock	temp. V.C's Shadwell and Kindersley.	......	6	roy. 8vo.	1815 to 1822
Simons and Stuart		......	2	roy. 8vo.	1822 to 1826
Simons		......	17	roy. 8vo.	1826 to 1849
Simons. *New series.*		......	2	roy. 8vo.	1850 to 1852
Drewry		......	4	roy. 8vo.	1852 to 1859
Drewry and Smale.		......	2	roy. 8vo.	1860 to 1861
Younge and Collyer	temp. V. C's. Knt. Bruce, Parker and Stuart.	......	2	roy. 8vo.	1841 to 1843
Collyer		......	2	roy. 8vo.	1844 to 1845
De Gex and Smale		......	5	roy. 8vo.	1846 to 1852
Smale and Giffard.		......	3	roy. 8vo.	1852 to 1857
Giffard		......	5	roy. 8vo.	1857 to 1865
Hare	temp. V. C's. Wigram, Turner and Wood.	......	11	roy. 8vo.	1841 to 1853
Kay		......	1	roy. 8vo.	1853 to 1854
Kay and Johnson		......	4	roy. 8vo.	1854 to 1858
Johnson		......	1	roy. 8vo.	1859 to 1860
Johnson & Hemm'g		......	2	roy. 8vo.	1860 to 1862
Hemming & Miller		......	2	roy. 8vo.	1862 to 1865
KING'S BENCH AND QUEEN'S BENCH.					
State Trials with Index		......	34	roy. 8vo.	1163 to 1820
Year Books		1679	11	folio.	1307 to 1537
Bellewe		1585	1	12mo.	1378 to 1400
Keilway		1688	1	folio.	1496 to 1531
Moore		1688	1	folio.	1512 to 1621
Dyer		1794	3	roy. 8vo.	1513 to 1582
Brooke's New Cases		1628	1	12mo.	1515 to 1558
March's Translation of Brooke		1651	1	12mo.	1515 to 1558
Benloe		1661	1	folio.	1531 to 1628
Leonard		1687	1	folio.	1540 to 1615
Plowden		1816	2	roy. 8vo.	1550 to 1580
Owen		1656	1	folio.	1556 to 1615
Noy		1669	1	folio.	1559 to 1649
Coke		1826	6	roy. 8vo.	1572 to 1616
Godbolt		1652	1	4to.	1575 to 1638
Croke		1790	4	roy. 8vo.	1582 to 1641
Goldesborough		1682	1	4to.	1586 to 1602
Popham		1682	1	folio.	1592 to 1627
Yelverton		1792	1	8vo.	1603 to 1613
Hobart		1724	1	folio.	1603 to 1625
Davies (Ireland)		1674	1	folio.	1604 to 1612
Ley		1659	1	folio.	1608 to 1629
Calthrop		1670	1	12mo.	1609 to 1618
Bulstrode		1688	1	folio.	1609 to 1639
Rolle		1675	2	folio.	1614 to 1625
Palmer		1721	1	folio.	1619 to 1629
Jones (W.)		1675	1	folio.	1620 to 1641
Latch		1662	1	folio.	1625 to 1628

Chronological List, English Reports—continued.

REPORTERS.	Date of last Edition.	No. of Vols.	Size.	Period.
KING'S & QUEEN'S BENCH—*con.*				
March, New Cases	1675	1	4to	1639 to 1643
Style	1658	1	folio.	1645 to 1656
Aleyn	1688	1	folio.	1646 to 1649
Siderfin	1714	2	folio.	1657 to 1670
Raymond (Sir T.)	1803	1	roy. 8vo.	1660 to 1684
Levinz	1793	3	8vo.	1660 to 1697
Keble	1685	3	folio.	1661 to 1679
Kelyng (J.)	1739	1	folio.	1662 to 1669
Saunders	1845	3	roy. 8vo.	1666 to 1673
Jones (T.)	1729	1	folio.	1667 to 1685
Ventris	1726	1	folio.	1668 to 1691
Pollexfen	1702	1	folio.	1669 to 1685
Modern	1793–6	12	roy. 8vo.	1669 to 1732
Freeman	1826	1	roy. 8vo.	1670 to 1704
Shower	1794	2	roy. 8vo.	1678 to 1695
Skinner	1728	1	folio.	1681 to 1698
Comberback	1724	1	folio.	1685 to 1699
Carthew	1743	1	folio.	1686 to 1701
Holt	1738	1	folio.	1688 to 1711
Salkeld	1795	3	roy. 8vo.	1689 to 1712
Raymond (Lord)	1790	3	roy. 8vo.	1694 to 1734
Fortescue	1748	1	folio.	1695 to 1738
Comyns	1792	2	roy. 8vo.	1695 to 1741
Sessions Cases	1760	2	8vo.	1710 to 1748
Gilbert's Cases in Law in Equity	1760	1	8vo.	1713 to 1715
Strange	1795	2	roy. 8vo.	1716 to 1749
Barnardiston	1744	2	folio.	1726 to 1735
Fitzgibbon	1732	1	folio.	1728 to 1733
Barnes' Cases of Practice	1790	1	roy. 8vo.	1732 to 1760
Ridgeway temp. Hardwicke	1794	1	roy. 8vo.	1733 to 1737
Cunningham	1770	1	folio.	1734 to 1736
Lee temp. Hardwicke	1815	1	roy. 8vo.	1733 to 1738
Andrews	1792	1	8vo.	1738 to 1740
Wilson	1799	3	roy. 8vo.	1742 to 1774
Blackstone (W.)	1828	2	roy. 8vo.	1746 to 1780
Sayer	1790	1	8vo.	1751 to 1756
Kenyon	1819–25	2	roy. 8vo.	1753 to 1760
Wilmot's Notes and Opinions	1802	1	4to.	1757 to 1770
Burrow	1812	5	roy. 8vo.	1757 to 1771
Lofft	1790	1	8vo.	1772 to 1774
Cowper	1800	2	roy. 8vo.	1774 to 1778
Douglas	1813–31	4	roy. 8vo.	1778 to 1784
Durnford and East	1817	8	roy. 8vo.	1785 to 1800
East	....	16	roy. 8vo.	1801 to 1812
Maule and Selwyn	....	6	roy. 8vo.	1813 to 1817
Barnewall and Alderson	....	5	roy. 8vo.	1817 to 1822
Barnewall and Creswell	....	10	roy. 8vo.	1822 to 1830
Barnewall and Adolphus	....	5	roy. 8vo.	1830 to 1834

Chronological List, English Reports—continued.

REPORTERS.	Date of last Edition	No. of Vols.	Size.	Period.
KING'S AND QUEEN'S BENCH—*con.*				
Adolphus and Ellis	......	12	roy. 8vo.	1834 to 1840
Queen's Bench (Adolphus and Ellis. New Series)	......	18	roy. 8vo.	1841 to 1852
Ellis and Blackburn	......	8	roy. 8vo.	1852 to 1859
Ellis, Blackburn and Ellis	......	1	roy. 8vo.	1858
Ellis and Ellis	......	3	roy. 8vo.	....
Best and Smith	......	10	roy. 8vo.	....
Dowling and Ryland	......	9	roy. 8vo.	1821 to 1827
Manning and Ryland	......	5	roy. 8vo	1827 to 1830
Nevile and Manning	......	6	roy. 8vo.	1831 to 1836
Nevile and Perry	......	3	roy. 8vo.	1836 to 1838
Perry and Davison	......	4	roy. 8vo.	1838 to 1841
Gale and Davison	......	3	roy. 8vo.	1841 to 1843
Davison and Merivale	......	1	roy. 8vo.	1843 to 1844
BAIL COURT.				
Chitty	......	2	roy. 8vo.	1819 to 1820
Dowling	......	9	roy. 8vo.	1830 to 1840
Dowling (New Series)	......	2	roy. 8vo.	1841 to 1842
Dowling and Lowndes	......	7	roy. 8vo.	1846 to 1849
Saunders and Cole	......	2	roy. 8vo.	1842 to 1848
Lowndes, Maxwell and Pollock	......	2	roy. 8vo.	1850 to 1851
Lowndes and Maxwell	......	1	roy. 8vo.	1852
COMMON PLEAS.				
Benloe and Dalison	1689	1	folio.	1486 to 1580
Anderson	1664	1	folio.	1534 to 1605
Brownlow and Goldesborough	1675	1	4to.	1569 to 1624
Saville	1688	1	folio.	1580 to 1594
Hutton	1682	1	folio.	1612 to 1639
Bridgman (Sir J.)	1659	1	folio.	1613 to 1621
Winch	1657	1	folio.	1621 to 1625
Littleton	1683	1	folio.	1626 to 1632
Hetley	1657	1	folio.	1627 to 1632
Bridgman (Sir Orlando)	1823	1	roy. 8vo.	1660 to 1667
Carter	1688	1	folio.	1664 to 1776
Vaughan	1706	1	folio.	1665 to 1674
Lutwyche	1704	2	folio.	1682 to 1704
Lutwyche, translated by Nelson	1718	1	folio.	1682 to 1704
Cooke	1747	2	8vo.	1706 to 1747
Willes	1800	1	8vo.	1737 to 1760
Blackstone (H.)	1827	2	roy. 8vo.	1788 to 1796
Bosanquet and Puller	1826	5	roy. 8vo.	1796 to 1807
Taunton	......	8	roy. 8vo.	1803 to 1819
Broderip and Bingham	......	3	roy. 8vo.	1819 to 1822
Bingham	......	10	roy. 8vo.	1822 to 1834
Bingham's New Cases	......	6	roy. 8vo.	1834 to 1840
Manning and Granger	......	7	roy. 8vo.	1840 to 1844

Chronological List, English Reports—continued.

REPORTERS.	Date of last Edition.	No. of Vols.	Size.	Period.
COMMON PLEAS—*continued.*				
Common Bench, with Index	....	19	roy. 8vo.	1845 to 1856
Common Bench, New Series	....	20	roy. 8vo.	1856 to 1865
Marshall	....	2	roy. 8vo.	1814 to 1816
Moore	....	12	roy. 8vo.	1817 to 1818
Moore and Payne	....	5	roy. 8vo.	1828 to 1831
Moore and Scott	....	4	roy. 8vo.	1831 to 1834
Scott	....	8	roy. 8vo.	1834 to 1840
Scott's New Reports	....	8	roy. 8vo.	1840 to 1845
EXCHEQUER.				
Jenkins	1777	1	folio.	1220 to 1623
Lane	1657	1	folio.	1605 to 1612
Hardres	1792	1	8vo.	1655 to 1669
Bunbury	1793	1	8vo.	1713 to 1742
Parker	1791	1	8vo.	1743 to 1767
Anstruther	1817	3	roy. 8vo.	1792 to 1797
Forest	....	1	roy. 8vo.	1801
Wightwick	....	1	roy. 8vo.	1810 to 1811
Price	....	13	roy. 8vo.	1814 to 1824
McCleland	....	1	roy. 8vo.	1824
McCleland and Younge	....	1	roy. 8vo.	1825
Younge and Jervis	....	3	roy. 8vo.	1826 to 1830
Crompton and Jervis	....	2	roy. 8vo.	1830 to 1832
Crompton and Meeson	.....	2	roy. 8vo.	1832 to 1834
Crompton, Meeson, and Roscoe	....	2	roy. 8vo.	1834 to 1836
Meeson and Welsby	....	16	roy. 8vo.	1836 to 1847
Exchequer Reports (Welsby, Hurlstone, and Gordon)	....	11	roy. 8vo.	1847 to 1856
Hurlstone and Norman	....	7	roy. 8vo.	1856 to 1861
Hurlstone and Coltman	....	4	roy. 8vo.	1862
Tyrrwhitt	....	5	roy. 8vo.	1830 to 1835
Tyrrwhitt and Granger	....	1	roy. 8vo.	1836
EXCHEQUER, EQUITY.				
Wilson. 1 part	....	......	roy. 8vo.	1817
Daniell	....	1	roy. 8vo.	1817 to 1819
Younge	....	1	roy. 8vo.	1830 to 1832
Younge and Collyer	....	4	roy. 8vo.	1833 to 1841
NISI PRIUS.				
Peake	1820–29	2	roy. 8vo.	1790 to 1812
Espinasse	....	6	roy. 8vo.	1793 to 1807
Campbell	....	4	roy. 8vo.	1808 to 1816
Holt	....	1	roy. 8vo.	1815 to 1817
Starkie; and Vol. III, part 1	....	2	roy. 8vo.	1815 to 1822
Gow	....	1	roy. 8vo.	1818 to 1820

Chronological List, English Reports—continued.

REPORTERS.	Date of last Edition	No. of Vols.	Size.	Period.
NISI PRIUS—continued.				
Dowling and Ryland. 1 part	......	.. ..	roy. 8vo.	1822 to 1823
Ryan and Moody	.....	1	roy. 8vo.	1823 to 1826
Carrington and Payne	......	9	roy. 8vo.	1823 to 1841
Moody and Malkin	......	1	roy. 8vo.	1827 to 1830
Moody and Robinson	......	2	roy. 8vo.	1831 to 1844
Carrington and Marshman	.....	1	roy. 8vo.	1840 to 1842
Carrington and Kirwan, and Vol. III, parts 1 and 2	......	2	roy. 8vo.	1843 to 1850
Foster and Finlason	......	4	roy. 8vo.	1858 to 1861
ECCLESIASTICAL.				
Lee	1833	2	roy. 8vo.	1752 to 1758
Haggard (Consistory)	1832	2	roy. 8vo.	1779 to 1821
Phillimore	......	3	roy. 8vo.	1809 to 1821
Addams; and Vol. III, part 1	......	2	roy. 8vo.	1822 to 1826
Haggard; and Vol. IV, parts 1 and 2	......	3	roy. 8vo.	1827 to 1833
Curteis	......	3	roy. 8vo.	1834 to 1844
Notes of Cases in the Ecclesiastical aud Maritime Courts	......	7	8vo.	1841 to 1850
Robertson; and Vol II, parts 1 and 2	......	1	roy. 8vo.	1844 to 1851
Spinks (Ecclesiastical and Admiralty)	......	2	roy. 8vo.	1853 to 1855
Deane	......	1	roy. 8vo.	1855 to 1857
PROBATE AND DIVORCE.				
Swabey and Tristram	.....	4	roy. 8vo.	1858 to 1865
ADMIRALTY.				
Mariott	......	1	8vo	1776 to 1779
Robinson	......	6	roy. 8vo.	1799 to 1808
Edwards	... ..	1	roy, 8vo.	1808 to 1810
Dodson	......	2	roy. 8vo.	1811 to 1822
Haggard	......	3	roy. 8vo.	1822 to 1837
Robinson: and Vol. III, parts 1 and 2	......	2	roy. 8vo.	1838 to 1852
Swabey	......	1	roy. 8vo.	1858 to 1859
Lushington	......	2	roy. 8vo.	
Browning and Lushington	......	1	roy. 8vo.	
BANKRUPTCY.				
Rose	......	2	roy. 8vo.	1810 to 1816
Buck	......	1	roy. 8vo.	1816 to 1820
Glyn and Jameson	......	2	roy. 8vo.	1821 to 1828
Montagu and M'Arthur	. ..	1	roy. 8vo.	1828 to 1830
Montagu	......	1	roy. 8vo.	1830 to 1832
Montagu and Bligh	......	1	roy. 8vo.	1832 to 1833
Montagu and Ayrton	......	3	roy. 8vo.	1833 to 1838
Montagu and Chitty	......	1	roy. 8vo.	1838 to 1840
Deacon and Chitty	......	4	roy. 8vo.	1832 to 1835

Chronological List, English Reports—continued.

REPORTERS.	Date of last Edition	No. of Vols.	Size.	Period.
BANKRUPTCY—continued.				
Deacon	......	4	roy. 8vo.	1836 to 1839
Montagu, Deacon, and De Gex	......	3	roy. 8vo.	1840 to 1844
De Gex	......	1	roy. 8vo.	1845 to 1848
De Gex, Macnaghten, and Gordon, parts 1 to 9	......			1851 to 1857
De Gex and Jones	......	1		1860
De Gex, Fisher and Jones	......	1		
Gazette of Bankruptcy	......	2	folio.	1862
RAILWAY AND CANAL CASES.				
Nicholl, Hare, Carrow, Oliver, Bevan, and Lefroy	......	7	roy. 8vo.	1835 to 1855
MERCANTILE CASES.				
Danson and Lloyd	......	1	roy. 8vo.	1828 to 1829
Lloyd and Welsby	......	1	roy. 8vo.	1829 to 1830
ELECTION CASES.				
Glanville	......	1	8vo.	1624
Douglas	......	4	8vo.	1774 to 1776
Fraser	......	2	8vo.	1776 to 1777
Luder	......	3	8vo.	1785 to 1790
Peckwell	......	2	8vo.	1802 to 1806
Corbett and Daniell	......	1	8vo.	1819
Cockburn and Rowe	......	1	8vo.	1832
Perry and Knapp	......	1	8vo.	1833
Knapp and Ombler	......	1	8vo.	1834
Falconer and Fitzherbert	......	1	8vo.	1837
Barron and Austin	......	1	8vo.	1842
Barron and Arnold	......	1	8vo.	1843 to 1846
Power, Rodwell and Dew	......	2	12mo.	1847 to 1856
Wolferstan and Dew	......	1	12mo.	1856 to 1858
O'Malley and Hardcastle	......	1		
REGISTRATION APPEAL CASES.				
Lutwyche	......	2	roy. 8vo.	1843 to 1853
Keane and Grant	......	1	roy. 8vo.	1854 to 1862
Hopwood and Philbrick	......	1	roy. 8vo.	1863 to
Hopwood and Coltman, Vol. 1, Parts 1 and 2.				
MAGISTRATES' CASES.				
Carrow, Hamerton, and Allen (New Sessions Cases); and Vol. IV, parts 1 to 4	......	3	roy. 8vo.	1844 to 1851

Chronological List, English Reports—continued.

REPORTERS.	Date of last Ed.	No. of Vols.	Size.	Period.
CROWN CASES.				
Foster	1809	1	roy. 8vo.	1743 to 1761
Leach	1815	2	roy. 8vo.	1730 to 1815
Russell and Ryan	......	1	roy. 8vo.	1799 to 1823
Lewin's Crown Cases on the Northern Circuit	......	2	12mo.	1822 to 1838
Moody	......	2	roy. 8vo.	1824 to 1844
Denison	......	2	roy. 8vo.	1844 to 1852
Dearsley	......	1	roy. 8vo.	1852 to 1856
Dearsley and Bell	......	1	roy. 8vo.	1856 to 1858
Bell	......	1	roy. 8vo.	1860
Leigh & Cave. Vol. 1, Parts 1–7	......	......	....	....
Cox's Criminal Law Cases	......	11	....	1843 to 1865
Temple and Mew's Criminal Appeal Cases	......	1	8vo.	1848 to 1851
REPORTS IN ALL THE COURTS.				
Jurist	......	18	imp. 8vo.	1837 to 1854
Jurist. *New series*	......	12	imp. 8vo.	1855 to 1866
Law Journal	......	9	4to.	1823 to 1831
Law Journal. *New series*	......	40	4to.	1832 to 1871
Law Times	......	33	folio.	1845 to 1859
Law Times Reports	......	24	roy. 8vo.	1859 to 1871
Weekly Reporter	......	19	imp. 8vo.	1853 to 1871
New Reports	......	6	4to.	1862 to 1865

CHRONOLOGICAL LIST OF REPORTS IN SCOTCH COURTS.

REPORTERS.	No. of Vols.	Size.	Period.
HOUSE OF LORDS.			
Robertson	1	roy. 8vo.	1707 to 1727
Craigie, Stewart and Paton	6	roy. 8vo.	1726 to 1821
Shaw	2	roy. 8vo.	1821 to 1824
Shaw, Wilson and Courtenay	7	roy. 8vo.	1825 to 1835
Shaw and Maclean	3	roy. 8vo.	1835 to 1838
Maclean and Robinson	1	roy. 8vo.	1839
Robinson	2	roy. 8vo.	1840 to 1841
Bell	7	roy. 8vo.	1842 to 1850
McQueen	4	roy. 8vo.	1851 to 1860
COURT OF SESSION CASES.			
Durie	1	folio.	1621 to 1642
English Judges	1	folio.	1655 to 1661

Chronological List, Scotch Reports—continued.

Reporters.	No. of Vols.	Size.	Period.
COURT OF SESSION CASES—continued.			
Stair	2	folio.	1661 to 1681
Gilmour and Falconer	1	4to.	1661 to 1685
Dirleton	1	folio.	1665 to 1677
Fountainhall	2	folio.	1678 to 1712
Harcarse	1	folio.	1681 to 1691
Dalrymple	1	folio.	1698 to 1726
Forbes	1	folio.	1705 to 1713
Bruce	1	folio.	1714 to 1715
Kames (Remarkable)	2	folio.	1716 to 1752
Edgar	1	folio.	1724 to 1725
Elchie	2	4to.	1733 to 1754
Clerk Home	1	folio.	1735 to 1744
Kilkerran	1	folio.	1738 to 1752
Falconer	1	folio.	1744 to 1751
Kames (Select)	1	folio.	1752 to 1768
Hailes	2	4to.	1766 to 1791
Bell	1	8vo	1790 to 1792
Bell	1	folio.	1794 to 1795
Hume	1	4to.	1781 to 1822
Brown's Supplement, containing the unpublished Decisions	5	4to.	1622 to 1794
Faculty of Advocates	14	folio.	1752 to 1808
Ditto	7	folio.	1808 to 1825
Ditto	16	roy. 8vo.	1825 to 1841
Shaw and Dunlop. (Court of Session Cases)	16	roy. 8vo.	1821 to 1838
Ditto. *Second series*	24	roy. 8vo.	1838 to 1861
Ditto. *Third series*	8	roy. 8vo.	1862 to 1871
Dees and Anderson	5	roy. 8vo.	1829 to 1833
Scottish Jurist	42	4to.	1829 to 1871
Scottish Law Reporter	7	....	....
Morrison's Dictionary of Decisions, with Synopsis and Indices	22	4to.	1540 to 1808
Brown's Synopsis of Decisions, including House of Lord's Appeals	4	4to.	1540 to 1827
Bell's Dictionary of Decisions	2	4to.	1808 to 1832
JUSTICIARY CASES.			
Shaw	1	roy. 8vo.	1819 to 1831
Syme	1	roy. 8vo.	1826 to 1830
Swinton	2	roy. 8vo.	1835 to 1841
Broun	2	roy. 8vo.	1842 to 1845
Arkley	1	roy. 8vo.	1846 to 1848
Shaw	1	roy. 8vo.	1848 to 1851
Irvine	5	roy. 8vo.	1851 to 1857
Couper	1	....	....
CONSISTORIAL COURT.			
Ferguson	1	8vo.	1811 to 1817

Chronological List, Scotch Reports——continued.

Reporters.	No. of Vols.	Size.	Period.
JURY COURT.			
Murray	5	8vo.	1815 to 1830
McFarlane	1	roy. 8vo.	1838 to 1839
TEIND COURT.			
Shaw	1	8vo.	1821 to 1831
STATUTE LAW.			
The Acts of Parliament of Scotland, made by King James I and his successors	3	12mo.	1424 to 1706
Acts of the Parliament of Scotland, Edited by Thomas Thompson	11	roy. folio.	1424 to 1707

CHRONOLOGICAL LIST OF REPORTS IN THE IRISH COURTS.

Reporters.	No. of Vols.	Size.	Period.
APPEALS AND WRITS OF ERROR.			
Ridgeway	3	8vo.	1784 to 1796
CHANCERY.			
Wallis, by Lyne	1	roy. 8vo.	1766 to 1791
Schoales and Lefroy	2	roy. 8vo.	1802 to 1806
Ball and Beatty	2	roy. 8vo.	1807 to 1814
Beatty	1	roy. 8vo.	1814 to 1830
Molloy ... and III, Part I,	2	roy. 8vo.	1827 to 1829
Lloyd and Goold, temp. Plunkett	1	roy. 8vo.	1834 to 1839
Drury and Walsh	2	roy. 8vo.	1837 to 1840
Connor and Lawson	2	roy. 8vo.	1841 to 1843
Lloyd and Goold ... temp. Sugden,	1	roy. 8vo.	1835
Drury and Warren ... temp. Sugden,	4	roy. 8vo.	1841 to 1843
Drury ... temp. Sugden,	1	roy. 8vo.	1843 to 1844
Jones and Latouche ... temp. Sugden,	3	roy. 8vo.	1844 to 1846
Continued by Irish Law and Equity Reports.			
ROLLS COURT.			
Hogan	2	roy. 8vo.	1816 to 1834
Sausse and Scully	1	roy. 8vo.	1837 to 1840
Flannegan and Kelly	1	roy. 8vo.	1840 to 1842
Continued by Irish Law and Equity Reports.			
KING'S BENCH AND QUEEN'S BENCH.			
Vernon and Scriven	1	8vo.	1786 to 1788
Ridgeway, Lapp and Schoales	1	roy. 8vo.	1793 to 1795
Fox and Smith	2	roy. 8vo.	1822 to 1824
Smith and Batty	1	roy. 8vo.	1824 to 1825
Batty	1	roy. 8vo.	1825 to 1826
Hudson and Brooke	2	roy. 8vo.	1827 to 1831
Alcock and Napier	1	roy. 8vo.	1831 to 1833
Cooke and Alcock ... I Part,		roy. 8vo.	1833 to 1834

Chronological List, Irish Reports—continued.

Reporters.	No. of Vols.	Size.	Period.
KING'S BENCH AND QUEEN'S BENCH CON.			
Jebb and Symes	2	roy. 8vo.	1838 to 1841
Jebb and Bourke	1	roy. 8vo.	1841 to 1842
Continued by Irish Law and Equity Reports.			
COMMON PLEAS.			
Smythe	1	roy. 8vo.	1839 to 1840
Continued by Irish Law and Equity Reports.			
NISI PRIUS.			
Armstrong, Macartney and Ogle	1	roy. 8vo.	1842
Blackham, Dundas and Osborne	1	roy. 8vo.	1846 to 1848
Continued by Irish Law and Equity Reports.			
EXCHEQUER.			
Hayes	1	roy. 8vo.	1830 to 1832
Hayes and Jones	1	roy. 8vo.	1832 to 1834
Jones	2	roy. 8vo.	1834 to 1838
Jones and Carey .... 2 Parts,		roy. 8vo.	1838 to 1839
Longfield and Townsend	1	roy. 8vo.	1841 to 1842
Continued by Irish Law and Equity Reports.			
REGISTRY CASES.			
Alcock	1	roy. 8vo.	1832 to 1837
Welsh	1	roy. 8vo.	1832 to 1840
CROWN CASES.			
Jebb	1	roy. 8vo.	1822 to 1840
ECCLESIASTICAL.			
Milward	1	roy. 8vo.	1819 to 1843
CIRCUIT CASES.			
Crawford and Dix, Abridged Cases	1	roy. 8vo.	1837 to 1838
Crawford and Dix	3	roy. 8vo.	1839 to 1846
Cases on the Six Circuits	1	roy. 8vo.	1841 to 1843
REPORTS IN ALL THE COURTS.			
Law Recorder, First Series	4	4to.	1827 to 1831
Glasscock	1	roy. 8vo.	1831 to 1832
Law Recorder, Second Series	6	roy. 8vo.	1833 to 1838
Irish Law, 13 vols. ...... } *not published* } Irish Equity, 13 vols ...... } *separately.* }	26	roy. 8vo.	1838 to 1850
Irish Law, New Series, 17 vols.. } *ditto.* } Irish Equity, New Series, 17 vols }	34	roy. 8vo.	1850 to 1861
Law Reports in the Irish Courts			1866 to 1871
STATUTES.			
The Irish Statutes, with two Indices, from 3 Edward II. to 40 Geo. III	21	folio.	1310 to 1800

PART THIRD.

DIGESTS OF JUDICIAL DECISIONS.

DIGESTS OF JUDICIAL DECISIONS.

Abbott. See United States Digests.

Abbott. See New York.

Alabama.

A Digest of the Alabama Reports. By T. Reavis. Volume 1. Tuskaloosa. 1850.

A Digest of Cases decided by the Supreme Court of the State of Alabama from Minor to VII. Alabama Reports, inclusive; with a Table of Titles. By P. Phillips. Mobile. 1846.

Digest of Cases decided by the Supreme Court of the State of Alabama, from seventh to thirteenth Alabama Reports, inclusive; with a complete Index of the whole body of Reports. By P. Phillips. Mobile. 1849.

Alexander. See Texas.

Anthon. See United States Digests.

Bacon. See Georgia.

Barclay. See Missouri.

Battle. See North Carolina.

Bell. See New Hampshire.

Benjamin and Slidell. See Louisiana.

Bennett and Heard. See Massachusetts.

Bigelow. See Massachusetts.

Brightly. See United States Digests.

California.

Digest of California Reports and Statutes. By Charles H. Parker. In two volumes. Vol. 1. Abandonment–Negligence. Vol. 2. New Trials–Writs. San Francisco. 1869.

CLERKE. See NEW YORK.

CLINTON. See NEW YORK.

COBB and LUMPKIN. See GEORGIA.

COFER. See KENTUCKY.

COHEN and LEE. See MARYLAND.

CONNECTICUT.

A Digest of the reported Decisions of the Superior Court, and of the Supreme Court of Errors, of the State of Connecticut, from the organization of said courts to the present time. By Thomas W. Waterman. New York. 1858.

A Digest of the reported Cases decided by the Supreme Court of Errors of the State of Connecticut, from 1786 to 1844, inclusive. With Tables of names of Cases and of the Titles. By Thomas Day. Hartford. 1846.

COOLEY. See MICHIGAN.

CORNWELL. See NEW YORK.

COXE. See UNITED STATES DIGESTS.

DAVIS. See INDIANA.

DAY. See CONNECTICUT.

DESLIX. See LOUISIANA.

DILLON. See IOWA.

EASTMAN. See MAINE.

FLORIDA.

Index to the Decisions of the Supreme Court of Florida, reported in Florida Reports, from Vol. 1 to 1st Number Vol. 11, inclusive. By John B. Galbraith. Tallahassee. 1866.

FREEMAN. See ILLINOIS.

GALBRAITH. See FLORIDA.

GEORGIA.

A General Digested Index to Georgia Reports; including 1, 2, 3 Kelley, 4–10 Georgia Reports, T. U. P. Charlton's Reports, Dudley's Reports, and Georgia Decisions, parts 1 and 2. Compiled by T. R. R. Cobb and W. W. Lumpkin. Athens, Ga. 1852.

Digest of the Decisions of the Supreme Court of Georgia, from Vols. 20 to 30, inclusive. Compiled by A. O. Bacon. Macon, Ga. 1867.

GHOLSON and OKEY. See OHIO.

GILCHRIST. See NEW HAMPSHIRE.

GILMAN. See INDIANA and ILLINOIS.

HALL. See VIRGINIA.

HALSTED. See NEW JERSEY.

HAMMOND. See IOWA.

HANES. See UNITED STATES DIGESTS.

HENNEN. See LOUISIANA.

HENRY and READ. See ILLINOIS.

ILLINOIS.

The "Illinois Digest:" being a full and complete Digest and Compilation of all the Decisions of the Supreme Court of the State of Illinois, from Breese's Rreports to the fifteenth volume of Illinois Reports, inclusive. By Norman L. Freeman. 2 vols. Cincinnati. 1856.

A Digest of the Illinois Reports, from the earliest period to the year, 1866; embracing in two volumes all the Decisions of the Supreme Court of the State, from Breese to the Thirty-eighth volume, both inclusive. By Charles H. Wood and Joseph D. Long, of the Illinois Bar. 2 vols. Chicago. 1867.

The Illinois Digest: being a full and completer Digest and Compilation of all the Decisions of the Supreme Court of the State of Illinois, from the fiteenth to the twenty-ninth volume, inclusive, of Illinois Reports. By Henry and Read, Counselors at Law. Vol. 3, being a continuation of Freeman's Digest. Chicago. 1865.

INDIANA.

A Digest of the Decisions of the Supreme Court of the State of Indiana. By Edwin A. Davis, LL. B., Counselor at Law. Second Edition. Cincinnati. 1866.

INDIANA AND ILLINOIS.

Digest of the Decisions of the Supreme Courts of the States of Indiana and Illinois, and the Circuit Court of the United States for the Seventh Circuit. By Charles Gilmore. Columbus. 1844.

IOWA.

Digest of the Decisions of the Supreme Court of the State of Iowa, from the organization of the Court in 1839, to 1860. Including the Decisions not yet reported. By John F. Dillon, one of the District Judges. Davenport. 1860. (Iowa Digest, Vol. 1.)

Digest of the Decisions of the Supreme Court of the State of Iowa, from the close of the year 1859 to the June Term, 1866. By William G. Hammond. Des Moines. 1866. (Iowa Digest, Vol. 2.)

IREDELL. See NORTH CAROLINA.

JOHNSON. See NEW YORK.

JONES. See NORTH CAROLINA.

KENTUCKY.

Digest of the Cases at Common Law and in Equity, decided by the Court of Appeals of Kentucky, from its organization in 1792, to the close of the Winter Term of 1852-3. By Ben. Monroe and James Harlan. 2 vols. Frankfort, Ky. 1853.

A Supplemental Digest of the Decisions of the Court of Appeals of Kentucky. 1853–1867. By Martin H. Cofer. Cincinnati. 1867.

LOUISIANA.

Digest of the reported Decisions of the Superior Court of the late Territory of Orleans, and of the Supreme Court of the State of Louisiana. Originally compiled by J. P. Benjamin and T. Slidell, and now Revised and Enlarged by Thomas Slidell. New Orleans. 1840.

Digest of the reported Decisions of the Supreme Court of the State of Louisiana, from December, 1838, to February, 1843. Compiled and Published by P. J. A. Deslix, Attorney-at-Law. New Orleans. 1845.

A Digest of the reported Decisions of the Supreme Court of the State of Louisiana, contained in the Louisiana Annual Reports, from the 15th to the 21st volume inclusive. By Sam'l R. & C. L. Walker. New York. 1870.

A Digest of reported Decisions of the Superior Court of the late Territory of Orleans; the late Court of Errors and Appeals; and the Supreme Court of the State of Louisiana. Contained in the sixty-five volumes of reports, from 1st Martin to 15th Louisiana Annual. By William D. Hennen. 2 vols. New Edition. Riverside. Cambridge. 1861.

MAINE.

Digest of the Decisions of the Supreme Judicial Court, of Maine, contained in Greenleaf's, Fairfield's, Appleton's and Shepley's Reports; and comprising twenty-six volumes of the Maine Reports. By Philip Eastman. Hallowell. 1849.

Digest of the Decisions of the Supreme Judicial Court of the State of Maine, contained in volumes 27–43 (both inclusive), of the Maine Reports. By William Wirt Virgin. Hallowell. 1859.

The Same. A Supplement containing the Decisions found in volumes 44–56 (both inclusive), of the Maine Reports. By William Wirt Virgin. Portland. 1870.

MARYLAND.

Digest of the Maryland Reports: comprising Harris & McHenry, four vols., Harris & Johnson, seven vols., Harris & Gill, two vols., Gill & Johnson, twelve vols., and Bland's Chancery Reports, three vols. By William Henry Norris, George William Brown, and Frederick William Brune, Jr., of the Baltimore Bar. 2 vols. Baltimore. 1847.

Digest of the Maryland Reports ; from the ninth to the twentieth volume inclusive. By J. J. Cohen and James Fenner Lee, Attorneys at Law. Baltimore. 1866.

Digest of the Maryland Reports : comprising Gill's Reports, Nine Vols., Maryland Reports, Eight Vols., Maryland Chancery Decisions, Four Vols. By J. Shaaf Stockett. Richard T. Merrick, and Oliver Miller. Baltimore, 1857.

MASSACHUSETTS.

A Digest of the Reported Cases argued and determined in the Supreme Judicial Court of the Commonwealth of Massachusetts. By Lewis Bigelow. 2 vols. Boston. 1825.

The Massachusetts Digest ; being a Digest of the Decisions of the Supreme Judicial Court of Massachusetts, from the year 1844 to the year 1857. By Edmund H. Bennett and Franklin F. Heard. 2 vols. Boston. 1862.

Digest of the decisions of the Supreme Judicial Court of Massachusetts, reported in the seven volumes of Massachusetts Reports, the twenty-four volumes of Pickering's Reports, and the first four volumes of Metcalf's Reports. Edited by George Minot. Boston. 1851.

The Same. Boston. 1844.

The Same. A Supplement. Containing the Cases reported in the last ten volumes of Metcalf's Reports and the first three volumes of Cushing's Reports. Edited by George Minot. Boston. 1852.

METCALF and PERKINS. See UNITED STATES DIGESTS.

MICHIGAN.

A Digest of the Reported Cases contained in the Michigan Reports. Embracing—
Harrington's Chancery Reports. 1 vol.
Walker's Chancery Reports. 1 vol.
Douglass' Michigan Reports. 2 vols.
Michigan Reports by Manning. 1 vol.
Michigan Reports by Gibbs. 3 vols.
Michigan Reports by Cooley. 8 vols.
Michigan Reports by Meddaugh. 1 vol.
By Thomas M. Cooley. Ann Arbor. 1866.

MINOT. See MASSACHUSETTS.

MISSISSIPPI.

A Digest of the Cases decided and reported in the High Court of Errors and Appeals and the Superior Court of Chancery of the State of Mississippi. From 1818 to 1847. By W. C. Smedes. Boston. 1847.

MISSOURI.

A Digest of the Decisions of the Supreme Court of the State of Missouri, contained in the first twenty-seven volumes of reports. By D. Robert Barclay. 2 vols. St. Louis. 1859.

MONROE and HARLAN. See KENTUCKY.

NASH. See OHIO.

NEW HAMPSHIRE.

A Digest of the Reports of Cases argued and determined in the Superior Court of Judicature of New Hampshire. Vols. 1–12. By John James Gilchrist. Concord. 1846. 2 copies.

A Digest of the Cases Determined in the Superior Court of Judicature of New Hampshire, and reported in New Hampshire Reports, Vols. 13, 14, 15, 19 and Foster's Reports, 1–11. By George Bell. Concord. 1858.

NEW JERSEY.

A Digested Index to the Decisions of the Superior Courts of the State of New Jersey. By William Halsted, Esq. Trenton. 1830.

The Same. Second Edition. 2 vols. Trenton. 1843.

NEW YORK.

A Digest of the Reports of Cases determined in the Supreme Court of Judicature, and the Court for the Correction of Errors of the State of New York; together with the reported cases of the Superior Court for the City and County of New York, from the organization of said Courts; including Coleman's Cases; Caine's Cases in Error, 2 vols.; Johnson's Cases, 3 vols.; Johnson's Reports, 20 vols.; Cowen's Reports, 9 vols.; Wendell's Reports, 26 vols.; Hill's Reports, 7 vols.; Denio's Reports, 5 vols.; Barbour's Law Reports, 4 vols.; Comstock's Reports, 1 vol.; Hall's Reports, 2 vols.; Sandford's Reports, 1 vol.; Anthon's Nisi Prius. By Thomas W. Clerke. Revised and continued to the present time by William Hogan. 4 vols. New York and Albany. 1850.

A Digest of Cases in Law and Equity, argued and determined in the Court of Appeals of the State of New York, during the first eleven years of its organization, as contained in sixteen volumes of its reports, from 1st Comstock to 16th New York Reports, inclusive, except 6th Selden not yet published. 1847–1859. By Francis E. Cornwall. Albany. 1859.

A Digest of the Cases decided and reported in the Supreme Court of Judicature of the Court of Chancery, and the Court for the Correction of Errors, of the State of New York; from 1799 to 1823. By William Johnson. Two volumes in one. Philadelphia. 1834.

A Digest of the Decisions at Law and in Equity, in the several Courts of the State of New York, contained in the one hundred and nine volumes of Reports, by Johnson, Caines, Cowen, Wendell, Hill, Davis, Comstock, Hopkins, Paige, Barbour and Sandford (Superior Court of New York), with a complete list of all Cases Reversed or Affirmed, and other useful matter. By Geo. W. Clinton. 3 vols. Albany. 1852.

A Digest of New York Statutes and Reports, from the earliest period to the year 1860. By Benjamin Vaughan Abbott and Austin Abbott. Comprising the Adjudications of all the Courts of the State, presented in the Reports by Abbott, Anthon, Barbour, Bosworth, Bradford, Caines, Clark, Coleman, Comstock, Cowen, Denio, Duer,

Edwards, Hall, Hill, Hilton, Hoffman, Hopkins, Howard, Johnson, Kernan, Paige, Parker, Sandford, Selden, E. D. Smith, E. P. Smith and Wendell; and in the Chancery Sentinel, the City Hall Recorder, etc., etc., etc. Together with the Statutes as embodied in the Revised Laws of 1813, the Revised Statutes, and the General Acts passed since 1829. Preceded by a Table of Cases criticised. 5 vols. With the supplements containing Digests of the later Reports up to 1870. In all 8 vols. New York. 1860–1870.

Condensed Digest of the Court of Appeals Decisions of the State of New York, as reported in Comstock's Reports, four volumes; Selden's Reports, six volumes; Kennan's Reports, four volumes; Smith's Reports, thirteen volumes; volumes 1 to 27 inclusive of New York Reports. By Joel Tiffany, State Reporter. Albany. 1866.

NORRIS, BROWN and BRUNE. See MARYLAND.

NORTH CAROLINA.

A Digest of all the reported Cases both in Law and Equity, Determined in the Courts of North Carolina, from the Earliest Period to the present year, together with a table of the names of the Cases. Prepared by William H. Battle. In three volumes. Vols. 1 and 2 containing the Law, and Vol. 3 containing the Equity Cases. Raleigh. 1866.

A Digest of reported Cases Determined in the Supreme Court of North Carolina, from the year 1845, (December,) to the year 1853, (August,) inclusive. 2 vols. in 1. Prepared by Hamilton C. Jones. Raleigh, N. C. 1854.

A Digest of all reported Cases Determined in the Courts of North Carolina, from the year 1778 to the year 1837, inclusive. Prepared by James Iredell, Esq. 3 vols. Raleigh. 1839–1846.

OHIO.

A Digest of the Decisions of the Supreme Court of Ohio, contained in the first twenty volumes of the Ohio Reports. By Simeon Nash. Cincinnati. 1853.

A Digest of the Decisions of the Supreme Court of Ohio, contained in Vols. 1–10 of the Ohio State Reports. By Simeon Nash. Columbus. 1861.

Digest of the Ohio Reports: embracing the twenty volumes of Ohio Reports, and fifteen volumes of the Ohio State

Rreports. Prepared by W. Y. Gholson and J. W. Okey. 2 vols. Cincinnati. 1867.

A Digest of the first sixteen volumes of the Ohio Reports. Vols. 13, 14, 15 and 16, by way of supplement. Containing together all the Cases ever reported at Law and Equity in the Supreme Court of the State of Ohio, in Bank. By P. B. Wilcox. Columbus. 1848.

PARKER. See CALIFORNIA.

PENNSYLVANIA.

A Digest of reported Cases adjudged in the several Courts held in Pennsylvania: together with some manuscript Cases. By Thomas J. Wharton. Fifth Edition. By Francis Wharton. 2 vols. Philadelphia. 1850.

The same. Second Edition. 2 vols. Philadelphia. 1829.

A Supplement to Wharton's Digest: containing the reported Cases during the years 1850, 1851 and part of 1852. Together with some manuscript Cases. By Henry Wharton. Philadelphia. 1858.

PETERS. See UNITED STATES DIGESTS.

PHILLIPS. See ALABAMA.

PUTNAM. See UNITED STATES EQUITY DIGEST.

REAVIS. See ALABAMA.

RICE. See SOUTH CAROLINA.

SHEFFIELD. See WISCONSIN.

SIMMONS. See WISCONSIN.

SMEDES. See MISSISSIPPI.

SOUTH CAROLINA.

A Digest of the Cases decided in the Superior Courts of Law of the State of South Carolina; from the earliest period to the present time. By William Rice. 2 vols. Charleston. 1838.

STOCKETT, MERRICK and MILLER. See MARYLAND.

TATE. See VIRGINIA.

TEXAS.

Digest of the Decisions of the Supreme Court of Texas; from January Term, 1840, to the close of the Spring Term, 1853. By William Alexander. Philadelphia. 1854.

TIFFANY. See NEW YORK.

UNITED STATES. See separate title, "UNITED STATES DIGESTS," *infra*, p. 209.

VERMONT.

A Digest of all the Cases decided in the Supreme Court of the State of Vermont, as reported in N. Chipman's, Tyler's, Brayton's, D. Chipman's and Aiken's Reports, and the first fifteen volumes of the Vermont Reports; together with many manuscript cases not hitherto reported. By Peter T. Washburn. 2 vols. Woodstock. 1845–1852.

VIRGIN. See MAINE.

VIRGINIA.

A Digested Index of the Virginia Reports, containing all the points argued and determined in the Court of Appeals of Virginia, from Washington to second Randolph inclusive. By Everard Hall. 2 vols. Richmond. 1825.

An Analytical Digested Index of the reported cases of the Court of Appeals and General Court of Virginia; from Washington to second Grattan inclusive. By Benjamin Tate. In two volumes. Richmond and Philadelphia. 1847.

WALKER. See LOUISIANA.

WASHBURN. See VERMONT.

WATERMAN. See CONNECTICUT.

WATERMAN. See UNITED STATES DIGESTS.

WHARTON. See PENNSYLVANIA.

WILCOX. See OHIO.

WISCONSIN.

A Complete Digest of the Decisions of the Supreme Court of the State of Wisconsin, in Law and Equity, from its organization, down to, and including the cases reported in Vol. 14, Wis. Reports. By William E. Sheffield. Chicago. 1865.

A Digest of Wisconsin Reports, from the earliest period to the year 1868; comprising all the published decisions of the Supreme Court of Wisconsin, presented in Burnett's, Chandler's and 20 vols. Wisconsin Reports, with references to the Statutes. By James Simmons. Albany. 1868.

WOOD and LONG. See ILLINOIS.

UNITED STATES DIGESTS.

ABBOTT (Benjamin Vaughan) and ABBOTT (Austin). A Digest of the Reports of the United States Courts, and of the Acts of Congress, from the organization of the Government to the year 1867. Comprising the Reports of the United States Supreme Court, those of the Circuit and District Courts, and of the various Territorial or Local Courts established by the United States; together with the leading provisions of the Statutes at Large, and important auxiliary information upon the National Jurisprudence. 4 vols. New York. 1867.

AMERICAN DIGEST. A Digested Index to the reported Decisions of the several Courts of Law in the United States. 5 vols.
Vol. 1. By John Anthon, Esq. New York. 1813.
Vol. 2. By Thomas Day, Esq. New York. 1816.
Vol. 3. By Thomas I. Wharton, Esq. Philadelphia. 1824.
Vol. 4. By Thomas I. Wharton, Esq. Philadelphia. 1825.
Vol. 5. By Thomas S. Smith and Francis J. Troubat. Philadelphia. 1830.

AMERICAN CHANCERY DIGEST: being an Analytical Digested Index of all the reported Decisions in Equity of the United States Courts and of the Courts of the several States, to the present time. By Thomas W. Waterman. Third Edition. 3 vols. New York and Albany. 1851.

BRIGHTLY (Richard C.) A Digest of the Decisions of the Federal Courts, from the organization of the Government to the present time. 2 vols. Philadelphia. 1868–1870.

COXE (Richard S.) A Digest of the Decisions in the Supreme Court, Circuit Courts, and District Courts of the United States. Philadelphia. 1829.

CURTIS (R. B.) Digest of the Decisions of the Supreme Court of the United States. From the origin of the Court to the close of the December Term, 1854. Boston. 1856.

HANES' (John L.) U. S. DIGEST OF CRIMINAL LAW. Digest of Decisions in Criminal Cases contained in the Reports of the Courts of the United States and the several State Courts: to which is appended a table of the Cases cited. New York. 1856.

PETERS (Richard.) A full and arranged Digest of the Decisions in Common Law, Equity, and Admiralty, of the Courts of the United States, from the organization of the Government in 1789 to 1847, in the Supreme Court, Circuit, District, and Admiralty Courts. 2 vols. Philadelphia. 1848.

UNITED STATES EQUITY DIGEST. Digest of the Decisions in the the Court of Equity in the United States. By John P. Putnam. 2 vols. Boston. 1851.

UNITED STATES DIGEST. Digest of the Decisions of the Courts of Common Law and Admiralty in the United States. Vol. 1. By Theron Metcalf and Jonathan C. Perkins. New Edition. Revised and corrected. Boston. 1847. Vol. 2. By George T. Curtis. 3d Ed. Boston. 1849. Vol. 3. By George T. Curtis. Boston. 1850. Vols. 4 and 5. A Supplement to the above in two vols. By By John Phelps Putnam. Boston. 1851. Vol. 6. A Table of the Cases contained in the foregoing five volumes. By George P. Sanger. Boston. 1852.

UNITED STATES DIGEST; being a Digest of Decisions of the Courts of Common Law, Equity and Admiralty in the United States. By John Phelps Putnam. Being an Annual Digest for the years 1847–1869. 29 vols. Boston. 1850–1871.

The Same. New Series. By Benjamin Vaughan Abbott. Vol. 1. Annual Digest for 1870. Boston. 1872.

ENGLISH DIGESTS.

BIDDLE (Geo. W.) and MCMURTRIE (Richard C.) A General Index to the English Common Law Reports. Vols. 1–83 inclusive. Second Edition. In two volumes. Philadelphia. 1857.

CHITTY (Edward). An Index to all the reported Cases decided in the several Courts of Equity in England and Ireland, the Privy Council, and the House of Lords; and to the Statutes on or relating to the Principles, Pleading and Practice of Equity and Bankruptcy; from the earliest period. The Third Edition, brought down to the year 1853, by James Macaulay, Esq. In four volumes. London. 1853.

COVENTRY (Thomas), and HUGHES (Samuel), Esqrs. An Analytical Digested Index to the Common Law Reports from the time of Henry III., to the commencement of the reign of George III. With Tables of the Titles and Names of Cases. In two volumes. First American from last London Edition. Philadelphia. 1832.

FISH (Asa J.) A General Digest of the Principal Matters contained in the Exchequer Reports, from 1824 to 1854, inclusive. Philadelphia. 1855.

HARRISON (R. Tarrant). Harrison's Analytical Digest of all the reported Cases determined in the House of Lords, the several Courts of Common Law, in Banc and at Nisi Prius, and the Court of Bankruptcy ; from Michaelmas Term, 1756, to Easter Term, 1843. To which are added spplements, continuing the work to the year 1851. In seven volumes. Philadelphia. 1853.

HARRISON (S. B.) An Analytical Digest of all the reported cases, determined in the House of Lords, the several Courts at Common Law, in Banc and at Nisi Prius; and the Court of Bankruptcy ; and also the Crown Cases reserved, from Mich. Term, 1756, to Mich. Term, 1834. 3 vols. Philadelphia. 1835.

PRITCHARD (William Tam). An Analytical Digest of all the reported Cases determined by the High Court of Admiralty of England, the Lords' Commissioners of Appeal in Prize Causes, and (on questions of maritime and international law) by the Judicial Committee of the Privy Council ; also of the analogous cases in the Common Law, Equity, and Ecclesiastical Courts, and of the Statutes applicable to the Cases reported. Harrisburg, Pa. 1848.

SMITH (Chauncey). A Digest of the Decisions of the Courts of England contained in the English Law and Equity Reports, from the first volume to the thirty-first inclusive. Boston. 1859.

PART FOURTH.

STATUTE LAW.

DIVISION 1.—REVISED OR COMPILED STATUTES, DIGESTS OF STATUTES, ETC.

DIVISION 2.—SESSION LAWS.

REVISED STATUTES, ETC.

ALABAMA.

The Code of Alabama. Prepared by John J. Ormond, Arthur P. Bagby, George Goldthwaite. With head notes and index by Henry C. Semple. Montgomery. 1852.

The Revised Code of Alabama. Prepared by A. J. Walker. Adopted by Act of General Assembly, approved February 19, 1867. Montgomery, Ala. 1867.

The Penal Code; prepared by G. W. Stone and J. W. Shepherd, and adopted by the General Assembly at the session 1865–6: together with the other Criminal Laws now in force. Montgomery. 1866.

ARIZONA.

The Compiled Laws of the Territory of Arizona; including the Howell Code and Session Laws from 1864 to 1871, inclusive. Compiled by Coles Bashford. Albany, N. Y. 1871.

ARKANSAS.

Revised Statutes of the State of Arkansas, adopted at the October Session of the General Assembly of said State, A. D. 1837. Revised by William McK. Ball and Sam. C. Roan. Notes and Index by Albert Pike. Boston. 1838.

A Digest of the Statutes of Arkansas; embracing all the Laws of a General and Permanent character, in force at the close of the Session of the General Assembly of 1846; with notes of the Decisions of the Supreme Court upon the statutes: by E. H. English. Examined and approved by Samuel H. Hempstead, Esq. Little Rock. 1848.

A Digest of the Statutes of Arkansas: embracing all laws of a general and permanent character, in force at the close of the session of the General Assembly of 1856; together with Notes by Josiah Gould. Examined and approved by Geo. C. Watkins. Little Rock. 1858.

CALIFORNIA.

The Statutes of California, passed at the first session of the Legislature. Begun the 15th Day of December, 1849, and ended the 22d Day of April, 1850, at the City of Pueblo de San José. With an Appendix and Index. San José. 1850.

Compiled Laws of the State of California: containing all the Acts of the Legislature of a Public and General Nature, now in force, passed at the session 1850-1-2-3. By S. Garfield and F. A. Snyder, Esqrs., Compilers. Benicia. 1853.

Digest of the Laws of California: containing all Laws of a general character which will be in force on the first day of January, 1858. Prepared by William H. R. Wood. San Francisco. 1857.

COLORADO.

The Revised Statutes of Colorado: as passed at the seventh session of the Legislative Assembly, convened December, 1867. Central City. 1868.

CONNECTICUT.

The Revised Statutes of the State of Connecticut. Hartford. 1849.

The Statutes of the State of Connecticut. New Haven. 1854.

The General Statutes of the State of Connecticut. New Haven. 1866.

DELAWARE.

Revised Statutes of the State of Delaware, to the year 1852, inclusive. Dover, Del. 1852.

FLORIDA.

A Manual or Digest of the Statute Law of the State of Florida, of a general and public character, in force on the sixth day of January, 1847. Digested and arranged by Leslie A. Thompson, Esq. Boston. 1847.

The Code of Procedure of the State of Florida. Approved Feb. 19, 1870, and taking effect July 1, 1870. Tallahasse. 1870.

GEORGIA.

A digest of the Laws of the State of Georgia, containing all the statutes of a General or Public Nature, now in force, which have been passed in said state from the year 1820 to the year 1829, inclusive. By Arthur Foster. Philadelphia. 1831.

A Codification of the Statute Law of Georgia, including the English Statutes of force: in Four Parts. Compiled, Digested and Arranged by William A. Hotchkiss. Savannah and New York. 1845.

A Digest of the State Laws of the State of Georgia, in force prior to the session of the General Assembly of 1851. Compiled and published by Thomas R. R. Cobb. Athens, Ga. 1851.

The Code of the State of Georgia. Prepared by R. H. Clark, T. R. R. Cobb and D. Irwin. Revised by D. Irwin. Atlanta, Ga. 1867.

Illinois.

Revised Statutes of the State of Illinois, adopted by the General Assembly of said state, at its regular session held in the years 1844–5. Revised and prepared for publication by M. Brayman. Springfield. 1845.

The Statutes of Illinois, embracing all the General Laws of the State in force December 1, 1857. Compiled by Samuel H. Treat, Walter B. Scates and Robert S. Blackwell. 2 vols. Chicago. 1858.

Indiana.

The Revised Statutes of the State of Indiana, adopted and enacted by the General Assembly at their Twenty-second Session. Indianapolis. 1838.

The Revised Statutes of the State of Indiana passed at the Twenty-seventh session of the General Assembly. Indianapolis. 1843.

The Revised Statutes of the State of Indiana, passed at the Thirty-sixth session of the General Assembly. 2 vols. Indianapolis. 1852.

The Statutes of the State of Indiana; containing the Revised Statutes of 1852, with the amendments thereto and subsequent legislation. Edited by James Gavin and Oscar B. Hord. (Second Edition.) 2 vols. Indianapolis. 1862.

Iowa.

The Code of Iowa, passed at the session of the General Assembly of 1850–1, and approved 5th February, 1851. Iowa City. 1851.

Revision of 1860; containing all the statutes of a general nature of the State of Iowa, which are now in force, or are to be in force as the result of the legislati o Eighth General Assembly. Des Moines. 186 0

KANSAS.

The Satutes of the Territory of Kansas, passed at the first session of the Legislative Assembly, 1855. Shawnee M. L. School. 1855.

The Laws of the State of Kansas, passed at the tenth session of the Legislature commenced January 17, 1870. Topeka, Kansas. 1870.

General Laws of the State of Kansas, in force at the close of the session of Legislature ending March 6th, 1862. Topeka, Kansas. 1862.

The General Statutes of the State of Kansas, revised by John M. Price, Samuel A. Riggs, and James McMahon. Lawrence. 1868.

KENTUCKY.

Code of Practice in Civil and Criminal Cases, for the State of Kentucky; pprepared by M. C. Johnson, James Harlan and J. W. Stevenson, Commissioners. Frankfort. 1854.

A Digest of the Statute Laws of Kentucky, of a public and permanent nature, from the commencement of the Government to the Session of the Legislature ending on the 24th February, 1834. By C. S. Morehead and Mason Brown. 2 vols. Frakfort, Ky. 1834.

The Revised Statutes of Kentucky, by C. A. Wickliffe, S. Turner and S. S. Nicholas, Commissioners appointed by the Legislature: approved and adopted by the General Assembly, 1851 and 1852. In force from July 1, 1852. Frankfort, Ky. 1852.

The Revised Statutes of Kentucky, approved and adopted by the General Assembly, 1851 and 1852, and in force from July 1, 1852. With an Appendix containing the acts of 1859 and 1860. By R. H. Stanton. 2 vols. Cincinnati. 1860.

A Digest of the General Laws of Kentucky, enacted by the Legislature, between December 4, 1859, and June 4, 1865. Embracing all the General Laws passed since the publication of Stanton's Edition of the Revised Statutes. With an Appendix containing the Laws of the Winter Session, 1865–66. By Harvey Myers. Cincinnati. 1866.

LOUISIANA.

A General Digest of the Acts of the Legislature of Louisiana: passed from the year 1804 to 1827, inclusive, and in force at this last period. By L. Moreau Lislet, Esq. 2 vols. New Orleans. 1828.

A System of Penal Law, for the State of Louisiana: consisting of a Code of Crimes and Punishments, a Code of Procedure, a Code of Evidence, a Code of Reform and Prison Discipline, a Book of Definitions. Prepared by Edward Livingston. Philadelphia. 1833.

Civil Code of the State of Louisiana; with Annotations by Wheelock S. Upton, LL.B., and Needler R. Jennings. New Orleans. 1838.

The Revised Statutes of Louisiana, compiled by U. B. Phillips. New Orleans. 1856.

The Revised Statute Laws of the State of Louisiana, from the Organization of the Territory to the year 1867, inclusive. New Orleans. 1870.

Civil Code of the State of Louisiana; with the Statutory Amendments from 1825–1866, inclusive. Compiled and edited by James O. Fuqua. New Orleans and New York. 1867.

Code of Practice in Civil Cases for the State of Louisiana: with Statutory amendments, from 1825 to 1865, inclusive. Compiled and edited by James O. Fuqua. New Orleans and New York. 1867.

The Same. New Orleans and New York. 1869.

The Code of Practice of the State of Louisiana. New Orleans. 1870.

The Revised Civil Code of the State of Louisiana. New Orleans. 1870.

MAINE.

The Revised Statutes of the State of Maine, passed October 2, 1840; to which are subjoined the other Public Laws of 1840 and 1841. Augusta. 1840.

The Revised Statutes of the State of Maine, passed April 17, 1857. Bangor. 1857.

The Revised Statutes of the State of Maine, passed January 25, 1871. Portland.

MARYLAND.

The General Public Statutory Law and Public Local Law of the State of Maryland, from the year 1692 to 1839, inclusive. By Clement Dorsey. 5 vols. Baltimore. 1840.

The Same, in three vols.

The Maryland Code. Public General Laws, compiled by Otho Scott, and Hiram McCullough, Commissioners; adopted by the Legislature of Maryland, January Session, 1860: the Acts of that Session being therewith incorporated. By Henry C. Mackall. 2 vols. Baltimore. 1860.

A Collection of the British Statutes in force in Maryland, according to the Report thereof made to the General Assembly by the late Chancellor Kilty. By Julian J. Alexander. Baltimore. 1870.

MASSACHUSETTS.

The Acts and Resolves, Public and Private, of the Province of Massachusetts Bay; to which are prefixed the Charters of the Province. Vol. 1. Boston. 1869.

The Revised Statutes of Massachusetts. 1836.

The General Statutes of the Commonwealth of Massachusetts. Boston. 1860.

MICHIGAN.

The Revised Statutes of the State of Michigan, passed and approved May 18, 1846. Printed under the Superintendence of Samuel M. Greene. Detroit. 1846.

The Compiled Laws of the State of Michigan. Compiled and Arranged by Thomas M. Cooley. 2 vols. Lansing. 1851.

MINNESOTA.

The Revised Statutes of the Territory of Minnesota, passed at the second session of the Legislative Assembly, commencing Jan. 1. 1851. Saint Paul. 1851.

The Public Statutes of the State of Minnesota, (1849–1858.) Compiled by Moses Sherburne and William Hollinshead, Esqrs., Commissioners. Saint Paul. 1859.

The General Statutes of the State of Minnesota. Revised by Commissioners, etc., etc. St. Paul. 1866.

MISSISSIPPI.

Code of Mississippi: being an Analytical Compilation of the Public and General Statutes of the Territory and State, with Tabular References to the Local and Private acts, from 1798 to 1848. By A. Hutchinson. Jackson, Miss. 1848.

The Revised Code of the Statute Laws of the State of Mississippi. Jackson, Miss. 1857.

The Revised Code of the Statute Laws of the State of Mississippi. Jackson, Miss. 1871.

MISSOURI.

The Revised Statutes of the State of Missouri. Revised by the Eighth General Assembly during the years 1834 and 1835. St. Louis. 1835.

The Revised Statutes of the State of Missouri. Revised and Digested by the Thirteenth General Assembly during the session 1844 and 1845. St. Louis. 1845.

The General Statutes of the State of Missouri By A. F. Denny. City of Jefferson. 1866.

NEBRASKA.

The Revised Statutes of the Territory of Nebraska. In force July 1, 1866. Revised by E. Estabrook. Omaha. 1866.

NEW HAMPSHIRE.

The Revised Statutes of the State of New Hampshire, passed Dec. 23, 1842. Concord. 1843.

The Compiled Statutes of the State of New Hampshire. Concord. 1853.

The General Statutes of the State of New Hampshire. Manchester. 1867.

NEW JERSEY.

Statutes of the State of New Jersey. Trenton. 1847.

A Digest of the Laws of New Jersey. By Lucius Q. C. Elmer. Third Edition, containing all the laws of general application now in force, from 1709 to 1861, inclusive, with the Rules and Decisions of the Courts. By John T. Nixon. Bridgeton and Trenton. 1861.

The Same. Second Edition; containing all the laws of general application now in force, from 1709 to 1855, inclusive. By John T. Nixon. Philadelphia. 1855.

NEW YORK.

Laws of the State of New York, comprising the Constitution and Acts of the Legislature since the Revolution, from the first to the twentieth session, inclusive. 3 vols. 1798.

Laws of the State of New York. Second Edition. Vol. 2. Albany. 1807.

Statutes of the State of New York of a public and general character, passed from 1829 to 1851, both inclusive. Compiled and arranged by Samuel Blatchford. Index arranged by Clarence A. Seward. 2 vols. Auburn. 1852.

The Revised Statutes of the State of New York, passed during the years 1827, 1828. 3 vols. Albany. 1829.

The Same. Second Edition. 3 vols. Albany. 1836.

The Revised Statutes of the State of New York, as altered by subsequent enactments; together with statutory provisions of a general nature passed between 1828 and 1845, inclusive. Prepared by John Duer, Benjamin F. Butler and John C. Spencer. Third Edition. 3 vols. Albany. 1846.

The Revised Statutes of the State of New York, as altered by subsequent legislation; together with unrepealed statutory provisions of a general nature, passed from the time of the revision to the close of the session of the Legislature of 1858. Prepared by Amasa J. Parker, George Wolford and Edward Wade. Fifth Edition. 3 vols. Albany and New York. 1859.

Supplement to the Fifth Edition of the Revised Statutes of New York; containing the Amendments and General Statutes passed since the Fifth Revision. Arranged by Isaac Edwards. Albany and New York. 1863.

General Index to the Laws of the State of New York. By T. S. Gillett. Albany. 1859.

The Code of Procedure of Pleadings and Practice of the State of New York, 1858–9. By Nathan Howard, Jr. New York and Albany. 1859.

The Code of Procedure of the State of New York, unabridged. By Nathan Howard, Jr. Vol. 1. New York. 1867.

Voorhies' Code of Procedure of the State of New York. 4th Ed. New York. 1855.

The Same. As amended to 1864. 8th Ed. By John Townshend. New York. 1864.

The Same. As amended to 1871. 10th Ed. By John Townshend. New York. 1871.

The Code of Procedure of the State of New York, as amended to 1871. By William Wait. Albany. 1871.

North Carolina.

Revised Code of North Carolina, enacted by the General Assembly at the session of 1854; together with other acts of a general naiure passsd at the same session. Prepared by Bartholomew F. Moore and Asa Biggs. Boston. 1855.

Ohio.

Statutes of the State of Ohio, of a general nature, in force, Dec. 7, 1840: also, the statutes of a general nature passed by the General Assembly at their Thiriy-ninth Session,

Commencing Dec. 7, 1840. Collated, with references to the Decisions of the Courts and to prior laws. By J. R. Swan. Columbus. 1841.

Statutes of the State of Ohio, of a general nature, in force August, 1854: with references to prior repealed laws. Collated and Compiled by Joseph R. Swan. Cincinnati. 1854.

The Revised Statutes of the State of Ohio, of a general nature, in force August 1, 1860. Collated by Joseph R. Swan. With notes to the decisions of the Supreme Court. By Leander J. Critchfield. 2 vols. Cincinnati. 1860.

Supplement to the Revised Statutes of the State of Ohio; embracing all Laws of a general nature passed since the publication of Swan & Critchfield's Revised Statutes, 1860, in force August 1, 1868. Collated by Joseph R. Swan. With notes to the decisions of the Supreme Court by Milton Sayler. Cincinnati. 1868.

OREGON.

The Statutes of Oregon, enacted and continued in force by the Legislative Assembly, at the Fifth and Sixth Regular Sessions thereof. Oregon. 1855.

The Organic and other General Laws of Oregon. 1845–1864. Compiled and annotated by M. P. Deady. Portland, Oregon. 1866.

The Code of Civil Procedure and other General Statutes of Oregon, enacted by the Legislative Assembly, 1862. Oregon. 1863.

PENNSYLVANIA.

A Digest of the Laws of Pennsylvania from the year 1700, to May 21, 1861. Originally compiled by John Purdon, Esq. Ninth Edition by Frederick C. Brightly, Esq. Philadelphia. 1862.

A Digest of the Laws of Pennsylvania from the year 1700 to June 16, 1836. Fifth Edition. Previous editions by John Purdon. Philadelphia. 1837.

RHODE ISLAND AND PROVIDENCE PLANTATIONS.

The Revised Statutes of the State of Rhode Island and Providence Plantations. Providence. 1857.

SOUTH CAROLINA.

The Statutes at Large of South Carolina; edited by Thomas

Cooper, M. D., LL. D. 9 vols. Columbia, S. C. 1836–1841.

An Alphabetical Digest of the Public Statute Law of South Carolina. 3 vols. By Joseph Brevard. Charleston, S. C. 1814.

A Digested Index of the Statute Law of South Carolina, 1837 to 1857. By Charles B. Flagg. Charleston. 1858.

TENNESSEE.

The Statute Law of the State of Tennessee, of a Public and General Nature; Revised and Digested by John Haywood and Robert L. Cobb. 2 vols. Knoxville, Tenn. 1831.

The Code of Tennessee; enacted by the General Assembly of 1857–8. Prepared and Edited by Return J. Meigs and William F. Cooper. Revised by a Sub-committee of the Legislature, composed of Joseph B. Heiskell, Chairman, Micajah Bullock and Samuel T. Bicknell. Nashville, Tenn. 1858.

TEXAS.

The Penal Code. Adopted by the Sixth Legislature. Galveston. 1857.

A Digest of the Laws of Texas. By Oliver C. Hartley. Philadelphia. 1850.

A Digest of the General Statute Laws of the State of Texas; to which are subjoined the repealed laws of the Republic and State of Texas, by or through which rights have accrued. Prepared by Williamson S. Oldham and Geo. W. White. Austin, Texas, 1859.

A Digest of the Laws of Texas; containing laws in force and repealed laws on which rights rest. Carefully annotated. By Geo. W. Paschal, of Austin, Texas. Galveston and New York. 1866.

UTAH.

Acts, Resolutions and Memorials, passed at the several annual sessions of the Legislative Assembly of the Territory of Utah. To which are prefixed the Declaration of Independence, the Articles of the Confederation, the Ordinance of 1787, the Constitution of the United States, the Naturalization Laws, the Constitution of the Provisional State of Deseret, the Deseret Laws, and the Organic Act of Utah. Great Salt Lake City. 1855.

VERMONT.

Laws of the State of Vermont, Revised and Compiled in the year 1797. Rutland. 1798.

The Revised Statutes of the State of Vermont, passed November 18, 1839. To which are added several public acts now in force. Burlington. 1840.

The Compiled Statutes of the State of Vermont, being such of the Revised Statutes, and of the Public Acts and Laws passed since, as are now in force. Burlington. 1851.

The General Statutes of the State of Vermont, passed at the annual session of the General Assembly commencing October 9, 1862; together with of the public acts of the year 1862. 1863.

The General Statutes of the State of Vermont: passed at the annual session of the General Assembly, commencing October 9, 1862. Second Edition. Comprising the public laws enacted since the annual session of 1862. Published by the State of Vermont. 1870.

VIRGINIA.

The Code of Virginia. Richmond. 1849.

Ordinances and Acts of the Restored Government of Virginia, prior to the formation of the State of West Virginia; with the Constitution and Laws of the State of West Virginia, to March 2, 1866. Wheeling. 1866.

WEST VIRGINIA.

The Code of West Virginia. Comprising Legislation to the year 1870. With an appendix containing Legislation of that year. Wheeling. 1868.

WISCONSIN.

Statutes of the Territory of Wisconsin, passed by the Legislative Assembly thereof at the session commencing November, 1838, and at an adjourned session commencing in January, 1839. Albany, N. Y. 1839.

The Revised Statutes of the State of Wisconsin, passed at the second session of the Legislature, commencing Jan. 10, 1849. Southport. 1849.

The Revised Statutes of the State of Wisconsin, passed at the annual session of the Legislature commencing Jan. 13, 1858, approved May 17, 1858. Chicago, Ill. 1858.

The Revised Statutes of the State of Wisconsin, altered and amended by subsequent legislation, together with the unrepealed statutes of a general nature, passed from the time of the revision of 1858 to the close of the Legislature of 1871. Prepared and arranged by David Taylor. 2 vols. St. Louis. 1871.

UNITED STATES OF AMERICA.

The Public Statutes of the United States of America, from the organization of the Government in 1789, to March 3, 1845. Arranged in chronological order, with references to the matter of each act, and to the subsequent acts on the same subject, and copious notes of the Decisions of the Courts of the United States construing those acts, and upon the subjects of the laws. With an index to the contents of each volume, and a full general index to the whole work, in the concluding volume. Edited by Richard Peters, Esq. 8 vols. Vols. 1–5 containing General Laws, etc.: Vol. 6, Private Laws; Vol. 7, Indian Treaties; Vol. 8, European Treaties. Boston. 1845–46.

The Statutes at Large and Treaties of the United States of America. Vols. 9 and 10. Edited by George Minot; Vol. 11, by George Minot and George P. Sanger; Vols. 12 to 16, by George P. Sanger. Vol. 9, from December, 1845 to 1851. Vol. 10, from December, 1851 to 1854. Vol. 11, from December, 1854, to 1858. Vol. 12, from December, 1858, to 1863. Vol. 13, from December, 1863, to 1865. Vol. 14, from December, 1865, to 1867. Vol. 15, from December, 1867 to 1869. Vol. 16, from December, 1869, to 1871.

"Story's Laws of the United States." From 1789 to 1836. 4 vols. Comprising—

1. The Public and General Statutes passed by the Congress of the United States of America, from 1789 to 1827, inclusive; whether expired, repealed or in force; arranged in chronological order, with Marginal References and a copious Index; to which is added the Constitution of the United States and an Appendix. Published under the inspection of Joseph Story, one of the Justices of the Supreme Court of the U. S. 3 vols. Boston. 1828.

2. The Public and General Statutes passed by the Congress of the United States of America, from 1828 to 1836, inclusive; whether expired, repealed or in force; arranged in Chronological Order, with Marginal References. Edited by George Sharswood. Philadelphia. 1837.

An Analytical Digest of the Laws of the United States from the Adoption of the Constitution to the Thirty-fourth Congress. 1789–1869. By Frederick C. Brightly, Esq. 2 vols. Philadelphia. 1858–1869.

An Analytical Digest of the Laws of the United States from the commencement of the Thirty-fifth to the end of the Thirty-seventh Congress. 1857–1863. Completing Brightly's United States Digest to the present time. By Frederick C. Brightly, Esq. Philadelphia. 1863.

Statutes of the United States relating to Revenue, Commerce, Navigation and the Currency. Compiled by Lewis Heyl, of the Treasury Department. Boston. 1868.

A Compendium of Internal Revenue Laws, with Decisions, Rulings, Instructions, Regulations and Forms. By J. B. F. Davidge and I. G. Kimball. Washington, D. C. 1871.

A Digest of the Decisions in the Office of the Second Comptroller of the Treasury. Compiled under the direction of Comptroller. By John W. Butterfield, of the Second Comproller's office. Third Edition. Washington, D. C. 1869.

The Military Laws of the United States, relating to the Army, Volunteers, Militia and to Bounty Lands and Pensions, from the foundation of the Government to the year 1863. By John F. Callan. Philadelphia. 1863.

A Digest of the Military Laws of the United States, from 1860 to 1867. Relating to the Army, Volunteers, Militia, etc. Compiled by Lieut. Col. J. S. Poland, U. S. A. Boston. 1868.

The American Diplomatic Code, embracing a collection of Treaties and Conventions between the United States and Foreign Powers; from 1775 to 1834. By Jonathan Elliot. 2 vols. Washington. 1834.

A Synoptical Index to the Laws and Treaties of the United States of America, from March 4, 1789, to March 3, 1851. Prepared under the Direction of the Secretary of State. Boston. 1852.

Public Lands. Laws of the United States, Resolutions of Congress under the Confederation, Treaties, Proclamations, Spanish Regulations, and other Documents respecting the Public Lands. Washington. 1828.

Public Lands. General Public Acts of Congress, respecting the Sale and Disposition of the Public Lands; with Instructions issued from time to time, by the Secretary of the Treasury and Commissioner of the General Land Office, and Official Opinions of the Attorney General on questions arising under the Land Laws. Part I, containing the Laws to the close of the 25th Congress. Part II, containing the Instructions and opinions to the 17th of August, 1838. 2 vols. Washington. 1838.

BRITISH STATUTES.

THE STATUTES AT LARGE, from Magna Charta to 33 Victoria. 47 vols. 4to. London. 1763–1869.

The Public General Statutes, with a list of the Local and Private Acts, passed in the 29th, 30th, 31st and 32d years of the reign of Her Majesty Queen Victoria, being the First, Second and Third Sessions of the Nineteenth Parliament of the United Kingdom of Great Britain and Ireland. 3 vols. London. 1866–68.

BIDDLE (John). A Table of References to unrepealed Public General Acts: arranged in the alphabetical order of their short or popular titles. 2d Ed. With a Supplement. London. 1870.

CANADIAN STATUTES.

The Consolidated Statutes for Upper Canada. Toronto. 1859.

The Consolidated Statutes of Canada. Toronto. 1859.

FRENCH STATUTES.

LOCRE (M. Le Baron). La Legislation Civile, Commerciale et Criminelle de la France. 16 Tomes. Paris. 1827–1829.

CODE NAPOLEON; or, The French Civil Code. Literally translated from the original and official edition, published at Paris in 1804. By a Barrister of the Inner Temple. New York. 1841.

SESSION LAWS.

ALABAMA.

Acts of the General Assembly of Alabama, held in the City of Montgomery, for the years 1850, 52, 53–4, 57–8, 59–60, 65–66, 66–7, 68, 69–70, 70–1. 10 vols.

ARIZONA.

Acts, Resolutions and Memorials, adopted by the Legislative Assembly of the Territory of Arizona, for the years 1864, 65, 66 and 68. 4 vols.

ARKANSAS.

Acts passed by the General Assembly of the State of Arkansas, during the years 1843, 5 and 6, 49 and 51, 53, 55, 56–7, 58–9, 66–7, 67, 68–9, 71. 10 vols.

CALIFORNIA.

The Statutes of California passed by the Legislature, during the years 1851, 52, 54, 55, 56, 57, 59, 60, 61, 62, 63, 63–4, 65–6, 67–8, 69–70. 15 vols.

Supplement to the Statutes of 1869–70, containing chapters 584–586. 2 copies. Sacramento. 1870.

CHOCTAW NATION.

Acts and Resolutions of the General Council of the Choctaw Nation, from 1852 to 1857, both inclusive. Fort Smith, Ark. 1858.

COLORADO.

General Laws, Joint Resolutions, Memorials, and Private Acts, passed by the Legislative Assembly of the Territory of Colorado, during the years 1861, 62 and 70. 3 vols.

CONNECTICUT.

Public Acts passed by the General Assembly of the State of Connecticut during the years 1847–9, 51, 52, 53, 55, 57, 58, 59, 60, 61, Spec. Sess. 61 and 62, Spec. Sess. 62, 63, 64, 65, 66, 67, 66–8, 69, 70, 71. 22 vols.

Resolutions and Private Acts of the General Assembly of the State of Connecticut during the years 1856, 57, 58,

59, 64, and Spec. Sess. 64, 60, 61, 61–2, 63, 65, 66, 67, 68, 69, 70, 71. 16 vols.

Resolves and Private Laws of the State of Connecticut from 1836 to 1865. 3 vols. Vols. 3–5. Hartford. 1857–71.

Laws of the State of Connecticut relating to Education. Hartford. 1868.

DAKOTA.

General Laws and Memorials, and Resolutions of the Territory of Dakota, passed during the years 1862, 62–3, 66–7, 70–71. 4 vols.

General and Private Laws and Memorials and Resolutions of the Territory of Dakota during the years 1863–4, 65–6, 67–8. 3 vols.

Laws, Memorials and Resolutions of the Territory of Dakota, passed by the Legislative Assembly of 1865–6.

DELAWARE.

Laws of the State of Delaware passed by the General Assembly, during the years 1837–43, 47–51, 59, 63, 66, 67, 69, 71. 8 vols.

FLORIDA.

The Acts and Resolutions adopted by the Legislature of Florida during the years 1849–51, 52, 55 56, 58, 59, 68, 69–71. 8 vols.

GEORGIA.

Acts of the General Assembly of the State of Georgia during the years 1839 and 42, 51–2, 53–4, 55-6, 57, 58, 59, 60, 61, 63, 63–4, 64–5, 65-6, 66, 68, 69. 16 vols.

IDAHO.

Laws, Memorials and Resolutions, passed by the Legislative Assembly of the Territory of Idaho during the years 1863–64, 66–7. 2 vols.

LLI NOIS.

Laws of the State of, passed by the General Assembly during the years 1839–40, 41, 42–3, 45, 47, 49, 2d Sess. 49, 51, 52, 53, 54, 55. 11 vols.

Public Laws of the State of, passed by the General Assembly during the years 1861, 63, 65, 67, 69. 5 vols.

Private Laws of the State of, passed by the General Assembly during the years 1861, 63 and 69. 6 vols.

Public and Private Laws of the State of, passed by the General Assembly at its first and second special sessions, June 11 and June 14, 1867.

INDIANA.

General Laws of the State of, passed by the General Assembly during the years 1843–6, 39–42, 47–9, 50–1. 4 vols.

Laws of a Local nature passed by the General Assembly of the State of Indiana during the year 1843, 45, 49. 3 vols.

Laws of the State of Indiana, passed by the General Assembly during the years 1853, 55, 57, Spec. Sess. 58, 59, 61, and Spec. Sess. 61, 63–4, 65, 67, 69, and Spec. Sess. 69, 71. 11 vols.

IOWA.

Acts, Resolutions and Memorials passed by the General Assembly of the State of Iowa during the years 1848, 52–3, 54–5, 57, 58.

Acts and Resolutions passed by the General Assembly of the State of Iowa during the years 1847–8, 49 and 51, 62, Ex. Sess. '62, 64, 66, 68, 70.

Special Acts and Resolutions passed at the Regular Session of the Eighth General Assembly of the State of Iowa, A. D. 1860.

KANSAS.

Laws of the Territory of, passed by the General Legislative Assembly during the years 1857, 57–8. 2 vols.

General Laws of the Territory of Kansas during the years 1859, 60. 2 vols.

General Laws of the State of Kansas during the years 1861, 63. 2 vols.

Laws of the State of Kansas during the years 1870, 1871. 2 vols.

KENTUCKY.

Acts of the General Assembly of the Commonwealth of Kentucky during the years 1836–7, 37–8, 40–1, 41–2, 42–3, 47–8, 48–9, 49–50, 51–2, 53–4, 55–6, 59–60, Called Sess. 61, 2d Called Sess. 61, 61–2 and 3, 63–4, 65. 18 vols.

LOUISIANA.

Acts passed by the Legislature of the State of Louisiana,

during the years 1828–9, 30–2, 33, 34, 35, 36, 37, 38–9, 40–1, 42, 43–4, 46, 47, 48, 50, 52, 53, 55, 56, 61, 64, Extra Sess. 65, 66, 67, 68, 69, 70.

MAINE.

Resolves of the Legislature of the State of Maine during the years 1837–38. 2 vols.

Acts and Resolves passed by the Legislature of the State of Maine, during the years 1840, 41, 42–3, 45–6, 48–9, 50–1, 52, 53, 55, 56, 57, 58, 59, 60, 61, 62, 63, 64, 65, 66, 67, 68, 69, 70, 71. 25 vols.

MARYLAND.

Laws made and passed by the General Assembly of the State of Maryland, during the years 1835, 39, 40 and 42, 41, 43, 49, 52, 53, 54, 56, 58, 60, 61, 61–62, 64, 65, 66, 67, 68, 70. 20 vols.

The New Constitution of the State of Maryland. 1864.

The Constitution of the State of Maryland. 1867.

MASSACHUSETTS.

Laws of the Commonwealth of Massachusetts, passed by the General Court during the years 1830, 38, 57–8.

Acts and Resolves passed by the General Court of Massachusetts during the years 1840 and 45, 45–46, 47–8, 49, 49–50, 52, 53, 55, 56, 57, 58, 59, 60, 65, 61, 62, 63, 64, 66, 67, 68, 69, 70, 71. 24 vols.

Private and Special Statutes of the Commonwealth of Massachusetts for years 1849–65. 3 vols. Vols. 9–11. Boston. 1860.

MICHIGAN.

Laws of the Territory of Michigan passed by the Legislative Council during the year 1833.

Acts of the Legislature of the State of Michigan passed during the years 1837–8, 38, 39, 40, 41, 42, 43, 44, 45, 46, 47, 48, 49, 50, 51, 53, 57, 59, 61, Ex. Sess. 63, Ex. Sess. 64, 65, 67, 69, Ex. Sess. 70, 71. 26 vols.

School Laws of Michigan. Lansing. 1859.

The Same. 1869.

MINNESOTA.

Session Laws of the Territory and State of Minnesota, passed by the Legislative Assembly during the years 1850, 51–52, 53, 55, 57, Ex. Sess. 57, 61, 62, Ex. Sess. 62, 63, 64 65, 66, 67, 68, 70, 71. 18 vols.

Special Laws of the State of Minnesota passed in 1858.

General Laws of the State of Minnesota passed in 1858.

MISSISSIPPI.

Laws of the State of Mississppi passed by the Legislature during the years 1838, 40, 46, 48, 50, 56–7, 59, 65, 67 70. 10 vols.

Constitution of the State of Mississippi as amended, with the Ordinance and Resolutions adopted by the Constitutional Convention, August, 1865. Jackson. 1865.

MISSOURI.

Laws of the State of Missouri, passed by the General Assembly during the years 1837, 38–9, 40–1, 47, 49, 51, 53, 57, 58–9, 60–1, 63, 63–4, 65, 67, 68, 69, 71. 17 vols.

Local Laws and Private Acts of the State of Missouri, passed at the first session of the Thirteenth General Assembly. 1845.

NEBRASKA.

Laws, Joint Resolutions, and Memorials, passed by the Legislative Assembly of the Territory of Nebraska during the year 1857, 57–8, 58, 59, 60, 61, 64, 65, 67. 9 vols.

NEVADA.

Laws of the Territory of Nevada passed by the Legislative Assembly during the years 1861, 62, 64. 3 vols.

Statutes of the State of Nevada, passed by the Legislature during the years 1864–5, 66, 67, 69, 71. 5 vols.

NEW HAMPSHIRE.

Laws of the State of New Hampshire, passed during the years 1838–45, 42–7, 47–50, 51, 52, 55, 56, 57, 59, 61, 62, 62, 64, 65, 66, 67, 68, 69, 70, 71. 20 vols.

NEW JERSEY.

Acts of the General Assembly of the State of New Jersey, during the years 1837–8, 42–5, 46–8, 49, 51, 52, 53, 54, 55, 56, 57, 58, 59, 60, 61, 63, 64, 66, 67, 68, 69, 70, 71. 23 vols.

NEW MEXICO.

Laws of the Territory of New Mexico, passed by the Legislative Assembly during the years 1851–2, 66–7. 2 vols.

NEW YORK.

Laws of the State of New York, passed by the Legislature during the years from the Revolution to 1798. 3 vols.

Laws of the State of New York, passed by the Legislature during the years 1848, 49, 50, 51, 52, 53, 54, 55, 56, 57, 58, 59, 60, 61, 62, 63, 64, 65, 66, 67, 68, 69, 70, 71. 31 vols.

General Index to the Laws of the State of New York. By T. S. Gillett. Albany. 1859.

Militia Law of the State of New York. Albany. 1854.

NORTH CAROLINA.

Laws of the State of North Carolina, passed by the General Assembly during the years 1837, 44–5, 48–9, 50–1, 52. 5 vols.

Public Laws of the State of North Carolina, passed by the General Assembly during the years 1854–5, 56–7, 58–9, 60–4, 65–6, 66–7, 68–9, 69–70, 70–1. 9 vols.

OHIO.

Acts of a General Nature passed by the General Assembly of the State of Ohio during the years 1836–7, 38, 39–40, 40–1, 41–2, 42–3, 43–4, 45–6, 46–7, 47–8, 48–9, 49–50, 50–1, 51, 52, 53, 54, 57, 58, 59, 60, 61, 62.

General and Local Laws and Joint Resolutions passed by the General Assembly of the State of Ohio during the years 1863, 64, 65, 66, 67, 68, 69, 70, 71. 9 vols.

Index to Ohio Laws, General and Local, and to the Resolutions of the General Assembly, from 1845–57, inclusive. By William T. Coggeshall. Columbus. 1858.

Chio School Laws. Second Edition. 1858. Columbus. 1858.

The Same. Third Edition. 1862. Columbus. 1862.

The Same. Fourth Edition. 1865.

Annual Report of the Commissioner of Railroads and Telegraphs, for the year 1870. With Railroad Laws and Charters. In two volumes. Prepared by Geo. B. Wright, Commissioner. Columbus. 1870.

OREGON.

Acts and Resolutions of the Legislative Assembly of the State of Oregon, passed during the years 1860, 66, 70. 3 vols.

Laws of the Territory of Oregon, enacted by the Legislative Assembly during the year 1858. 1 vol.

PENNSYLVANIA.

Laws of the Commonwealth of, during the years 1822–5, 27–8, 37, 38, 38–9, 40, 41, 43, 44, 45, 46, 48, 50, 51, 52, 53, 54, 55, 56, 57, 58, 59, 60, 61, 62, 63, 64, 65, 66, 67, 68, 69, 70, 71. 34 vols.

The Election Laws of Pennsylvania. Harrisburg. 1868.

RHODE ISLAND AND PROVIDENCE PLANTATIONS.

Public Laws of the State of Rhode Island and Providence Plantations, during the years 1835–46, 44, 48–51, 58–9, 57–68, Supplements 63–5, 67–9, 69–71. 8 vols.

Acts and Resolves of the General Assembly of the State of Rhode Island and Providence Plantations, passed during the years 1850–53, 51–2, 55, 56, 55–7, 57, 58, 59, 60, 61, 62, 63, 65, 67–68, 68–9. 21 vols.

Index to the printed Acts and Resolves, and of the Petitions and Reports to the General Assembly of the State of Rhode Island and Providence Plantations, from the year 1758 to 1850. By John Russell Bartlett. Providence. 1856.

SOUTH CAROLINA.

Acts of the General Assembly of the State of South Carolina, passed during the years 1845–6, 61, 63, 64–5, 66, Extra Sess. 66, 68–9, 69–70, 71.

TENNESSEE.

Acts of the General Assembly of the State of Tennessee passed during the years 1839–40, 41–2, 47–8, 51–2, 53–4, 65, 65–6, Ex. Sess. 66, 66–7, 67–8, Ex. Sess. 68, 69–70, 71. 13 vols.

Public Acts of the State of Tennssee passed during the years 1857–8, 59–60, Ex. Sess. 61. 3 vols.

The Militia Law of the State of Tennessee, passed Jan. 28, 1840. Nashville. 1840.

TEXAS.

Laws and Decrees of the State of Coahuila and Texas, in Spanish and English, during the years 1821–36, 39. 2 vols.

Laws passed by the State of Texas during the years 1846, 48, 50, 52, 53–4. 5 vols.

General Laws of the State of Texas passed during the years 1855–6, 57 and 8, 59–60, 59–64, 66. Called Sess. 70. 6 vols.

UTAH.

Acts and Resolutions passed by the Legislative Assembly o the Territory Utah, during the years 1852, 52–3, 61–2f 3 vols.

VERMONT.

Acts and Laws passed by the Legislature of the State of Vermont during the years, 1802, 10, 11, 12, 13, 14, 15, 16, 17, 18, 19, 20, 21, 22, 23, 24, 25, 26, 27, 28, 29, 30, 31, 32, 33, 34, 35, 36, 37, 38, 39, 40, 41. 33 vols.

The Acts and Resolves passed by the Legislature of the State of Vermont during the years 1842, 43, 44, 45, 46, 47, 48, 46–8, 49–50, 51, 52, 53, 54, 55, 56, 57, 58, 59, 60, 61, 62, 63, 64, 65, 66, 67, 68, 69, 70. 29 vols.

VIRGINIA.

Acts of the General Assembly of Virginia, passed during the year 1839–40, 39, 42, 47–8, 49–50, 48–9, 50–1, 52, 52–3, 55–6, 57–8, 59–60, 61, 61–2, 62 and 63, 63 and 64, 62, 65–66, 66–7, 69–70, 70–1. 21 vols.

WASHINGTON.

Statutes of the Territory of Washington, being the Code passed by the Legislative Assembly at their first session, 1854.

Laws of the Territory of Washington. 1856.

Acts of the Legislative Assembly of the Territory of Washington passed during the years 1857–8, 58–9.

Session Laws of the Territory of Washington, and the Resolutions and Memorials of the Legislative Assembly at its session 1860–61.

WEST VIRGINIA.

Acts of the Legislature of West Virginia, passed during the years 1866, 67, 68, 69, 70, 71. 6 vols.

WISCONSIN.

Acts of the Legislature of Wisconsin during the years 1836–8, 40–52. 9 vols.

General Laws passed by the Legislature of Wisconsin during the years 1853–71. 21 vols.

Private and Local Laws passed by the Legislature of Wisconsin, during the years 1853–71. 16 vols.

Election Laws of the State of Wisconsin, with extracts from the Constitution, together with forms and instructions for the use of Clerks, Inspectors, etc. Prepared under the direction of David W. Jones, Sec'y of State, by John W. Hunt, Ass't Sec'y. Madison. 1857.

The Code of Procedure of the State of Wisconsin, as passed by the Legislature in 1856, and amended in 1856 and 1857. Published by direction of David W. Jones,

Sec'y of State, with corrections and a complete Index, by John W. Hunt, Assistant Secretary. Madison. 1857.

Laws of Wisconsin relating to the organization and Government of Towns, and the Powers and Duties of Town Officers, with Practical Forms. By J. C. Spooner and E. E. Bryant, Counsellors-at-Law. Madison, Wis. 1869.

Laws of Wisconsin relating to Common Schools. 1857. Paper.

The Same. 1870.

School Code of Wisconsin for the year 1867.

Laws of Wisconsin relating to the Organization and Government of Towns, etc. By Elijah M. Haines. 1858. Paper.

CANADA SESSION LAWS.

Statutes of the Province of Canada, passed during the years 1860, 61, 62, 63, 64, 65, 66. 7 vols. Quebec. 1860–1866.

Statutes of the Dominion of Canada, passed during the years 1867–68, 70–71. 4 vols. Quebec. 1867–1871.

PART FIFTH.

LEGISLATIVE AND EXECUTIVE
DOCUMENTS.

DOCUMENTS, ETC.

ALABAMA.

Journals of the House of Representatives of the State of Alabama during their sessions in the years 1857–8, 59–60. 2 vols. Paper.

Journals of the Senate of the State of Alabama at their sessions held in the years 1857–8, 59–60. 2 vols. Paper.

ARKANSAS.

Journals of the House of Representatives, for the sessions of the General Assembly of the State of Arkansas, held during the years 1858–9, 66–7, 68, 68–9, 71. 5 vols. Paper.

Journals of the Senate for the sessions of the General Assembly of the State of Arkansas, held during the the years 1858–9, 64, 64–5, 65, 66–7, 68–9, 71. 5 vols. Paper.

Messages of Elias N. Conway, Governor of Arkansas, to both Houses of the General Assembly; Nov. 4, 1856, and Nov. 3, 1858. 2 vols. Paper.

Journal of the Convention of Delegates of the people of Arkansas, assembled at the Capitol, Jan. 4, 1864; also Journals of the House of Representatives of the sessions 1864, 64–5, 65. Paper. Little Rock. 1870.

Debates and Proceedings of the Convention which assembled at Little Rock, January 7, 1868, under the Provisions of an Act of Congress of March 2d, 1867, and the Acts of March 23d and July 19th, 1867, to form a Constitution for the State of Arkansas. Official: John G. Price, Secretary. Little Rock. 1868.

ARIZONA.

Journals of the 1st, 2d, and 3d Legislatures of the Territory of Arizona, 1864, 65, 66. 3 vols.

CALIFORNIA.

Journals of the Legislature of the State of California, at its second session, 1851.

Journals of the Assembly during the sessions of the Legislature of the State of California, for the years 1854, '56 '57, '58 '59, '60, '61, '62, '63, '63-4, '65-6, '67-8, '69-70. 13 vols.

Journals of the Senate during the sessions of the Legislature of the State of California, for the years 1854, '55, '56, '57, '58, '59, '60, '61, '62, '63, '63-4, '65-6, '67-8, '69-70. 14 vols.

Appendix to the Journals of the Assemby during the sessions of the Legislature of the State of California for the years 1856, '57, '58, '59, '60, '61. 6 vols.

Appendix to the Journals of the Senate during the sessions of the Legislature of the State of California for the years 1855, '58, '59, '60, '61. 6 vols.

Appendix to the Journals of the Senate and Assembly during the sessions of the Legislature of the State of California for the years 1862, '63, '63-4, '65-6, '67-8, '69-70. 6 vols.

First and Third Biennial Reports of the Superintendent of Public Instruction of the State of California, for the school years 1864 and 1865, 1868 and 1869. 2 vols.

Catalogue of the California State Library, prepared by W. C. Stratton, State Librarian. Sacramento. 1866.

Bibliotheca Californiae. A Descriptive Catalogue of books in the State Library of California. 2 vols. Vol. 1, Law Library; Vol. 2, General Library. Sacramento. 1870.

Relacion de los Debates de la Convencion de California, sobre la Formacion de la Constitucion de Estado, en Setiembre y Octobre de 1849. Por J. Ross Browne. Nueva York. 1851.

Report of the Debates in the Convention of California on the Formation of the State Constitution, in September and October, 1849. By J. Ross Browne. Washington. 1850.

Transactions of the California State Agricultural Society during the year 1858. Sacramento. 1859.

COLORADO.

Council Journals of the Legislative Assembly of the Territory of Colorado. Sessions during the years 1861, '62, '70. 3 vols. Paper.

House Journals of the Legislative Assembly of the Territory of Colorado. Sessions during the year 1861, '62, '70. 3 vols. Paper.

CONNECTICUT.

Journals of the Senate of the State of Connecticut, for the sessions of the years 1853, '58, '58,' 59, '60, '62, '63, '63–4, 64, '65, '66, '67, '68,'69, '70, '71. 15 vols. (All paper except those for 1867, '68, '69.)

Journals of the House of Representatives of the State of Connecticut for the sessions of the years 1856, '57, '58, '59, '60, '61, Spec. Sess. '61, '63–64, '64, '65, '66, '67 '68, '69, '70, '71. 15 vols. (All paper except those for 1867, '68, '71.)

The Public Records of the Colony of Connecticut, from August, 1689, to May, 1706, transcribed and edited, in accordance with with Resolutions of the General Assembly, by Charles J. Hoadley. Hartford. 1868.

Messages, Reports, &c., communicated to the Legislature of Connecticut, at the sessions for the years 1857, '58, '60, '61, '62, '64, '66, '67, '68, '69, '70, '71. 12 vols.

The Transactions of the Conn. State Agricultural Society, for the year 1857–58, with the Reports of the County Societies, for the same year. Hartford. 1858.

Third and Fourth Annual Reports of the Connecticut Board of Agriculture. 1868–9, 1869–70. 2 vols.

Report of the Bank Commissioners to the General Assembly. May session, 1859. Paper. New Haven. 1859.

Annual Report of the Superintendent of Common Schools of Connecticut to the General Assembly. Pamphlet. 1859.

Report of the Commissioner of the School Fund to the General Assembly, May session, 1859. Pamphlet. New Haven. 1859.

Report of the Directors of the Connecticut State Prison to the General Assembly. May session, 1859. Pamphlet. New Haven. 1859.

Seven Annual Report of the Board of Trustees of the State Reform School of Connecticut, for the year 1859, to the General Assembly. May session, 1859. New Haven. 1859.

Annual Report of the Trustees of the State Normal School to the General Assembly. May session, 1859. With a Catalogue of the School. Pamphlet. New Haven. 1859.

The Thirty-fifth Annual Report of the Officers of the Retreat for the Insane, at Hartford, Conn., April, 1859. Pamplet. Hartford. 1859.

Addresses Delivered on the occasion of the Dedication of the Hartford Hospital in Hartford, Conn., on the 18th of April, 1859. Pamphlet. Hartford. 1859.

The Forty-third Annual Report of the Directors of the American Asylum at Hartford for the Education and Instruction of the Deaf and Dumb. Pamphlet. Hartford. 1859.

Connecticut Common School Journal, published under direction of the Commissioners of Common Schools, from 1838 to 1842. Vols. 1–4 in one. Edited by Henry Barnard. 4to. Hartford. 1842.

DAKOTA.

Council Journals of the sessions of the Legislative Assembly of the Territory of Dakota held during the years 1862, '63-4, '64–5, '65–6, '66–7, '67–8. 6 vols. (All paper except 1863–64, 65–6.)

House Journals of the sessions of the Legislative Assembly of the Territory of Dakota held during the years 1862, '63–4, '64–5, '65–6, '66–7, '67–8. 6 vols. (All paper except 1863–4.)

DELAWARE.

Annual reports of the Wilmington Institute. Incorporated January, 1859. 1862, 1863, 1865 and 1866. Wilmington, Delaware. Three pamphlets.

FLORIDA.

A Journal of Proceedings of the Senate of the General Assembly of the State of Florida, at the Ninth session, 1858, and at an adjourned session, 1859. Paper.

A Journal of Proceedings of the House of Representatives of the General Assembly of the State of Florida at the Ninth session, and at an adjourned session, 1859. Paper.

A Journal of Proceedings of the House of Representatives of the General Assembly of the State of Florida, at its Eighth session, begun November 24, 1856.

GEORGIA.

Journals of the Senate of the State of Georgia at the sessions of the General Assembly held during the years 1858–59. Called Sessions '68, '69. 4 vols. Paper.

Journals of the House of Representatives of the State of Georgia, at the Sessions of the General Assembly held during the years 1858–59. Called Sessions '68, 69.

Catalogue of the Georgia State Library. 1869. By John L. Conley, State Librarian. Atlanta, Georgia. 1869.

IDAHO.

Council Journals of the Sessions of the Legislative Assembly of the Territory of Idaho, held during the years 1863–4, '70–1. 2 vols. Paper.

House Journals of the sessions of the Legislative Assembly of the Territory of Idaho, held during the years 1863–4, '70–1. 2 vols. Paper.

Journals of the Council and House of Representatives of the fourth session of the Legislative Assembly of the Territory of Idaho, held 1866–7. Paper.

ILLINOIS.

Journals of the Senate of the General Assembly of the State of Illinois at the sessions held during the years 1849–51, '61, '63, '65, '67, '69. 7 vols.

Journals of the House of Representatives of the General Assembly of the State of Illinois, at their sessions held during the years 1861, '63, '65, '67, '69. 8 vols.

Journals of the Senate and House of Representatives of the State of Illinois, at the sessions of the General Assembly held 1867.

Journal of the Constitutional Convention of the State of Illinois, convened at Springfield, January 7, 1862.

Reports made to the General Assembly of Illinois, at its sessions held during the years 1861, '65, '67, '69. 7 vols.

Journal of the Constitutional Convention of the State of Illinois, convened at Springfield, Dec. 13, 1869. Springfield. 1870.

Debates of the Constitutional Convention of the State of Illinois, convened at Springfield, Dec. 13, 1869. Springfield. 1870.

Reports of the Adjutant General of the State of Illinois. 8 vols. Containing the Reports for the years from 1861 to 1866, inclusive.

Transactions of the Illinois Agricultural Society, with Reports from County Agricultural Societies and Kindred Associations. Edited by John P. Reynolds, Sec'y. Vol. VII. 1867–8. Springfield. 1870.

Third Annual Report of the Board of Trustees of the Illinois Industrial University, for the Academic year commencing Sept. 13, 1869, and closing June 4, 1870. With a Report of the Agricultural Lectures and Discussions at Champaign, Centralia and Rockford, etc. Springfield. 1870.

First Biennial Report of the Board of State Commissioners of Public Charities of the State of Illinois. Presented to the Governor, December, 1870. Springfield. 1871.

Eighth Biennial Report of the Superintendent of Public Instruction of the State of Illinois. 1869–70.

Message of his Excellency, Richard Yates, Governor of Illinois, to the General Assembly, Jan. 2, 1865. Pamphlet.

Biennial Report of the Auditor of Public Accounts of the State of Illinois to the twenty-second General Assembly. Springfield. 1861. Pamphlet.

Geological Survey of Illinois. 4 vols., 4to. Vol. 1, Geology. Vol. 2, Paleontology. Vols. 3 and 4, Geology and Paleontology. A. H. Worthen, Director. Assistants, F. B. Meek, J. S. Newberry, Leo Lesquereux, Henry Engelmann, H. C. Freeman, H. M. Bannister. Chicago. 1866–70.

INDIANA.

Documents of the General Assembly of Indiana, at the thirty-third and thirty-ninth sessions, 1849 and 1857. 3 vols.

Journal of the Senate of Indiana during the thirty-ninth session of the General Assembly, 1857.

Journal of the House of Representatives of the State of Indiana, during the thirty-ninth session of the General Assembly. 1857.

Twentieth Annual Report of the Trustees and Superintendent of the Indiana Institute for the Education of the Blind. To the Governor. Indianapolis. 1866. Pamphlet.

Report of the Adjutant General of the State of Indiana. 8 vols. Containing Indiana in the War of the Rebellion, and Statistics and Documents. Indianapolis. 1869.

IOWA.

Journals of the Senate at the sessions of the General Assembly held during the years 1862, 68, 70. 3 vols.

Journals of the House of Representatives at the sessions of the General Assembly held during the years 1862, 68, 70. 3 vols.

Legislative Documents submitted to the General Assembly of the State of Iowa during the years 1868 to 1870. 4 vols.

Reports of the Adjutant General and Acting Quartermaster General of Iowa. 8 vols. 1861 to 1865, 1868. (1861, paper.)

Census of the State of Iowa. 1856.

Report on the Geological Survey of the State of Iowa, to the Thirteenth General Assembly, January, 1870, containing results of examinations and observations made within the years 1866 to 1869. By Charles A. White, M.D. Geological Survey: Charles A. White, State Geologist. Orestes H. St. John, Assistant. Rush Emery, Chemist. 2 vols. 4to. Des Moines. 1870.

Report on the Geological Survey of the State of Iowa; embracing the results of investigations made during portions of the years 1855, 56, 57. By James Hall, State Geologist; J. D. Whitney, Chemist and Mineralogist. 2 vols. Vol. 1, Geology. Vol. 2, Paleontology. 1858.

Geological Survey of Iowa. 1858.

KANSAS.

Journals of the House of Representatives of the Territory of Kansas, held during the years 1855, '57, '59 (paper,) '60 (paper.) In all 4 vols.

Journals of the House of Representatives of the Commonwealth of Kentucky, held during the years 1847–8, '48–9, '59–50, '53–4, '65, '65–6. 6 vols.

Council Journals of the Legislative Assembly of Kansas Territory, held during the years 1855, '57, 59 (paper,) '60 (paper.) 4 vols.

Journals of the House and Council of the Legislative Assembly of Kansas Territory, at their session held in 1860. Lecompton, Kansas. 1860. 4 vols.

Journals of the Senate of the State of Kansas, at their session held in the year 1870.

Journal of the House of Representatives at their session held in the year 1870.

State of Kansas. Public documents of the State Officers and State Institutions for the year 1870. Topeka, Kansas, 1870.

KENTUCKY.

Journals of the Senate of the Commonwealth of Kentucky, held during the years 1847–8, '48–9, '49–50, '53–4, '65, '65–6. 6 vols.

Reports communicated to both branches of the Legislature of Kentucky at the sessions held during the years 1847

-8, '48-9, '49-50, '52, '53-4, '55-6, '63-4, '64, '65. 10 vols.

Annual Reports of the Auditor of Public Accounts of the State of Kentucky, for the years 1860, '62, '65. 3 vols.

Annual Report of the Adjutant General of the State of Kentucky, for the year 1864.

Reports of the Superintendent of Public Instruction of the State of Kentucky, for the years 1859, '60, '62, '63, 64. 5 vols. Paper.

Reports of the Kentucky Agricultural Society to the Legislature of Kentucky for the years 1856 and '57 and '58 and '59. 2 vols.

Report of the Board of Managers of the Eastern Lunatic Asylum, at Lexington, Ky., for the year 1864-5. Frankfort. 1856.

Report of the Geological Survey in Kentucky, made during the years 1854 and 1855, by David Dale Owen, Principal Geologist; assisted by Robert Peter, Chemical Assistant; Sydney S. Lyon, Topographical Assistant. Frankfort, Ky. 1856.

LOUISIANA.

Journals of the Senate of the State of Louisiana. Sessions held during the years 1860, '64-5, Ex. Sess. '65, '66, '67. 5 vols. all paper.

Journals of the House of Representatives of the State of Louisiana. Sessions held during the years 1860, '64-5, Ex. Sess. '65, '66, '67. 5 vols. all paper.

Documents of the sessions of the Legislature of Louisiana, held during the years 1860, '66, '67, '68, '69, '70. 6 vols. all paper. Also Documents of 1866 bound. 1 vol. In all 7 vols.

Journals of the Senate and House of Representatives of the State of Louisiana, at the sessions held during the year 1870. Together with the Documents of that year. New Orleans. 1870.

Debates of the House of Representatives of the State of Louisiana. Session of 1870. Paper. New Orleans. 1870.

Debates of the Senate of the State of Louisiana. Session 1870. Paper. New Orleans. 1870.

Report of Joint Committee of the General Assembly of Louisiana on the Conduct of the Election of April 17 and 18, 1868, and the condition of Peace and Order in the State. Paper. New Orleans. 1870.

Catalogue of the Louisiana State Library, 1869. Albert Bovee, State Librarian. New Orleans. 1869.

Official Journal of the Proceedings of the Convention for the Revision and Amendment of the Constitution of the State of Louisiana. New Orleans. 1864.

MAINE.

Documents printed by order of the Legislature of the State of Maine during its sessions A. D. 1841, '61–'62, '63, '64, '65. 8 vols.

Annual Reports of the Adjutant General of the State of Maine, for the years 1861, '62, '63. 3 vols. 1861. Paper.

Journal of the Constitutional Convention of the District of Maine: with the Articles of Separation and Governor Brooks' Proclamation, prefixed. 1819–20. Augusta. 1856.

Annual Reports of the Superintendent of Common Schools of the State of Maine, for the years 1862, '63, '69. (Reports of 1862, '69, Paper.) 3 vols.

Annual Reports of the Secretary of the Maine Board of Agriculture. 1860, '63, '64, '68, '69. (Report of 1869, Paper.) 5 vols.

The Water Power of Maine. By Walter Wells, Superintendent of the Hydrographic Survey of Maine.

Reports of the Commissioners of Fisheries of the State of Maine for the years 1867 and 1868. Paper. Augusta. 1869.

Agriculture and Geology of Maine. 1861. Augusta. 1861.

MARYLAND.

Journals of the Proceedings of the Senate of Maryland at the sessions of the General Assembly held during the years 1853, '54, '61, '68. 4 vols.

Journals of the Proceedings of the House of Delegates of the State of Maryland at the sessions of the General Assembly held during the years 1853, '54, '56, '60, '61, '68, '70. 7 vols.

Maryland State Documents. By the House of Delegates read and ordered to be printed. For the years 1852, '53, '56. 3 vols.

Journals of the Proceedings of the Senate of Maryland at

the sessions held during the years 1856, '58, '60, '61–2, '64, '65, '66. Together with the Documents of those years, by the Senate read and ordered to be printed. 7 vols.

Journals of the Proceedings of the House of Delegates at the sessions held during the years 1858, '61–2, '64, '65, '66. Together with the Documents of those years, by by the House read and ordered to be printed. 5 vols.

House and Senate Documents. By the House and Senate read and ordered to be printed. For the years 1861, '68, '70. 3 vols.

The Debates of the Constitutional Convention of the State of Maryland, assembled at the City of Annapolis, Wednesday, April 27, 1864. 3 vols. Annapolis. 1864.

The Proceedings of the State Convention of Maryland to Frame a New Constitution. Commenced at Annapolis, April 27, 1864. Annapolis. 1864.

Proceedings of the State Convention of Maryland to Frame a New Constitution. Commenced at Annapolis, May 8, 1867. Annapolis. 1867.

MASSACHUSETTS.

Public Documents of Massachusetts; being the annual reports of various Public Officers and Institutions, for the years 1858, 1859 (Vol. 2), 1860 (2 vols.), 1861 (3 vols.), 1862 (6 vols.), 1863 (4 vols.), 1864 (4 vols.), 1865 (4 vols), 1866 (4 vols.), 1867 (4 vols.), 1868 (4 vols.), 1869 (4 vols.), 1870 (Vols. 1, 3, 4). In all 44 vols.

Journal of the Constitutional Convention of the Commonwealth of Massachusetts, begun and held in Boston May 4, 1853. Boston. 1853.

Statistics of the condition and Products of certain Branches of Industry in Massachusetts, for the years ending April 1, 1845 and May 1, 1865. 2 vols.

Fifteenth Report of the Legislature of Massachusetts relating to the Registry and Return of Births, Marriages, and Deaths, in the Commonwealth, for the year ending December 21, 1856. By Francis De Witt. Paper. Boston. 1857.

Report on Insanity and Idiocy in Massachusetts, by the Commissioner on Lunacy, under Resolve of the Legislature of 1854. Boston. 1855.

Report of a General Plan for the Promotion of Public and personal Health. Devised, Prepared and Recommended by the Commissioners appointed under a Resolve of the Legislature of Massachusetts relating to a Sanitary Survey of the State. Boston. 1850.

Fourth Annual Report of the Trustees of the State Lunatic Hospital, at Northampton, October, 1859. Pamphlet. Boston. 1859.

Report of the Auditor of Accounts of the Commonwealth of Massachusetts, for the year ending December 31, 1861. Paper. Boston. 1862.

Catalogue of the State Library of Massachusetts. Boston. 1858. 2 copies.

Twenty-fifth and thirty-third Annual Reports of the Board of Education, togother with the twenty-fifth and thirty-third Annual Reports of the Secretary of the Board. Boston. 1862–70.

Address of His Excellency, John A. Andrew, to the Legislature of Massachusetts, Jan. 9, 1863. Pamphlet.

Annual Report of the Adjutant and Acting Quartermaster-General of the Commonwealth of Massachusetts, for the year ending December 31, 1860. Pamphlet. Boston. 1860.

Report of the Legislative Committee on the Pleuro-Pneumonia at the extra session of the Legislature. 1860. Paper.

Transactions of the Massachusetts Agricultural Society, 1859.

Geology of Massachusetts. By Edward Hitchcock. 4to. Boston. 1858.

MICHIGAN.

Joint Documents of the State of Michigan, for the years 1859, '64, '65, '66, '67, '68, '69, '70. 9 vols.

Documents accompanying the Journal of the House of Representatives of the State of Michigan at the Biennial Session of 1859. Lansing. 1859.

Journals of the Senate of the State of Michigan, for the years 1865, 1869 (2 vols.), 1871 (2 vols.), and Extra Sess. 1870.

Journals of the House of Representatives of the State of Michigan, for the years 1865 (2 vols.), 1869 (3 vols.), 1871 (3 vols.), and Extra Sess. 1870.

Annual Report of the Adjutant General of the State of Michigan for the year 1865–6. 2 vols. Lansing. 1866.

Census and Statistics of the State of Michigan, 1864. Lansing. 1865.

Transactions of the State Agricultural Society of Michigan; with Reports of County Agricultural Societies for the year 1857. Vol. IX. Lansing. 1859.

Annual Reports of the Secretary of the State Board of Agriculture of the State of Michigan, for the years 1867, '68, '69. 3 vols.

Reports of the Superintendent of Public Instruction of the State of Michigan, for the years 1855, '56, and '57, '62, '63, '65 (paper), '66, '67, '68, '69, '70. 9 vols.

Catalogue of the Michigan State Library for the years 1870–71. Prepared by H. A. Tenney, State Librarian, Nov. 30, 1870. Paper. Lansing. 1870.

Report of the State Librarian of the State of Michigan, for the years 1869 and 1870. Two Pamphlets.

Michigan Geological Survey. 1852.

MINNESOTA.

Journals of the House of Representatives during the sessions of the Legislature of the State of Minnesota, held during the years 1857, '61, '62, '63, '64, '65, '67, '68, '69, '70, '71. 11 vols., all paper.

Journals of the Senate during the sessions of the Legislature of the State of Minnesota, held during the years 1857, '61, '62, '63, '64, '65, '67, '68, '69, '70, '71. 11 vols., all paper.

Executive Documents of the State of Minnesota for the years 1860, '61, '62, '63, '64, '65, '66, '68, '68–9, '69, 70. 12 vols. Pasteboard covers.

Journals of the Council and House of Representatives of the Territory of Minnesota, during the second session of the Legislative Assembly held 1851. Saint Paul. 1851.

Debates and Proceedings of the Constitutional Convention for the Territory of Minnesota, to form a State Constitution preparatory to its admission into the Union as a State. By T. F. Andrews. Saint Paul. 1858.

Journal of the Constitutional Convention of the Territory of Minnesota, held in the year 1857. Saint Paul. 1857.

Annual Report of the Adjutant General to the Governor of Minnesota, 1863. St. Paul. 1863. Paper.

MISSISSIPPI.

Journals of the House of Representatives of the State of Mississippi, at the sessions held during the year 1858 and 1870. 2 vols. Paper.

Journals of the Senate of the State of Mississippi, at the

sessions held during the years 1858 and 1870. 2 vols. Paper.

Constitution of the State of Mississippi, as Amended, with the Ordinances and Resolutions adopted by the Constitutional Convention, August, 1865. Pamphlet. Jackson, Miss. 1865.

Journal of the Proceedings and Debates in the Constitutional Convention of the State of Mississippi, August, 1865. 1865. Paper. Jackson, Miss. 1865.

MISSOURI.

Annual Report of the Adjutant General of the State of Missouri, for the year 1863.

First Report of the Board of Immigration of the State of Missouri to the twenty-fourth Assembly, for the years 1865 and 1866. Jefferson City. 1867.

Geology of Missouri. 1855.

First and Second Annual Reports of the Geological Survey of Missouri. By C. G. Swallow, State Geologist. Jefferson City. 1855.

NEBRASKA.

Journals of the Council at the sessions of the General Assembly of the Territory of Nebraska, held during the years 1857, '58, '60, '61, '64, '65. 6 vols., all paper.

Journals of the House of Representatives at the sessions of the General Assembly of the Territory of Nebraska, held during the years 1857, '58, '59, '60, '61, '64, '65. 7 vols., all paper.

Senate Journal of the State Legislature of Nebraska. First, Second and Third Sessions. Held during the years 1866–7. Paper.

House Journal of the State Legislature of Nebraska. First, Second and Third Sessions. Held during the years 1866–7. Paper.

Annual Message of Governor Saunders, to the Legislative Assembly of the Territory of Nebraska, at its tenth regular session. With the accompanying documents. Pamphlet. Omaha City, Nebraska. 1865.

NEVADA.

Journals of the Senate at the sessions of the Legislature of the State of Nevada, held during the years 1864–5, '66, '69, '71. 5 vols.

Journals of the Assembly at the sessions of the Legislature

of the State of Nevada, held during the years 1864–5, '66, '67, '71. 4 vols.

Appendix to Journals of Senate of the first session of the Legislature of the State of Nevada. 1864–5. Carson City.

Official Report of the Debates and Proceedings in the Constitutional Convention of the State of Nevada, Assembled at Carson City, July 4th, 1864, to form a Constitution and State Government. Andrew J. Marsh, Official Reporter. San Francisco. 1866.

Catalogue of the Nevada State Library, for the year 1865. Pamphlet. Carson City. 1865.

NEW HAMPSHIRE.

Journals of the Honorable Senate and House of Representatives of the State of New Hampshire, at their sessions held during the years 1857, '58, '59, '60, '61, '62, '65, '67, '68, '69, '70. 11 vols., all paper.

Transactions of the New Hampshire State Agricultural Society, for the years 1857, '58, '59. 3 vols.

Annual Report upon the Common Schools of New Hampshire; being the Annual Report of the Board of Education for the years 1858, '59, '60, '61, '62, '64, '65, '67. 8 vols. (Reports of 1858 and '61–67, in paper covers.)

Reports of the Board of Visitors, Trustees, Treasurer and Superintendent of the New Hampshire Asylum for the Insane, for the years 1860, '61, '67. (All pamphlets.)

Annual Reports of the Bank Commissioners of the State of New Hampshire, made to his Excellency, the Governor, sessions of 1860 and '67. 2 Pamphlets.

Reports of the Insurance Commissioners, made to his Excellency, the Governor, June sessions, 1860, 1867. 2 Pamphlets.

Report of the Railroad Commissioners of the State of New Hampshire, June, 1860. Pamphlet.

Report of the Warden of the New Hampshire State Prison, accompanied by the Reports of the Chaplain and Physician, together with other documents relating to the affairs of the Institution. June sessions, 1860 and '67. Pamphlets.

Report of the Adjutant General, made to his Excellency, the Governor. June session, 1860. Pamphlet.

Report of the Board of Trustees of the House of Reformation, for Juvenile and Female Offenders against the

Laws; together with the Reports of the Superintendent and Treasurer. June session, 1860. Pamphlet.

Litigation Statistics: furnished by Clerks of several Counties to Commissioners appointed by the Governor upon the subject of Town or Local Courts, and printed under an order of the House. June 14, 1860. Pamphlet.

The New Hampshire Annual Register and United States Calendar for the year 1861. By G. Parker Lyon. No 40. No. 17, New Series. 16mo. Concord.

NEW JERSEY.

Journals of the Senate of the State of New Jersey at the sessions of the Legislature held during the years 1866, '67, '68, '69, '70, '71. 6 vols.

Minutes of Votes and Proceedings of the General Assembly of the State of New Jersey at its sessions during the years 1866, '67, '68, '69, '70, '71. 6 vols.

Appendix to the Journal of the Fifteenth Senate of the State of New Jersey. Hoboken, N. J. 1859.

Appendix to the Minutes of the Eighty-fourth General Assembly of the State of New Jersey. Freehold, N. J. 1860.

Legislative Documents of the State of New Jersey, for the years 1862, '63, '64, '65, '66, '67, '68, '69, '70, '71. 10 vols.

Journal of the Proceedings of the Convention to form a Constitution for the Government of the State of New Jersey; begun at Trenton May 14, 1844. Trenton. 1844.

Annual Report of the Superintendent of Public Schools of the State of New Jersey, for the year 1862. Paper. Trenton, N. J. 1863.

Register of the Commissioned Officers and Privates of the New Jersey Volunteers, in the service of the United States. Jersey City. 1863.

NEW YORK.

Journals of the Legislative Council of the State of New York. From 1691–1775. 2 vols. 4to. Albany. 1861.

Journal of the Assembly of the State of New York at the first meeting of the fourth session. 1780. 4to. Albany. 1859.

Journals of the Senate of the State of New York at the sessions held during the years 1850, '51, '52, '53, '55, '56, '57, '58, '59, '60, '61, '62, '63, '64, '65, '66, '67, '68, '69, '70. 20 vols.

Journals of the Assembly of the State of New York at the sessions held during the years 1850, 51 (2 vols.), 52, 53 (2 vols.), 55 (2 vols.), 56, 57, 58, 59, 60, 61, 62, 63, 64, 65, 66 (2 vols.), 67 (2 vols.), 68 (2 vols.), 69 (2 vols.), 70 (2 vols.) 28 vols.

Documents of the Senate of the State of New York, Sessions held during the years 1850–1870. 1850, 3 vols.; 1851, 3 vols.; 1852, 3 vols.; 1853, 3 vols.; 1855, 3 vols.; 1856, 3 vols.; 1857, 4 vols.; 1858, 3 vols.; 1859, 2 vols.; 1860, 1 vol.; 1861, 2 vols.; 1862, 6 vols.; 1863, 5 vols.; 1864, 4 vols.; 1865, 2 vols.; 1866, 2 vols.; 1867, 3 vols.; 1868, 7 vols.; 1869, 8 vols.; 1870, 4 vols. In all 71 vols.

Documents of the Assembly of the State of New York. Sessions held during the years 1850–1870. 1850, 8 vols., 1–3, 5–9; 1851, 5 vols., 2–6; 1852, 6 vols., 2–7; 1853, 7 vols.; 1855, 6 vols., 1, 3–7; 1856, 6 vols., 2–7; 1857, 5 vols.; 1858, 6 vols.; 1859, 5 vols.; 1860, 6 vols.; 1861, 8 vols.; 1862, 10 vols.; 1863, 9 vols.; 1864, 12 vols.; 1865, 10 vols.; 1866, 10 vols.; 1867, 18 vols.; 1868, 15 vols., Vol. 15, 2 pts.; 1869, 12 vols.; 1870, 13 vols. In all, 178 vols.

Catalogue of the New York State Library, January 1, 1846. Paper. Albany. 1846.

Catalogue of the New York State Library. January 1, 1850. 2 vols. Vol. 2 containing the Miscellaneous Books.

Catalogue of the New York State Library. Vol. 1. General Library, 1855. Vol. 2. Law Library, 1855. Vol. 3. Maps, Mss., Medals, etc. 1856.

The Same. Catalogue of Books on Bibliography, Typography and Engraving. 1858.

The Same. General Library: First Supplement. 1861.

The Same. Law Library: First Supplement. 1865.

Transactions of the American Institute of the City of New York, for the year 1850. Albany. 1851.

Transactions of the New York State Agricultural Society, with an abstract of the Proceedings of the County Agricultural Societies. For the years 1848, 50, 62, 65. 4 vols.

Report of the Secretary of Criminal Statistics of the State of New York. Transmitted to the Legislature March 14, 1855. Paper. Albany. 1855.

Annual Report of the Regents of the University of the State of New York, for the years 1855, 57, 58, 61, 64, 65, 66, 67, 68, 69, 70. 11 vols. (1857 and 66, in paper.)

Annual Report of the Governors of the Alms House of New York, for the years 1854, 55, 56. 3 vols., all paper.

Report of the State Engineer and Surveyor on the Railroads of the State of New York, for the fiscal year ending September 30, 1857. Transmitted to the Assembly, March 5, 1858. Paper. Albany. 1858.

Annual Report of the Trustees of the New York State Library, for the years 1857, 58, 61, 62, 63, 64, 65, 66, 67, 69, 70, 71. 12 vols. All paper except 1858, 63 and 64.

Annual Reports of the Regents of the University of the State of New York, on the condition of the State Cabinet of Natural History, etc., etc. 1858, 60, 61, 64, 66, 67, 69. (All paper except 1867.)

Annual Report of the Superintendent of the Insurance Department of the State of New York for the years 1861, '64. 3 vols.

Annual Report of the Adjutant General of the State of New York, for the years 1860, '62, '64. 3 vols. Report of 1864, Pamphlet.

Annual Report of the Executive Committee of the Prison Association of New York. Transmitted to the Legislature, Jan. 29, 1864, and Jan. 29, 1868. 2 vols. Albany. 1864 and 1868.

Transactions of the Homœpathic Medical Society of the State of New York, for the year 1868. Vol. 6. Albany. 1868.

A Compilation of Cases of Breach of Privilege of the House, in the Assembly of the State of New York, with the Reports of standing and special committees and the Proceedings and Judgments thereon, together with full reference to all action in each case, from 1777 to 1871. Prepared by C. W. Armstrong. Albany. 1871.

Annual Report of the Superintendent of Public Instruction of the State of New York. Transmitted to the Legislature Jan. 28, 1864. Albany. 1864.

Census of the State of New York, 1855. Prepared from the original returns, under the direction of Joel T. Headley, Secretary of State, by Francis T. Hough, Superintendent of the Census. 4to. Albany. 1857.

North Carolina.

Proceedings and Debates of the Convention of North Carolina, called to amend the Constitution of the State, which assembled at Raleigh, June 4, 1835, etc., etc. Raleigh. 1836.

Geological Report of the Midland Counties of North Carolina. By Ebenezer Emmons. New York and Raleigh. 1856.

OHIO.

Journals of the Senate of the State of Ohio, at the sessions of the General Assembly held during the years 1856, 58, 59, 60, 61, 62, 63, 64, 65, 66, 67, 68, 69, 70. 14 vols.

Journals of the House of Representatives of the State of Ohio, at the sessions of the General Assembly held during the years 1856, 58, 59, 60, 61, 62, 63, 64, 65, 66, 67, 68, 69, 70. 14 vols.

Messages and Reports made to the General Assembly and Governor of the State of Ohio, for the years 1857, 58, 59, 60, 61, 62, 63, 64, 65, 66, 67, 68, 69, 70, each year 2 pts. 28 vols.

Report of the Investigating Commission appointed to enquire into the causes of the Defalcation in the State Treasury and other matters specially named in the Act of the General Assembly of the State of Ohio, passed April 12, 1858.

Annual Reports of the Ohio State Board of Agriculture, with abstracts of the Proceedings of the County Agricultural Societies, made to the General Assembly of Ohio for the years 1857, 58, 59, 60, 61, 62, 63, 64, 65, 66, 68, 69. 12 vols.

Annual Reports of the Commissioners of Statistics of the General Assembly of Ohio for the years 1857, 58, 59, 60, 61, 62, 63, 64, 65, 66. 10 vols.

Annual Reports of the Commissioners of the Ohio State Library for the years 1858, 63, 65, 66, 67, 69. (Reports of 1863, 65, 66, 67, 69, pamphlets.)

Annual Reports of the Auditor of State to the Governor of the State of Ohio, for the years 1863, 64, 65, 66, 67. (Reps. of 1866, 67 and 70, in paper.)

Annual Reports of the Commissioners of Railroads and Telegraphs, to the Governor of the State of Ohio, for the years 1867, 68. 2 vols. Columbus, 1868–70.

59 pamphlets.

Ohio Geological Survey for 1869. Columbus, 1871.

Geological Survey of the State of Ohio for 1870. Columbus, 1871.

Maps accompanying the above. (Package.)

OREGON.

Journal of the House of Representatives of the Territory of Oregon, during the Eighth Regular Session, 1856–7. Paper.

The Same. Ninth Regular Session. 1857–8.

Journal of the Council of Oregon Territory. Ninth Regular Session, 1857–8.

Journals of the House Proceedings of the Legislative Assembly of the State of Oregon, at the sessions of 1860, 1862. 2 vols. Paper.

The Same. Session of 1870.

Journals of the Senate Proceedings of the Legislative Assembly of the State of Oregon, at the sessions of 1860, 1862. 2 vols. Paper.

The Same. Session of 1870.

Governor's Message and Accompanying Documents, for 1870.

PENNSYLVANIA.

Journal of the Senate of the Commonwealth of Pennsylvania, of the sessions held during the years 1860, 63, 64, 65, 66, 67, 68, 69, 71. 9 vols.

Journal of the House of Representative of the Commonwealth of Pennsylvania, of the sessions held during the years 1860, 63, 64, 65, 66, 67, 68, 69, 71. 9 vols.

Executive Documents. Reports of the heads of Departments transmitted to the Governor of Pennsylvania, in pursuance of law, for the Financial years ending Nov. 30, 1862, 63, 64, 65, 66, 67, 68, 69, 71. 13 vols.

Legislative Documents. Miscellaneous Docnments read in the Legislature of the Commonwealth of Pennsylvania, during the sessions held during the years 1860, 63, 64, 65, 66, 67, 68, 69, 71. 11 vols.

Annual Report of the Superintendent of Common Schools for the State of Pennsyalvania, for the years 1855, 65, 66.

Catalogue of the Pennsylvansa State Library. Compiled and Classified by Wallace De Witt. Harrisburg. 1859.

Thirty-eighth Annual Report of "The Controllers of the Public Schools of the First School District of Pennsylvania," comprising the city and county of Philadelphia, for the year ending Dec. 31, 1856, with their accounts. Paper. Philadelphia. 1857.

The Journal of Prison Discipline and Philanthropy. Published Quarterly under the direction of "The Philadelphia Society for alleviating the miseries of Public Prisons;" instituted in 1787. July, 1857. Pamphlet.

Annual Report of the Managers of the Pennsylvania Institute of the Blind. Presented to the Corporators at their annual meeting, 1860. Pamphlet.

Annual Report of the Executive Office, Military Department, of the Commonwealth of Pennsylvania, for the years ending December 1, 1864 and 1865. 2 vols. Harrisburg, 1865–66.

Annual Report of the Adjutant General of Pennsylvania, transmitted to the Governor in pursuance of law, for the years 1864, 65, 66. 3 vols. Harrisburg. 1865–67.

Reports of the Several Railroad and Canal Companies of Pennsylvania, for the year 1865. Communicated to the Auditor General. Isaac Slenker, Auditor General. Charles Connor, Railroad Clerk. Harrisburg. 1866.

Revised Report made to the Legislature of Pennsylvania, relative to the Soldiers' National Cemetery at Gettysburg, embracing an account of the origin of the undertaking; address of Hon. Edward Everett, at its consecration, with the dedicatory speech of President Lincoln, and the other exercises of that event; together with the address of Maj. Gen. O. O. Howard, delivered July 4, 1864, upon the dedication of the Soldiers' National Monument, and other proceedings upon that occasion. Harrisburg. 1867.

The Geology of Pennsylvania. A Governmental Survey by Henry Darwin Rogers, State Geologist. In two volumes. 4to. Philadelphia. 1858.

Maps accompanying the above.

RHODE ISLAND.

Reports to the General Assembly of Rhode Island, relating to the Registry and Returns of Births, Marriages and Deaths, in the State, for the years 1855, '56, '57, '60. 4 Pamphlets.

Report of the Quartermaster General, DeWitt C. Remington, made to the General Assembly of the State of Rhode Island, at its session in 1865. Pamphlet.

Manual with Rules and Orders for the use of the General Assembly of the State of Rhode Island. 1867–68. Providence. 1868.

SOUTH CAROLINA.

Acts, Reports and Resolutions of the General Assembly of South Carolina, passed during the years 1847, 48, 49, 50, 51, 52, 53, 55, 56, 57, 58, 59. 12 vols.

Acts, Reports, Resolutions and Journals of the General Assembly of South Carolina, passed at the session of 1854.

Reports and Resolutions of the General Assembly of South Carolina, passed at the sessions of the years 1869–70, 70–1. 2 vols. (1869–70, paper.)

Journal of the General Assembly of the State of South Carolina at the regular session of 1869–70. Paper.

Journal of the Senate of the General Assembly of the State of South Carolina at the session of 1870–71.

Journal of House of Representatives of the State of South Carolina at the session of 1870–1.

TENNESSEE.

Journal of the Proceedings of the Legislative Council of the Territory of the United States of America, South of the river Ohio. Begun and held at Knoxville, Aug. 25, 1794.

Appendix, 1857–8. Containing the Public Documents for that year.

Senate Journals of the Sessions of the General Assembly of the State of Tennessee held during the years 1859–60, 65, 65–6, 66, 67–8, Ex. Sess. 68, 68–9, 69–70. 8 vols.

House Journals of the Sessions of the General Assembly of the State of Tennessee held during the years 1859–60, 65, 65–6, 66, 67–8, Ex. Sess. 68, 68–9, 69–70. 8 vols.

Journals of the Extra Sessions of the Thirty-third General Assembly of the State of Tennessee, which convened at Nashville, January, 1861.

Appendix. For the years 1865–6, 67–8. 2 vols.

Appendices to the Journals of the Senate of the State of Tennessee, for the years 1867–8, 68–9, 69–70. 3 vols.

Appendices to the House Journals of the State of Tennessee for the years 1868–9, 69–70. 2 vols.

Senate Journal of the first session of the Thirty-seventh General Assembly of the State of Tennessee, convened at Nashville, October, 1871. With Appendix. Nashville, Tenn. 1871.

House Journal of the first session of the Thirty-seventh General Assembly of the State of Tennessee, convened at Nashville, October, 1871. With Appendix. Nashville, Tenn. 1871.

Reports from Public Officers and Institutions made to the General Assembly of the State of Tennessee. Session of 1859–60. Nashville, Tenn. 1860.

Nashville City and Business Directory, for the years 1860–'61. Vol. 5.

First Report of the Superintendent of Public Instruction of the State of Tennessee, ending Thursday, October 7th, 1869. John Eaton, Jr., Superintendent of Public Instruction. Nashville. 1869.

Catalogue of the General and Law Library of the State of Tennessee. Prepared by order of the Judges of the Supreme Court. Mrs. Paralee Haskell, State Librarian. Nashville, Tenn. 1871.

Journal of the Proceedings of the Convention of Delegates elected by the people of Tennessee, to Amend, Revise, or Form and Make a New Constitution for the State. Assembled in the city of Nashville, January 10, 1870. Nashville. 1870.

139 Pamphlets.

TEXAS.

Journals of the House of Representatives of the State of Texas, at the sessions held during the years 1855, '57, '59–60, '66, '70. 5 vols.

Journals of the Senate of the State of Texas at the sessions held during the years 1855, '57, '59–60, '66, '70. 5 vols.

Journal of the Texas State Convention, assembled at Austin, Feb. 7, 1866. Adjourned April 2, 1866. Austin. 1866.

UTAH.

Journals of the Legislative Assembly of the Territory of Utah, for the year 1869. Salt Lake City.

Report of the Superintendent of Common Schools of the Territory of Utah. 1864.

VERMONT.

Journals of the Senate of the State of Vermont, for the sessions held during the years 1856 to 1870, inclusive. Extra session of 1861. 16 vols.

Journals of the House of Representatives of the State of Vermont, for the sessions held during the years 1854, 1856 to 1870; and extra session of 1861. 17 vols.

Vermont Legislative Documents and Official Reports. Annual sessions of the General Assembly, 1866 to 1870–71. 5 vols.

Annual Reports to the Legislature of Vermont, relating to Registry and Returns of Births, Marriages and Deaths, in this State, for the years 1857 to 1867. 11 vols.

Annual Reports of the Secretary of the Vermont Board of Education, made to the board, 1858 to 1865. 8 vols. (All paper.)

Annual Reports of the Auditor of Accounts of the State of Vermont for the years 1858 to 1865. 8 vols. (All paper.)

Annual Report of the Railroad Commissioner of the State of Vermont to the General Assembly for the years 1858, '59, '61, '62, '63, '65. 6 vols. (All paper.)

Annual Directory for the use of the General Assembly; containing the Rules and Orders of the Senate and House, etc., etc. For the years 1865 and 1868. 2 vols. 16mo.

Collections of the Vermont Historical Society. Vol. 2. Montpelier. 1871.

13 Pamphlets.

Geology of Vermont. By Edward Hitchcock, L. L. D., Edward Hitchcock, Jr., M. D., Albert D. Hager, A. M., Charles Hitchcock, A. M. Published under authority of the State Legislature. By Albert D. Hager. Claremont, N. H. 1861.

VIRGINIA.

Journals of the House of Delegates of Virginia for the sessions held dnring the years 1850–1, 52–3, 55–6, 57–8, 59–60, 65–6. 6 vols.

Journal of the Senate of the Commonwealth of Virginia, at the session held during the year 1852.

Journal of the Senate of the Commonwealth of Virginia at the session held during the years 1865-6, 66–7. With Documents. 2 vols.

Proceedings and Debates of the Virginia State Convention of 1829–30. To which are subjoined the New Constitution of Virginia, and the votes of the people. Richmond. 1830.

Governor's Messages and Annual Reports of the Public Officers of the State, and of the Boards of Directors, Visitors, Superintendents, and other agents of Public Institutions or Interests of Virginia. For the years 1847, 49–50, 50–1, 52–3, 53–4, 55–6, 57–8, 59–60, 65–6. 26 vols.

Journal of the House of Delegates of the Commonwealth of Virginia for the session held 1866–7. With Documents.

WASHINGTON.

Journals of the Council of the Territory of Washington: at the sessions of the Legislative Assembly held during the years 1855, 56, 57, 58, 60. 5 vols. (All paper.)

Journals of the House of Representatives of the Territory of Washington, at the sessions of the Legislative Assembly, held during the years 1855, 56, 57, 60. 4 vols. (All paper.)

Message of the Governor of Washington Territory. Also, the Correspondence with the Secretary of War, Major General Wood, the Officers of the Regular Army, and of the Volunteer Service of Washington Territory. Olympia. 1857.

WEST VIRGINIA.

Journals of the Senate of the State of West Virginia, for the sessions held in the years 1866, 68, 70. 3 vols.

Journals of the House of Delegates of the State of West Virginia, for the sessions held during the years 1870, 71. 2 vols.

Journal of the House of Delegates of the State of West Virginia for the Sixth session, commencing Jan. 21, 1868. With Documents. Wheeling. 1868.

Annual Message of Gov. Wm. E. Stevenson, with accompanying Documents, to the Legislature of West Virginia. Session of 1871. Wheeling. 1871.

WISCONSIN.

Title and Year.	No.	Title and Year.	No.
Journals of the Council.		Journal of Senate—con.	
1836-37	12	1859	25
1836	25 paper.	1860	26
1837-38	25 paper.	1861	28
1838	23 paper.	1862. Vol. 1	26
1839	26 paper.	1862. Vol. 2	28
1838-39-40	8	1863	25
1839-40	30 (24 pap'r)	1864	25
1840—special session.	25 paper.	1865	25
1840-41	32 (16 pap'r)	1866	25
1841-42	18 (13 pap'r)	1867	25
1842-3	29 (17 pap'r)	1868	25
1843-4	28 (22 ap'r)	1869	25
1845	19 paper.	1870	25
1844-45	6	1871	25
1846	14 (8 paper.	Journal of the Assembly	
1847	26 (18 pap'r)	1848	2
1847—special session.	25 paper.	1849	4 (1 paper.)
1848	26 (20 pap'r)	1850	4 (2 paper.)
Journals of the House		1851	28 (25 pap'r)
of Representatives.		1852	5 (1 paper.)
1837	18 paper.	1853	4 (2 paper.)
1836-37-38	16	1854	11 (1 paper.)
1838-39-40	11	1855	25
1838	25 paper.	1856	24
1838—special session.	25 paper.	1857	20
1839	21 paper.	1858. Vol. 1	24
1839-40	11 paper.	1858. Vol. 2	24
1840—special session.	27 paper.	1859	21
1840-41	33 (18 pap'r)	1860	25
1841-42	26 (14 pap'r)	1861	29
1842-43	23 (10 pap'r)	1862. Vol. 1	27
1843-44	19 (17 pap'r)	1862. Vol. 2	28
1845	39 (14 pap'r)	1863	25
1846	15 paper.	1864	24
1847	15 (13 pap'r)	1865	25
1847—special session.	24 paper.	1866	25
1848	25 (19 pap'r)	1867	25
Journal of the Senate.		1868	25
1848	5 (1 paper)	1869	4
1849	7 (3 paper)	1870	25
1850	6	1871	25
1851	28 (22 pap'r)	Journal of the General	
1852	6 (2 paper)	Assembly.	
1853	14 (8 paper)	1846	9
1854	23 (1 paper)	Journal of the Constitu-	
1855	26	tional Convention.	
1856	28	1846	18
1857	7	Journal and Debates of	
1858. Vol. 1	27	Constitutional Con.	
1858. Vol. 2	25	1847-8	23

Wisconsin—continued.

Title and Year.	No.	Title and Year.	No.
Appendix to Journals.		Gov. Mess. & Acc. Docs.	
1852.	5 (1 paper)	1856.	28
Appendix to Assembly		1857. Vol. 1.	11
Journal.		1857. Vol. 2.	14
1853.	3 paper.	1858.	25
1854.	3 paper.	1859.	25 (23 pap'r)
1855.	10	1860.	28
1856.	15	1861.	28
1857. Vol. 1.	20	1862	27
1857. Vol. 2.	29	1862–3.	27
1859.	8	1863.	25
1869. Vol. 1.	2	1865.	12
1869. Vol. 2.	2	1865–6. Vol. 1. . . .	25
App. to Senate Journal.		1865–6. Vol. 2. . . .	25
1855.	10	1866.	25
1856.	6	1867.	25
1857.	11	1869. Vol. 1.	25
1858.	19	1869. Vol. 2.	25
Wisconsin Documents.		1870.	25
1854.	11	1871. Vol. 1.	25
1855.	6	1871. Vol. 2.	25

Wisconsin Horticultural Collections. 1854–55–56–57. 7 copies.

Transactions of Wisconsin State Agricultural Society for 1858–9. One copy.

Same for 1869. 49 copies.

Same for 1870. 48 copies.

Report of the Geological Survey of the State of Wisconsin. James Hall on Geology and Paleontology, and J. D. Whitney on the Upper Mississippi Lead Region. January, 1862.

UNITED STATES DOCUMENTS.

Journals of the American Congress for the years 1774–88. 4 vols. Washington. 1823.

Secret Journals of the Acts and Proceedings of Congress from the first meeting thereof to the dissolution of the Confederation by the adoption of the Constitution of the United States. Vols. 2–4. Boston. 1820.

Journals of the Senate of the United States of America at its sessions held during the years 1789–93, 1793–99, 1799–1805, 1811–15, 1815–16, 16–17, 17, 18–19, 19, 20, 21, 22, 23–4, 24–5, 25–6, 26–7, 27–8, 28–9, 29–30, 30–31, 31–2, 32–3, 33–4, 34–5, 35–6, 36–7, 37, 38–9, 39–40, 40–41, 41, 42–3, 44–5, 45–6, 46–7, 47–8, 48–9, 50–51, 51–2, 52–3, 53–4, 54–5, 55–6, 56–7, 57–8, 58–9, 59–60, 60–61, 61, 61–2, 62–3, 63–4, 64–5, 65–6, 66–7, 67, 67–8, 68–9, 69–70. 58 vols.

Journals of the House of Representatives of the United States at the sessions held during the years 1789–92, 93–97, 1797–1801, 1801–4, 1804–7, 1807–9, 1809–11, 11–13, 13–15, 15–16, 16–17, 17–18, 18–19, 19–20, 20–21, 21–22, 22–3, 23–4, 24–5, 25–6, 26–7, 27–8, 28–9, 29–30, 30–31, 31–2, 33–4, 34–5, 35–6, 36–7, 37, 38–9, 39–40, 40–41, 41, 41–2, 42–3, 43–4, 44–5, 45–6, 46–7, 47–8, 48–9, 50–51, 51–2, 52–3, 53–4, 54–5, 55–6, 56–7, 57–8, 58–9, 59–60, 60–61, 61, 61–2, 62–3, 63–4, 64–5, 65–6, 66–7, 67, 67–8, 68–9, 69–70. 67 vols.

CONGRESSIONAL DOCUMENTS. In 8vo.

Cong.	Sess.	Year.	Title.	Vols.
23	1	1833–4	Senate Documents. Vols. 12–14. Pension Roll.	3
24	1	1835–6	Executive Documents. Vols. 1–7.......... ...	7
			Senate Documents. Vols. 1–6...............	6
			Senate Reports of Committees and Journal	1
			Reports of Committees. Vols. 1–3.......	3
24	2	1836–7	Executive Documents. Vols. 1–4............	4
			Senate Documents. Vols. 1–3...............	3
			Senate Reports of Committees and Journal	1
			Reports of Committees. Vols. 1–3.......	3
25	1	1837	Executive Documents......................	1
			Executive Documents and Reports of Committees	1
			Senate Documents	1
25	2	1837–8	Senate Documents. Vol. 1	1
25	3	1838–9	Executive Documents. Vols. 1–6	6
			Senate Documents. Vols. 1–5...............	5
			Reports of Committees. Vols. 1–2............	2
22–25	2	1831–39	Index to House Documents	1
26	1	1839–40	Executive Documents. Vols. 1–7............	7
			Senate Documents. Vols. 1–8	8
			Reports of Committees. Vols. 1–4...........	4
26	2	1840–41	Executive Documents. Vols. 1–6	6
			Senate Documents. Vols. 1–4. Pt. 1, vol. 5 ..	5
			Reports of Committees	1
27	1	1841	Executive Documents and Reports of Committees	1
			Senate Documents	1
27	3	1842–3	Executive Documents. Vols. 1–8	8
			Senate Documents. Vols. 1–4	4
			Reports of Committees. Vols. 1–4...........	4
28	1	1843–4	Senate Documents. Vol. 7	1
28	2	1844–45	Executive Documents. Vols. 1–4. Vol. 4, 2 pts.	5
			Senate Documents. Vols. 1–11. Vol. 10, 2 pts.	12
			Reports of Committees. Vols. 1, 2	2
29	1	1845–6	Executive Documents. Vols. 1–8............	8
			Senate Documents. Vols. 1–9	9
			Reports of Committees. Vols. 1–4	4
29	2	1846–47	Executive Documents. Vols. 1–4	4
			Senate Documents. Vols. 1–3	3
			Reports of Committees	1
30	1	1847–48	Executive Documents, Vols. 1–9	9
			Senate Documents. Vols. 1–8	8
			Senate Reports of Committees...............	1
			Senate Miscellaneous Documents............	1
			Reports of Committees. Vols. 1–4	4
			House Miscellaneous Documents............	1
30	2	1848–49	Executive Documents. Vols. 1–7	7
			Senate Documents. Vols. 1–4	4
			Senate Reports of Committees	1
			Senate Miscellaneous Documents. Vols. 1–2..	2
			House Miscellaneous Documents............	1
			Reports of Committees. Vols. 1–2	2
	S. S.	1849	Senate Documents	1
			Senate Reports............	1
31	1	1849–50	Senate Documents. Vols. 11, 12.............	2

Congressional Documents. In 8vo.—continued.

Cong.	Sess.	Years.	Title.	Vols.
31	2	1850–51	Ex. Docs. Vols. 1–8. Vols 6 and 7, each, 2 prts.	10
			Senate Documents. Vols. 1–5	5
			Reports of Committees	1
			House Miscellaneous Documents	1
			Senate Miscellaneous Documents	1
			Senate Reports of Committees	1
32	S. S.	1851	Senate Documents. Vols. 1, 3	2
	1	1851–2	Ex. Docs. Vols. 1–14. Vol. 2, 3 pts. Vols. 4 and 10, each 2 pts	18
			Ex. Docs. Tables of Com. & Nav. of U. S. for 1851	1
			Senate Documents. Vols. 1–16. Vol. 5, 2 pts.	17
			Senate Reports. Vols. 1–2	2
			Senate Miscellaneous Documents	1
			House Miscellaneous Documents	1
			Reports of Committees	1
	2	1852–53	Ex. Docs. Vols. 1-7, 9–11. Vols. 1 & 9, each 2 pts	12
			Senate Documents. Vols. 1, 3–10. Vol. 1, 2 pts	10
			Senate Reports of Committees	1
			Senate Miscellaneous Documents	1
			Reports of Committees	1
			House Miscellaneous Documents	1
	S. S.	1853	Senate Documents	1
33	1	1853–54	Ex. Docs. Vols. 1–3, 5–8, 10–14, 17, 19. Vol. 1, 3 pts. Vol. 7, 2 pts	17
			Ex. Docs. Maps accompanying Message	1
			Sen. Docs. Vols. 1–6, 8–10, 12. Vol. 12, 2 pts.	11
			Sen. Repts. of Coms. Vols. 1, 1. Vol. 2, 2 pts.	3
			Senate Miscellaneous Documents	1
			House Miscellaneous Documents	1
			Reports of Committees. Vols. 1–3	3
	2	1854–55	Ex. Docs. Vols. 3–5, 7–10, 11 pts. 1, 2, 5, 6, 8 11, 12, pts. 1–3; 13, pts. 3, 4, 6, 9–11; 14, pt. 3; 15, pts. 3, 6; 16	28
			Senate Documents. Vols. 1–9, , 11	10
			Senate Reports of Committees	1
33	2	1854–55	Senate Miscellaneous Documents. Vols. 2, 3	2
			Reports of Committees	1
			House Miscellaneous Documents	1
34	1	1855–56	Ex. Docs. Vols. 1, 2, 4–9, 11–13, 14, pt. 3: 15, 16. Vol. 1, 4 pts. Vol. 6, 3 pts	19
	1&2		Senate Documents. Vols. 1–16	16
	1		Senate Reports. Vols. 1–2	2
	1&2		Senate Miscellaneous Documents	1
			Reports of Committees. Vols. 1–3	3
			House Miscellaneous Documents. Vols. 1–2	2
			Reports from the Court of Claims. Vols. 1–2.	2
34	3	1856–57	Ex. Docs. Vols. 1–3, 5, 6, 8–13. Vol. 1, 2 pts, Vol. 8, 4 pts	15
			Senate Documents. Vols. 1–13	13
			Senate Reports of Committees	1
			Senate Miscellaneous Documents	1
			House Miscellaneous Documents	1
			Reports of the Court of Claims	1
			Reports of Committees. Vols. 1–3	3
	S. S.	1857	Senate Documents	1

Congressional Documents. In 8vo.—continued.

Cong.	Sess.	Years.	Title.	Vols.
35	1	1857-58	Executive Documents. Vols. 1–4, 7–14. Vol. 2, 4 pts. Vol. 8, 4 pts	18
			Senate Documents. Vols. 1–14	14
			Senate Reports. Vols. 1–2	2
			Senate Miscellaneous Documents. Vols. 1–4	4
			Reports of Committees. Vols. 1–6	6
			Miscellaneous Documents. Vols. 1–3	3
			Reports Court of Claims. Vols. 1–3	3
	2	1858–59	Executive Documents. Vols. 1–5, 7, 9–13. Vol. 2, 5 pts. Vol. 10. 4 pts	18
			Senate Documents. Vols. 1–15. Vol. 6, 2 pts	16
			Senate Reports	1
			Senate Miscellaneous	1
			Miscellaneous Documents. Vols. 1–2	2
			Reports of Committees. Vols. 1–3	3
			Reports Court of Claims	1
36	1	1859–60	Executive Documents. Vols. 1, 3–6, 8, 9, 10, pt. 1, 12, 13, 15	11
			Senate Documents. Vols. 1–12	12
			Senate Reports. Vols. 1–2	2
			Senate Miscellaneous	1
			Reports of Committees. Vols. 1–5	5
			Miscellaneous Documents. Vols. 1–7	7
			Reports Court of Claims. Vols. 1–5	5
		1861	Exec. Documents. Reports of Committees	1
	2	1860–61	Exec. Documents. Vols. 1–6, 9, 10	8
			Senate Docs. Vols. 1–8. Vols. 3 and 7 each 2 pts.	10
			Senate Reports	1
			Senate Miscellaneous Documents	1
			Repts. of Committees. Vols. 1–3. Vol. 3, 2 pts	4
			House Rep. No. 78. Abs. Ind. Trust Bds. Paper.	1
			Miscellaneous Documents	1
			Reports Court of Claims. Vols. 1–3	3
37	1	1861	House Miscellaneous Documents	1
			Exec. Documents. Reports of Committees	1
			Senate Executive and Miscellaneous Documents and Reports of Committees	1
	2	1861–62	Exec. Docs. Vols. 1–3, 5, 7–12. Vol. 5, 3 pts	12
			President's Message. Maps	1
			Senate Documents. Vols. 1–6	6
			Senate Reports of Committees	1
			Senate Miscellaneous Documents	1
			Reports of Committees. Vols. 1–4	4
			House Miscellaneous Documents	1
			Reports Court of Claims. Vols. 1, 2	2
	3	1862–63	Exec. Docs. Vols. 1–8, 10–12. Vol. 10, 2 pts	12
			Exec. Docs. President's Message. Maps	1
			Senate Miscellaneous Documents	1
			Senate Reports. Vol. 1	1
			House Miscellaneous Documents. Vols. 1–2	2
			House Reps. Committees and Ct. of Claims	1
			Commerce and Navigation	1
			Report on the Conduct of the War. Vols. 2, pt. 1, 3, pt. 2, 4, pt. 3	3

Congressional Documents. In 8vo—continued.

Cong.	Sess.	Year.	Title.	Vol.
37	S. S.	1863	Senate Documents...	1
38	1	1863	Commerce and Navigation...	1
			Patent Office Report, Vols. 1–3...	3
		1863–64	Executive Documents, Vols. 1–7, 9, 10, 13–16..	3
			Executive Documents, Maps...	1
			Senate Documents...	1
			Senate Reports...	1
			Senate Micellaneous Documents...	1
			House Miscellaneous Documents, Vols. 1–3....	3
			Reports of Committees, Vols. 1–2...	2
			Smithsonian Report...	1
	2	1864–65	Executive Documents, Vols. 1–15, Vol. 8, 2 pts.	16
			Senate Documents...	1
			Senate Miscellaneous Documents...	1
			Senate Reports...	1
			Honse Reports...	1
			Reports of Committees, Vols. 1–4...	4
			House Miscellaneous Documents...	1
			Contested Elections, 1864–65...	1
			Smithsonian Report...	1
			Report on the Conduct of the War, Parts 1–3..	3
39	1	1865–66	Executive Documents. Vols. 1–16, Vol. 1, 4 pts, Vols. 4 and 11, each 2 pts., Vol. 9, 3 pts....	23
			Senate Documents...	2
			Commerce and Navigation...	1
			Rpt. on Conduct of the War. Supple't. Vols. 1–2	2
			House Micellaneous Documents...	3
			Senate Miscellaneous Documents...	1
			Senate Reports...	1
			Reports of Committees, Vols. 1–3...	3
	2	1866–67	Ex. Doc'ts. Vols. 1–12, 13, 15. Vol. 1, 3 pts..	16
			Senate Documents. Vols. 1–2...	2
			Senate Reports...	1
			Senate Miscellaneous Documents...	1
			House Miscellaneous Documents...	1
			Reports of Committees. Vols. 1–4...	4
			Commerce and Navigation...	1
			Patent Office Report. Vols. 1–3...	3
40	1	1867	Executive Documents...	1
			Senate Documents...	1
			Senate Reports and Miscellaneous Documents.	1
			Reports of Committees...	1
			House Miscellaneous Documents. Vols. 1–2..	2
	2	1867–68	Ex. Doc'ts. Vols. 1–14, 16–18, 20. Bound in 23	23
			Senate Documents...	2
			Senate Reports...	1
			Senate Miscellaneous Documents...	1
			House Miscellaneous Documents...	2
			Reports of Committees...	2
			Reports of Commiss'rs to the Paris Exposition	6
			Commerce and Navigation...	1
			Report of Department of Agriculture...	1

Congressional Documents. In 8vo.—continued.

Cong.	Sess.	Year.	Title.	Vol.
40	3	1868–69	Ex. Docs. Vols. 1–4, except Vol. 11. In 18 parts	18
			Senate Documents	1
			Senate Reports	1
			Senate Miscellaneous	1
			House Miscellaneous	1
			Reports of Committees. Vols. 1–3	3
			Report on the Treatment of Prisoners of War by Rebel Authorities	1
			Commerce and Navigation	1
			Report of Department of Agriculture	1
41	1	1869	Claims of the U. S. against Great Britain	5
			Executive Documents	1
			Senate Documents	1
			Senate Reports and Miscellaneous	1
			Reports of Committees	1
			House Miscellaneous	1
			Index to Reports of Committees, 26th to 40th Congress (1839–1869)	1
			Index to Executive Documents, 26th to 40th Congress (1839–1869)	1
41	2	1869–70	Executive Documents. 13 vols., excepts vols. 8 and 9. In 11 parts	11
			Commerce and Navigation	1
			Report of the Department of Agriculture	1
			Senate Documents	3
			Senate Reports	1
			Reports of Committees	3
			QUARTO DOCUMENTS.	
		1850	The Seventh Census of the United States. 1850	1
		1851	Sketches accompanying Coast Survey Report.	1
		1852	Report of Superintendent of the Coast Survey.	1
		1853	House List of Private Claims, 1st to 31st Congress. Vols. 1–3	3
32	2	1852–53	Ex. Docs. Vol. 8, Coast Survey Report	1
			Senate Docs. Vol. 11, Coast Survey Reports	1
33	1	1853	Report of Superintendent of the Coast Survey	1
		1853–54	Executive Documents. Vol. 15. Parts 3 and 6	2
		1853–54	Reports of Explorations and Surveys to Ascertain themost practicable and economical route for a railroad from the Mississippi river to the Pacific ocean. Vols. 1 and 5	2
		1854–55	The Same. Vols. 6, 9, and 12	3
		1854	U. S. Naval Astronomical Ex. Vol. 1. Chile	1
			The Same. Vol. 2. Andes and Pampas. Nat. His.	1
			Report of Superintendent of the Coast Survey.	1
	2	1854–55	Ex. Docs. Vols. 11 pts. 2, 4, 7, 9; 12 pts. 1–3	7
			Senate Docs. Vols. 12, 13, pts. 3, 4, 8, 10, 11; 14 pt. 3	7
		1855	Report of Superintendent of Coast Survey	1
		1855–56	House Doc. Military Commission to Europe	1
			Senate Doc. Military Commission to Europe	1

Quarto Documents--continued.

Cong.	Sess.	Years.	Title.	Vols.
34	1	1855-56	Ex. Docs. Vol. 3; 10 pts. 1-4; 14 pts. 1 and 3..	7
			Senate Documents. Vol. 18................	1
	1&2		Senate Docs. Vols. 17, 18; 19 pts. 2-4; 20 pt. 3	6
		1856	Report of the Superintendent of the Coast Survey	1
34	3	1856-57	Executive Documents. Vols. 4, 7...........	2
			Senate Documents. Vol. 15	1
		1857	Report of the Superintendent of the Coast Survey	1
			House Documents. Commercial Relations. Vols. 2, 4. Pts. 2, 3..........................	2
35	1	1857-58	Executive Documents. Vols. 5, 6	2
			Senate Documents. Vol. 15............... .	1
		1858	Report of the Superintendent of the Coast Survey	1
35	2	1858-59	Executive Documents. Vols. 6, 8...........	2
			Senate Documents. Vols. 16, 17...........	2
			Senate Documents. Results of Meteorological Observations	1
		1859	Report of the Superintendent of the Coast Survey	1
36	1	1859-60	Executive Documents. Vols. 2, 7, 10 pt. 2, 11 pts. 1 and 2, 14	6
			Senate Documents. Vols. 13, 14. 15..........	3
		1860	Report of the Superintendent of the Coast Survey	1
			Art of War in Europe. By Mark Delafield ...	1
	2	1860-61	Executive Documents. Vol. 7..............	1
			Senate Documents. Vol. 4	1
37		1861-62	Executive Documents. Vols. 4, 6............	2
	3	1862-63	Executive Documents. Vol. 9................	1
			Eighth Census of the United States..........	6
38	1	1863	Report of United States Coast Survey.........	1
	2	1864-65	United States Coast Survey Report...........	1
37	1	1865-66	Report of United States Coast Survey........	1
	2	1866-67	United States Coast Survey.................	1
40	2	1867-8	United States Coast Survey.................	1

SEPARATE DOCUMENTS IN 8vo.

Annual Message of the President of the United States, with accompanying Documents, for the years 1849-50, 50-51, 52, 53, 54-5, 55-6, 56-7, 57-8, 59-60, 60-61, 61-2, 62-3. 28 vols.

The Same. Abridgments for the years 1857-58, 59-60, 60-61, 62-63, 69. 8 vols.

Annual Report of the Commissioner of Patents for the years 1847, 48, 49–50, 50–51, 51–52, 52–53, 53, 56, 59. 14 vols.

Annual Report of the Superintendent of the Coast Survey, for the years 1852, 55, 57. 3 vols.

Andrews' Report on Colonial and Lake Trade. 1852. Washington. 1853.

Annual Report of the Regents of the Smithsonian Institution, for the years 1856, 57, 58, 60, 61, 62. 6 vols.

Commerce and Navigation. Report of the Secretary of the Treasury, transmitting a Report from the Register of the Treasury of the Commerce and Navigation of the United States, for the years 1851, 52, 53, 54, 60. 5 vols.

Condition of the Banks of the United States for the years 1854, 1860. 2 vols.

Insurance Report for the year 1860.

Letter of the Secretary of State, transmitting a Report on the Commercial Relations of the United States with Foreign Nations, for the year 1865. Washington. 1866.

Maps accompanying Gibbons' Report. 1854.

Papers relating to Foreign Affairs accompanying the Annual Message of the President of the United States, to the Third Session, Fortieth Congress. 2 vols. Washington. 1869.

Report of the Secretary of the Treasury on the State of the Finances, for the years 1849–50, 51–2, 52–3, 53–4, 56–7, 57–8, 59–60, 66. 8 vols.

Report of the Special Commissioner of Internal Revenue, for the years 1866, 67, 68, 69. 4 vols.

Report of the Commissioner of Internal Revenue, on the operations of the Internal Revenue System, for the year ending June 30, 1863.

Report on Interoceanic Canals and Railroads between the Atlantic and Pacific Oceans. By Rear Admiral Chas. H. Davis. Washington. 1867.

Report of the Commissioner of Agriculture for the year 1867. Washington. 1868.

Report of the Secretary of War, being part of the Message and Documents communicated to the two Houses of Congress, for the years 1868, 71. 2 vols.

Report of the Commissioner of Indian Affairs, for 1862.

Reports and Charts of the United States Brig Dolphin, made under direction of the Navy Department, by S. P. Lee, U. S. N. Washington. 1854.

Report of the Commissioners of the General Land Office, accompanying the Annual Report of the Secretary of the Interior. For the years 1860, 1865. 2 vols.

Report of the Superintendent of the Census for December 1, 1852; to which is appended the Report for Dec. 1, 1851. Washington. 1853.

Preliminary Report on the Eighth Census, 1860. By Jos. C. G. Kennedy, Superintendent. Washington. 1862.

MISCELLANEOUS PUBLICATIONS

Issued by authority of Congress, or relating to Congressional History.

Annals of the Congress of the United States. The Debates and Proceedings in the Congress of the United States, with an Appendix containing important State Papers and Public Documents, and all the Laws of a Public nature. From the first to the eighteenth Congress. 1789–1824.

Register of Debates in Congress. Comprising the leading debates and incidents of Congress from the session of the Eighteenth Congress to the second session of the twenty-second Congress: together with an Appendix containing all the important State Papers and Public Documents. To which are added all the laws enacted during those sessions, with a copious Index to the whole. 9 vols. Vols. 2, 4, 6 and 9, each two parts; Vol. 8, 3 parts. Washington. 1825–1833.

Abridgment of the Debates of Congress from 1789 to 1856. By Thos. H. Benton. Vols. 1–16. 1789–1850. New York and London. 1857–1861.

American Archives. Fourth Series, Vols. 1–6. Fifth Series, Vols. 1, 2. In all 8 vols. Folio.

American State Papers. Documents, Legislative and Executive, of the Congress of the United States, in relation to the Public Lands. Edited by Walter Lowrie. Vols. 1–8.

In relation to Finances. Vols. 1–5.

In relation to Naval Affairs. Vols. 1–4.

In relation to Military Affairs. Vols. 3–7.

In relation to Foreign Relations. Vols. 1–6.

Documents of the United States Sanitary Commission. 3 vols. Paper.

Astronomical and Meteorological Observations made at the United States Naval Observatory during the years 1864, 66, 67, 68, 69. 4to. Washington. 1866–1872.

Navy of the United States, from the commencement in 1775 to 1853. Including captures and services performed, and the fate of each vessel, etc.

Army Meteorological List for twelve years, from 1843 to 1854, inclusive, compiled from observations made by officers of the Medical Department of the Army at the Military Posts of the United States. Prepared under the direction of Brevet Brigadier General Thomas Lawson. Washington. 1855.

A Census of Pensioners for Revolutionary or Military Services; with their names, ages and places of residence, as returned by the Marshals of the several Judicial Districts. Washington. 1844.

A Report on Amputation at the Hip Joint in Military Surgery. Circular No. 7. War Department. Surgeon General's Office. Washington. 1867.

Smithsonian Miscellaneous Collections. Catalogue of the described Diptera of North America. Prepared for the Smithsonian Institution by R. Osten Sacken. Also, Catalogue of Publications of Societies and of other Periodical works in the Library of the Smithsonian Institution, July 1, 1859. 2 vols. Paper. Washington. 1858–1859.

Also, Directions for collecting, preserving, and transporting Specimens of Natural History, prepared for the use of the Smithsonian Institution. 3d Ed. Pamphlet.

Report on the History and Progress of the American Coast Survey, up to the year 1858. Pamphlet.

Report of Joint Committee on Reconstruction. Pamphlet.

Laws to encourage Immigration, to Regulate the Carrying of Passengers, and to secure Homesteads to actual settlers, etc. Pamphlet. Also printed in German and French.

Sanitary Commission No. 40. A Report to the Secretary of War of the operations of the Sanitary Commission, and upon the sanitary condition of the Volunteer Army, its Medical Staff, Hospitals and Hospital Supplies. Dec., 1861. Pamphlet. Washington, D. C. 1861.

Maps. Andrews' Report. House of Representatives, U. S.

Reports on the Extent and nature of the Materials available for the preparation of a Medical and Surgical History of the Rebellion. Philadelphia. 1865. Paper. 4to.

Smithsonian Miscellaneous Collections. Vols. 1–8. Paper. Washington. 1861–1869.

Alphabetical Catalogue of the Library of Congress. Authors. Washington. 1864.

Catalogue of Additions made to the Library of Congress from December 1, 1864 to December 1, 1865. Washington. 1865.

Alphabetical List of Post Offices in the United States, with the names of Post-Masters, (except at suspended offices) as published by the Post Office Department; also names of new Post offices, &c., arranged alphabetically; with an Appendix containg the rates of Domestic and Foreign Postage; List of Money Order Post Offices, and latest Post Office Laws; together with the Post Offices in Canada. Table of Distances from Washington, D. C., to the County Seats of the Several States and Territories, &c. Revised and corrected by J. Disturnell to October 1st, 1865. 4to. Paper. New York and Washington, D. C.

The Same. Revised and Corrected by the Post Office Department to October 20, 1867. 4to. Paper. Washington. 1868.

Congressional Globe and Appendix. 1858–59, Parts 1, 2. 1860–61, Parts 1, 2. 1861. 1861–62, Parts 1–4. 1862–63, Parts 1, 2. 1865–6, Parts 1–5. 1869–70, Parts 1–7. In all 23 vols. 4to. Washington. 1860–71.

Maps of Washington.

History of the Condition and Prospects of the Indian Tribes of the United States, by H. R. Schoolcraft, LL.D. Illustrated by S. Eastman, U. S. A. Parts 1–5.

Smithsonian Contributions to Knowledge. Vols. 3–9, 11–17. 14 vols.

United States Exploring Expedition during the years 1838, 1839, 1840, 1841, 1842, under Command of Charles Wilkes, U. S. N. Vols. 1–8, 11–16, 20. Vols. 8 and 13 each 2 parts. With an atlas accompanying the narrative. 17 vols. 4to. Also 8 vols. of engravings and atlases in folios. In all 25 vols. Philadelphia. 1844–1858.

Art of War in Europe. 1854, 55, 56. By Maj. R. Delafield. 4to.

The Sixth Census or enumeration of the inhabitants of the United States, as corrected at the Department of State in 1840. Washington. 1840.

Compendium of the Sixth Census. Washington. 1841.

Statistics of the United States, Census of 1850. 4to.

The Eighth Census of the United States. 1860. Population. Agriculture, Manufactures and Mortality. 4 vols. 4to. Washington. 1864–6.

CANADA DOCUMENTS.

Sessional Papers. Sessions of 1859 to 1866 of the Parliament of the Province of Canada. Appendix to Vol. 17, Nos. 1, 2, 3, 5, 1859; Vol. 18, Nos. 1–4, 1860; Vol. 19, Nos. 1–4, 1861; Vol. 20, Nos. 1–5, 1862; Vol. 21, Nos. 1, 2, 4–6, 1863; Vol. 22, 1863; Vol. 23, Nos. 1–4, 1864; Vol. 24, Nos. 1–3, 1865: Vol. 25, Nos. 1–2, 1865; Vol. 26, Nos. 1–4, 1866. 36 volumes.

Session Papers. Sessions of 1867–1871 of the Parliament of the Dominion of Canada. Vol. 1, Nos. 1–9, 1867–68; Vol. 2, Nos. 1–6, 1869; Vol. 3, Nos. 1–6, 1870; Vol. 4, Nos. 1–4, 6, 1871. 26 vols.

Parliamentary Debates on the subject of the Confederation of the British Provinces of North America. 3d Session, 8th Parliament of Canada. Quebec. 1865.

Journals of the Legislative Council of the Province of Canada. Vols. 17–26. 1859–1866. 10 vols.

Journals of the Legislative Assembly of the Province of Canada. Vols. 17–26, except 22. 1859–1866. 9 vols.

Journals of the House of Commons of the Dominion of Canada. From 1867 to 1871. Vols. 1–4.

Journals of the Senate of Canada. 1867–1871. Vols. 1–4.

General Report of the Commissioner of Public Works for the half year ending June 30, 1864. Quebec. 1864.

Tables of the Trade and Navigation of the Province of Upper Canada, for the years 1858 and 1859. 2 vols. Quebec and Toronto. 1859–1860.

Report of the Post Master General for the nine months ending June 30, 1864. Quebec. 1865.

Report of the Minister of Agriculture for the Province of Canada for the 1864. Quebec. 1865.

Patents of Canada, from 1849 to 1855. Toronto. 1865.

Census of the Canadas, 1860–61. 2 vols. Quebec. 1864.

Geological Survey of Canada. Report of Progress from its commencement to 1863. With an atlas of Maps and Sections. Officers of the Survey: Sir William E. Logan, LL.D., F. R. S., F. G. S., Director; T. Sterry Hunt, LL.D., F. R. S., Assistant Geologist; E. Billings, F. G. S., Paleontologist. 2 vols. Montreal. 1865.

The Same. Report of Progress from 1863 to 1866. Ottowa. 1866.

PART SIXTH.

MISCELLANEOUS BOOKS:

WORKS RELATING TO HISTORY, BIOGRAPHY, PHILOSOPHY, POLITICAL ECONOMY, THE MATHEMATICAL AND PHYSICAL SCIENCES, BELLES LETTRES, ETC., WITH CYCLOPÆDIAS, DICTIONARIES, ETC., ETC.

MISCELLANEOUS BOOKS.

ABRIDGMENT OF THE DEBATES OF CONGRESS. See BENTON.

ADAMS (John). Life and works of John Adams, second President of the United States. By his Grandson, Charles Francis Adams. Boston. 1851–54. 10 vols.

ADAMS (John Q.) The Duplicate Letters, The Fisheries and the Mississippi. Documents relating to the Transactions at the Negotiation of Ghent. Washington. 1822.

ADDISON (Joseph). See SPECTATOR.

ADLER (J. G.) Dictionary of the German and English Languages. New York. 1856.

AGASSIZ (Lewis) and GOULD (Augustus A.) Principles of Zoology, etc., for the use of Schools and Colleges. Part I.

Comparative Physiology. Boston. 1853.

Lake Superior: its Physical Character, Vegetation and Animals, etc., with a narrative of the tour by J. C. Cabot. Boston. 1850.

Contributions to the Natural History of the United States. Boston. 1857. 2 vols.

AGRICULTURE. See NEW YORK.

AIKIN (John). British Poets, from Ben Jonson to Beattie. Philadelphia. 1831.

AIKEN (Lucy). Memoirs of the Court of James the First. Boston. 1822. 2 vols.

Memoirs of the Court of Charles the First. Philadelphia. 1853. 2 vols.

ALABAMA, History of. Pickett. Charleston. 1857. 2 vols.

ALISON (Archibald). History of Europe from the Commencement of the French Revolution to the Restoration of the Bourbons. New York. 1856. 4 vols.

History of Europe from the Fall of Napoleon to the Accession of Louis Napoleon. New York. 1856. Vols. 2, 3, 4.

Essay on the Nature and Principles of Taste. New York. 1830. 1 vol.

See MODERN BRITISH ESSAYISTS.

ALLAN (Robert). A Manual of Mineralogy. Edinburgh. 1834.

ALLIBONE (S. Austin). Dictionary of English Literature and British and American Authors. Philadelphia. Vol. 1.

ALMANAC (The National) and Annual Record. 1863–4. Philadelphia. 1863–4. 2 vols.

(The American) and Repository of Useful Knowledge for 1857. Boston. 1856.

(Merchant's and Banker's). 1869.

AMERICAN CONSPIRACIES. History of. See VICTOR (Orville J.)

AMERICAN ETHNOLOGICAL SOCIETY, Transactions of. 1845–48. 2 vols.

AMERICAN INSTITUTE of the City of New York. Transactions. 1850.

AMERICAN LITERARY GAZETTE AND PUBLISHER'S CIRCULAR. Philadelphia. 6 vols.

AMERICAN QUARTERLY REVIEW. Philadelphia. 1827–36. 20 vols.

AMERICAN STATESMEN. A Political History. By Andrew W. Young. New York. 1857.

AMERICUS VESPUCIUS. Life and Voyages of. By C. Edwards Lester. 4th ed. New Haven. 1854.

AMES (Fisher.) Works of, with a selection from his Speeches and Correspondence. Boston. 1854. 2 vols.

ANDREWS (E. A.) A Copious and Critical Latin Lexicon, founded on the larger Latin Lexicon of Freund. New York. 1856.

ANNALS OF THE CONGRESS of the United States, with an Appendix containing important State Papers and Public Documents, and all the laws of a Public nature. From the first to the Eighteenth Congress, inclusive. 1789–1824. 42 vols. (Duplicate set, not complete.)

ANTHON (Charles.) Classical Dictionary. New York. 1856.

Works of Horace. New York. 1853.

A Dictionary of Greek and Roman Antiquities. New York. 1854.

ANTIETAM NATIONAL CEMETERY. History of; including a descriptive list of all Loyal Soldiers buried therein. Baltimore. 1869.

APPLETON'S Dictionary of Mechanics, Machines, Engine-work and Engineering, with 4,000 engravings. New York. 1852. 2 vols.

Cyclopædia of Biography. New York. 1856.

ARCADIA. See SYDNEY (Sir Philip.)

ARISTOTLE. Aristotle's Ethics. Translated with notes, by R. R. W. Brown. London. *Bohn.* 1853.

The Organon; or Logical Treatises. Translated by O. F. Owen. London. *Bohn.* 1853. 2 vols.

The Politics and Economics. Translated by E. Walford. London. *Bohn.* 1853.

ASTOR LIBRARY. Alphabetical Index to the Astor Library. New York. 1851.

ATLAS. See COLTON (J. H.) HUMBOLDT. JOHNSON.

AUSTRIA in 1848–49. By William H. Stiles. New York. 1852. 2 vols.

BACON (Francis.) Works of. A new edition. With Life of the Author, by Basil Montagu. Philadelphia. 1856. 3 vols.

BAKER (George E.) The Works of William H. Seward. New York. 1853. 3 vols. (Vol. 1 wanting.)

BANCROFT (George.) A History of the United States, from the Discovery of the American Continent to the Present Time. Boston. 9 vols.

Literary and Historical Miscellanies. New York. 1855.

BANKS (John). A Treatise of Mills. London. 1815.

BARNARD (Henry.) Journal of the Rhode Island Institute of Instruction. Providence. 1846. 4 vols.

The American Journal of Education. Hartford. 1859. Vol. 6.

National Education in Europe. New York. 1859.

Reformatory Education. Papers on Preventive, Correctional and Reformatory Institutions and Agencies in Different Countries. Hartford. 1857.

Report of the Commissioner of Education. Washington. 1868.

Normal Schools and other Institutions, Agencies and Means. Hartford. 1851.

Educational Biography, Memoirs of Teachers, Educators and Promoters and Benefactors of Education, Literature and Science. New York. 1859.

School Architecture. New York. 1854.

Pestalozzi and Pestalozzianism. Life, Educational Principles and Methods of John Henry Pestalozzi. New York. 1859.

Tribute to Gallaudet. A discourse in commemoration of the Life, Character and Services of the Rev. Thomas H. Gallaudet, LL. D. New York. 1859.

BARNUM (Rev. Samuel W.) A Comprehensive Dictionary of the Bible. New York. 1869.

BARTH (Henry). Travels and Discoveries in North and Central Africa. New York. 1857. 3 vols. (Vol. 1 wanting.)

BARTLETT (John Russell). Records of the Colony of Rhode Island and Providence Plantations in New England. 1707 to 1740. Providence. 1859.

BAYLE (Peter). The Dictionary, Historical and Critical of. 2d Ed. With Life of the Author. London. 1735. 5 vols. Folio.

BECCARIA ON CRIMES. An Essay on Crimes and Punishments. Translated from the Italian of Caesar Bonesana, Marquis Beccaria. Philadelphia. 1819.

BEMIS (George). American Neutrality—Its Honorable Past, Its Expedient Future. A Protest against the Proposed Repeal of the Neutrality Laws, and a plea for their Improvement and Consolidation. Boston. 1866.

BENTHAM (Jeremy.) Rationale of Judicial Evidence, Specially applied to English Practice. London. 1827. 6 vols.

BENTON (Thomas H.) Abridgement of the Debates of Congress from 1789 to 1856. Vols. 1–16, 1789–1850. New York and London. 1851–1861.

Thirty Year's View; or, a History of the Working of the American Government from 1820 to 1850. New York. 2 vols.

BECHE, DE LA (Henry T.) Geological Manual. Philadelphia. 1832.

BERKELEY (George D. D.) Works of; to which is added some Account of his Life. London. 1820. 3 vols.

BIBLE (Holy.) Philadelphia. 1853.

BIGELOW (Erastus B.) The Tariff Question considered in regard to the Policy of England and the interests of the United States. Boston. 1862.

BLACKWOOD'S EDINBURGH MAGAZINE. New York. 1865–1870. 11 vols. 97–108 (Vol. 104 missing.)

BLAKE (J. L.) General Biographical Dictionary. New York. 1854.

BLATCHFORD (Thos. W.) Hydrophobia; Its Origin and Development. Philadelphia. 1856. Paper.

BLODGET (Lorin.) Climatology of the United States and of the Temperate Latitudes of the North American Continent. Philadelphia. 1857.

BOBRIK (Eduard, Dr.) Allgemeines Nautisches Worterbuch, mit Sacherklarungen. Leipzig. 1850.

BOECKH (Augustus.) The Public Economy of Athens, with a Dissertation on the Silver Mines of Laurion. Boston. 1857. (Duplicate.)

BOETHIUS. Consolations of Philosophy. (Missing.)

BOKER (George H.) Plays and Poems. Boston. 1856. 2 vols.

BONAPARTE (Charles Lucien.) American Ornithology. Philadelphia. 1825–33. 4 vols.

Note.—Volumes 1 and 4 are wanting.

BOOK OF THE WORLD. New York. 1852. 2 vols.

BOSWELL (James.) The Life of Samuel Johnson; with additions and notes, by John Wilson Croker. New York. 1835. 2 vols.

BOSWORTH (Rev. Joseph.) A Compendious Anglo-Saxon and English Dictionary. London. 1860.

BOTANY. See NEW YORK.

BOWEN (Francis.) The Principles of Political Economy. Boston. 1863.

BOYNTON (C. B.) English and French Neutrality, and Anglo-French Alliance, in their relations to the United States and Russia. Cincinnati. 1864.

BRAND (John.) Observations on the Popular Antiquities of Great Britain. London. 1854. Vols. 2 and 3.

BRANDE (W. T.) A Dictionary of Science, Literature and Art. New York. 1856.

BRINDLEY (Robert.) A Compendium of Civil Architecture. Devonport. 1832.

BRITISH ESSAYISTS. London. 1831. Vols. 3-5. Vol. 3. The Rambler; The Idler; The Adventurer. Vol. 4. The World; The Mirror; The Lounger. Vol. 5. The Observer; The Connoisseur; Knox's Essays; The Microcosm; The Olla Podidra.

See MODERN BRITISH ESSAYISTS.

BRITISH ESSAYISTS (The Modern). Smith, Allison, Jeffrey, Macaulay, Mackintosh, Wilson, Philadelphia. 6 vols.

BRITISH POETS. Goldsmith and Dryden. Boston. 5 vols.

BROCKETT (L. P.) The Life and Times of Abraham Lincoln. Philadelphia. 1865.

BROUGHAM (Henry, Lord). Political Philosophy. London. 3 vols.

BROUGHAM (Henry, Lord). Speeches of, upon questions relating to Public Rights, Duties and Interests. Edinburgh. 1838. 4 vols.

BROWN (David Paul). The Forum, or Forty Years full Practice at the Philadelphia Bar. Philadelphia. 1856. 2 vols.

BROWN (Thomas.) Lectures on the Philosophy of the Human Mind. Hallowell. 1836. 2 vols.

BROWN (Samuel Gilman.) See CHOATE (Rufus).

BRYANT (William Cullen.) Poems, with Illustrations by E. Leutze. Philadelphia. 1848.

BUCKLE (Henry Thomas.) History of Civilization in England, New York. 1862. 2 vols. (Vol. 1 wanting.)

BURKE (Edmund). The Works of. Revised edition. Boston. 1865. 12 vols. (Vols. 1 and 3 wanting.)

BURKE (Edmund). The Works of; with a Memoir. New York. 1837. 3 vols.

Note.—Vol. 1 is wanting.

See CHATHAM.

BURNET (Bishop). History of his Own Time, from the Restoration of Charles the I, to the Settlement of King William and Mary, at the Revolution. London. 1724. 2 vols.

BURNS (Robert). The Complete works of. Boston. 1854.

The Works of; with his life, by Allen Cunningham. 4 vols.

Note.—Vols. 1 and 2 are wanting.

BURR (Aaron). Memoirs of; with Miscellaneous Selections from his Correspondence. By Matthew L. Davis. New York. 1855. 2 vols.

Life and Times of, by J. Parton. New York. 1858.

The Private Journal of, during his residence of four years in Europe. Edited by Matthew L. Davis. New York. 1856. 2 vols.

BURTON (William E.) Cyclopaedia of Wit and Humor, containing selections from the writings of the most eminent Humorists of America, Ireland, Scotland and England. New York. 1858. 2 vols. (Vol. 2 wanting.)

Butler (Samuel). Hudibras, with notes by the Rev. Treadway Russel Nash, D. D. New York. 1847.

Byron (Lord). The Complete Works of. New York.

Calhoun (John C.) Works: edited by R. C. Cralle. Columbia. 1851. New York. 1853. 6 vols. (Vol. 5 wanting.)

California. Catalogue of the State Library of. Sacramento. 1860.

Campbell (John, Lord). The Lives of the Lord Chancellors and Keepers of the Great Seal of England. Philadelphia. 1851. 7 vols.

The Lives of the Chief Justices of England, from the Norman Conquest till the death of Lord Mansfield. Philadelphia. 1851. 2 vols.

Canning (George). Select Speeches of, with a Preliminary Biographical Sketch. Philadelphia. 1835. 1 vol.

Carlyle (Thomas). Critical and Miscellaneous Essays, collected and republished. Boston. 1860. 4 vols. (Vols. 1 and 4 wanting.)

Oliver Cromwell's Letters and Speeches. New York. 1868. 2 vols.

French Revolution. 2 vols.

History of Frederick the Great. New York. 1859. Vols. 1 and 2.

Casgrain (H. R.) Un Coutemporain. F. X. Garneau. Quebec. 1866.

Cervantes. The History of the Ingenious Gentleman Don Quixote. Lockhart's Edition. Boston. 1856. 4 vols.

Chalmers (Alexander.) The Spectator. A new Edition, carefully revised. New York. 1853. 6 vols.

Chancellors of England. Lives of the Lord Chancellors and Keepers of the Great Seal of England, from the earliest times till the reign of King George IV., by John (Lord) Campbell. Philadelphia. 1851. 7 vols.

Channing (William E.) Works: 12th complete edition, with an introduction. Boston. 1853. 6 vols.

Chatham, Burke and Erskine. Celebrated Speeches, to which is added the Argument of Mr. Mackintosh in the case of Peltier. Philadelphia. 1835.

Chaucer (Geoffrey.) Poetical Works of. London. 1843.

Chemistry of the Arts. See Porter (Arthur L.)

CHEVALIER (Michael.) On the Probable Fall in the Value of Gold. New York. 1859.

CHOATE (Rufus.) The Works of, with a Memoir of his Life, by Samuel Gilman Brown. Boston. 1862. 2 vols.

CICERO. Bohn's Translation, 5 vols.

Three Books of Offices, or Moral Duties. London. 1856.

The Academic Questions. London. 1853.

The Orations. London. 1852. 4 vols. (Vols. 1 and 2 wanting.)

On Oratory. London.

CIRCLE OF THE SCIENCES. See under CYCLOPÆDIA.

CLAPPERTON (Commander.) Journal of a Second Expedition into the Interior of Africa,—to which is added the Journal of Richard Lander. Philadelphia. 1829.

CLARENDON (Edward, Earl of.) History of the Rebellion and Civil War in England, begun in 1641,—with all the suppressed passages, and the unpublished notes of Bishop Warburton. 1827. 6 vols. (Volume 2 is wanting.)

CLARKE (Mary Cowden.) Concordance to Shakspeare.

CLARKE (James Freeman.) Revolutionary Services and Civil Life of General William Hull. New York and Philadelphia. 1848.

CLAY (Henry.) See COLTON (Calvin) and MALLORY (Daniel.)

CLOUGH (A. H.) Plutarch's Lives. The Translation called Dryden's. Boston. 1859. 5 vols.

COLERIDGE (Samuel Taylor.) The Works of, in Prose and Verse. Philadelphia. 1853.

COFFIN (William F.) The War of 1812, and its Moral. A Canadian Chronicle. Montreal. 1864.

COLTON (Calvin.) The Life, Correspondence and Speeches of Henry Clay. New York. 1857. 6 vols.

COLTON (J. H.) Atlas of the World. Vol. 1. North and South America. Vol. 2. Europe, Asia and Africa. 4to. 1855.

COMTE (Auguste.) The Positive Philosophy of. New York. 1858.

CONGRESS. See ANNALS OF CONGRESS.

CONGRESSIONAL DEBATES. See BENTON (Thos. H.), and REGISTER OF DEBATES IN CONGRESS.

CONNECTICUT. The Public Records of the Colony of, from 1689 to 1716. By Charles S. Hoadley. Hartford. 1870. 2 vols.

CONSTITUTIONS of the several States of the Union and United States. New York. 1857.

CONVERSATIONS LEXIKON. Leipzig. 1843. 15 vols.

Note.—Vols. 3, 13, 14 and 15 are wanting.

COOPER (James Fennimore.) The Pioneers.

COPELAND (James.) A Dictionary of Practical Medicine. New York. 1860. 3 vols.

CORPUS POETARUM LATINORUM. Edidit Gul. Sidney Walker. London. 1854.

COUSIN (Victor.) Course of the History of Modern Philosophy. Translated by O. W. Wight. New York. 1857. 2 vols.

Lectures on the True, Beautiful and Good. Translated by O. W. Wight. New York. 1854. 1 vol.

COWPER (William.) The Complete Poetical Works of. New York. 1853. 1 vol.

And James Thomson. Works of; with a new and interesting Memoir of the Life of Thomson. Philadelphia. 1837.

CRABB (George.) English Synonyms. New York. 1857.

CROFFUT (W. A.) and MORRIS (J. M.) Military and Civil History of Connecticut, during the War of 1861–65. New York. 1869.

CROMWELL (Oliver.) See CARLYLE (Thomas.)

CULTIVATOR (The.) A Monthly Journal devoted to Agriculture. New Series. Vol. III. Albany. 1846. 1 vol.

CUNNINGHAM (Allan.) The Works of Robert Burns, with his Life. Boston. 1834. 4 vols. (Vols. 1 and 2 wanting.)

CURTIS (George Ticknor.) History of the Origin, Formation and Adoption of the Constitution of the United States. New York. 1854. 2 vols.

The Life of Daniel Webster. New York. 1870. 2 vols.

CUSHING (Luther Stearns.) Elements of the Law and Practice of Legislative Assemblies in the United States. Boston. 1856.

CUVIER (Baron G.) Animal Kingdom. Translated from the French, with Notes and Additions, by H. M. Murtrie. New York. 1831. 4 vols.

Animal Kingdom. London. 1851.

CYCLOPAEDIAS.

Cyclopaedia of the Physical Sciences. London. 1857. 1 vol.

Cyclopaedia of Geography. By Hugh Murray. Philadelphia. 1837. 3 vols.

Lardner's Cabinet Cyclopædia. Philadelphia. 1832. 23 vols.

Cyclopaedia (Appleton's) of Biography; embracing a series of Original Memoirs of the most distinguished presons of all times. Revised American Edition, by Francis L. Hawks. New York. 1856.

Cyclopædia of Bibical, Theological and Ecclesiastical Literature. By John McClintock and James Strong. New York. Vols. 1–4.

Cyclopædia of Wit and Humor; containing selections from the Writings of the most Eminent Humorists of America, Ireland, Scotland and England. By William E. Burton. New York. 1858. 2 vols. (Vol. 2 wanting.)

The English Cyclopædia. By Charles Knight. Geography. London and New York. 1854. 4 vols.

Cyclopædia of Commerce and Commercial Navigation. By J. Smith Homans. New York. 1859.

The New American Cyclopædia. A Popular Dictionary of General Knowledge. New York. 1861. 16 vols.

The American Annual Cyclopedia and Register of Important Events. New York. 10 vols., from 1861 to 1870.

Cyclopædia of American Literature. By Evert A. Duyckinck. New York. 1856. 2 vols.

Cyclopædia of the Physical Sciences. By J. P. Nichol. London and Glasgow. 1857.

Cyclopædia of Science, Literature and Art. By W. T. Brande. New York. 1856.

The Circle of the Sciences; with an Introductory Discourse of the Objects, Pleasures and Advantages of Science. By Henry, Lord Brougham. Vol. 1: Parts 1 and 2. Vol. 2: Parts 1 and 2. (Bound in 4 volumes.)

Davis (Matthew L.) The Private Journal of Aaron Burr, during his Residence of Four Years in Europe. New York. 1856. 2 vols.

Memoirs of Aaron Burr, with Miscellaneous Selections from his Correspondence. New York. 1855. 2 vols.

Davis (W. W. H.) History of the 104th Pennsylvania Regiment, from August 22, 1861, to September 30, 1864. Philadelphia. 1866.

DAWSON (Henry B.) The Fœderalist: A Collection of Essays, written in favor of the New Constitution as agreed upon by the Federal Convention, September 17, 1787. New York. 1864. Vol. 1.

"DEBATES ON THE JUDICIARY."—Debates in the Congress of the United States on the Bill for Repealing the Laws "For the more convenient Organization of the Courts of the United States." Albany. 1802.

DEBATES OF CONGRESS. See BENTON and REGISTER OF DEBATES, etc.

DE BOW (J. B.) The Industrial Resources, etc., of the United States, and more particularly of the Southern and Western States. New York and London. 1854.

DE FOE (Daniel). The Works of; with a Biographical Account of the author. Vol. 1, Robinson Crusoe. Vol. 2, Religious Courtship, etc. New York. 1857-8.

DE HAUSSEZ (Baron.) Great Britain in 1833. Phil. 1833.

DE LA BECHE (Sir H. T.) Geological Manual. Phil. 1832.

DE LIEFDE (John.) Six Months among the Charities of Europe. London. 1865. 2 vols.

DENHAM (Major), and Captain CLAPPERTON. Travels and Discoveries in Northern and Central Africa, in 1822-23-24. London. 1831. 4 vols. (Vols. 1, 2 and 3 wanting.)

DE PEYSTER (John Watts.) Personal and Military History of Philip Kearney. New York. 1869.

DE QUINCY (Thomas.) Philosophical Writers. 2 vols. Boston. 1854.

Narrative and Miscellaneous Papers. Vol. 2. Boston. 1853.

Literary Reminiscences. Vol. 2. Boston. 1854.

Essays on Philosophical Writers and other Men of Letters. Boston. 1854. 2 vols.

DERBY (Edward, Earl of.) The Iliad of Homer, translated by. New York. 1865. 2 vols.

DE RETZ (Cardinal.) Memoirs of. Philadelphia. 1817. 3 vols.

DE VRIES (David Petersen.) Voyage from Holland to America, A. D. 1632–44. Translated by Henry C. Murphy. New York. 1853. 1 vol.

DICTIONARIES.

Adler's German and English Dictionary.

Allibone's Dictionary of English Literature and of English and American Authors.

Andrew's Latin and English Lexicon.

Anthon's Classical Dictionary.

Anthon's Smith's Dictionary of Greek and Roman Antiquities.

Appleton's Dictionary of Mechanics, Machines, Engine Work and Engineering.

Barnum's Smith's Dictionary of the Bible.

Bayle's Critical and Biographical Dictionary.

Blake's Biographical Dictionary.

Bosworth's Anglo-Saxon and English Dictionary.

Copeland's Dictionary of Practical Medicine.

Halliwell's Dictionary of Archaic and Provincial Words, etc.

Johnson's (Samuel) Dictionary of the English Language.

Lanman's Dictionary of the United States Congress.

McCulloch's Commercial Dictionary.

Mozin's Dictionnaire Allemand - Francais. Francais - Allemand.

Seoane's Newman and Baretti's Spanish and English Pronouncing Dictionary.

Spier's and Surenne's French Pronouncing Dictionary.

Ure's Dictionary of Arts, Manufactures and Mines.

Walker's Pronouncing Dictionary.

DRYDEN (John). The Poetical Works of. Boston. 1854. 3 vols.

The Comedies, Tragedies, and Operas of John Dryden. London. 1701. 2 vols. Folio.

DUER (William Alexander). A Course of Lectures on the Constitutional Jurisprudence of the United States, delivered annually in Columbia College, New York. Boston. 1856.

DUYCKINCK (Evert A.) Cyclopedia of American Literature. New York. 1856. 2 vols.

EDGEWORTH (Maria). Tales and Novels by. New York. 1836. Vol. 1, Castle Rackrent. Vol. 5, Tales of Fashionable Life, etc. Vol. 7, Leonora, and Patronage. Vol. 8, Patronage, etc.

EDINBURGH REVIEW. Boston. 1802–1834. 59 vols.

EDINBURGH REVIEW OR CRITICAL JOURNAL. (American Edition). 1861–1871. New York.

ELIOT (Samuel). History of Liberty: The Early Christians. Boston. 1853. 2 vols.

History of Liberty: The Ancient Romans. Boston. 1853. 2 vols. (Vol. 1 wanting.)

ELLIOTT (Charles W.) The New England History from the Discovery of the Continent by the Northmen, A. D. 986, to the period when the Colonies declared their independence, A. D. 1776. New York. 1857. 2 vols.

ELLIOT (Jonathan.) The Debates, Resolutions and other Proceedings in Convention, on the adoption of the Federal Constitution, as recommended by the General Convention at Philadelphia, September 17, 1787. Vol. I. Debates in Massachusetts and New York. Vol. II. Virginia. Vol. III. North Carolina and Pennsylvania. Vol. IV. Journal and Debates of the Federal Convention, held at Philadelphia, from May 14 to September 17, 1787. Washington. 1827–28, and 1830. 4 vols. 8vo.

EMERSON (Ralph Waldo.) Essays. Second Series. Boston. 1855.

Poems. 1856.

EMMONS (Ebenezer.) Geological Report of the Midland Counties of North Carolina. New York and Raleigh. 1856.

ENCYCLOPÆDIAS.

Encyclopædia Americana. By Francis Lieber, assisted by E. Wigglesworth and T. G. Bradford. Boston. 1854. 13 vols. (Vol. 10 wanting.)

Encyclopædia Brittanica, or Dictionary of Arts, Sciences, and General Literature. Boston. 1855. 22 vols.

Encyclopædie Neue der Wissenschafter and Kunste fur die Deutsche Nation. Stuttgart. 1852. 4 vols.

Encyclopædia of Geography. By Hugh Murray. Philadelphia. 1837. 3 vols.

Icongraphic Encyclopædia. (See that title.)

ENGLAND.

See BURNETT, CLARENDON, FROUDE, FULLER, HUME, MACKINTOSCH, RUSSELL, SMOLLETT, etc.

The Parliamentary History of England from the Earliest Period to the year 1803. London. 1806. 36 vols.

ENGLISH POETS. The Works of, from Chaucer to Cowper, including the Series edited, with Prefaces, Biographical and Critical, by Dr. Samuel Johnson, and the most approved Translations. The additional Lives by Alexander Chalmers, F. S. A. London. 1810. 21 vols.

ENGLISH CYCLOPÆDIA OF GEOGRAPHY. By Charles Knight. London. 1853. 4 vols.

ERSKINE (T.) See CHATHAM.

Speeches of Lord Erskine while at the Bar. Edited by James Lambert High. Chicago. 1870. 4 vols.

ESSAYS on the Formation and Publication of Opinions, and on other subjects. Philadelphia. 1831.

EVERETT (Edward). Orations and Speeches of. Boston. 1865. 4 vols.

FAIRBAIRN (Henry.) A Treatise upon the Political Economy of Railroads. London. 1836.

FEDERALIST (The), on the New Constitution. Written in the year 1788. Hallowell. 1837. See DAWSON.

FERRIS (John Alexander). The Financial Economy of the United States Illustrated. San Francisco. 1867.

FISHER (Richard Swainson). New and Complete Gazetteer of the United States. New York. 1853.

FISHER (Richard S.) The Book of the World: being an account of all Republics, Empires, Kingdoms and Nations, in reference to their Geography, Statistics, Commerce etc. New York. 1852. 2 vols.

FLANDERS (Henry). The Lives and Times of the Chief Justices of the Supreme Court of the United States. First series. Philadelphia. 1855, 1858. 2 vols.

FOREST CULTURE. See SCHNEIDER, VON HAGEN.

FORMAN (J. G.) The Western Sanitary Commission. St. Louis. 1864.

FORSTER (John.) The Statesmen of the Commonwealth of England. New York. 1855.

FORSYTHE (William.) History of Trial by Jury. London. 1852.

FOSS (Edward.) A Biographical Dictionary of the Judges of England, from the Conquest to the Present Time, 1866–1870. Boston. 1870.

FOSTER (John Y.) New Jersey and the Rebellion. A History of the Services of the Troops and People of New Jersey in Aid of the Union Cause. Newark. 1868.

FRANKLIN (Benjamin.) The Works of; containing several Political and Historical Tracts, not included in any former edition; with Notes and a Life of the Author. Boston. 10 vols. (Vol. 1 wanting.)

FROUDE (James Anthony.) History of England from the fall of Wolsey to the death of Elizabeth. New York. 1865. 10 vols.

FULLER (Thomas.) The History of the Worthies of England. London. 1840. 3 vols.

GALLOWAY (Elijah.) History and Progress of the Steam Engine, with a Practical Investigation of its Structure and Application, to which is added an extensive Appendix. By Luke Hebert. 1 vol.

GENIN (Sylvester.) Selections from the Works of, with a Biographical Sketch. New York. 1855.

GENIN (Thomas Hedges.) Selections from the Writings of, with a Biographical Sketch. New York. 1869.

GEOLOGY. See NEW YORK.

GETTYSBURG. Report of the Committee relative to the Soldiers' National Cemetery. 1865.

GIBBON (Edward.) History of the Decline and Fall of the Roman Empire. New York. 1836. 4 vols.

Note.—Vol. 1 is wanting.

Miscellaneous Works of, with Memoirs of his Life and Writings, composed by himself. London. 1814. 5 vols.

GIDDINGS (Joshua R.) The Exiles of Florida, or The Crimes Committed by our Government against the Maroons who fled from South Carolina and other Slave States, seeking protection under Spanish Laws. Columbus. 1858.

GIESELER (John C. L.) A Text Book of Church History. New York. 1857. 3 vols.

GILLIES (John.) The History of Ancient Greece, its Colonies and Conquests, including the History of Literature, Philosophy and Fine Arts. Philadelphia. 1835.

GODWIN (Parke.) The History of France. New York. 1860. Vol. 1.

GOETHE (John Wolfgang). Sammtliche Werke. Stuttgart & Tubingen. 1850. 30 vols. (Vols. 3, 4, 5, 6 and 11 missing)

Faust. Stuttgart & Tubingen. 1854. Folio.

GEGENWART (Die). Ein encyclopædische Darstellung der Neuesten Zeitgeschichte fur alle Stande. Leipzig. 1849. 5 vols. (Vol 1 missing.)

GOLDSMITH (Oliver).) A History of the Earth and Animated Nature. Philadelphia. 1848. 4 vols in 2.

Works of, with Life and Notes. London. 1852. 4 vols. (Vol. 1 wanting.)

Life of, by James Prior. Philadelphia. 1837.

GOOD (John Mason). The Book of Nature. New York. 1836·

GORDON (Thomas F.) The History of Pennsylvania from its Discovery to the Delaration of Independence. Philadelphia. 1829.

GRATTAN (Hon. Henry). The Speeches of. Edited by Daniel Owen Madden. Dublin. 1867.

GRAY (Asa). A Manual of the Botany of the United States. Boston. 1848.

GRAZIER. (Complete) ; or Farmer's and Cattle-Breeder's and Dealer's Assistant. London. 1833.

GREENLEAF (Simon). Examination of the Testimony of the Four Evangelists, by the rules of evidence administered in Courts of Justice; with an Account of the Trial of Jesus. London. 1847.

GREGORY (John). Industrial Resources of Wisconsin. Chicago. 1853.

GREELY (Horace). The American Conflict. History of The Great Rebellion in the United States. Hartford. 1864. 2 vols.

GRIFFIN (John Joseph). Chemical Recreations. A Popular Compendium of Experimental Chemistry. London. 1849.

GRIFFITH'S Marine and Naval Architecture. New York. 1854.

GROTE (George). History of Greece. New York. 1857. 12 vols.

GUIZOT (F.) The History of Civilization from the fall of the Roman Empire to the French Revolution. New York. 1859. 4 vols.

GUROWSKI (Adam G.) America and Europe. New York. 1857

HALL (James) and WHITNEY (J. D.) Report of the Geological Survey of Iowa. 2 vols.

HALL (James). Report of the Geological Survey of Wisconsin. 1862. 2 copies.

HALL (Hiland). The History of Vermont from its discovery to its admission into the Union in 1791. Albany. 1868.

HALLAM (Henry). The Constitutional History of England from the Accession of Henry VII., to the death of George II. Boston and New York. 1864. 3 vols.

The Constitutional History of England from the Accession of Henry VII., to the death of George II. Boston. 1829. 3 vols. (Vol. 1 is wanting.)

View of the State of Europe during the Middle Ages. Paris. 1835. 2 vols. (Vol. 1 is missing.)

Introduction to the Literature of Europe in the Fifteenth, Sixteenth and Seventeenth Centuries. New York. 1856. 2 vols.

HALLIWELL (James Orchard). A Dictionary of Archaic and Provincial Words, Obsolete Phrases, Proverbs and Ancient Customs, from the fourteenth century. London. 1855. 2 vols.

HAMILTON (John C.) History of the Republic of the United States, as traced in the writings of Alexander Hamilton and of his Cotemporaries. New York. 1858. 6 vols. (Vol. 1 wanting.)

The Life of Alexander Hamilton. New York. 1834.

HAMILTON (Sir William). Lectures on Metaphysics. Boston. 1859.

HARRINGTON (James). The Oceana and other works, with an Account of his Life. By John Toland. London. 1837. Folio.

HASTED (Frederick). The Writings, etc., of. 1863.

HAZLITT (William). The Miscellaneous Works of. New York. 1857. 5 vols. (Vols. 2 and 3 wanting.)

HEADLEY (J. T.) Grant and Sherman: their Campaigns and Generals. New York. 1865.

HEBER (Reginald, Bishop). Narrative of a Journey through the Upper Provinces of India. Philadelphia. 1829. 2 vols.

HECK (J. G.) See ICONOGRAPHIC ENCYCLOPÆDIA.

HELPS (Arthur.) The Spanish Conquest in America, and its Relations to the History of Slavery and to the Government of Colonies. New York. 1856. 3 vols.

HERODOTUS. The History of Herodotus. A New English Version. Edited, with copious Notes, etc., by Geo. Rawlinson, M. A., assisted by Col. Sir Henry Rawiinson, K. C. B., and Sir J. G. Wilkinson, F. R. S. New York. 1859. 4 vols.

HERSCHEL (Sir J. F. W.) Outlines of Astronomy. Philadelphia. 1853.

HEYSE (Dr. J. C. A.) Theoretisch-Praktische deutsche Schulgrammatik. Hanover. 1842.

HIGH (James Lambert.) See ERSKINE.

HILDRETH (Richard.) The History of the United States of America. New York. 1856. 6 vols.

Theory of Politics. New York. 1853.

HINDS (H. Y.) Canadian Exploration Expeditions. 2 vols.

HOADLEY (Charles S.) The Public Records of the Colony of Connecticut, from 1689–1716. Hartford. 1870. 2 vols.

HOBBES (Thomas.) The Moral and Political Works of. London. 1750. Folio.

HOEY (John Cashel.) See PLUNKET.

HOLLAND (J. G.) The Life of Abraham Lincoln. Massachusetts. 1866.

HOMANS (J. Smith.) Cyclopædia of Commerce and Commercial Navigation. New York. 1859.

HOMER. The Iliad of. Translated by William Cowper. London. 1809. 2 vols.

Odyssey. Translated by William Cowper. London. 1809. 2 vols.

The Iliad. Translated by Edward, Earl of Derby. New York. 1865. 2 vols.

HOOKER (Richard.) Works of; containing eight Books of the Laws of Ecclesiastical Polity, and several other Treatises, with a Life of the Authur, by Isaac Walton. Oxford. 1807. 3 vols.

HORACE. The Works of, with English Notes, critical and explanatory, by Charles Anthon, L.L.D. New York. 1853.

HOUGH (Franklin B.) Census of the State of New York for 1865. Albany. 1867.

HOYT (John W.) Addresses on University Progress. New York. 1870.

HULL (Gen. William.) Revolutionary Scenes and Civil Life, by his daughter, Mrs. Maria Campbell; together with the History of the Campaign of 1812, and Surrender of the Post of Detroit ; by his grandson, James Freeman Clark. New York. 1848. 1 vol.

HUMBOLDT (Alexander Von.) Aspects of Nature. Translated by Mrs. Sabine. Philadelphia. 1850.

Kosmos. Stuttgart and Tuebingen. 1845. 3 vols.

Cosmos. Translated by E. C. Otte. London. 4 vols.

Kritische Untersuchungen. Berlin. 1335. 2 vols.

Letters of Alexander Von Humboldt to Varnhagen Von Ense. Translated by Friedrich Kapp. New York. 1860.

Kleinere Schriften. Stuttgart and Tuebingen. 1853.

Atlas der Kleineren Schriften. Stuttgart and Tuebingen. 1853.

HUME (David.) The History of England from the Invasion of Julius Cæsar to the Abdication of James the Second, 1688. New York. 1868.

Essays. Edinburg. 1825. 2 vols.

Philosophical Works. Edinburg. 1826. 4 vols. (Vol 4 wanting.)

HUNT'S Merchants' Magazine. 1871.

HUNT (John Warren.) Wisconsin Gazetteer.

HUSKISSON (William.) See WINDHAM.

INCONOGRAPHIC ENCYCLOPÆDIA of Science, Literature and Art, systematically arranged, by J. G. Heck. Translated from the German, and edited by S. F. Baird. New York. 1857. 6 vols.

IRVING (Washington.) Life of George Washington. 5 vols. New York. 1856.

The Works of. New York. 1853.
Vol. 1. Knickerbocker's New York.
Vols. 3–5. Life and Voyages of Columbus.
Vol. 7. Tales of a Traveller.
Vol. 9. Crayon Miscellany.
Vol. 10. Bonneville's Adventures.
Vol. 11. Oliver Goldsmith.
Vols. 12, 13. Mahomet and His Successors.
Vol. 14. Conquest of Granada.

JAY (John.) A Statistical View of American Agriculture. New York. 1859.

JEFEERSON (Thomas.) The Writings of. Edited by H. A. Washington. New York. 1853. 9 vols.

Life of. By Henry S. Randall, LL. D. New York. 1858. 3 vols.

JEFFREY (Francis.) See MODERN BRITISH ESSAYISTS.

JOHNSON (Samuel.) Dictionary of the English Language. Philadelphia. 1818. 2 vols.

Works of ; with an Essay on his Life and Genius, by Arthur Murray. New York. 1856. 2 vols.

See also ENGLISH POETS.

JOHNSON'S New Illustrated Family Atlas, with Physical Geography, etc. Edited by Richard S. Fisher, M. D. New York. 1864. 4to.

JONSON (Ben.) Works of. London. 1692. Folio.

JOSEPHUS (Flavius.) Translated by Whiston. Philadelphia. 1829. 2 vols. Philadelphia. 1854. 1 vol.

JUNIUS. Including Letters by the same Author under other Signatures. London. 1850. 2 vols.

Note—Vol. 1 is wanting.

KANE (Elisha Kent.) The U. S. Grinnell Expedition in Search of Sir John Franklin. New York. 1854.

KAPP (Friedrich.) The Life of Frederick William Von Steuben. New York. 1859.

Letters of Alexander Von Humboldt to Varnhagen Von Ense. New York. 1860.

KARSTEN (Dr. C. J. B.) Handbuch der Eisenhuettenkunde. Berlin. 1827. 4 vols. in 2.

KEATING (William H.) Long's Expedition to the Source of St. Peter's River, Lake Winnepeek, Lake of the Woods, etc., etc. Philadelphia. 1824. 2 vols. (Vol 1 wanting.)

KENNEDY (John P.) Memoirs of the Life of William Wirt, Attorney General of the United States. Philadelphia. 1856. 2 vols. (Vol. 1 wanting.)

KENTUCKY. Report of the Geological Survey in 1854–55.

KLOPSTOCK (Friedrich Gottlieb.) Sammtliche Werke. Leipzig. 1844. 10 vols. in 5.

KNAPP (Dr. F.) Lehrbuch der Chemischen Technologie. Braunschweig. 1847. 2 vols.

Chemical Technology, translated by Dr. Edmund Ronalds and Dr. Richardson. Philadelphia. 1848. 2 vols.

KNIGHT (Charles.) The English Cyclopædia. Geography. London and New York. 1854. 4 vols.

KINGSLEY (Charles). The Voyage and Adventures of Sir Amyas Leigh, Knight. Boston. 1857.

LAMARTINE (Alphonse de). History of the Girondists. New York. 1854. 3 vols.

Restoration of the Monarchy in France. New York. 4 vols.

LANMAN (Charles). Dictionary of the United States Congress, containing Biographical Sketches of its Members from the foundation of the Government. Philadelphia. 1859.

LARDNER (Dionysius, Rev.) Cabinet Cyclopædia. Philadelphia. 1832.

[*Contents:* 1 British Statesmen.
2 England, Mackintosh's History of. 3 vols.
3 France, Crowe's History of. 3 vols.
4 Herschel's Natural Philosophy.
5 Hydrostatics and Pneumatics.
6 Italian Republics, Sismondi's History of.
7 Mechanics.
8 Netherlands, Grattan's History of the.
9 Outlines of History.
10 Porcelain and Glass Manufacture.
11 Scotland, Scott's History of. 2 vols.
12 Spain and Portugal, History of. 5 vols.]

Natural Philosophy and Astronomy. First Course. Philadelphia. 1854.

Natural Philosophy. Second Course. 1854.

Natural Philosophy. Third Course. 1854.

Museum of Science and Art. London. 1854. 12 vols.

Steam Engine Familiarly Explained and Illustrated. Philadelphia. 1836.

LAS CASES (Count De.) Memoirs of the Life, Exile and Conversations of the Emperor Napoleon. New York. 1855. 4 vols. (Vols. 1 and 2 wanting.)

LAYARD (Austin H.) Discoveries among the Ruins of Nineveh and Babylon. New York. 1856.

LEMAY (Leon Pamphile.) Essais Poetiques. Quebec. 1865.

LE MOINE (J. M.) Ornithologie Du Canada. Quebec. 1861.

LESSING (Gotthold Ephraim.) Gesammelte Werke. Leipzig. 1841. 10 vols. in 5. (Vols. 5 and 6 missing.)

LIDDELL (Henry G.) A History of Rome from the earliest times to the establishment of the Empire. London. 1855. 2 vols.

LIEBER (Francis). The Penitentiary System in the United States and its application in France. Philadelphia. 1833.

LINGARD (John). History of England from the first invasion of the Romans. Philadelphia. 1827. 7 vols.

LIPPINCOTT'S Pronouncing Gazetteer of the World. Philadelphia. 1857.

LIVIUS (Titus). History of Rome, translated by George Baker. Philadelphia. 1836. 2 vols. (Vol. 1 wanting.)

LOCKE (John). Essays. Philadelphia.

LODGE (G. Henry). See WINCKELMANN.

LOGAN (W. E.) Geological Survey of Canada from its commencement to 1863. 2 vols. Montreal. 1865.

Geological Survey of Canada from 1863 to 1866. Ottawa. 1866.

LONDON QUARTERLY REVIEW. (*American Edition.*) 1861–1871. 11 vols. New York.

LONG'S Expedition. 1824. 2 vols. (Vol. 1 wanting.)

LONGFELLOW (Henry Wadsworth.) Poems. Boston. 1854. 2 vols.

LOSSING (B. J.) Pictorial Field Book of the Revolution. New York. 1855. 2 vols.

LOVE (William De Loss.) Wisconsin in the War of the Rebellion; a History of all Regiments and Batteries the State has sent to the Field. Chicago. 1866.

LYELL (Sir Charles.) Principles of Geology. New York. 1854.

MACAULAY (T. Babington.) See MODERN BRITISH ESSAYISTS.

History of England from the accession of James II. Philadelphia. 1861. 5 vols.

MACHIAVELLI (Nicholas). The Works of, Citizen Secretary of Florence. London. 1680. Folio.

MACKAY (Charles). Memoirs of Extraordinary Popular Delusions. London. 1841. 3 vols. (Vol. 1 is wanting.)

MACKINTOSH (Sir James). See MODERN BRITISH ESSAYISTS.

See CHATHAM.

A General View of the Progress of Ethical Philosophy. Philadelphia. 1834. 1 vol.

The Cabinet History of England. Philadelphia. 1830. 3 vols.

MADDEN (Daniel Owen). See GRATTAN.

MADISON (James). The Papers of. Washington. 1840. 3 vols.

Letters and other Writings of. Philadelphia. 1865. 4 vols.

History of the Life and Times of, by W. C. Rives. Boston. 1859. Vols 1 and 3.

MADISON City Directory. 1858.

MAHON (Lord). History of England from the Peace of Utrecht to the Peace of Paris. New York. 1849. 2 vols.

MAINE. Catalogue of the State Library of Maine. Augusta. 1850.

Documentary History of the State of Maine. By Wm. Willis. Portland. 1869. Vol. 1.

MALLORY (Daniel.) The Life and Speeches of Hon. Henry Clay. New York. 1843. 2 vols.

MALTE-BRUN. Universal Geography. Philadelphia. 1827. 6 vols.

MALTHUS (Rev. T. R.) Essay on the Principle of Population. London. 1826. 2 vols.

MARSH (G. P.) Man and Nature. New York.

MARSHALL (John.) The Life of George Washington, with Map. Philadelphia. 1832. 2 vols.

MARTINEAU (Harriet.) The Positive Philosophy of Auguste Comte. New York. 1858.

MASSACHUSETTS. Records of, 1644–1686. Vols. 1–5. Vol 4 in 2 parts. In all 6 vols. 4to. Boston. 1854.

Plymouth Colony Records 1633–1682. 11 vols. in 9. 4to. Boston. 1855–1861.

Catalogue of the State Library of Massachusetts. 1858.

Records of the Governor and Company of the Massachusetts Bay in New England. Edited by Nathaniel Shurtleff, M. D. Vols. I–VIII. 1628. Boston. 1853–54. Royal 8vo. 8 vols.

Report of Sanitary Commission of Boston. 1850.

MASSON (David.) The Life of John Milton narrated in connection with the Political, Ecclesiastical and Literary History of his Time. Boston. 1859. Vol 1.

MATHER (Cotton). Magnalia Christi Americana. Hartford. 1855. 2 vols.

MAUNDER (Samuel). The Treasury of Geography. London. 1856.

The Treasury of History. London. 1853.

The Treasury of Knowledge. London. 1855.

Biographical Treasury. London. 1856.

MAURY (M. F.) The Physical Geography of the Sea. New York. 1857.

MAY (Thomas Erskine). The Constitutional History of England since the Accession of George Third. 1760–1860. Boston. 1862. 2 vols.

McCLINTOCK (John) and STRONG (James). Cyclopaedia of Biblical, Theological and Ecclesiastical Literature. New York. Vols. 1–4.

McCULLOCH (J. R.) A Descriptive and Statistical Account of the British Empire. London. 1854. 2 vols.

McCULLOCH (J. R.) Dictionary of Commerce and Commercial Navigation. London. 1837.

McCULLOCH (J. R.) Principles of Political Economy. Edinburg. 1825.

McGREGOR (John). Progress of America, from the Discovery by Columbus to the year 1846. London. 1847. 2 vols.

Commercial Statistcs of all Nations. London. 1850. 5 vols.

MENZEL (Wolfgang.) History of Germany, translated by Mrs. George Horrock. London. 1853. 3 vols.

MERIVALE (Charles). History of The Romans under the Empire. London. 1852. 7 vols.

METEOROLOGY. See NEW YORK.

MICHAUD (Joseph Francis.) History of the Crusades. New York. 1853. 3 vols.

MIGNET (A. F.) History of the French Revolution from 1789 to 1814. York. 1827.

MILL (James.) History of British India. London. 1826. 6 vols.

MILLER (J. R.) History of Great Britain from the Death of George II. to the Coronation of George IV. Philadelphia. 1836.

MILLER (Hugh.) The Works of. Boston. 1859. 7 volumes, viz.:

The Cruise of the Betsey, or a Summer Ramble Among the Fossiliferous Deposits of the Hebrides.

First Impressions of England and its People.

My Schools and Schoolmasters; or the Story of My Education. An Autobiography.

The Foot-Prints of the Creator; or The Asterolepis of Stromness.

The Testimony of the Rocks; or Geology in its Bearings on the Two Theologies, Natural and Revealed.

Popular Geology. A Series of Lectures Read before the Philosophical Institution of Edinburgh.

The Old Red Sandstone, or New Walks in an Old Field.

MILMAN (Rev. H. H.) History of the Jews. New York. 1836. 3 vols.

MILTON (John.) The Poetical Works of. Boston. 1836. 2 vols.

The Life and Times of. See MASSON.

MINERALOGY. A Manual of. By Robert Allen. Edinburgh. 1834.

MINERALOGY. See NEW YORK.

MISSOURI. The First and Second Annual Reports of the Geological Survey of. By G. C. Swallow, State Geologist. Jefferson City. 1855.

MITFORD (William.) The History of Greece. Boston. 1823. 8 vols.

MODERN EUROPE. History of. By William Russell, and a Continuation by William Jones. New York. 1833. 3 vols.

MODERN BRITISH ESSAYISTS. Philadelphia. 6 vols., including ALISON, JEFFREY, MACAULAY, MACKINTOSH, SIDNEY SMITH, WILSON.

MODERN TRAVELLER. A Popular Description, Geographical, Historical and Topographical, of the Various Countries of the Globe. Boston. 1830. 10 volumes. (Vol. 1 wanting.)

MOHR (Francis.) Practical Pharmacy. Philadelphia. 1849.

MONTAGUE (Lady Mary Wortley.) The Letters and Works of. Philadelphia. 1837. 2 vols.

MONTAGU (Basil.) See BACON.

MONTAIGNE (Michael de.) Works of. By Wm. Hazlitt. London. 1853. 1 vol.

MONTESQUIEU. Spirit of Laws. 2 vols.

MOORE (Thomas.) Letters and Journals of Lord Byron, with notices of his Life. New York. 1836. 2 vols. (Vol. 1 wanting.)

MORE (Sir Thomas.) A most pleasant, fruitful, and witty Work, of the best state of a Public weal, and of the new Isle called Utopia. Written in Latin by the Right Worthy and Famous Sir Thomas More, Knight, and translated into English by Raphe Robinson, A. D. 1551. A new Edition, by the Rev. T. F. Dibdin, F. S. A. London. 1808. 2 vols. 12mo.

MORRIS (Gouverneur.) Life of, with Selections from his Correspondence. Boston. 1832. 3 vols. (Vol 1 wanting.)

MOSHEIM (John Lawrence.) An Ecclesiastical History, Ancient and Modern. Baltimore. 1834. 2 vols. (Vol. 1 wanting.)

MOTLEY (John Lothrop.) The Rise of the Dutch Republic. A History. New York. 1856. 3 vols.

MOZIN'S Vollstandiges Worterbuch fur der Deutschen and Franzosichen Sprache. Stuttgart & Tubingen. 1846. 4 vols.

MULFORD (E.) The Nation—The Foundation of Civil Order and Political Life in the United States. New York. 1871.

MULLER (J.) Principles of Physics and Meteorology. Philadelphia. 1848.

MURPHY (Arthur.) The Works of Samuel Johnson, LL. D., with an Essay on his Life and Genius. New York. 1856. 2 vols.

The Works of Cornelius Tacitus, with an Essay on his Life and Genius. Philadelphia. 1836.

MURRAY (Hugh.) Encyclopædia of Geography. Philadelphia. 1837. 3 vols.

NAPOLEON (*Emperor.*) Memoirs of the Life. Exile and Conversations of. New York. 1855. 4 vols. (Vols. 1 and 2 wanting.)

NATIONAL ALMANAC AND ANNUAL RECORD. 1863–4. 2 vols.

NATURAL HISTORY. See NEW YORK.

NEAL (Daniel.) The History of the Puritans. New York. 1856. 2 vols.

NEW AMERICAN CYCLOPÆDIA. A Popular Dictionary of General Knowledge. New York. 1861. 16 vols.

NEW DICTIONARY OF QUOTATIONS, from the Greek, Latin and Modern Languages. Translated into English, and occasionally accompanied with Illustrations, Historical, Poetical and Anecdotical. Philadelphia. 1860.

NEW HAVEN. Colonial Records. 1653–65. Hartford. 1850.

NEWTON (Isaac.) Principia. New York. 1 vol.

NEW YORK.

Documentary History of. Arranged under the direction of the Hon. Christopher Morgan, Secretary of State, by E. B. O'Callaghan, M. D., with Engravings and Plans. Albany. 1850. 4to. 4 vols.

Documents relative to the Colonial History of the State of New York; procured in Holland, England and France, by John Romeyn Brodhead, Esq., agent. Edited by E. B. O'Callaghan, with a general introduction by the agent. Albany. 1853–57. 4to. 10 vols. and index.

Proceedings and Debates of the Third National Quarantine and Sanitary Convention. New York. 1859.

Natural History of New York.
Part 1. Zoology, by James E. De Kay. 4 vols.
2. Botany, by John Torrey. 2 vols.
3. Mineralogy, by Lewis C. Beck. 1 vol.
4. Geology, by James Hall, Wm. H. Mather, E. Emmons and Gardner Vanixan. 1 vol.
5. Agriculture, by E. Emmons. 4 vols.
6. Paleontology, by James Hall. 3 vols. With an extra volume containing plates.
In all 16 vols. 4to. Albany.

Meteorology. 1826–1850. By F. B. Hough. 4to. 2 copies.

Nichol (J. P.) Cyclopaedia of the Physical Sciences. London and Glasgow. 1857.

Nicholson (John). The Operative Mechanic and Machinist. Philadelphia. 1831. 2 vols.

Nicholson (Peter). Principles of Architecture. London. 1836. 3 vols.

Niebuhr (B. G.) Lectures on Ancient History. London. 1852. 3 vols.

Lectures on the History of Rome. London. 1852. 3 vols.

History of Rome. Philadelphia. 1835. 2 vols.

Noctes Ambrosianae. New York. 1857. 4 vols. (Vol. 3 wanting.)

North Carolina. Geological Report of the Midland Counties of, by Ebenezer Emmons. New York. 1856.

North American Review. 1820–37. Boston. Vols. 1–35.

The same. Vols. 82–112, inclusive. 30 vols. (Vol. 108 missing.)

North British Review. (American Edition.) 1861–1871. 11 Vols.

Nott (J. C.) and Gliddon (George R.) Indigenous Races of the Earth. Philadelphia. 1857.

Types of Mankind, or Ethnological Researches. Philadelphia. 1855.

OKEN (Prof.) Allgemeine Naturgeschichte fur alle Stande. 1833. 9 vols.

OLIVER (Peter). The Puritan Commonwealth. An Historical Review of the Puritan Government in Massachusetts in its Civil and Ecclesiastical Relations, from its rise to the Abrogation of the First Charter. Boston. 1856.

OPINION, Essays on the Formation and Publication of. Philadelphia. 1831.

OVERMAN (Frederick). A Treatise on Metallurgy, comprising Mining and General and Practical Metallurgical Operations. New York. 1854.

OWEN (David Dale). First Report of a Geological Reconnoissance of the Northern Counties of Arkansas. Little Rock. 1858.

Report of the Geological Survey in Kentucky. Frankfort. 1856.

PAGE (Thomas J.) La Plata, the Argentine Confederation and Paraguay. A Narrative of the Exploration of the Tributaries of the River La Plata and Adjacent Countries. New York. 1859.

PAINE (Martyn). The Institutes of Medicine. New York. 1867.

PALEONTOLOGY. See NEW YORK.

PALFREY (John Gorham). History of New England. London. 1859. 2 vols.

PALEY (William). Works, with a Life of the Author, by Rev. Edmund Paley. Cambridge. 1830. 6 vols. (Vol. 5 missing.)

PARKMAN (Francis, Jr.) History of the Conspiracy of Pontiac, and the War of the North American Tribes against the English Colonies. Boston. 1851.

PARLIAMENTARY HISTORY. See ENGLAND.

PARNELL (Sir Henry.) A Treatise on Roads. London. 1833. 1 vol.

PARTINGTON (Charles F.) A Manual of Natural and Experimental Philosophy. London. 1828. 2 vols. (Vol. 1 wanting.)

PARTON (James.) The Life of Andrew Jackson. New York. 1860. 3 vols.

PERCY (Thomas.) Reliques of Ancient English Poetry. London. 3 vols. (Vol. 1 wanting.)

PERIODICALS.

Edinburgh Review. (American Edition.) 1861–1871. 11 vols.

Edinburgh Review. Vols. 1–59.

Quarterly Review. Vols. 1–51. (Vol. 40 missing.)

Blackwood's Edinburgh Magazine. Vols. 97–108. (Vol. 104 missing.)

North British Review. (American Edition.) 1861–1871. 11 vols.

London Quarterly Review. (American Edition.) 1861–1871. 11 vols.

Westminster Review. (American Edition.) 1861–1871. 11 vols. New York.

North American Review. Vols. 82–112. (Vol. 108 missing.)

North American Review. 1820–37. 35 vols.

American Literary Gazette and Publishers' Circular. Philadelphia. 1868–1870. Vols. 1–10, 15, 16, bound in 6 vols.

American Quarterly Review. Vols. 1–20. Philadelphia. 1827–36.

Siliman's American Journal. Vols. 1–31. 1819–37.

PICKETT (Albert James.) History of Alabama, and incidentally of Georgia and Mississippi, from the earliest period. Charleston. 1851. 2 vols.

PLATEN (August von.) Gesammelte Werke. Stuttgart und Tuebingen. 5 vols. in 3. 16mo. (Vol. 1 missing.)

PLATO. Translated by Henry Cary, George Burges and Henry Davis. London. 6 vols.

PLUNKET (Wm. Conyngham,) Lord High Chancellor of Ireland. Speeches at the Bar and in the Senate. Edited, with a Sketch of his Life, by John Cashel Hoey. Dublin. 1865.

PLUTARCH'S LIVES. The Translation called Dryden's; by A. H. Clough. Boston. 1859. 5 vols.

POLLARD (Edward A.) Southern History of the War. New York. 1864. 3 vols.

PONTIAC. History of the Conspiracy of, and the War of the North American Tribes against the English Colonies, by Francis Parkman, Jr. Boston. 1851.

POOLE (Wm. Fred.) Index to Periodical Literature. New York. 1853.

POPE (Alexander.) The Works of; to which are added a New Life of the Author, an Estimate of his Poetical Character and Writings. By William Roscoe, Esq. London. 1847. 8 vols. (Vol. 5 wanting.)

POPE (Thomas.) A Treatise on Bridge Architecture. New York. 1811.

PORTER (Arthur L.) The Chemistry of the Arts. Philadelphia. 1830. 2 vols.

POULTRY BOOK (The.) London. 1853.

PRESCOTT (William H.) Biographical and Critical Miscellanies. Boston. 1857.

History of the Reign of Ferdinand and Isabella, the Catholic. New York. 1852. 3 vols.

History of the Conquest of Mexico, etc., with the Life of the Conqueror Fernando Cortez. Boston. 1856. 3 vols.

History of the Conquest of Peru, with a Preliminary View of the Civilization of the Incas. New York. 2 vols.

History of the Reign of Philip the II. King of Spain. Boston. 1857. Vols. 1 and 2.

PRIOR (James.) The Life of Oliver Goldsmith. Philadelphia. 1837.

PROVANCHER (P. L'Abbe L.) Flore Canadienne. Quebec. 1862. 2 vols.

PYRKER (Johann Ladislav.) Sammtliche Werke. Stuttgart & Tubingen. 1845. 3 vols.

QUARTERLY (The) Review. Vol. 1–51. 1809–1824. 51 vols. (Vol. 40 wanting.)

QUINER (E. B.) Military History of Wisconsin. A Record of the Civil and Military Patriotism of the State. Chicago. 1866.

RAMSEY (J. G. M.) The Annals of Tennessee to the end of the Eighteenth Century. Charleston. 1853.

RANDALL (Henry S.) The Life of Thomas Jefferson. New York. 1858. 3 vols.

RANKE (Leopold.) The History of the Popes, their Church and State. London. 1853. 3 vols.

Civil Wars and Monarchy in France in the Sixteenth and Seventeenth Centuries. New York. 1853.

RAUMER (Karl Von.) Contributions to the History and Improvement of the German Universities. New York. 1859.

RAWLINSON (George.) The History of Herodotus. New York. 1859. 4 vols.

REGISTER OF DEBATES IN CONGRESS, comprising the leading debates and incidents of Congress, from the second session of the Eighteenth Congress to the second session of the Twenty-second Congress; together with an Appendix containing all the important State Papers and Public Documents. To which are added all the laws enacted during those sessions, with a copious Index to the whole. 9 vols. Vols. 2, 4, 6 and 9 each two parts; vol. 8, 3 parts. Washington. 1825–1833. Bound in 15 vols.

REGISTER OF OFFICERS AND AGENTS, Civil Military and Naval, in the service of the United States on the 30th of September, 1861. Washington. 1862.

REID (Whitelaw). Ohio in the War—Her Statesmen, Her Generals and Soldiers. Cincinnati. 1868.

REVENUE, Report of the Special Commissioner of, for 1866, '67, '68 and '69. 4 vols.

RHODE ISLAND. Journal of the Institute of Instruction. 1845–6. Providence. 1846.

Colonial Records of the Colony of Rhode Island. Vols. 3–6, 8, 10. 1707–1792. 6 vols.

Rhode Island in the Continental Congress, with the Journal of the Convention that adopted the Constitution. 1765–1790. By Wm. R. Staples, LL.D. Providence. 1870.

Records of the Colony of Rhode Island and Providence Plantations in New England. 1707–1740. By John Russell Bartlett. Providence. 1859.

RICHARDSON (Albert D.) The Secret Service—The Field, The Dungeon and The Escape. Hartford. 1865.

RIVES (William C.) History of the Life and Times of James Madison. Boston. 1859. Vols. 1 and 3.

ROBERTSON (William.) The History of the Discovery and Settlement of America. New York. 1835.

The History of the Reign of the Emperor Charles V. New York. 1836.

The History of Scotland during the Reign of Queen Mary and of King James VI. Also, an Historical Disquisition concerning the Knowledge which the Ancients had of India. New York. 1836.

ROGERS (Henry Darwin.) The Geology of Pennsylvania. Philadelphia. 1858. 2 vols. 4to.

ROGET (Peter Mark.) Thesaurus of English Words and Phrases. Boston. 1856.

ROLLIN (Charles.) The Ancient History of the Egyptians, Carthagenians, and Assyrians. New York. 1836. 2 vols.

ROORBACH (O. A.) Catalogue of American Publications from 1820–52. New York. 1852.

RUFFIN (Edward.) An Essay on Calcareous Manures. Shellbank's. 1835. 1 vol.

RUSKIN (John.) Modern Painters. New York. 1856. 5 vols.

Seven Lamps of Architecture. New York. 1857.

Lectures on Architecture and Painting. New York. 1856.

The Two Paths—being Lectures on Art and its Application to Decoration and Manufacture. New York. 1859.

RUSSELL. The History of Modern Europe. New York. 1836. 3 vols.

RUSSELL, (John Earl.) An Essay on the History of the British Government and Constitution from the Reign of Henry VII. to the present time. London. 1866.

SABINE (Lorenzo.) Biographical Sketches of Loyalists of the American Revolution. Boston. 1864. 2 vols.

SAFFORD (Wm. H.) The Blennerhassett Papers. Cincinnati. 1861.

SAFFORD (James M.) Geology of Tennessee. Nashville. 1869.

SALE (George.) The Koran, commonly called The Alcoran of Mohammed. Philadelphia. 1859.

SANGSTER (Charles.) Hesperus and other Poems and Lyrics. Montreal. 1860.

SCHILLER'S Sammtliche Werke. Stuttgart & Tubingen. 1844. 10 vols. (Vols. 1, 5 and 7 wanting.)

SCHLEGEL (Augustus William.) A Course of Lectures on Dramatic Art and Literature. Philadelphia. 1833.

SCHLOSSBERGER (J. E.) Lehrbuch der Organischen Chemie. Stuttgart. 1852.

SCHNEIDER (Dr. F. W.) Lehrbuch der Preussischen Forst und Yagd-Gesetsgebung. Vols. 1–3, and Vol. 4, Part 1. Paper.

SCHOOLCRAFT (Henry Rowe.) Historical and Statistical Information, respecting the History, Condition and Prospects of the Indian Tribes of the United States; collected and prepared under the direction of the Bureau of Indian Affairs, illustrated by S. Eastman, Captain U. S. N. Philadelphia. 4 vols. 1851–54. 4to. [Plates.]

SCHOULER (William). History of Massachusetts in the Civil War. Boston. 1868.

SCHUBERT (Dr. F.) Lehrbuch der Organischen Chemie. Erlangen. 1854.

SCOTT (Sir Walter). Works. Philadelphia. 1852. Vols. 1, 8, 9, 10.

SEOANE and NEWMAN. A Pronouncing Dictionary of the Spanish and English Languages. New York. 1852.

SEGUR (Count Philip de). History of the Expedition to Russia. London. 1855. 2 vols.

SEWARD (William H.) The Works of, edited by George E. Baker. New York. 1853. 3 vols. (Vol. 1 wanting.)

SHAKESPEARE (William). Dramatic Works. Boston. 1836. 7 vols. (Vol. 5 wanting.)

SIDNEY (Algernon). Discourses Concerning Government, to which are added Memoirs of his Life, and an Apology for Himself. London. 1751. Folio.

SIDNEY (Sir Philip). The Countess of Pembroke's Arcadia, written by Sir Philip Sidney, Knight, with the Defense of Poesie, Sonnets, etc. Thirteenth Edition. London. 1674. Folio.

SILLIMAN (Benjamin). American Journal of Science. New York. 1819–1837. 31 vols.

SINDING (Paul C.) History of Scandinavia from the early times of the Northmen and Vikings to the present day. Pittsburg. 1862.

SISMONDI (J. C. L. Simonde). Literature of Southern Europe. London. 1823. 4 vols.

SMITH (Adam). An Inquiry into The Nature and Causes of the Wealth of Nations. Edinburg. 1863.

SMITH (William). History of the Peloponnesian War. Translated from the Greek of Thucydides. Philadelphia. 1836.

SMITH (Sidney). See MODERN BRITISH ESSAYISTS.

SMITHSONIAN Institution. Smithsonian Contributions to Knowledge. 1848–70. 4to. Vols. 3–10, 14–17.

Annual Report of Board of Regents. 1855, '56, '58, '61, '62. 5 vols.

SOUTHEY (ROBERT). The complete Poetical Works of. New York. 1846.

SPARKS (Jared). The Writings of Washington with a Life of the Author. Boston. 1834. 11 vols.

Correspondence of the American Revolution, being Letters of Eminent Men to George Washington, from the time of his taking Command of the Army, to the end of his Presidency. Boston. 1853. 4 vols.

Diplomatic Correspondence of the United States . . . from the signing of the Definitive Treaty of Peace, 10th of September, 1783, to the adoption of the Constitution, March 4, 1789, being the Letters of the Presidents of Congress, the Secretary of Foreign Affairs, American Ministers at Foreign Courts, Foreign Ministers near Congress, Reports of Committees of Congress and Reports of the Secretary of Foreign Affairs, and various Letters and Communications, together with Letters from Individuals on Public Affairs. Washington. 1834. 7 vols.

Diplomatic Correspondence of American Revolution, being the Letters of Benjamin Franklin, Silas Deane, John Adams, John Jay, Arthur Lee, William Lee, Ralph Izard, Francis Dana, William Carmichael, Henry Laurens, John Laurens, M. De Lafayette, M. Dumas, and others . . . Boston. 1830. 12 vols.

The works of Benjamin Franklin, with notes and Life of the Author. Boston. 1836. 10 vols. (Vol. 1 wanting.)

The Life of Governeur Morris, with Selections from his Correspondence and Miscellaneous Papers. Boston. 1832. 3 vols. (Vol. 1 is wanting.)

SPECTATOR (The). Edited by Alexander Chalmers—with Prefaces Historical and Biographical. New York. 1853. 6 vols.

SPENSER (Edmund). Poetical Works. Boston. 1848. 5 vols. (Vol. 1 wanting.)

SPIERS & SURRENNE. French Pronouncing Dictionary. New York. 1852.

SQUIERS (E. G.) Notes on Central America, particularly the States of Honduras and San Salvador ; their Geography, Topography, Climate, Population, Resources, Productions, &c. New York. 1855.

STAPLES (William R.) Rhode Island in the Continental Congress, with the Journal of the Convention that adopted the Constitution. 1765–1790. Providence. 1870.

STEUBEN (Baron.) See KAPP.

STEWART (Dugald). Works. Cambridge. 1829. 7 vols.

STILES (William H.) Austria in 1848–49. A History of the late Political Movements in Vienna, Milan, Venice and Prague. New York. 1852. 2 vols.

STORY (Joseph). Life and Letters. Boston. 1851. 2 vols. (Vol. 1 wanting.)

Miscellaneous Writings. Boston. 1852.

SUETONIUS (Caius Tranquillus.) C. Suetonii Tranquilli XII. Cæsares, with a free translation by John Clarke. London. 1732.

SULLIVAN. Familiar Letters on Public Characters and Public Events, from the Peace of 1783 to the Peace of 1815. Boston. 1834.

SWIFT (Jonathan,) D.D., Works. Arranged by Thomas Sheridan, A. M., with Notes Historical and Critical. London. 1803. 24 vols.

Note—Vols. 6, 7 and 9 are wanting.

SWALLOW (G. C.) Annual Report of the Geological Survey of Missouri. Jefferson City. 1855.

TACITUS (Cornelius), with an Essay on his Life and Genius, by Arthur Murphy, Esq. Philadelphia. 1836.

TAYLOR (Jeremy). The Whole Works of; with an Essay Biographical and Critical. London. 1853. 3 vols.

TEMPLE (Sir William.) The Works of, to which is prefixed The Life and Character of Sir William Temple, written by a particular friend. London. 1750. 2 vols.

TENNEY (W. J.) The Military and Naval History of the Rebellion in the United States. New York. 1865.

THIERS (M. A.) The History of the French Revolution. New York. 1854. 4 vols.

History of the Consulate and the Empire of France, and of Napoleon. Philadelphia. 1856. Vols. 1–3.

THOMSON (Thomas.) An Outline of the Sciences of Heat and Electricity. London. 1830.

THOMSON (James.) See COWPER.

THUCYDIDES. History of the Peloponnesian War, translated by William Smith, A. M. Philadelphia. 1836.

TICKNOR (George.) History of Spanish Literature. New York. 1854. 3 vols.

TOLAND (John.) See HARRINGTON.

TILLOTSON (Dr. John.) Works of. London. 1752. 3 vols. Folio.

TOOKE (Horne.) Diversions of Purley. 2 vols.

TOUR OF H. R. H. THE PRINCE OF WALES, through British America and the United States. Montreal. 1860.

TRANSACTIONS of the American Ethnological Society. New York. 1845. 2 vols.

TRANSACTIONS of the American Institute of the City of New York for the year 1850. Albany. 1851.

TRAVELLER (The) Modern. A Popular Description, Geographical, Historical and Topographical, of the Various Countries of the Globe. Boston. 1831. 10 vols. (Vol. 1 wanting.)

TRESCOTT (William Henry.) The Diplomatic History of the Administrations of Washington and Adams. 1789–1801. Boston. 1857.

TUCKER (George.) History of the United States from the Colonization to the end of the Twenty-sixth Congress in 1841. Philadelphia. 1856. 2 vols.

TUCKERMAN (Henry T.) Essays Biographical and Critical, or Studies of Character. Boston. 1857.

TURNER (Edward.) Elements of Chemistry, including the Recent Discoveries and Doctrines of the Science. Philadelphia. 1835.

URE (Andrew.) A Dictionary of Arts, Manufactures, and Mines. New York. 1846. 2 vols.

UTOPIA. See More (Sir Thomas.)

VERMONT. The History of, from its discovery to its admission into the Union in 1791. By Hiland Hall. Albany. 1868.

VICTOR (Orville J.) History of American Conspiracies. A Record of Treason, Insurrection, Rebellion, etc., in the United States, from 1760 to 1860. New York. 1863.

VON HAGEN (Otto.) Die Forstlichen Verhaltnisse Preussens. By Otto Von Hagen, Oberlandforstmeister. Berlin. 1867. 1 vol. 4to. Paper.

WALKER (Gulielmus Sidney.) Corpus Poetarum Latinorum. London. 1854.

WALKER (John.) A Critical Pronouncing Dictionary. New York. 1836.

WALPOLE (Horace.) The Letters of, including Numerous Letters now first published from Original Manuscripts. London. 1840. 14 vols.

WALSH (Robert.) Select Speeches of The Right Honourable George Canning, with Biographical Sketches. Philadelphia. 1835.

Select Speeches of The Right Honourable William Windham and The Right Honourable William Huskisson, with Biographical Sketches. Philadelphia. 1837.

WASHINGTON (H. A.) The Writings of Thomas Jefferson, being his Autobiography, Correspondence, Reports, Messages, Addresses, and other writings, Official and Private. New York. 1853. 9 vols.

WATSON (Robert.) The History of the Reign of Philip II., King of Spain. New York. 1818. 2 vols.

WEBSTER (Daniel.) The Works of. Boston. 1854. 6 vols.

The Private Correspondence of. Boston. 1857. 2 vols.

WEISBACH (Julius.) Principles of the Mechanism of Machinery and Engineering, edited by Walter R. Johnson, A. M. Philadelphia. 1848. 2 vols.

WELLS (William V.) Explorations and Adventures in Honduras, comprising sketches of Travel in the Gold Regions of Olancho, and a review of the History and General Resources of Central America. New York. 1857.

WESTMINSTER REVIEW (American Edition.) 1861–1871. 11 vols. New York.

WHISTON (William.) The Works of Flavius Josephus. Philadelphia. 1833. 2 vols.

The Same in one volume. Philadelphia. 1854.

WIELAND (C. M.) Sammtliche Werke. Leipzig. 1839. 36 vols. in 18.

WILKES (Charles.) Narrative of the United States Exploring Expedition, during the years 1838–42. By Charles Wilkes, U. S. N., Commander; with an Atlas. Vol. I.–V. Vol. VI. Ethnography and Philology. By Horatio Hale. Vol. VII. Zoophytes. By James G. Dana, with a folio Atlas containing 61 plates. Vol. VIII. Mammalia and Ornithology. By Titan R. Peale. Vol. IX. The

The Races of Men, and their Geographical Distribution. By Charles Pickering, M. D. Vol. X. Geology. By James D. Dana, with a folio Atlas of 21 plates. Vol. XI. Meteorology. By Charles Wilkes, with 25 Illustrations. Vol. XII. Mollusca and Shells. By Augustus A. Gould, with an Atlas of plates. Vols. XIII., XIV. Crustacea. By James D. Dana, with a folio Atlas of 96 plates. Parts I., II. Vol. XV. Botany. By Asa Gray, M D., with a folio Atlas of 100 plates. Part I. Vol. XVI. Botany. By William D. Brackenridge, with a folio Atlas of 46 plates. Philadelphia. 1844–54. 16 vols. 4to.

WILKINSON (J. Gardner). A Popular Account of the Ancient Egyptians. New York. 1854. 2 vols.

WILLARD (Joseph). Willard Memoir; or Life and Times of Major Simon Willard. Boston. 1858.

WILLIAMS (Edwin). The Addresses and Messages of the Presidents of the United States, Inaugural, Annual and Special, from 1789 to 1846. New York. 1846. 2 vols.

WILLIS (William). Documentary History of the State of Maine. Portland. 1869. Vol. 1.

WILSON (Alexander). American Ornithology, or the Natural History of the Birds of the United States, with a Sketch of the Author's Life. New York and Philadelphia. 1829. 3 vols

WILSON (John). See MODERN BRITISH ESSAYISTS.

WILSON (John). Noctes Ambrosianae. New York. 1857. 4 vols. (Vol. 3 wanting.)

WINCKELMANN (——). History of Ancient Art. By G. Henry Lodge. Boston. 1856. 2 vols.

WINDHAM (William) and HUSKISSON (William). Select Speeches. Philadelphia. 1837.

WINTHROP (John). History of New England from 1630 to 1649; from original manuscript, with notes. 2 vols. Boston. 1853.

WIRT (William). Mémoirs and Life of, by John P. Kennedy. Philadelphia. 1856. 2 vols. (Vol. 1 wanting.)

WISCONSIN. Industrial Resources of. Chicago. 1853.

Gazetteer. Madison. 1853.

Annual Report of Adjutant General of Wisconsin for 1865. Madison, Wis. 1866.

WOOD (Nicholas.) A Practical Treatise on Railroads and Interior Communication in General. Philadelphia. 1832.

WOODBURY (Levi.) Writings, Political, Judicial, and Literary. Boston. 1852. 3 vols.

WORDSWORTH (William.) Poetical Works. New Haven. 1836.

WORTHEN (A. H.) Geological Survey of Illinois. 1866. 3 vols.

WYCHERLY'S Plays. Vol. 2. Folio.

XENOPHON. The whole Works of, translated by Ashley Cooper, Spelman, Smith, Fielding, and others. Philadelphia. 1836.

YOUNG (Alexander.) Chronicles of First the Planters of The Colony of Massachusetts Bay, from 1623 to 1636. Boston. 1846.

YEAMAN (George H.) The Study of Government. Boston. 1871.

ZOOLOGY. See NEW YORK.

www.ingramcontent.com/pod-product-compliance
Lightning Source LLC
LaVergne TN
LVHW020224110826
845151LV00003B/817

* 9 7 8 1 4 2 5 5 3 1 8 9 8 *